Lecture Notes in Computer Science 11819

More information about this series at http://www.springer.com/series/7411

Karim Djemame · Jörn Altmann ·
José Ángel Bañares · Orna Agmon Ben-Yehuda ·
Maurizio Naldi (Eds.)

Economics of Grids, Clouds, Systems, and Services

16th International Conference, GECON 2019
Leeds, UK, September 17–19, 2019
Proceedings

 Springer

Editors
Karim Djemame ⓘ
University of Leeds
Leeds, UK

Jörn Altmann ⓘ
Seoul National University
Seoul, Korea (Republic of)

José Ángel Bañares ⓘ
University of Zaragoza
Zaragoza, Spain

Orna Agmon Ben-Yehuda ⓘ
Technion – Israel Institute of Technology
and University of Haifa
Haifa, Israel

Maurizio Naldi ⓘ
LUMSA University
Rome, Italy

ISSN 0302-9743   ISSN 1611-3349   (electronic)
Lecture Notes in Computer Science
ISBN 978-3-030-36026-9   ISBN 978-3-030-36027-6   (eBook)
https://doi.org/10.1007/978-3-030-36027-6

LNCS Sublibrary: SL5 – Computer Communication Networks and Telecommunications

This Springer imprint is published by the registered company Springer Nature Switzerland AG
The registered company address is: Gewerbestrasse 11, 6330 Cham, Switzerland

Preface

We are glad to introduce the proceedings of the 16th International Conference on the Economics of Grids, Clouds, Systems, and Services (GECON 2019). GECON 2019 was held during September 17–19, 2019, hosted by the University of Leeds, UK. The conference, held annually, is now firmly established as a place of convergence among economics and computer science researchers, with the ultimate aim of building a strong multidisciplinary community in the increasingly important areas of future ICT systems and economics.

Nowadays, economics plays a pervasive role in the ICT world and is essential in strategic decisions concerning the development of new technologies. It influences its deployment, rollout plans, and is concerned in everyday operations and resource allocation optimization. However, the relationship between ICT and economics is really a two-way street, since the development of technologies such as blockchain is going to change the way economic transactions are carried out. A conference such as GECON, therefore, plays a leading role due to its blending of skills and knowledge from both worlds.

We received 48 submissions in response to our call for papers. Each paper was peer-reviewed by at least three members of the international Program Committee (PC). Based on significance, novelty, and scientific quality, we selected 12 full papers (a 25% acceptance rate), which are included in this book. Additionally, ten shorter work-in-progress papers and four extended abstracts describing the work shown on posters during the conference were integrated in the volume.

The full papers were organized around four themes:

- Blockchain Technology and Smart Contracts
- Resource, Service, and Communication Federations
- Economic Assessment, Business and Pricing Models
- Resource Management

The work-in-progress papers gathered around the following themes:

- Cost-Based Computing Allocation
- Blockchain and Network Function Virtualization Technologies
- Economic Models for Cyber-Physical Systems, Industry 4.0 and Sustainable Systems

Keynotes

This year's GECON featured three keynotes, evenly distributed across the three days of the conference, addressing topics that span social, economic, and financial issues in the ICT world.

The keynote speaker on the first day was Prof. Aad Van Moorsel, from the University of Newcastle, UK.

Prof. Van Moorsel's keynote, "Benchmarks and Models for Blockchain: The Incentives Layer," dealt with the mechanisms, protocols, and software architecture associated with fees, costs, and other considerations that either entice or discourage participants to the blockchain scheme, i.e. the so-called incentives layer.

The keynote speaker on the second day was Prof. Dieter Kranzlmüller, from Ludwig-Maximilians-Universität München, Germany, where he is Head of the Munich Network Management Team.

His keynote, "Economic Observations of the Leibniz Supercomputing Centre," was concerned with his appointment at the Leibniz Supercomputing Center, where he provided generic IT-services for sciences, including everything from the desktop of the scientist via arbitrary cloud services to the large-scale high performance computers. While scientific output is typically considered as a key performance indicator, his talk focused on the economic aspects of the center and its energy efficiency, which play a key role in determining its future sustainability.

The speaker on the third and final day was Dr. Paul Townend, co-founder and CTO of Edgetic.

His keynote, "Data Center Growth, Challenges, and Inefficiencies in a Connected World," focused on data centers as the engine of smart cities and highly connected mobile devices, addressing the economic and environmental consequences of their evergrowing power consumption. The talk examined a range of holistic solutions to manage both the complexity and inefficiencies of data centers, reporting a case study of a data center facility located in northern Sweden.

Acknowledgments

Any conference is the fruit of the work of many people, and GECON 2019 was no exception. In particular, we wish to thank the authors, whose papers made up the body of the conference, as well as the members of the PC and the reviewers, who devoted their time to review the papers on a tight time schedule. We wish to thank the invited speakers, for bringing new viewpoints and inputs to the GECON community. Furthermore, we would like to thank Alfred Hofmann, Anna Kramer, and the whole team at Springer, who continue an established tradition of publishing GECON proceedings in the renowned LNCS series. Finally, we wish to thank the attendees, whose interest in the conference is the main driver for its organization.

September 2019

Karim Djemame
Jörn Altmann
José Ángel Bañares
Orna Agmon Ben-Yehuda
Maurizio Naldi

GECON2019 – Organization

Conference Chair

Karim Djemame   University of Leeds, UK

Conference Vice Chairs

Jörn Altmann   Seoul National University, South Korea
Orna Agmon Ben-Yehuda   Technion, Israel
José Angel Bañares   Zaragoza University, Spain

Public Relations Chair

Orna Agmon Ben-Yehuda   Technion, Israel

Industrial Session Chair

Jie Xu   University of Leeds, UK

Proceedings Chair

Maurizio Naldi   LUMSA Università, Italy

Posters Session Chair

Orna Agmon Ben-Yehuda   Technion, Israel

Roundtable Session Chair

Konstantinos Tserpes   Harokopio University of Athens, Greece

Special Session Chairs

Aurilla Aurelie Arntzen   University of South-Eastern Norway, Norway
Maurizio Naldi   LUMSA Università, Italy

Programme Chairs

Franz Lehner   University of Passau, Germany
Vlado Stankovski   University of Ljubljana, Slovenia

Steering Committee

Jörn Altmann	Seoul National University, South Korea
Jose Ángel Bañares	Zaragoza University, Spain
Orna Agmon Ben-Yehuda	Technion, Israel
Steven Miller	Singapore Management University, Singapore
Omer F. Rana	Cardiff University, UK
Gheorghe Cosmin Silaghi	Babes-Bolyai University, Romania
Konstantinos Tserpes	Harokopio University of Athens, Greece
Maurizio Naldi	LUMSA Università, Italy

Program Committee

Alvaro Arenas	IE University, Spain
Aurilla Aurelie Arntzen	University of South-Eastern Norway, Norway
Unai Arronategui	University of Zaragoza, Spain
Ashraf Bany Mohamed	University of Jordan, Jordan
Stefano Bistarelli	Università di Perugia, Italy
Rajkumar Buyya	University of Melbourne, Australia
María Emilia Cambronero	University of Castilla-La Mancha, Spain
Emanuele Carlini	ISTI-CNR, Italy
Jeremy Cohen	Imperial College London, UK
Massimo Coppola	ISTI-CNR, Italy
Costas Courcoubetis	SUTD, Singapore
Daniele D'Agostino	CNR-IMATI, Italy
Patrizio Dazzi	ISTI-CNR, Italy
Alex Delis	University of Athens, Greece
Karim Djemame	University of Leeds, UK
Patricio Domingues	ESTG-Leiria, Portugal
Giancarlo Fortino	Università della Calabria, Italy
Felix Freitag	Universitat Politècnica de Catalunya, Spain
Saurabh Kumar Garg	University of Tasmania, Australia
Daniel Grosu	Wayne State University, USA
Netsanet Haile	Seoul National University, South Korea
Chun-Hsi Huang	University of Connecticut, USA
Bahman Javadi	Western Sydney University, Australia
Odej Kao	TU Berlin, Germany
Stefan Kirn	University of Hohenheim, Germany
Tobias Knoch	Erasmus MC, The Netherlands
Bastian Koller	HLRS, Universität Stuttgart, Germany
Somayeh Koohborfardhaghighi	University of Amsterdam, The Netherlands
Harald Kornmayer	DHBW Mannheim, Germany
George Kousiouris	National Technical University of Athens, Greece
Dieter Kranzlmüller	Ludwig-Maximilians-Universität München, Germany
Joerg Leukel	University of Hohenheim, Germany

Leonardo Maccari	University of Trento, Italy
Ivan Merelli	ITB-CNR, Italy
Roc Meseguer	Universitat Politècnica de Catalunya, Spain
Paolo Mori	IIT-CNR, Italy
Leandro Navarro	Universitat Politècnica de Catalunya, Spain
Marco Netto	IBM, Italy
Mara Nikolaidou	Harokopio University of Athens, Greece
Alberto Nuñez Complutense	University of Madrid, Spain
Frank Pallas	TU Berlin, Germany
Dana Petcu	West University of Timisoara, Romania
Ioan Petri	Cardiff University, UK
Congduc Pham	Université de Pau et des pays de l'Adour, France
Ilia Pietri	Intracom S.A. Telecom Solutions, Greece
Radu Prodan	University of Klagenfurt, Austria
Omer Rana	Cardiff University, UK
Ivan Rodero	Rutgers University, UK
Rizos Sakellariou	University of Manchester, UK
Benjamin Satzger	Microsoft, USA
Lutz Schubert	University of Ulm, Germany
Arun Sen	Arizona State University, USA
Jun Shen	University of Wollongong, Australia
Gheorghe Cosmin Silaghi	Babes-Bolyai University, Romania
Aleksander Slominski	IBM, USA
Stefan Tai	TU Berlin, Germany
Rafael Tolosana-Calasanz	University of Zaragoza, Spain
Bruno Tuffin	INRIA, France
Iraklis Varlamis	Harokopio University of Athens, Greece
Dora Varvarigou	National Technical University of Athens, Greece
Luís Veiga	Universidade de Lisboa, Portugal
Stefan Wesner	University Ulm, Germany
Phillipp Wieder	GWDG, University of Göttingen, Germany
Ramin Yahyapour	GWDG, University of Göttingen, Germany
Dimitrios Zissis	University of the Aegean, Greece

Abstracts

Benchmarks and Models for Blockchain: The Incentives Layer

Aad van Moorsel

School of Computing, Newcastle University, UK
aad.vanmoorsel@ncl.ac.uk

Abstract. In this presentation we consider blockchains from a performance engineering perspective, with an emphasis on the incentives layer. The incentives layer in the blockchain software stack [5] refers to the mechanisms, protocols and software architecture associated with fees, costs, and other considerations that either entice or discourage participants. The presentation builds on two earlier keynotes that consider blockchain performance engineering in general [7] and in the consensus layer [8], respectively. We start the presentation with an illustration that incentives need to be aligned to ensure the reliable operation of permissionless blockchains [4]. This forms the motivation behind a list of main topics that require further attention from the research community. We will distinguish two categories of issues at the incentives layer: issues related to the dependable operation of blockchains in general, and issues related to incorporating incentives in novel blockchain applications. With respect to the first category, we report on an extensive benchmarking study of Ethereum smart contracts [3], which explores the relation between the rewarded fee and the computational cost [1, 2]. With respect to the second category, we include an in depth discussion of recent work in game-theoretic economic mechanism design for accountable cloud computing [6].

Keywords: Blockchain · Incentives · Economic mechanisms · Models · Benchmarks · Discrete-event simulation

Biography. Aad van Moorsel is Professor at the School of Computing in Newcastle University. He worked in industry from 1996 until 2003, first as a researcher at Bell Labs/Lucent Technologies in Murray Hill and then as a research manager at Hewlett-Packard Labs in Palo Alto, both in the United States. He got his PhD in computer science from Universiteit Twente in The Netherlands (1993) and has a Masters in mathematics from Universiteit Leiden, also in The Netherlands. After finishing his PhD he was a postdoc at the University of Illinois at Urbana-Champaign, Illinois, USA, for two years. He is the author of over 100 peer-reviewed research papers, and holds three US patents. His research group at Newcastle University conducts research in security, privacy and trust, with applications in payment, blockchain and smart systems. All the group's research contains elements of quantification, be it through system measurement, predictive modelling or on-line adaptation.

References

1. Aldweesh, A., Alharby, M., Mehrnezhad, M., van Moorsel, A.: OpBench: a CPU performance benchmark for Ethereum smart contract operation code. In: Proceedings of the IEEE International Conference on Blockchain, July 2019
2. Aldweesh, A., Alharby, M., Solaiman, E., van Moorsel, A.: Performance benchmarking of smart contracts to assess miner incentives in Ethereum. In: Proceedings of the First International Workshop on Blockchain Dependability. IEEE (2018)
3. Alharby, M., Aldweesh, A., van Moorsel, A.: Blockchain-based smart contracts: a systematic mapping study of academic research. In: Proceedings of the 2018 International Conference on Cloud Computing, Big Data and Blockchain (2018)
4. Alharby, M., van Moorsel, A.: The impact of profit uncertainty on miner decisions in blockchain systems. Electron. Notes Theor. Comput. Sci. **340**, 151–167 (2018). http://www.sciencedirect.com/science/article/pii/S1571066118300665. The proceedings of UKPEW 2017, the thirty third Annual UK Performance Engineering Workshops (UKPEW)
5. Alharby, M., van Moorsel, A.: BlockSim: a simulation framework for blockchain systems. SIGMETRICS Perform. Eval. Rev. **46**(3), 135–138 (2019). https://doi.org/10.1145/3308897.3308956
6. Dong, C., Wang, Y., Aldweesh, A., McCorry, P., van Moorsel, A.: Betrayal, distrust, and rationality: smart counter-collusion contracts for verifiable cloud computing. In: Proceedings of the 2017 ACM SIGSAC Conference on Computer and Communications Security, pp. 211–227. ACM (2017)
7. van Moorsel, A.: Benchmarks and models for blockchain. In: Proceedings of the 2018 ACM/SPEC International Conference on Performance Engineering, ICPE 2018, p. 3. ACM, New York, NY, USA (2018). https://doi.org/10.1145/3184407.3184441
8. van Moorsel, A.: Benchmarks and models for blockchain: consensus algorithms. SIGMETRICS Perform. Eval. Rev. **46**(3), 113–113 (2019). https://doi.org/10.1145/3308897.3308949

Economic Observations of the Leibniz Supercomputing Centre

Dieter Kranzlmüller

Ludwig Maximilians Universität, Munich, Germany
Kranzlmueller@ifi.lmu.de

Abstract. The Leibniz Supercomputing Centre (LRZ) is home of SuperMUC-NG, one of the top 10 supercomputers of the world, and offers its computing capabilities to scientists in Bavaria, Germany and Europe. However, its task is more holistic in providing generic IT-services for sciences, including everything from the desktop of the scientist via arbitrary cloud services to the large-scale high performance computer. This talk addresses the economical aspects of LRZ as an example from academia, where key performance indicators are scientific output and not stakeholder revenue. We will take a look at actual costs of the services, accounting of user activities, and sustainability measures for the future. As power usage is a large cost factor, LRZ is also leading in energy-efficient computing with hot-water cooling and heat reuse.

Keywords: Supercomputer · Cloud · Power usage · Sustainability · Leibniz · Heat reuse

Biography. Prof. Dieter Kranzlmüller is from Ludwig Maximilians Universität, Munich, Germany, where he is Head of the Munich Network Management Team. In addition, he has also been Chairman of the Scientific Advisory Board of the Heidelberg Institute for Theoretical Studies since 2014, and Chairman of the Board of the Leibniz Supercomputing Center of the Bavarian Academy of Sciences since 2017. After studying and obtaining a doctorate at Johannes Kepler University Linz, Kranzlmüller he initially worked for E. Eisenbeiss and Söhne in the IT sector. In 1993, he returned to the Institute of Computer Science as an assistant to the same university and remained there until 2003. After holding some positions at the universities in Reading, Dresden and Lyon and a position as deputy project manager at CERN, he joined Ludwig Maximilians Universität in 2008.

Data Center Growth, Challenges, and Inefficiencies in a Connected World

Paul Townend

Edgetic, UK
paul.townend@edgetic.com

Abstract. The rise of smart cities and highly connected mobile devices is driving enormous growth in the data center industry. Data centers are the fundamental infrastructure that supports smart, distributed and connected systems; they currently consume 3Like the smart systems that they support, data centers are highly complex systems-of-systems with interacting hardware, software, power, and thermal components connected to a wide range of service and business models. There is a huge need to address the growing power consumption of the industry (and its resulting financial and environmental impact) but effective solutions are challenging, requiring intelligent and automated reasoning across extremely large volumes of data in a range of disciplines. This talk focuses on the importance of data centers in supporting modern smart systems, and highlights their growth and inefficiencies. We examine a range of holistic solutions that mark some of the first steps towards managing both the complexity and inefficiencies of data centers. We finish with a case study showing how with advanced behavioural modelling, a scheduling mechanism has been developed that has led to significant power reductions in a data center facility located in northern Sweden.

Keywords: Smart cities · Data centers · Power consumption · Efficiency · Sweden

Biography. Dr. Paul Townend is co-founder and CTO of Edgetic, an early-stage technology company developing AI/ML solutions for improving throughput and reducing cost in the data center industry. His team specialises in taking a holistic approach to data center systems, with scheduling decisions made based on reasoning across hardware, software, and environmental conditions. During the 2004–2017 years, Dr Townend was Team Leader of the Distributed Systems and Services Group at the University of Leeds, UK, and lead architect and co-author of over £4 million in successful research projects. He has authored over 70 internationally peer-reviewed articles, which have been cited over 1200 times. His interests span a wide range of topics within the distributed systems domain, with an emphasis on big data analytics, cloud computing, decision support, energy-efficient computing, and dependability.

Contents

Resource Management

Poster Session: Emerging Ideas

Blockchain Technology and Smart Contracts

Exploiting Blockchain Technology for Attribute Management in Access Control Systems

Damiano Di Francesco Maesa[1,2]([✉]), Alessio Lunardelli[2], Paolo Mori[2],
and Laura Ricci[3]

[1] Department of Computer Science and Technology, University of Cambridge,
Cambridge, UK
d.difrancesco@for.unipi.it
[2] Istituto di Informatica e Telematica, Consiglio Nazionale delle Ricerche,
Pisa, Italy
{alessio.lunardelli,paolo.mori}@iit.cnr.it
[3] Department of Computer Science, University of Pisa, Pisa, Italy
ricci@di.unipi.it

Abstract. Access Control systems are a key resource in computer security to properly manage the access to digital resources. Blockchain technology, instead, is a novel technology to decentralise the control and management of a shared state, representing anything from a data repository to a distributed virtual machine. We propose to integrate traditional Access Control systems with blockchain technology to allow the combined system to inherit the desirable properties blockchain technology provides, mainly transparency and, consequently, auditability. Depending on the application scenario considered, for some systems it may not be desirable to employ a fully decentralised approach. As such, in this paper we outline how our proposal can be adapted to allow for the minimal possible integration of blockchain technology in a traditional Access Control system. In particular, we consider the scenario where Attribute Managers only may be managed on chain through smart contracts. We provide a proof of concept implementation based on Ethereum, and show its performance through experimental results.

Keywords: Distributed ledger · Blockchain · Smart contract · Ethereum · Access Control · XACML

1 Introduction

Thanks to the wide availability of Internet connection, a very large number of digital resources of any kind are nowadays shared among a potentially huge number of users. Guaranteeing the security of such resources is a main concern resulting from their sharing, and regulating the related accesses is one of the security measures which must be taken. Several Access Control models have been proposed in the scientific literature to define which factors have to be taken into account in the decision process to determine whether a given user should be granted the right to access a resource in a certain environment, and several Access Control systems have been developed to implement such models. A widely adopted Access Control model is the Attribute-Based Access Control one (ABAC) [1], where the decision process exploits the attributes describing the features of the subject, resource and environment involved in the access context. Examples of attributes of subjects could be: their IDs, the IDs of the companies they work for, their role in such companies, the name of the projects assigned to them. Examples of resources could be: documents, computers, and Internet of Things devices, while some examples of attributes could be: the project a document belongs to or the privacy level assigned to such document (e.g., *public*, *internal* or *confidential*). A very simple example of ABAC policy exploiting the previous attributes could be the following: a subject S is allowed to access a given document D if D belongs to one of the projects assigned to S.

The attributes required for the evaluation of ABAC policies are stored and managed by Attribute Managers (AMs), which are queried by the Access Control system to get the current values of such attributes when an access decision has to be taken. AMs can be embedded in the Access Control systems and/or they can be external, such as third party services (e.g., companies' attribute Data Bases, LDAP services or SAML Attribute Authorities for subjects' attributes).

This paper proposes to exploit blockchain technology for implementing Attribute Managers, and to integrate them in traditional Access Control systems alongside traditional ones. The main advantage introduced by blockchain based AMs is the auditability of attribute values. As a matter of fact, the blockchain eternally keeps trace of all the changes in the attribute values. This way, at any moment, the subject could check the values of the attributes at any time in the past, in order to verify whether the response to an access request he submitted was correct or not. It is important to notice that integrating blockchain based AMs in an Access Control system to manage some attributes would not prevent such system to use, alongside them, also traditional AMs to manage other attributes.

The rest of the paper is structured as follows. Section 2 provides some background about Access Control systems and blockchain technology. In Sect. 3 we analyze the available related works. Our proposal is presented in detail in Sect. 4, while Sect. 5 evaluate its main advantages and drawbacks. In Sect. 6 we measure the experimental performance of our proof of concept implementation. Finally, Sect. 7 presents our conclusions and possible future work.

2   Background

2.1   XACML Based Access Control Systems

The eXtensible Access Control Markup Language (XACML) standard defines a XML based language to write policies, access requests and responses, and a reference architecture for policy evaluation and enforcement (Fig. 1). In the

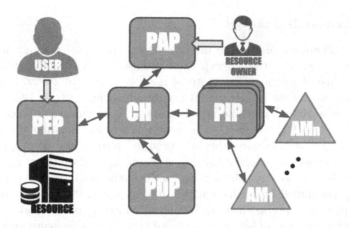

Fig. 1. XACML reference architecture (an arrow represents a communication link between different components).

following, we give a brief overview of the reference architecture, while a detailed description of the XACML standard can be found in [2].

The *Policy Enforcement Point (PEP)* is the component of the XACML reference architecture tasked with intercepting the access requests performed by users, in order to trigger the policy evaluation process and to enforce the related result by actually performing or blocking the execution of the requested access. The *Context Handler (CH)* receives requests from the PEP and it coordinates the execution of the decision process interacting with the other components. The *Policy Administration Point (PAP)* is in charge of storing and managing policies, in order to retrieve them when they are necessary for evaluating access requests. The *Policy Decision Point (PDP)* is the engine that takes an access request and the current attribute values as input, and evaluates the policy to return to the CH the related access decision. *Attribute Managers (AMs)* are the components that actually store and manage the attributes of subjects, resources, and environment. They are queried each time an access request must be evaluated in order to retrieve the updated values of the required attributes. AMs could be part of the Access Control system itself, they could be run by the resource owner, or they can be services run by third parties. In the latter case, the resource owner should trust these AMs, because they could alter the decision process by providing malicious attribute values. Existing services, such as LDAP services, SAML Attribute Authorities, or Attribute Data Bases can be exploited as AMs. *Policy Information Points (PIPs)* act as plugins of the Access Control System, providing the interfaces for interacting with each AM, thus allowing the Access Control System to retrieve the latest values of attributes and to update them.

2.2   Blockchain Technology

Blockchain technology allows the distributed creation and management of an unique data repository (the ledger), thus maintaining a common state among different untrusted parties. The state of a blockchain can be as simple as a collection of records, as in traditional cryptocurrencies such as Bitcoin [3], or as complex as a virtual machine representation, as in smart contract enabling blockchains such as Ethereum [4]. The state updates are recorder through data structures named *transactions* that are grouped into *blocks* cryptographically linked to each other in a ordered list, i.e., a *chain*. To update the state means to add new blocks, and so new transactions, to the chain. Such process is performed by mutually untrusted byzantine entities, and so a distributed consensus algorithm is employed. The consensus algorithm guarantees, under certain conditions (often on the percentage of honest participant) that the chain keeps growing with honest majority in control [5]. Coupling the distributed consensus with a P2P communication network that anyone can join to listen or submit information and chain replication among the peers provides *decentralisation*. The fact that transactions once written in the chain can not be changed (unless the distributed consensus algorithm is overcome by malicious entities), guarantees *persistency* (information remains publicly visible), *timestamping* (information exists at a given discrete time) and *immutability* (information can not be changed). The previous three properties altogether provide *auditability*, i.e., proof that a given information do exist at a given time and cannot be changed later.

Transactions submitted to be included in new blocks are first validated by the consensus participants. Depending on the blockchain protocol, the transaction payload can be a simple record update, or an executable code. In the latter case the code is executed by the validators to update the common state accordingly. Such blockchain protocols are called *smart contract supporting* protocols. A *smart contract* can be, in general, any kind of executable code. The code can be stored on chain organized into callable functions of programmable objects, named *contracts*. Transactions can either create new contracts or invoke functions of existing ones, specifying the possible parameters. The execution of such calls is replicated among all nodes taking part in the consensus and so, the call results are beyond the control (and can not be tampered with) by the transaction creator. It is the contracts' code that deterministically determines the outcome. A reward mechanism for the validation effort is often enforced by blockchain protocols, e.g., the smart contract supporting Ethereum protocols uses the concept of *gas* to price contracts execution. Each basic operation has a gas cost, and the total gas of a given code execution is calculated as sum of all its basic operations costs. Transaction creators can then specify a voluntary *gasprice* to advertise how much they are offering for each unit of gas spent. The transaction gas cost times the advertised gas price is the total amount spent (in the blockchain backed cryptocurrency) to have the transaction validated, i.e., inserted in a new block.

3   Related Work

This work follows the same line of our previous works [6,7] whose main contribution is the idea of merging a traditional access control system with blockchain technology. Such generality is unique in the current literature. A preliminary attempt [8] only used the blockchain as secure repository and log for policies management. In [9], instead, the entire decision process is delegated to the blockchain. The current work starts from the insight obtained by such previous work, as well as the intuition that a fully blockchain integrated system might not be desirable for some scenarios. As such we show how integrating AMs only on chain would still provide interesting properties.

Research on blockchain solutions for Access Control systems have mainly been proposed in the IoT field [10–12]. In [13] the authors propose an entire blockchain protocol with modified transactions dedicated only to the Access Control management. Differently, in our proposal we leverage an already existing, and, potentially, well established and secured, blockchain, without any change needed. Another interesting proposal is [14] where the blockchain is used to distribute the access control process, but there is no traditional access policy involved. Instead a single global policy is used and adapted through machine learning to allow the policy to dynamically self adjust. The proposal uses a novel concept of policy, differently from our aim of disrupting traditional Access Control systems as little as possible. Also no experimental evaluation is provided in [14] to evaluate the actual feasibility of the proposal.

Another research field that has sparked a lot of interest is to try and apply blockchain technology to Access Control systems in health care [15–17]. Such proposals revolve around the implementation of an Electronic Medical Record, and the advantages of security, availability and interoperability that blockchain integration could provide. In such a sensitive field, the potential privacy issues introduced by blockchain use need to be properly addressed. The main difference of such systems from our proposed one is their lack of generality. We provide a possible integration with blockchain technology of any traditional Access Control system independently of their application scenario. Our proposal is not tailored for IoT or health care applications, it can be applied wherever a traditional system already is.

4   Blockchain-Based Attribute Managers

This paper proposes to enhance traditional XACML based Access Control systems by integrating smart contract managed Attribute Managers (called SMART AMs). SMART AMs are smart contracts able to store, compute, and manage attributes values, and they are invoked by Access Control systems to retrieve the current values of such attributes when required for evaluating access control policies. The integration of SMART AMs within XACML based Access Control systems is straightforward, since the XACML reference architecture has been designed to be modular and to allow the integration of any kind of AM. In other words, this paper proposes to use a traditional XACML Access Control system, where the PEP, the CH, the PDP, the PAP, and a set of AMs are deployed off chain (e.g., on the machine related to the resource to be protected, or on a VM running on the Cloud), and to extend this system by introducing a set of blockchain-based AMs, which will be enabled to interact with the rest of the Access Control system through the development of a proper set of PIPs (as required by the XACML standard).

With respect to our previous solution described in Sect. 3 which, instead, moves the entire Access Control system on the blockchain, the approach proposed in this paper allows for the minimal disruption while still retaining the blockchain benefits, even if only applied to the management of attributes, instead of to the whole access decision process. As a matter of fact, this solution also allows an Access Control system to exploit traditional AMs and SMART AMs at the same time, thus being applicable to real application scenarios where some of the attributes required for the policy evaluation are already available through existing traditional AMs.

4.1   Integration in the XACML Reference Architecture

This section shows how SMART AMs can be integrated within a traditional XACML Access Control System to retrieve the attribute values required for the decision process.

First, we note that the XACML reference architecture (see Sect. 2.1) is already designed to integrate external AMs in the decision process. In fact, in several real application scenarios, AMs are usually third party services (e.g., attribute Data Bases, LDAP services or SAML Attribute Authorities). The way for integrating SMART AMs in XACML Access Control systems is through PIPs, the pluggable components for interacting with AMs. Hence, we only need to define new PIPs capable of interacting with the blockchain in order to invoke smart contracts, and to integrate such PIPs with the CH which will invoke them when necessary to carry on the decision process, as shown in Fig. 2. Obviously, an Access Control system can exploit traditional AMs and SMART AMs at the same time, simply integrating a set of proper PIPs.

We imagine an already existent ecosystem of SMART AMs advertised by their respective owners. We assume the owner lets the potential users know at least the contract address and the mean to retrieve attribute values from it, e.g., they could advertise the signature of its public methods returning values for certain attributes. Of course it is in the interest of the owner to make those information reachable to potential users (customers in case of pay to use SMART AMs). Furthermore, the owner can optionally also advertise the source code of the contract to increase its transparency, if this is a property required.

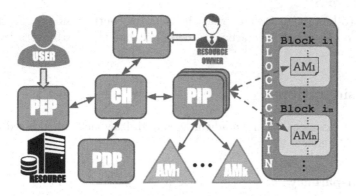

Fig. 2. Architecture of the proposed system.

4.2 Implementation Details

To validate our proposal, we have developed a proof of concept implementation based on the WSO2 OASIS `balana`[1] framework, acting as Policy Decision Point, and on a PIP written in Java, same as the other components of the XACML based Access Control system.

The PIP has been integrated in the `balana` based Access Control system by extending the *Functionbase* `balana` class[2]. In particular, the *evaluate* function of the extended class is the one which includes the code for accessing the blockchain. Assuming that our PIP wants to retrieve the current value of an attribute, say a, from a SMART AM, say am, it only needs to call the corresponding function of the smart contract am. This means sending a transaction to the blockchain (that can result in a simple read of a value from its state). The PIP then uses the `web3j` library [18] to send the request to a `geth` client that will use it again to send back the answer to the PIP.

It is worth noting that the basic function of an AM, returning the attribute value, would be natural to be implemented as a *constant* function (also known as *pure* function in Ethereum), i.e., a function that does not cause any state update. This may not hold in all scenarios (e.g. when the request for an attribute causes some logging inside the attribute manager, for example for statistical purposes), but in general a fetch request of some value, should not modify an AM state. Furthermore it is not true if some pricing of value read is in place, since the micro-payment exchange needs to be recorded. In general having constant functions only, leads to huge advantages. In fact, no transaction needs to be sent to the network, since the user's client can execute the contract function code locally (it has no need to notify the other nodes since the result does not affect the common state). No transactions validation means no fees to be paid and no wait

---

[1] http://xacmlinfo.org/category/balana/.
[2] https://github.com/wso2/balana/blob/master/modules/balana-core/src/main/
java/org/wso2/balana/cond/FunctionBase.java.

for blocks to be mined. Do note that the relevant contract function code is still executed and it can still be arbitrary complex, not necessarily just "reading a value".

5 Considerations

This section discusses the main advantages and drawbacks introduced by using SMART AMs instead of traditional AMs.

5.1 Transparency

In case of public blockchain, the adoption of SMART AMs allows increased transparency since the attribute values cannot be tampered by the AM owner. In practice, using a public blockchain to manage AMs has the effect of making attribute values and their updates publicly visible (unless an obfuscation layer is purposely introduced). This allows auditability, in the sense that any given attribute is proven to have had a certain value in any point in time. Moreover, the actual attribute value fetch is executed in a distributed fashion, so the AM owner can not intervene or tamper with the process. The AM owners do still retain the ability to update their controlled attribute values, but such updates' history is remembered by the chain, exposing any fraudulent behaviours. The other side of the coin is of course a lack of privacy. All values publicly visible are readable by all users. AMs managing sensible data can not follow this simple approach.

5.2 Data Replication

In a blockchain, data are replicated among all the participants. This has the clear advantage that AMs information is locally retrievable by querying an updated local copy of the blockchain (as noted in Sect. 4.2). Hence, SMART AMs guarantee availability by removing the problem of single point of failure and attack. The obvious drawback is that more resources (computational power, memory, bandwidth and storage) need to be dedicated at maintaining the system. Such burden can, however, be eased, for the client, by employing a *light client*. A light client is a minimalistic client that does not locally store the entire chain, but instead relies on other nodes to know of the information it requires. The advantage is a dramatic reduction in the resources needed at the expense of a communication delay (since the required information needs to be fetched by remote nodes, see Sect. 6) and possible privacy leaks (since the queried nodes can infer private information by knowing what the client is interested in).

5.3 Smart Contracts

Another novel advantage of using SMART AMs instead of traditional AMs concerns the automatization capabilities granted by smart contract. Due to the self executing nature of smart contracts, entirely new scenarios are possible. For example, a SMART AM could be defined to automatically update its attribute values depending on some events happening on chain. In a traditional system, users need to trust the managers of the AMs they are retrieving attribute values from. Using an automatic SMART AM would instead require users to only inspect and trust the code that defines it, relieving any need for trusted third parties. The novel ability of creating trust between byzantine entities is a main contribution of blockchain technology, and it could be leveraged in the Access Control field by making trustworthy AMs possible.

6 Experimental Results

In order to validated the proposed approach, we performed a set of experiments with our proof of concept implementation. The goal of the experiments is to measure the time required to evaluate XACML policies exploiting SMART AMs, comparing this time with the one required employing a traditional Attribute Manager, i.e., a database service. We do remark that the proof of concept modifies a traditional Access Control system only to allow it to also recover attribute values from Ethereum smart contracts. So the same general system is used for both tests, the only thing we change is the policy considered, i.e., whether it contains references to traditional AMs or to SMART AMs.

For the experiments involving traditional AMs we used a PHP web server operating a MySQL DataBase. Do note that the `balana` framework and the PHP web server are deployed on distinct machines. The PIP for interacting with this AM simply requests the required attribute via a http get operation.

For the SMART AM tests we considered three different options. First of all, we performed our experiments on an official Ethereum testnet, i.e., *Rinkeby* [19], not to bloat the main net with temporary test data. On such network we deployed a few hundred contracts representing each a different SMART AM. For this experiment we chose to keep the SMART AMs as simple as possible, and so they only advertise two methods without parameters, to return a boolean and an integer respectively, and a single method accepting one parameter, representing an user name, and returning the value of an integer attribute associated to that user (remembered by a map inside the contract). All of the methods are constant (see Sect. 4.2).

Rinkeby is one of the official global test nets used by the Ethereum community. To connect to such network we need a client to receive and send messages (including transactions) as well as read the data on the blockchain. Different type of clients are possible. For the first blockchain test we decided to use the less invasive solution possible. As such we relied on a third party node, i.e., a remote node with respect to the one where the Access Control system is deployed, that we connect to through `http` requests. We chose *Infura* [20], the most widespread such service at the time of writing. The advantage of relieving the user from any need to deploy and maintain a local blockchain node, provided by such approach, is paid with the time spent waiting for `http` requests. For the second and third tests we installed, respectively, a blockchain light node and full node (see Sect. 5)

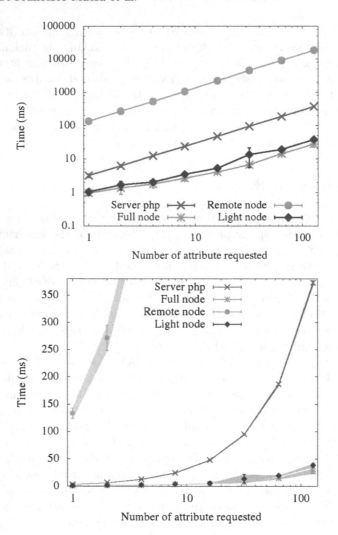

Fig. 3. Time required to fetch attributes with SMART AMs and traditional AMs. The results are shown for a traditional AM implemented as a PHP server operating a MySQL DataBase, a remote *Infura* node, a `geth` light node and a `geth` full node. The upper graph represents the complete results in logarithmic scale, while the bottom graph shows a zoom in linear scale, focusing the scale on the three fastest methods only (PHP server, full node and light node).

with which we interact through the `geth` client installed on the same machine as the `balana` framework.

Figure 3 compares the results of our experiments. We measured the overall time to fetch the attribute values needed to evaluate XACML policies requiring to collect the values of {1, 2, 4, 8, 16, 32, 64, 128} attributes in each of the four scenarios detailed above. For each experiment we perform one hundred executions and we show the mean and standard deviation. We note that when a light node needs a given smart contract code, it has to request it to other nodes but, once collected, it stores it locally (*caching*) and it has no need to query it again until it is updated on chain. As such, by repeating the same attribute request many times, the client would actually use the local value instead of requesting it again. This results in very efficient information collection, as long as the attribute values considered are fairly static. In fact such a solution has the advantage that only the information actually needed is stored locally (and updated fairly rarely), while a full node would have to store the entire blockchain and keep it updated all the time. To test the effectiveness of light node caching we performed a worst case experiment, i.e., we prevented caching. We deployed one hundred SMART AMs, each in a different block, to avoid possible block caching. We then updated a given attribute value once for SMART AM, making sure that each update transaction would end up in a different block. For each of those SMART AMs we defined a policy requiring only the attribute value which has been previously updated. The resulting average wait time to evaluate all hundred policies with only one attribute value (one from every different SMART AM) is 227.25 ms, about one hundred times higher that the time needed to evaluate a policy only using one cached attribute value, i.e., 2.7625 ms. So a light node is an highly efficient solution, but mainly in the case of several requests to the same, fairly static, Attribute Providers. Of course, maintaining a local full node is the better solution in terms of time performance (since all the blockchain data is kept locally by the node), but it is costly in terms of resources needed to be maintained (see Sect. 5).

7   Conclusions and Future Work

In this paper we have presented an approach to exploit blockchain based Attribute Managers in traditional Access Control systems. A relevant advantage of this approach is that it is not disruptive, i.e., it can be adopted in those scenarios where traditional Attribute Based Access Control systems are already in place, by simply integrating new Policy Information Points.

As future work, we are planning to compare the performance of blockchain based Attribute Managers with other services typically exploited as Attribute Managers, such as LDAP services, and to extend the adoption of blockchain based Attribute Managers to more complex Access Control systems, such as the one implementing the Usage Control model [21], where the role of attributes is crucial because they change their values as normal consequence of the system operation, thus requiring the repeated evaluation of the Access Control policies while an access is in progress.

References

1. Hu, V.C., et al.: Guide to attribute based access control (ABAC) definition and considerations (2014)
2. OASIS: eXtensible Access Control Markup Language (XACML) version 3.0, January 2013
3. Nakamoto, S.: Bitcoin: a peer-to-peer electronic cash system (2008)
4. Wood, G.: Ethereum: a secure decentralised generalised transaction ledger. Ethereum Project Yellow Paper **151**, 1–32 (2014)
5. Miller, A., LaViola Jr., J.J.: Anonymous byzantine consensus from moderately-hard puzzles: a model for bitcoin (2014). http://nakamotoinstitute.org/research/anonymous-byzantine-consensus
6. Di Francesco Maesa, D., Mori, P., Ricci, L.: Blockchain based access control services. In: IEEE International Symposium on Recent Advances on Blockchain and Its Applications (BlockchainApp), 2018 IEEE International Conference on Blockchain, pp. 1379–1386. IEEE (2018)
7. Di Francesco Maesa, D., Ricci, L., Mori, P.: Distributed access control through blockchain technology. Blockchain Eng. 31 (2017)
8. Di Francesco Maesa, D., Mori, P., Ricci, L.: Blockchain based access control. In: Chen, L.Y., Reiser, H.P. (eds.) DAIS 2017. LNCS, vol. 10320, pp. 206–220. Springer, Cham (2017). https://doi.org/10.1007/978-3-319-59665-5_15
9. Di Francesco Maesa, D., Mori, P., Ricci, L.: A blockchain based approach for the definition of auditable access control systems. Comput. Secur. **84**, 93–119 (2019)
10. Novo, O.: Blockchain meets IoT: an architecture for scalable access management in IoT. IEEE Internet Things J. **5**(2), 1184–1195 (2018)
11. Dukkipati, C., Zhang, Y., Cheng, L.C.: Decentralized, blockchain based access control framework for the heterogeneous internet of things. In: Proceedings of the Third ACM Workshop on Attribute-Based Access Control, pp. 61–69. ACM (2018)
12. Tapas, N., Merlino, G., Longo, F.: Blockchain-based IoT-cloud authorization and delegation. In: 2018 IEEE International Conference on Smart Computing (SMARTCOMP), pp. 411–416. IEEE (2018)
13. Ouaddah, A., Abou Elkalam, A., Ait Ouahman, A.: Fairaccess: a new blockchain-based access control framework for the internet of things. Secur. Commun. Netw. **9**(18), 5943–5964 (2016)
14. Outchakoucht, A., Hamza, E., Leroy, J.P.: Dynamic access control policy based on blockchain and machine learning for the internet of things. Int. J. Adv. Comput. Sci. Appl. **8**(7), 417–424 (2017)
15. Azaria, A., Ekblaw, A., Vieira, T., Lippman, A.: MedRec: using blockchain for medical data access and permission management. In: International Conference on Open and Big Data (OBD), pp. 25–30. IEEE (2016)
16. Dias, J.P., Reis, L., Ferreira, H.S., Martins, Â.: Blockchain for access control in e-health scenarios. arXiv preprint arXiv:1805.12267 (2018)
17. Dagher, G.G., Mohler, J., Milojkovic, M., Marella, P.B.: Ancile: privacy-preserving framework for access control and interoperability of electronic health records using blockchain technology. Sustain. Cities Soc. **39**, 283–297 (2018)
18. Svenson, C.: Blockchain: using cryptocurrency with Java. Java Mag. 36–46 (2017)
19. Rinkeby Ethereum Testnet. https://github.com/ethereum/EIPs/issues/225. Accessed 15 Feb 2019
20. Infura - Scalable Blockchain Infrastructure. https://infura.io/. Accessed 15 Feb 2019
21. Carniani, E., D'Arenzo, D., Lazouski, A., Martinelli, F., Mori, P.: Usage control on cloud systems. Future Gen. Comput. Syst. **63**(C), 37–55 (2016)

GENEVIZ: A Visual Tool for the Construction and Blockchain-Based Validation of SFC Packages

Muriel F. Franco[1](✉), Martin J. J. Bucher[1](✉), Eder J. Scheid[1](✉),
Lisandro Z. Granville[2](✉), and Burkhard Stiller[1](✉)

[1] Communication Systems Group CSG, Department of Informatics IfI,
University of Zürich UZH, Binzmühlestrasse 14, 8050 Zürich, Switzerland
{franco,scheid,stiller}@ifi.uzh.ch, martin.bucher2@uzh.ch
[2] Computer Networks Group, Institute of Informatics INF,
Federal University of Rio Grande do Sul UFRGS,
Av. Bento Gonçalves, Porto Alegre 9500, Brazil
granville@inf.ufrgs.br

Abstract. Network Functions Virtualization (NFV) decouples the network package performed by network functions from dedicated hardware appliance by running Virtual Network Functions (VNF) on commercial off-the-shelf hardware. Network operators can create customized network services by chaining multiple VNFs, defining a so-called Service Function Chaining (SFC). Because NFV became technically mature recently, the building of such SFCs still needs in-depth knowledge about NFV technology and its descriptors. Furthermore, there is a lack of tools that help to simplify the creation of SFCs. This paper, introduces *GENEVIZ*, a tool that provides a user-friendly interface for the creation of new SFCs as well as for importing and adjusting acquired SFCs (*e.g.*, from marketplaces of VNFs), in order to create new SFCs based on existing ones. Therefore, this work addresses as well data integrity and provides the functionality to store and validate SFCs through the use of blockchains. Three case studies are presented to provide evidence of the technical feasibility of the solution proposed.

Keywords: Network Functions Virtualization · Blockchain · Service Functions Chaining · Virtual Network Functions-as-a-Service

1 Introduction

The paradigm of Network Functions Virtualization (NFV) has gathered significant attention over the last years both from academia and industry [11]. NFV decouples packet processing from dedicated hardware middleboxes and handles it within Virtual Network Functions (VNF) that run on off-the-shelf

© Springer Nature Switzerland AG 2019
K. Djemame et al. (Eds.): GECON 2019, LNCS 11819, pp. 15–28, 2019.
https://doi.org/10.1007/978-3-030-36027-6_2

programmable hardware [10]. NFV offers several benefits, including simplified network operations, a potential of speeding up service delivery, and significant reductions in Operational Expenditures (OPEX) and Capital Expenditures (CAPEX) [8]. Also, NFV allows network operators to create customized network services by chaining together multiple VNFs (*e.g.*, firewalls, load balancers, and DHCP servers). Such network services can provide, for example, different levels of protection, performance, and connectivity for end-users, while the NFV-based virtualization reduces costs and increase the flexibility of the network (*e.g.*, accelerated time-to-market and dynamic resources allocation). Such aggregation of different VNFs building up a network service is represented as a Service Function Chaining (SFC).

As of today, a network operator must have in-depth knowledge about the NFV technology and its corresponding descriptors in order to create an SFC, which can be deployed on an NFV-enabled infrastructure to provide novel network services. In NFV an SFC is represented as a forwarding graph of VNFs and should take into account different descriptors representing the configurations and dependencies of each VNF that compound an SFC [5], such as the VNF Descriptor (VNFD) and the Network Service Descriptor (NSD). The task of dealing with each one of these descriptors is not trivial and requires efforts to configure each one of them manually. The process of constructing such an SFC is not intuitive, many manual steps are necessary for descriptors handling and editing, and the creation can be quite error-prone. This might even lead to a negative impact on a broader adoption of the NFV technology. Furthermore, by considering the prospective market growth of VNF-as-a-Service (VNFaaS) [2] and its potential to simplify the way how end-users obtain services in general, the lack of intuitive solutions has to be addressed when considering the potential of SFCs for end-users with no expertise in the NFV technology.

In this context, information visualization techniques are considered to be a viable tool to help network administrators understand the behavior of the managed network or service, in a faster and easier way [7]. Even though the analysis of such data can be almost fully automated, human interpretation plays a crucial role in decision-making process for network and service management. Especially in NFV environments an enormous amount of data is available and the understanding of it represents a challenging task itself [6]. Although past work exploited visualization techniques to simplify the identification of problems in SFCs, there is still a lack of research addressing the simplification of SFC construction. The visualizations can provide several benefits in NFV environments, such as *(a)* an intuitive way to select VNFs that will compound the forwarding graph and *(b)* a quick configuration of the SFC through its corresponding VNFs. Thus, the visual interface designed here also provides opportunities to reuse already available SFCs and check their integrity relying on the blockchains [1], making it easier to build a new SFC based on an existing one and also contributing to the expansion of the NFV business models (*e.g.*, marketplaces implementing VNFaaS approaches).

This paper introduces *GENEVIZ*, a visual solution allowing the construction of a new SFC Package based on multiple VNF Packages' information (*e.g.*, descriptors of each VNF) and other inputs defined through interactive visualizations (*e.g.*, minimum resources and dependencies to run the service). The tool proposed provides an easy way to create new SFCs as well as to configure properties of VNFs that will compound an SFC. Also, *GENEVIZ* is able to store the hash of the content of such an SFC package on a public blockchain to enable the verification of their integrity and origin (*i.e.*, the developer information) of an already existing SFC configuration before it will be deployed inside the network.

The remainder of this paper is structured as follows. Section 2 reviews related work. Section 3 introduces the *GENEVIZ*'s general architecture and prototype. An evaluation based on case studies is conducted together with a discussion in Sect. 4 in order to provide evidence of the effectiveness of *GENEVIZ*. Section 5 concludes this paper and outlines future work.

2   Related Work

The management of networks and services demands a multitude of methods, activities, procedures, and tools, with the goal to ensure a proper functioning of systems observed. Such tools enable a network administrator to retrieve management information from corresponding devices, analyze the obtained data, and take decisions to optimize or repair services. Within this workflow, visualizations can provide a way to represent a large amount of data in a way perceivable much faster by the human user than via raw and often abstract data. In such a direction, the information visualization allows to perform cognitive work more efficiently and hence in less time [3].

The field of information visualization applied to NFV environments [7] discusses the current applications of visualization and how it should be explored in different topics, such as NFV and Software-defined Networks (SDN). [15] examined specifically the process of configuring virtualized networks, making it clear that no tools existed to assist the configuration, deployment, and testing of virtualized networks by 2016. Specifically, they found no single graphical tool for the creation of a network map directly from a configuration as given by the various descriptors in an SFC configuration. [6] presented the *VISION* platform, which provides interactive and selective visualizations to assist NFV management. *VISION* not only helps network operators to identify and alleviate problems in the context of VNFs, but also provides a complete forwarding graph visualization. Although it provides useful information on incorrect VNF placements or performance problems using visualizations, it only focuses on services already deployed and monitoring systems previously configured, thus not addressing the creation of new network services through the help of visualization tools.

In the context of SFC visualization, [13] introduced SFCPerf, an automatic performance evaluation tool for SFCs. SFCPerf ensures the repeatability of the performance measurements by defining a testing workflow; thus, allowing the performance comparison among different SFC configurations based on the same test. The visualization module included in the tool provides a user-readable interface to visualize throughput, round-trip time, and request rate of a given SFC. Based on their scenarios, they discovered that the main impact factors on the overall performance of an SFC were *(i)* the number of physical link hops between different nodes, and *(ii)* the competition for resources on shared physical nodes. These visualizations can be useful, especially during the construction phase of an SFC, while considering different topologies and NFV platforms, ensuring that the performance meets the desired requirements. [4] presented the *SFC Path Tracer*, a troubleshooting tool for SFC environments that enables the visualization of the trace of network packets in SFC domains. This trace generation is accomplished by mirroring probe packets as they traverse through the chain. Hence, SFC Path Tracer can be useful for the identification of problems within an SFC configuration, as it pinpoints the origin of a possible problem by providing packet trace information. The authors also argue that the tool can be expanded in the near future to a more comprehensive measurement tool.

Although different solutions as discussed above address different aspects related to SFC (*e.g.*, placement, resources allocation, and performance), none of them is focusing on the simplification of the process of an SFC construction by providing intuitive tools (*e.g.*, based on information visualization) for end-users, who construct SFCs and configure their acquired VNFs before the start of the deployment.

3   GENEVIZ

This section introduces GENEVIZ (Generation, Validation, and Visualization of SFC Packages) and its conceptual architecture combined with relevant details of the prototype's implementation. *GENEVIZ* architecture is composed of separated, but interconnected components, providing flexibility to allow replacement of existing modules or adding new modules without affecting remaining components.

White blocks with solid borders of Fig. 1 represent internal components and grey blocks with dashed borders represent external components (*i.e.*, decentralized). *GENEVIZ* is divided into three main layers: *User Layer*, *Data Layer*, and *Blockchain Layer*, respectively. Although the *Blockchain Layer* is not part of *GENEVIZ* itself, it is an integral part of the solution proposed, since it plays a crucial role for validate and trust in SFCs. *GENEVIZ (i)* simplifies the process of creating new network services (*i.e.*, SFCs) in general, and *(ii)* ensures data integrity of previously created services by validating them using blockchain.

An end-user accesses the tool through the *User Interface*, which provides interactive visualizations depending on data provided by the *Visualization Manager*. An integral part of this data is given by the *Template Catalog*, which retrieves templates from the *Templates Collector*. The *Collector* retrieves data from different sources (*e.g.*, marketplaces, independent catalogs, or a manual upload from the local machine). While creating an SFC through the *Service*

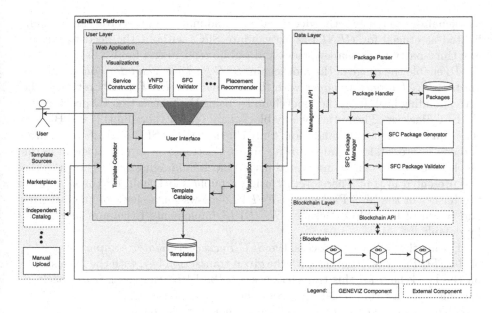

Fig. 1. GENEVIZ architecture

Constructor visualization, VNF Templates from the *Template Catalog* are transmitted through the *Visualization Manager* to the *Management API* and stored through the *Package Handler* on the *Packages Database*. When an SFC Package is generated, the *SFC Package Generator* creates a package based on the information provided (*e.g.*, the list of included VNFs containing their descriptors, the forwarding graph, and properties of the NSD). Besides, the end-user creating the package are able to select the option to store the hash of the SFC Package in the blockchain. If select and configure the blockchain information (*e.g.*, end-user's address and private key), the hash of such an SFC Package will be available on blockchain. After the transaction be sent to the blockchain, the transaction ID is stored in a descriptor called *geneviz.json*, which is included inside of the SFC Package, thus providing useful information to validate the hash during further validation by others.

The validation of the SFC Packages relies on the blockchain to verify the integrity of files representing the SFC Package. Blockchain was initially developed as a distributed ledger to be the backbone of the Bitcoin cryptocurrency [12]. Blockchain is an ordered list of blocks that uses cryptographic hashes to chain and identify the blocks. Each block has a dependency with the others on the chain, thus, if one wants to modify a data on the blockchain, he/she must change every block until the beginning of the chain. Because of the cryptography scheme implemented, this task is arduous and not viable in terms of computational resources. Based on that, blockchain ensures that one data stored cannot be removed, while the address of the account that stored the data and the data itself can be publicly available as well. Thus, among the benefits provided by blockchains, the trustworthy, decentralized, and immutable records can be high-lighted as crucial for *GENEVIZ* to validate SFCs without the need to rely on any third-party (*e.g.*, marketplaces and public repositories for VNFs).

To enable the usage of the blockchain, *SFC Package Validator* communicates via the *SFC Package Manager* with the *Blockchain API*. The API retrieves the corresponding hash from the blockchain by using the transaction ID provided by the SFC Package. Theoretically, any blockchain (*e.g.*, Ethereum [17] and Bitcoin [12]) can be used for this validation. Only the hash of the SFC Package is required and can be stored, for example, using Smart Contracts or as a transaction in the blockchain. It also can be integrated with a blockchain-agnostic API, such as the one presented in [14]. Therefore, by using a public blockchain for the storage of the hashes of the SFC Packages, *GENEVIZ* allows for a check of the integrity and origin of that SFC Package. *GENEVIZ* implements Ethereum blockchain by default.

During the validation process, the *SFC Package Validator* compares the hash of the SFC Package, together with the given transaction key, with the hash stored on the blockchain for this transaction key, *GENEVIZ* can check if the package content matches the initial one from the creator of the SFC Package. Three possible states are defined: *(i)* Valid meaning that the hash of a SFC Package matches the one stored on the blockchain for the given transaction key, *(ii)* Invalid, when the SFC Package was modified and the hash of the downloaded package does not match with the one stored on the blockchain for the given transaction key; and *(iii)* Unknown represents that the SFC Package's hash was not stored in the blockchain during its creation because special reasons (*e.g.*, the developer decided to not use the blockchain validation upon constructing the SFC), thus, there is no transaction key or hash available for verification. In this case, *GENEVIZ* cannot make any statement about the integrity of the content (*cf.* Sect. 4.3 below).

3.1   Prototype and Implementation

The *GENEVIZ* prototype was implemented using JavaScript on the *User Layer* and Python 3.7.0 together with Flask 1.0.2 on the *Data Layer*. For the *Blockchain Layer*, Ethereum blockchain was used, supported by Ganache [16] its latest version as the development environment. For the SFC Package, the VNFD following the European Telecommunications Standards Institute (ETSI) standards and the codes to execute each VNF was considered. The prototype implemented considering those components previously defined, serving as a Proof-of-Concept (PoC) for the *GENEVIZ*'s architecture. The prototype's source-code and its documentation are publicly available online [9].

The left side of the *GENEVIZ* interface (*cf.* Fig. 2) offers a menu, allowing the user to manually upload zipped VNF and SFC Packages by using the dropzone (depicted with the dashed border). By clicking on the respective buttons for *VNFs* and *SFCs*, the user can switch between these two catalogs. Only ZIP files containing VNF-related files are allowed to be uploaded. At the bottom of the menu, the blue button allows for the generation of an SFC Package based on the SFC constructed. This button only appears if the constructed SFC is valid. Hence, the button is not visible at the initial start of the application, as an empty SFC is considered to be invalid. The User Interface shows an alert on the top right corner if any error message has to be passed to the user. This can especially be helpful during the graph construction or import of new packages, since there is feedback from the application if an action fails or is not allowed. Examples include a wrong format of the VNF Template (*e.g.*, the *Package Parser* cannot find the VNFD) or the attempt to create a loop during the forwarding graph construction.

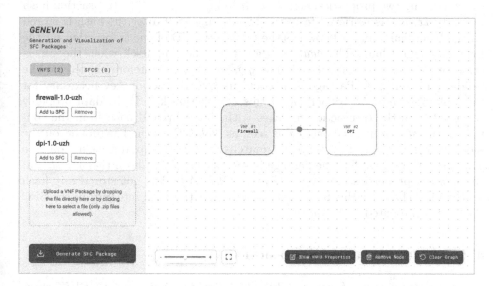

Fig. 2. GENEVIZ dashboard (Color figure online)

GENEVIZ provides also feedback during the construction of the SFC (*i.e.*, chaining recommendation). When a new edge is being placed between two nodes on the graph plane, the edge color is defined based on the two properties *target_recommendation* and *target_caution* inside the VNFD of the source VNF. Such properties are an extension provided by *GENEVIZ* for the ETSI VNFD standard. These properties can be defined by the developer of the VNF inside of the respective VNFD. For example, dependencies of VNFs can be listed (*e.g.*, ensure that two complementary VNFs will be chained) and suggestions for performances improvement (*e.g.*, avoid the chaining of conflicting VNFs) can be described. Based on this information, *GENEVIZ* highlights wrong connections or possible bottlenecks during the SFC construction. Edges can be described as *(a)* green dot for a *recommended* target VNF, *(b)* red dot for *not recommended* target VNF, and *(c)* blue/white for neutral targets. The latter is especially important, since a VNF does not hold the entire list of all possible VNFs as targets in their properties, leaving the statement on the chaining recommendation neutral.

The structure of an SFC Package generated and handled by the *GENEVIZ* prototype is described as a *sfc.zip* file, which contains one or more VNF Packages. Each VNF composing the SFC has a separate folder for its respective content (*e.g.*, descriptors and source-code). For an SFC Package with multiple VNFs from the same template (*i.e.*, reuse of VNFs with different configurations), multiple VNFDs with different IDs will be available in the same *Descriptors* folder of the respective VNF. In addition, the *sfc.zip* file has a file named *nsd.json*, which represents the Network Service Descriptor (NSD) of the SFC.

Also, the *sfc.zip* file contains the *geneviz.json*, which is a *GENEVIZ* descriptor containing two properties, namely *txHash* and *address*. The transaction hash property *txHash* is retrieved from the blockchain itself after the hash is stored on the blockchain, and is known as the transaction ID of the transaction for the Ethereum blockchain. The *address* is given by the user itself when the generation of the package is requested. The *geneviz.json* is therefore needed for the validation of an SFC Package as it contains the transaction key necessary for the lookup of the data properties for this transaction key. If the data property retrieved from the transaction matches with the computed hash from the content of the *sfc.zip* file, the package is seen as *Valid*. Does the hash found on the blockchain for the given *txHash* not match with the computed hash from the content of the *sfc.zip* file, the package is seen as *Invalid*. If both the *txHash* and the *address* properties are empty strings, *GENEVIZ* has not stored any hash on the blockchain for this SFC Package and thus the data integrity of the SFC Package is presented as *Unknown*.

4   Evaluations and Discussion

In order to validate key features and the technical feasibility of *GENEVIZ*, three case studies on: *(i)* the process of the construction of SFCs, outlining benefits of the visualization to simplify the process of SFC construction, *(ii)* the generation of an SFC package, which means the merging of different VNF packages and configurations defined in previous steps. Also, the storage of the SFC package on the blockchain is shown, via an *(iii)* import of an existent SFC package (*e.g.*, available on online marketplaces or public repositories) and its validation of integrity and origin using the hash stored in the Ethereum blockchain. In addition, a discussion is provided to highlight the main benefits and limitations of the presented solution.

4.1   Case Study #1 - Construction of an SFC

Case study #1 considers a user with the specific demand to create a new network service, which shall be deployed in an NFV environment. Thus, the user bought three different VNF Packages from an external source (*e.g.*, from a marketplace), which are needed to create the SFC. The VNFs acquired implement a Deep Packet Inspection (DPI), a Firewall, and a Load Balancer (LB), respectively.

In a first step, the three VNFs are imported via the manual upload of the *GENEVIZ* Web application. After uploading them, all *VNF Packages* appear in the left menu as *VNF Templates*, since they could be added multiple times for the same SFC. By selecting the blue-bordered "Add to SFC" button for each *VNF Template* once, each template is added as a VNF Package to the SFC and appears as a node within the graph on the right side of the Web application. Next, the user constructs a connection between two VNFs selecting the DPI and Firewall. This leads to the creation of an edge between the DPI and the Firewall node. By connecting the Firewall with the LB node with the same approach, the second edge is created (*cf.* Fig. 3).

This first draft of the SFC can be seen as a misconfiguration, although it would not be wrong to create such an SFC. The current construction also shows that the user is not experienced with the creation of SFCs, since a red dot on the edge between the DPI and the Firewall node appears. This red dot is part of the chaining recommendation of the *GENEVIZ*'s Prototype and indicates that the connection is not recommended for an SFC. In this case, this red dot highlights that a DPI allocated before a Firewall can generate a bottleneck in the service chaining. Hence, based on such an alert, the user changes the current construction and swaps the DPI and the Firewall node by deleting the two edges created, then swapping the position of the DPI and the Firewall node, and finally connecting the three nodes again by creating two new edges. As a result, the first edge will see a green dot, indicating a recommended connection. This recommendation is based on the information being part of the VNFDs, determining an additional as an extension of *GENEVIZ*.

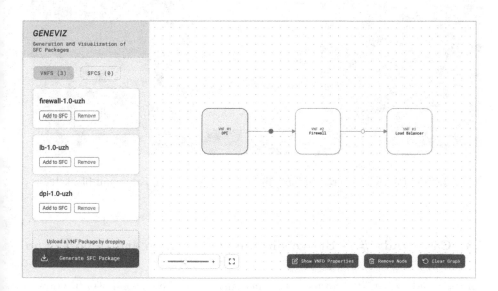

Fig. 3. SFC construction user interface for case study 1 (Color figure online)

4.2   Case Study #2 - Generation of an SFC Package

The case study #2 evaluates the generation of an SFC Package and assumes a correct construction of the forwarding graph within the graph as constructed within case study #1. If such a constructed SFC is valid, a blue button with the label "Generate SFC Package" appears at the bottom left corner. By selecting on that a popup window appears, requesting the user to define the name, vendor, and version for SFC Package. If the end-user decided to store the hash of the SFC Package on the Ethereum blockchain for further validations, additional information are requested (*cf.* Fig. 4). For this, the end-user needs to provide both the address of an Ethereum account as well as the private key for this account in order to sign the transaction properly.

As a next step, the user selects the blue-bordered "Download" button, which generates the SFC Package and stores the hash of the package on the Ethereum blockchain. The *GENEVIZ* will automatically trigger the download of a ZIP file, containing both an *sfc.zip* file for the deployment of the SFC as well as a *geneviz.json* file to be used for further validations of the SFC Package. The

Fig. 4. SFC Package generation including its storage on the Ethereum blockchain

4.3   Case Study #3 - Blockchain-Based Validation and Import of an SFC Package

For case study #3 a different user is being considered. This second user has downloaded three SFC Packages before (*e.g.*, from a marketplace or a public catalog of VNFs), without any information on their integrity and origin (*i.e.*, developers). As these packages contain different folders and nested files representing each VNF that compose the service, for which a check of their content may be time-consuming, the user leaves the validation of these package up to *GENEVIZ*. Here the user refers to use the SFC Package named *sfc-package-evaluation*, but he also considers the *sfc-package-other* and the *sfc-package-other-2* packages in case the first one turns out to be invalid.

In the first step, the user selects the "SFCS" button in the menu on the left side to switch to the SFC section. This section allows for the manual upload of SFC Packages through the browser as it is performed for the upload of VNF Packages. The SFC Packages uploaded appear on the SFC list as *SFC Templates* in a similar way uploaded VNF Packages are handled as *VNF Templates*. The validation of the packages uploaded is triggered automatically and the response depends on the current block time of the blockchain. For the package named *sfc-package-other-2* no statement on its data integrity can be made, since no information for the retrieval on the blockchain is provided, hence, it is marked as *Unknown*. The second package *sfc-package-other* appears to be marked as *Invalid*, which means the content of this package was modified. The third package *sfc-package-evaluation* is the package created within case study #2. Since the hash of this package was stored in the Ethereum blockchain during the generation of the package by the first user and the transaction ID is part of the SFC Package downloaded, *GENEVIZ* finds a hash for the given transaction ID, which matches with the hash of the content from the SFC Package uploaded. Hence, *GENEVIZ* marks the SFC Package uploaded as *Valid*, and shows the green "Valid" label, as shown in Fig. 5 within the white boxes of the *SFC Templates*.

Fig. 5. Blockchain-based validation of SFCs

For this third SFC Package, an acceptable level of trust was established, thus, the user decides to import this SFC Package as a new SFC into *GENEVIZ* in order to adjust VNFD properties of the VNFs involved, since they fit his/her demands. By selecting on the blue-bordered "Import" button on the left menu an alert appears, warning the user that the currently drafted SFC will be cleared and replaced by the new SFC. This is adequate for the user, since the drafted SFC previously is not relevant anymore. Now, the SFC will be imported and, if the SFC Package can be extracted, the visualization will be constructed to show the corresponding graph. This is considered helpful for the user, since the forwarding graph is now directly visible and can also be modified if needed. In turn, the user decides to open the *VNFD Editor* for the DPI, which lies between the Firewall and the LB. By selecting on the "Show VNFD Properties" at the bottom of the user interface (*cf.* Fig. 3), a popup window appears, displaying current VNFD properties of the DPI. The user decides to change the memory size to "8 GB" and the number of CPUs to "2" to fulfill his/her demands for the new network service. After applying these changes, the new VNFD properties are directly updated. Finally, the user selects the option to generate the SFC Package, forcing the generation and download of the adjusted SFC Package based on the SFC Package created by the first user. Finally, the customized SFC Package can be used to be deployed as a new network service.

4.4   Discussion

These three case studies investigate and evaluate different set-ups, while applying *GENEVIZ*. Both, the construction of a new network service based on selected VNF Packages as well as the adjustment of properties of a certain VNF being part of the SFC, simplify the process for the user compared to existing support solutions. The graphical user interface for the service construction and the chaining recommendation address the critical issue of VNF chaining, helping the user to draft suitable SFCs. Furthermore, by storing the hash of the content of the newly created package on the blockchain, the verification of the package's originality can be performed by any user through *GENEVIZ* as well. All tasks can be performed separately, consuming an unnecessary manual effort for users being inexperienced in the NFV market. The unified thus simplified approach at one single place is achieved by the *GENEVIZ*.

Since this current evaluation is based on case studies only, quantitative evidence on the performance of *GENEVIZ* in terms of intuitiveness and simplification to create SFCs will be performed in future steps. In this sense, a usability evaluation with real users is planned to validate the benefits of *GENEVIZ* and provide quantitative details about the effectiveness, while these evaluations will be based on System Usability Scale (SUS) questionnaires. Also, by constructing SFCs through *GENEVIZ*, specific quantitative gains can be articulated through measurements in a real-world deployment.

The application of a blockchain ensures data integrity of a previously created SFC Package. The block time is assumed to be within in a reasonable amount of time for the end-user, which is not always guaranteed for certain blockchains (*e.g.*, Ethereum may show block time peaks with up to 30 s). Although the integrity of content can be guaranteed through the hash verification, the package can already contain malicious code at the moment of the creation of the new package or during the creation of the VNF Package, being part of the SFC Package downloaded. Hence, *GENEVIZ* provides evidence for the end-users trust in a download package from the Internet, since the author and the content can be verified by using the information available in the blockchain.

5   Summary and Future Work

As NFV becomes technically more mature and its infrastructure widely adopted, the demand for specific network services based on the chaining of different virtualized network functions will increase in the years to come. Thus, this paper introduced *GENEVIZ*, a tool for the generation, validation, and visualization of SFC Packages. The graphical user interface proposed leads to a more intuitive and easier construction of new network services. *GENEVIZ* potentially can also lead to fewer mistakes during the creation of new or the adjustment of existing services, as there are fewer steps required to be taken to generate an SFC Package. Thus, visualizations had been proposed within a single Web application to deal with *(i)* the construction of an SFC by chaining different VNFs through a single, directed, and acyclic graph, *(ii)* the adjustment of VNFD properties of VNFs being part of the SFC, *(iii)* supporting the user to create better SFCs by providing a chaining recommender, and *(iv)* the ability to validate, supported by blockchains, a previously created SFC to check its integrity and origin.

GENEVIZ runs as a Web-based application, which can be deployed on a local machine, hence allowing end-users to create and adjust SFC Packages locally. Although *GENEVIZ* provides the possibility to validate data integrity of the content of a package by using blockchains trust in the individual VNF Packages offered by third-parties is still necessary. All visualizations provided by the solution proposed can foster both the growth of the NFV market and business models introduced by marketplaces for VNF-as-a-Service (VNFaaS). Thus, *GENEVIZ* shows the potential to support not only experienced network operators, but also end-users acquiring VNFs from marketplaces. Therefore, a possible positive effect on a broader adoption of NFV technology may become possible.

As future work, existing visualizations can be expanded in order to support different recommendations for the chaining of VNFs inside the service function chaining by using, for example, the affinity between pairs of VNFs. Also, the VNFD Editor can be made configurable to support the editing of additional properties from the VNF Descriptor. Since input fields in the popup window map directly match the properties of a VNFD, *GENEVIZ* can maintain these inputs, too. SFCs created can be offered to other users through a blockchain-based marketplace for SFCs. Finally, the validation of SFCs can be improved not only to ensure data integrity, but also to increase the level of trust for an SFC Package from an unknown source by scanning the content for malicious content. This can be performed during the construction of an SFC, while VNF Packages are imported, or during the import of an existing SFC Package.

References

1. Aste, T., Tasca, P., Di Matteo, T.: Blockchain technologies: the foreseeable impact on society and industry. IEEE Comput. **50**, 18–28 (2017)
2. Bondan, L., et al.: FENDE: marketplace-based distribution, execution, and life cycle management of VNFs. IEEE Commun. Mag. **57**, 13–19 (2019)
3. Ware, C.: Information Visualization: Perception for Design; 3rd edn, pp. 1–536. Elsevier (2012)
4. Eichelberger, R.A., Ferreto, T., Tandel, S., Duarte, P.A.: SFC path tracer: a troubleshooting tool for service function chaining. In: IFIP/IEEE Symposium on Integrated Network and Service Management (IM 2017), Lisbon, Portugal, May 2017, pp. 568–571 (2017)

5. ETSI GS NFV-MAN: Network Functions Virtualisation (NFV); Management and Orchestration, December 2014
6. Franco, M.F., dos Santos, R.L., Schaeffer-Filho, A., Granville, L.Z.: VISION - interactive and selective visualization for management of NFV-enabled networks. In: IEEE 30th International Conference on Advanced Information Networking and Applications (AINA 2016), Crans-Montana, Switzerland, March 2016, pp. 274–281 (2016)
7. Guimarães, V.T., Freitas, C.M.D.S., Sadre, R., Tarouco, L.M.R., Granville, L.Z.: A survey on information visualization for network and service management. IEEE Commun. Surv. Tutorials. **18**, 285–323 (2015)
8. Han, B., Gopalakrishnan, V., Ji, L., Lee, S.: Network function virtualization: challenges and opportunities for innovations. IEEE Commun. Mag. **53**, 90–97 (2015)
9. Bucher, M., Franco, M., Scheid, E.: GENEVIZ Prototype - Source Code. https://gitlab.ifi.uzh.ch/franco/geneviz. Accessed May 2019
10. Chiosi, M., et al.: Network functions virtualisation: an introduction, benefits, enablers, challenges and call for action. In: SDN and OpenFlow World Congress, Düsseldorf, Germany, October 2012, vol. 48, pp. 1–16 (2012)
11. Mijumbi, R., Serrat, J., Gorricho, J., Bouten, N., De Turck, F., Boutaba, R.: Network function virtualization: state-of-the-art and research challenges. IEEE Commun. Surv. Tutorials **18**, 236–262 (2016)
12. Nakamoto, S.: Bitcoin: A Peer-to-Peer Electronic Cash System (2009). https://bitcoin.org/bitcoin.pdf. Accessed June 2019
13. Sanz, I.J., Mattos, D.M.F., Duarte, O.C.M.B.: SFCPerf: an automatic performance evaluation framework for service function chaining. In: IEEE/IFIP Network Operations and Management Symposium (NOMS 2018), Taipei, Taiwan, April 2018, pp. 1–9 (2018)
14. Scheid, E., Rodrigues, B., Stiller, B.: Toward a policy-based blockchain agnostic framework. In: IFIP/IEEE Symposium on Integrated Network and Service Management (IM 2019), Washington, DC, USA, April 2019, pp. 609–613 (2019)
15. Soles, L.R., Reichherzer, T., Snider, D.H.: A tool set for managing virtual network configurations. In: IEEE SoutheastCon (SoutheastCon 2016), Norfolk, UK, March 2016, pp. 1–4 (2016)
16. Truffle Blockchain Group: Ganache Website. https://truffleframework.com/ganache. Accessed May 2019
17. Wood, G.: Ethereum: a secure decentralised generalised transaction ledger. Ethereum Project Yellow Paper **151**, 1–32 (2014)

A Smart Contract Based Recommender System

Andrea Lisi[1], Andrea De Salve[2,3(✉)], Paolo Mori[3], and Laura Ricci[1]

[1] University of Pisa, Largo Bruno Pontecorvo, 3, 56127 Pisa, Italy
andrealisi.12lj@gmail.com, laura.ricci@unipi.it
[2] University of Palermo, Via Archirafi, 34, 90123 Palermo, Italy
andrea.desalve@unipa.it
[3] Consiglio Nazionale delle Ricerche - IIT, via G. Moruzzi, 1, 56124 Pisa, Italy
paolo.mori@iit.cnr.it

Abstract. Nowadays information available on the World Wide Web has reached unprecedented growth and it makes difficult for users to find the most relevant for them. In order to alleviate such issue, Recommender Systems (RSs) have been proposed to collect opinions and preferences about a set of items, process such preferences and build a personalized information access.

While the most part of current RSs exploit centralized architecture to provide the service, in this manuscript we propose an alternative approach for building a general purpose RSs that provides to users with more transparent and decentralized rating strategy. Indeed, the proposed framework is built on top of a Distributed Ledger technology platform that runs without any centralized authority and it supports both decentralized ratings and ranking of different items. A preliminary evaluation on the Ethereum test network demonstrates the feasibility of the framework in terms of performance and cost.

Keywords: Distributed Ledger Technology · Recommender system · Blockchain · Smart contract

1 Introduction

Information available on the World Wide Web are continuously growing and users are allowed to share any kind of content more quickly and easily. However, the proliferation of such information makes it difficult for users to find the most relevant for them. In order to alleviate such issue, Recommender Systems (RSs) have been proposed and they are used to enable intelligent and personalized information access [13].

A RS collects opinions and preferences from its users about a set of items, and exploits such information to suggest the items that are most favoured and that are of potential interest according to the actions performed by its users. The collection of items' preferences is one of the most important step for a RS,

© Springer Nature Switzerland AG 2019
K. Djemame et al. (Eds.): GECON 2019, LNCS 11819, pp. 29–42, 2019.
https://doi.org/10.1007/978-3-030-36027-6_3

and it is typically carried out by allowing users to express a numerical vote (e.g., number of stars) and a textual opinion about items, based on their experiences. As for instance, read or write a review on TripAdvisor[1], currently one of the most popular RSs, is among the top-10 most popular daily social media activities performed by users of the United States[2] and, based on TripAdvisor Global Report[3], 49% of travellers were inspired to visit a new destination by a personalized recommendation on TripAdvisor. Besides classical products, restaurant, and hotel recommendation and advertising, RSs are also used to recommend relevant information related to different types of items: such as movies preferences [5],professionals who join LinkedIn, videos uploaded on YouTube [3], songs provided on Spotify, or the best time for a user to send a message [4].

The most part of current RSs are based on a centralized architecture where the service provider controls and manages all the preferences given by users. Such preferences are used by the service provider to return a ranked list of items based on their global relevance aimed to affect the consumer decisions [11]. Hence, one of the main issues of current RS are the difficulty to obtain knowledge about the whole set of preferences and how the final score of an item is computed. Consequently, users are not aware of both the mechanisms and the information used by the RS to suggest them items.

In order to solve the previous issues and to provide users with more transparent rating strategy, we propose an alternative approach for building a general purpose RSs which is based on the Distributed Ledger Technology [15]. The proposed framework supports decentralized ratings, ranking of different items and it is built on top of a platform that runs smart contracts on a public blockchain, without any centralized authority. Since it is based on a public blockchain which provides an immutable, public, and ordered ledger, the proposed RS prevents censorship, downtime, and alteration in a second moment of the preferences and opinions. Furthermore, we have extended the framework's capabilities by integrating an authorization module that collects preferences only from users entitled to rate the item. To prove the feasibility of the proposed approach we developed and deployed a prototype of such decentralized recommendation framework on an Ethereum TestNet and we conducted an extensive set of experimental evaluations to measure its performance.

The rest of the manuscript is organized as follows: Sect. 2 introduces the reader to the fundamental concepts related to the Blockchain, Smart Contract, and RSs while Sect. 3 presents the related works. Section 4 provides the general architecture of our framework while in Sect. 5 we show in detail the framework instantiation process to the case of Ethereum platform. Section 6 focuses on the performance of the proposed framework. Finally, in Sect. 7 we draw conclusions and future improvements.

---

[1] https://www.tripadvisor.com.
[2] Statista 2019: https://bit.ly/2BYJf1U.
[3] TripAdvisorInsights: https://bit.ly/2UaE8Tn.

2   Background

In this section we introduce the reader to the fundamental concepts related to the Blockchain, Smart Contract technology, and Recommendation System.

2.1   Smart Contract and Blockchain

A *blockchain* is an append-only list of blocks which contains immutable records. Immutability is achieved by a combination of cryptographic techniques and a P2P consensus protocol, such as Proof of Work or Proof of Stake, a collaborative approach that defines the rules of who will be elected to update the ledger (e.g. miners or validators) by appending the new block and be finally rewarded for the contribution to the validation of the transactions. As consequence, the blocks of the chain are protected against modification and the underlying peer-to-peer network is used to replicate the blockchain on different peers. Bitcoin [12] uses the blockchain to mint and transfer a cryptocurrency, bitcoin[4], in a distributed fashion; Ethereum [15] hosts decentralized statefull applications (named smart contracts) written through a Turing-complete programming language (e.g. Solidity[5]) and running on a virtual machine where transactions represent a change from a state to another. In particular, a smart contract [14] is a piece of software with the property to run transactions without involving third parties. The cryptocurrency used by Ethereum is named Ether (ETH) and it must also be used to pay the fees for the execution of smart contracts. The modification of the state of a smart contract, by calling one of its functions, will cost units of *gas* to the caller, a fee which amout is proportional to the complexity of the computation. The caller can decide how much ETH assign to every unit of gas (*gas price*) and how many units of gas provide for that execution (*gas limit*). In case many transactions are issued to the network, higher the gas price higher the probability to be executed in a short time. If the execution exceeds the gas limit the contract will be reverted to the original state and all gas spent will not be refunded. In contrast, a state query[6] does not need to be placed in a block and thus does not consume ETH to the caller, even though the gas is computed and the gas limit rule still applies. At the time of writing both Ethereum and Bitcoin use as consensus the Proof of Work (PoW) algorithm [6].

2.2   Recommender Systems

A Recommender system (RS) is a software application which collects and analyzes the preferences (named *ratings*) given by *users* to different *items* in order to enable reliable recommendation of *items* to interested users [13]. RSs can influence and help users in everyday decisions concerning the acquisition of products. Furthermore, RSs go beyond the traditional marketing applications because, in

---

[4] The protocol starts with a capital "B", the cryptocurrency does not.

[5] Solidity docs: https://bit.ly/2S5X2La.

[6] A smart contract function which does not change the contract's state.

addition to banners and advertisements, the subjects of the RSs can be various types of items which depend on the application domain (such as, travel destinations, web sites, music and videos or influencers).

One of the most important features of these systems is the need to collect ratings in order to determine if some item may be suitable or not for a user, such as, preferences, inclinations, opinions, choices, etc. The ratings can be represented by a *score* in different ways: *(i)* numerical ratings, such as a numbered stars between 1 and 5 (Amazon), *(ii)* binary ratings, the presence of either "like" and "dislike" buttons (YouTube), and *(iii)* unary ratings, only the "like" button (Instagram). Often, text information is paired with the ratings (such as comment or review) in order to explain the reasons of the score. All of this information is collected and processed by RSs to build personalized recommendations to users.

3   Related Works

The problem of recommending the most appropriate item is not trivial and several techniques to rank items based on different factors have been proposed [1]. The most part of current RSs are implemented exploiting a centralized architecture where a single authority collects the ratings submitted by users and performs recommendation for the other users. As for instance, Tripadvisor and Amazon are among the most popular centralized RS which collect feedbacks on destinations and products in order to recommend new items to users, and Linkedin which acts like an Online Social Network where companies are recommended to users if they fit users skills.

However, such centralized architecture introduces the several issues and risks for the users of the services:

– the data related to items (such as reviews) could not be entirely accessible and verified by users, because the central authority could make available only a subset of them to its users;
– users of the centralized RS need to trust the central authority controlling the service which, for instance, could alter or delete existing reviews to properly modify the rank of an item;
– users of the RSs are unaware of (or cannot verify) the method used by the centralized authority to compute the rank of the items.

In order to solve the previous problems, decentralized RSs [9] have been proposed and their aim is to avoid unnecessary centralized entities. In the following, we will focus only on RSs involving blockchain solutions. Gastroadvisor[7], a Tripadvisor like platform focusing only on restoration, exploits the blockchain to store a special type of reviews, gold reviews, that a user can leave if he previously booked and paid through FORK tokens, the platform currency. Friendz[8], an Instagram like photo platform focusing on product campaigns, exploits the blockchain to make the system transparent and decentralized.

---

[7] Gastroadvisor whitepaper: https://bit.ly/2YfIs6v.
[8] Friendz whitepaper: https://bit.ly/2FdKolK.

Both Gastroadvisor and Friendz have their own tokens built on top of the architecture and a reward system to make the platform more appealing than the competitors. In contrast to the previous solutions, the approach proposed in this manuscript does not focus on a specific context, neither introduces a new sub-currency for the users, but it analyzes whether the DLT would be a suitable architecture to build decentralized RS, offering a set of smart contracts implementing the major operations concerning RSs, such as information storage, rating and a flexible and customizable score computation.

Another relevant work is proposed in [7] where blockchain is used as Personal Data Management System. The users' personal data relevant for the recommendation task are stored in encrypted form on the blockchain and they can be used by companies, i.e., third-parties interested in recommending their products and services. A company can propose a contract that define how users' data are utilized by the recommendation task. If the users agrees such contract, the company will have access to perform the recommendation. However, the proposed approach has an important limitation, it requires the use of expensive mechanisms (such as homomorphic encryption) to perform simple computations on encrypted data.

4 A Framework for Recommender System

To address the issues of current centralized RSs (see Sect. 3) and to provide the user with more transparency and flexibility, we propose a framework which brings together blockchain technology and recommendation system. The proposed framework builds up a decentralized component for a RS implemented through smart contracts on top of a blockchain, thus being:

- Public: the *items*, the *ratings*, and the *rating functions*, are visible to all users and replicated on all the nodes of the blockchain.
- Decentralized: the framework relies on untrusted environment where there is no central authority which manages the rates and the score of items.
- Tamper-proof: the ratings submitted by the users and the rating functions stored in the blockchain cannot be altered.
- Persistent: the ratings and the smart contracts deployed on the blockchain are always available i.e., they cannot be removed.
- Customizable rating function: anyone is free to define his own method to compute the rating, since the data are available on the blockchain (see *Score module* paragraph of Sect. 5 for more information).

In this paper we focus our attention on *public* blockchains as underlying architecture hosting the smart contracts composing our framework.

4.1 System Model

The proposed solution is built on top of a blockchain protocol supporting smart contracts. Figure 1 shows high level overview of the components proposed by our

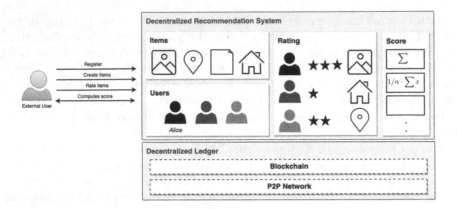

Fig. 1. General architecture of a decentralized recommendation system.

approach, each of them reflecting the entities involved in the recommendation systems scenario, i.e. *items*, *users*, the *ratings* given by users to items, and the *scores* paired to items and computed taking into account the ratings (Sect. 2.2). The main operations provided by the system concern the registration of a new user (**Register**), the creation of a new item (**Create item**), the rating of an existing item (**Rate item**) and the computation of the score of an existing item (**Compute score**).

A user can register to the system with the **Register** operation, choosing a pseudonym that does not reveal nothing about the real. Each user can add new items to the system with the **Create item** operation, assigning to such items the public information needed to recognize them. An item could be a virtual representation of a place (such as restaurant, hotel, or store) or of a service (such as financial instruments, web services, or another smart contract). Each user can leave a rating on an item through the **Rate item** operation. We assume that a rating record consists of the identifier of the item, the identifier of the user, a timestamp, and a numeric score representing the opinion of user with respect to the item.

Finally, the **Compute score** operation allows users to get the overall score of an item, computed in real-time over the total ratings attached to that item. Relying on an open and public blockchain, and being the RS ratings visible, anyone can implement his own methods, rating functions, to compute the final score of the item. To help the RS users to choose a method, the framework provides a registry of functions approved by the RS owner. The approval prevents unnecessary spam of functions. All of these operations and components are implemented and executed by using the underlying Decentralized Ledger guaranteeing the benefits previously listed.

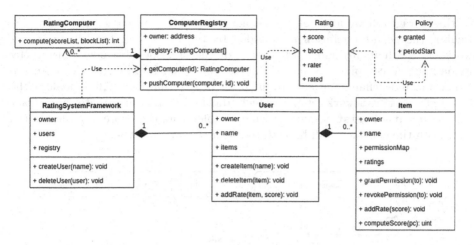

Fig. 2. Overview of the main contracts

5   Architecture and Implementation

To implement the proposed system we rely on Ethereum because it provides stable and participated testing networks, plus tools for the development of smart contracts. The contracts composing the proposed solution have been implemented in Solidity and are shown in Fig. 2. The `RatingSystemFramework` contract is responsible of storing, creating, and deleting `User` contracts which model the users of the RS: this contract is supposed to be a singleton and can be seen as entry point of the system. The `User` contract is responsible of storing, creating, deleting and rating items exploiting `Items` contracts, which model the items of the RS. A person can own one or more `User` contracts. Finally, the `Item` contract is responsible of storing the received `Rating` and a permission map of (`address`, `Policy`) pairs describing whether a RS user has the permissions to rate the item, plus it provides the functions to accept a new rating and update the permission map. Each item should be represented by its own `Item` contract. The `ComputerRegistry` contract is in charge to store the rating functions which implement the `Compute Score` operation in Fig. 1. This contract should be a singleton. To simplify the description of the proposed framework, we introduce the following actors: *(i)* Alice, who wants to deploy a recommendation service for different types of establishments (such as restaurants, bars, and pubs); *(ii)* Bob, who is the owner of a bar; *(iii)* Carl, a customer of Bob's bar. We assume that Alice, Bob and Carl use Metamask[9] to interact with the smart contracts of the framework and we assume they have addresses *0xalice*, *0xbob* and *0xcarl*, respectively.

System Deployment. Figure 3 shows how the contracts previously listed are deployed, who is in charge of the deployment and how they are interconnected.

---

[9] Metamask: https://bit.ly/2DIukHT.

In this paragraph we focus on the deployment of the system by Alice. In particular, the *deploy* operation is provided by the underlying blockchain framework (i.e., Ethereum) and it takes care of the creation of a new contract by uploading the compiled version of the contract (i.e., EVM bytecode) onto the Ethereum blockchain. Initially, by help of an external tool, Alice deploys the `RatingSystemFramework` (step 1) which, during its creation, creates a contract called `ComputerRegistry` (step 2) which implements the Score module. At the end, both the contracts will have stored *0xalice* as their owner.

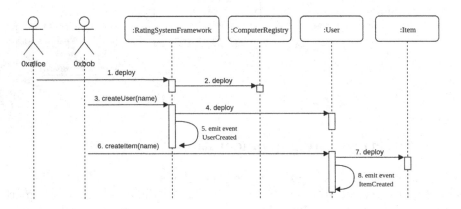

Fig. 3. Creation flow of `RatingSystemFramework`, `User` and `Item`

User Module. Bob can register to the RS with the `createUser()` operation (step 3 in Fig. 3) provided by `RatingSystemFramework` smart contract (deployed by Alice): the operation deploys a new instance of `User` contract (step 4) at address *0xbobUser*, and emits a new event to notify the network about the presence of the new user (steps 5). The contract *0xbobUser* stores *0xbob* as its owner. Thanks to this contract, Bob is officialy an user of Alice's platoform.

To create an item representing his own bar, Bob needs to call the `createItem()` operation on his `User` contract (step 6). Such operation checks if the caller is *0xbob* and, if successfull, it deploys a new instance of `Item` contract (step 7) storing *0xbob* in the owner field, and emits a new event to notify the network about the presence of this new item (steps 8). Now is possible, for other users, to rate Bob's bar.

Item and Rating Modules. We assume Carl to be registered to Alice's RS, thus having his own `User` contract with address *0xcarlUser*. In order to rate an `Item`, Carl needs the permissions to be properly set by that item owner. Bob, an item owner, gives permissions to other users to rate his items through the `grantPermission()` operation provided by the `Item` contract. The permission policy, modeled by the `Policy` struct, consists of a boolean flag together with the starting period expressed as the block which contains the transaction

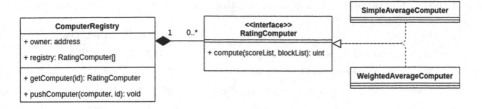

Fig. 4. `RatingComputer` implementations

triggered by `grantPermission()`. Once Carl has the permissions set by Bob, he can rate Bob's bar by invoking the `addRate()` operation on his `User`, at address *0xcarlUser*, within a time window expressed in number of blocks. The `User.addRate()` expects the score value and the address of the `Item` to rate, and it will invoke `Item.addRate()` function: this double step prevents external users of the RS from rating items. The `Item.addRate()` checks whether the caller has the permissions and, if it does, it stores the new rating modeled as the `Rating` struct shown in Fig. 2.

Score Module. A *rating function* is a function which computes the score of an item according to a specific formula. In our framework, Rating functions implement the `RatingComputer` interface, a smart contract exposing only one method called `compute()` which calculates the overall score of an item by using the list of ratings of the item (*scoreList*) and the list of the blocks indexes containing those ratings (*blockList*). The `ComputerRegistry` contract is in charge to store `RatingComputer` implementations and can be populated only by who deployed the RS (Alice in our example): this should keep the registry clean by unnecessary implementations, such as bad or repeated ones. Figure 4 shows the relationships among the listed contracts. To compute the score, the `Item` contract provides the `computeScore()` operation which accepts as input a `RatingComputer` to compute the score of that item. Carl can choose a `RatingComputer` from the registry and use it to compute the score of Bob's bar.

6 Evaluations

To validate the proposed approach we deployed the previously described smart contracts on an Ethereum testing blockchain. Among the test networks officially provided by Ethereum we chose Ropsten[10] because it uses the same consensus of the Ethereum main network at the time of writing. Instead of running an Ethereum node with tools such as Geth[11], our evaluations rely on the Infura service[12], which allows to connect to an Ethereum node and call the smart contract functions.

---

[10] Ropsten: https://bit.ly/2E9bfjV.
[11] Geth: https://bit.ly/2Isky2b.
[12] Infura: https://bit.ly/2L5t4pJ.

Table 1. Operations cost in gas and in Eth considering a gas price of 15 Gwei

Contract	Operation	Cost (gas)	Eth-15Gw
RatingSystemFramework	Deploy	4,347,987	0.0652
RatingSystemFramework	createUser	2,282,844	0.0342
User	createItem	1,038,614	0.0155
User	addRate	166,337	0.0025
Item	grantPermission	78,735	0.0012
ComputerRegistry	pushComputer	75,125	0.0011
SimpleAverageComputer	Deploy	197,603	0.0030
WeightedAverageComputer	Deploy	220.611	0.0033
RatingComputer	Compute	0	0

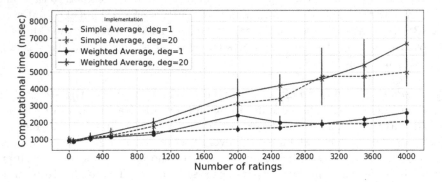

Fig. 5. Evaluation of the `compute(scores,blocks)` operation of the contract `RatingComputer` by varying the input size

Gas Analysis. We evaluate the gas consumed for the deployment and execution of the main contracts' functions of our framework. Table 1 shows the cost in gas and the related cost in Ether that will be charged to the caller for the execution of the main operations of our framework with a gas price of 15 Gwei. The creation and deployment of a contract are the most expensive ones but their execution occurs only a few times for each user. The `compute()` operation of the `RatingComputer` contract does not change the state of the network, and hence its execution does not consume gas. For what concerns the number of transactions that can be accommodated in a single block, at the time of writing the blocks of Ropsten test network can contain transactions for at most 8M units of gas. As a result, in case of a free network, we expect to have at most around 7/8 `createItem()` transactions or around 100 `grantPermission()` transactions inside a block.

Scalability Analysis. We evaluate the scalability of the `compute()` operation provided by the `RatingComputer` contract because it is supposed to be the most

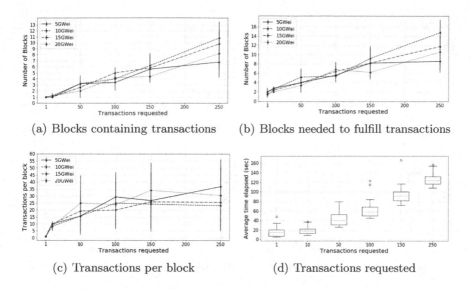

(a) Blocks containing transactions   (b) Blocks needed to fulfill transactions

(c) Transactions per block   (d) Transactions requested

Fig. 6. Testing the resolution of multiple `grantPermission()` transactions

frequent function to be invoked. Such operation requires to loop over the input arrays in order to compute the score of an item, and this could cause the operation to run out of gas if the dimension of such arrays is high. Since we did not evaluated the smart contracts locally on our machines, but on a remote node, we measured how the latency increases by considering different number of ratings for the computation of the score of an item. Furthermore, we tested two distinct implementations of `compute()`: a simple average of the score list and a weighted average which assigns a higher weight to the scores belonging more recent blocks: such implementations are showed in Fig. 4. Figure 5 shows on the x-axis the number of ratings and on the y-axis the mean and the standard deviation of the time (ms) needed to get result. Each point on the plot is computed over 25 samples and with a gas limit of 4.7M units. Both the functions run out of gas with an input size higher than of 4000 elements. This means that the current implementation can take into account no more than 4000 ratings to compute a score. However, more sophisticated implementations could be developed. The dashed lines concern the simple average computation, the continuous line the weighted average, the circle markers concern a single request sent, the cross markers concern a sequence of 20 execution requests sent simultaneously. The plot indicates that when querying multiple executions the time does not add up linearly, and that the execution time does not increase exponentially.

Throughput Analysis. In this paragraph we focus on how many blocks are required to execute a certain amount of transactions[13]. We consider the

---

[13] We remark that a smart contract function which changes the state has to be stored in a transaction, and thus has to be mined.

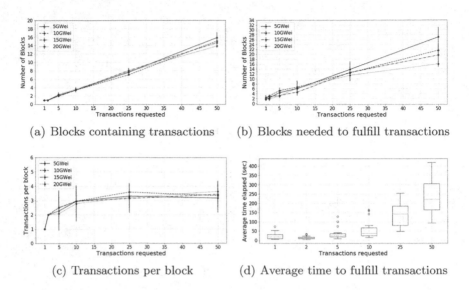

(a) Blocks containing transactions   (b) Blocks needed to fulfill transactions

(c) Transactions per block   (d) Average time to fulfill transactions

Fig. 7. Testing the resolution of multiple `createItem()` transactions

`createItem()` and `grantPermission()` functions because they are more likely to be invoked. The `addRate()` function is omitted because its complexity is comparable to `grantPermission()`. We performed our tests by triggering multiple transactions and we kept track of the blocks where these transactions have been placed. Figure 6 shows the evaluation results concerning the execution of the `grantPermission()` function. For each plot, the x-axis reports a batch of transactions we issued to the network in a single time window while the y-axis shows the mean and the standard deviation got by 5 samples. Such analyses have been performed four times for four different gas prices: 5, 10, 15 and GWei. Figure 6(a) shows how many blocks of the Ropsten blockchain contains our transactions. The number of blocks increases as long as more transactions need to be processed. However, it is possible that such blocks are not contiguous. For this reason, we show in Fig. 6(b) how many blocks elapsed from the time all the transactions are submitted to the time all the transactions are stored in the blockchain. The plot has a trend similar to that of Fig. 6(a) but the number of blocks slightly increases because there are some blocks (between 2 and 4 on average) that do not contain any of the submitted transactions. We investigate in more detail the average number of transactions recorded in each block in Fig. 6(c). The results indicate that the average number of transactions per blocks ranges between 15 and 35 as long as the total number of transactions is more than 50. As shown from the previous analysis, in the Ropsten testnet the change of the gas price does not affect the number of blocks and the number of transactions per block considerably because there is no transaction congestion. Indeed, at the time of writing, Ropsten has in general blocks half full[14] while the main network fills

---

[14] Ropsten blocks, blocksout.com: https://bit.ly/2TQt6C4.

most of its blocks up[15]. We investigate in Fig. 6(d) the average time necessary to grant permission to multiple users by considering the time Ropsten takes to mine the corresponding blocks. The average time to mine an individual transaction is between 10 to 20 s and it is equal to the expected mining time of the Ethereum network (13–14 s[16] at the time of writing). The execution of 250 and 150 `grantPermission()` operations takes on average 125 and 80 s respectively, i.e., about 0.5 s for each transaction.

Figure 7 shows the same evaluations concerning the `createItem()` function. Like in the previous case, the blocks containing these transactions are not contiguous (Figs. 7(a) and (b)). Figure 7(a) shows that, independently from the gas price, the number of blocks mined with such transactions are roughly the same meanwhile Fig. 7(b) shows that with higher gas price the total number of blocks waited are fewer on average, as expected. Finally, Fig. 7(d) confirms that the time to mine transactions does not scale linearly with the number of transactions until they reach a certain threshold from which the number of transactions per block stabilizes, which is 10 in our case as shown in Fig. 7(c).

7   Conclusion and Future Work

In this paper we proposed a context-free smart contract based framework that can be used as external module by a RS and which is aimed at enhancing current RSs by adding the properties of transparency, decentralization, and immutability of the data involved in the process. With respect to traditional RSs, the proposed approach has the advantage that users do not need to trust the entity running the RS, because both the ratings given by the users and the algorithms exploited to compute the score of the items are stored on the blockchain, thus being publicly visible and not alterable.

The proposed framework includes a simple access control mechanism to enable users to rate an item. However, the current implementation relies on a "off chain" agreement between customer and item owner to leave a rating. This prevents massive negative review attacks because such users would not have the permissions to rate an item, but it does not prevent a collusion between the customer and the item owner. Moreover, since creating new Ethereum accounts is cheap, the service owner and is vulnerable to shilling attacks [8]. To mitigate such issues, as a future work, we plan to provide a more sophisticated access control support, integrating other proposals such as [10], and we aim to test the proposal on different ledgers running consensus algorithms focused on locations instead of mining, such as [2]. Finally, we plan to study different approaches with the purposes of increasing the scalability of the Score module implementing it with a pagination technique[17]. Since the proposed `compute()` function, implemented by a smart contract, cannot execute for too long in networks such as

---

[15] Ethereum blocks, blocksout.com: https://bit.ly/2uANLj9.
[16] Insight from Etherscan: https://bit.ly/2H6uLB3.
[17] Pagination in solidity: https://bit.ly/2CksK0B.

Ethereum, a real world platform may rely on smart contracts only when users explicitly ask to do so and not for every execution.

References

1. Bobadilla, J., Ortega, F., Hernando, A., Gutiérrez, A.: Recommender systems survey. Knowl.-Based Syst. **46**, 109–132 (2013)
2. Brambilla, G., Amoretti, M., Zanichelli, F.: Using blockchain for peer-to-peer proof-of-location (2016). arXiv preprint arXiv:1607.00174
3. Davidson, J., et al.: The youtube video recommendation system. In: Proceedings of the Fourth ACM Conference on Recommender Systems, pp. 293–296. ACM (2010)
4. De Salve, A., Guidi, B., Mori, P.: Predicting the availability of users' devices in decentralized online social networks. Concurr. Comput.: Pract. Exp. **30**(20), e4390 (2018)
5. De Salve, A., Guidi, B., Ricci, L., Mori, P.: Discovering homophily in online social networks. Mob. Netw. Appl. **23**(6), 1715–1726 (2018)
6. Dwork, C., Naor, M.: Pricing via processing or combatting junk mail. In: Brickell, E.F. (ed.) CRYPTO 1992. LNCS, vol. 740, pp. 139–147. Springer, Heidelberg (1993). https://doi.org/10.1007/3-540-48071-4_10
7. Frey, R.M., Wörner, D., Ilic, A.: Collaborative filtering on the blockchain: a secure recommender system for e-commerce. In: 22nd Americas Conference on Information Systems, AMCIS 2016, 11–14 August 2016, San Diego, CA, USA (2016)
8. Gunes, I., Kaleli, C., Bilge, A., Polat, H.: Shilling attacks against recommender systems: a comprehensive survey. Artif. Intell. Rev. **42**(4), 767–799 (2014)
9. Han, P., Xie, B., Yang, F., Shen, R.: A scalable P2P recommender system based on distributed collaborative filtering. Expert Syst. Appl. **27**(2), 203–210 (2004)
10. Maesa, D.D.F., Mori, P., Ricci, L.: A blockchain based approach for the definition of auditable access control systems. Comput. Secur. **84**, 93–119 (2019)
11. De Veirman, M., Cauberghe, V., Hudders, L.: Marketing through instagram influencers: the impact of number of followers and product divergence on brand attitude. Int. J. Advert. **36**, 798–828 (2017)
12. Nakamoto, S.: Bitcoin: a peer-to-peer electronic cash system (2009). https://bitcoin.org/bitcoin.pdf
13. Ricci, F., Rokach, L., Shapira, B.: Recommender systems: introduction and challenges. In: Ricci, F., Rokach, L., Shapira, B. (eds.) Recommender Systems Handbook, pp. 1–34. Springer, Boston (2015). https://doi.org/10.1007/978-1-4899-7637-6_1
14. Szabo, N.: Formalizing and securing relationships on public networks. First Monday **2**(9) (1997)
15. Wood, G., et al.: Ethereum: a secure decentralised generalised transaction ledger. Ethereum Proj. Yellow Pap. **151**, 1–32 (2014)

Cost-Based Computing Allocation

Cost-Optimized Parallel Computations Using Volatile Cloud Resources

Jens Haussmann[1,2]($\boxtimes$), Wolfgang Blochinger[1]($\boxtimes$), and Wolfgang Kuechlin[2]

[1] Parallel and Distributed Computing Group, Reutlingen University,
Reutlingen, Germany
{jens.haussmann,wolfgang.blochinger}@reutlingen-university.de
[2] Symbolic Computation Group, University of Tuebingen, Tuebingen, Germany
wolfgang.kuechlin@uni-tuebingen.de

Abstract. In recent years, the parallel computing community has shown increasing interest in leveraging cloud resources for executing parallel applications. Clouds exhibit several fundamental features of economic value, like on-demand resource provisioning and a pay-per-use model. Additionally, several cloud providers offer their resources with significant discounts; however, possessing limited availability. Such volatile resources are an auspicious opportunity to reduce the costs arising from computations, thus achieving higher cost efficiency. In this paper, we propose a cost model for quantifying the monetary costs of executing parallel applications in cloud environments, leveraging volatile resources. Using this cost model, one is able to determine a configuration of a cloud-based parallel system that minimizes the total costs of executing an application.

Keywords: Cloud computing · Parallel computing · Cost model

1 Introduction

On-site compute clusters built of commodity hardware are a very popular platform for executing a broad range of HPC applications. However, this type of parallel platform requires considerable upfront investments and furthermore, scalability is limited to static scaling (by manually adding cluster nodes). In the last years, the cloud has emerged to a powerful and versatile platform for building parallel execution environments, establishing a promising alternative to conventional HPC clusters. In particular, cloud computing opens up new opportunities to explicitly control and optimize monetary costs on the level of individual parallel application runs. One can employ typical IaaS (Infrastructure-as-a-Service) cloud offerings to construct (virtual) parallel environments that share many characteristics with traditional on-site compute clusters. This holds especially when using the performance-optimized cloud resources designed for HPC workloads, recently introduced by many cloud providers. By employing a simple "copy & paste" approach, users can substitute their HPC cluster infrastructure with cloud-based virtual clusters, harnessing the on-demand self-service and pay-per-use characteristics of cloud offerings.

© Springer Nature Switzerland AG 2019
K. Djemame et al. (Eds.): GECON 2019, LNCS 11819, pp. 45–53, 2019.
https://doi.org/10.1007/978-3-030-36027-6_4

The pay-per-use model turns out to be especially beneficial for institutions which otherwise would have to deal with underutilized resources or have a restricted budget that prevents an investment for on-site clusters. Moreover, the *on-demand self-service* characteristic of cloud offerings allows novel execution scenarios. For example, jobs submitted to HPC clusters are typically handled by a scheduling system, stored in a queue and executed later when resources become available. In contrast, virtually unlimited and immediately available resources of cloud environments allow the execution of all jobs in parallel at the same cost but without delays. There already exists a number of activities on utilization of cloud environments for HPC workloads from both industry and academia. Large scale experiments in public cloud environments where over 150k processing units have been utilized give evidence of the feasibility of cloud based HPC [3].

However, there is still a tremendous untapped potential for savings, which can be harnessed for higher cost efficiency. Particularly promising in this context are low priced *volatile* resources, which, however, possess limited availability. Cloud providers offer such resources with significant discounts, in order to prevent idle cloud infrastructures. Users can seize these resources for a fraction of the usual price, under the limitation of having no guarantee of availability. Volatile resources are well suited for a variety of parallel applications. Decisive factors are the degree of coupling and scalability. The better an application meets these properties, the higher is the potential to decrease the costs of executions. Among others, this includes discrete optimization, graph search, constraint satisfaction solving, and MapReduce. Several published studies have considered the utilization of volatile resources for HPC in cloud environments [5,16,17]. However, relationship and impact on the cost efficiency is not yet fully understood.

The work presented in this paper is motivated by the following hypothesis: Due to their high pricing, it is not adequate to solely rely on traditional *reserved* cloud resources. We argue that cost-efficient computations require a fine-tuned and balanced execution environment configuration, consisting of both volatile and reserved resources. Which combination of volatile and reserved resources offers the best cost efficiency depends on the characteristics of both application as well as resources. In particular, we make the following contributions: (1) The key research question of our study is to find the number of processors and, more importantly, the concrete type (reserved or volatile) for which the total monetary costs of a parallel computation are minimal. (2) To address this question, we propose a novel cost model for quantifying the monetary costs of parallel computations employing a mix of reserved and volatile processors.

The remainder of the paper is organized as follows: In Sect. 2, we briefly address the background topics of our work. Furthermore, in Sect. 3, we discuss in more detail the specific problem we are addressing. Next, Sect. 4 describes our cost model for parallel computations in cloud environments. Later, in Sect. 5, we evaluate the cost model and investigate the effects of individual parameters on the total costs. Section 6 gives an overview of related work. Finally, Sect. 7 concludes the paper and outlines directions for future research.

2   Background

Analytical Modeling of Parallel Systems - Performance metrics of parallel systems (a particular combination of application and architecture) are an essential instrument for evaluation purposes. The most fundamental metrics are the *sequential execution time* T_{seq} and the *parallel execution time* $T_{par}(p)$. While the former is the time required to solve a given problem by the fastest known sequential algorithm, the latter is the time required to solve the same problem in parallel, using p processors. Based on these two fundamental metrics, additional metrics can be derived. *Speedup* $S(p) = \frac{T_{seq}}{T_{par}(p)}$ indicates the performance improvement of solving a problem in parallel over a sequential execution. *Parallel efficiency* $E(p) = \frac{S(p)}{p}$ represents the fraction of processing time spent on essential work. For economic considerations, parallel efficiency is of particular interest, as it indicates the capitalized fraction of the invested processing capacity. Besides the ideal case, parallel systems exhibit *overhead* which manifests itself as processor idling, inter-processor communication, and excess computation. The parallel overhead negatively impacts the parallel efficiency and thus also the *scalability* of a parallel system, which is characterized by $E(p)$ within a range of different numbers of processors p [10].

Volatile Cloud Resources - More and more cloud providers offer volatile resources, including *spot-instances* of *Amazon EC2* [6], *preemptible VMs* of *Google Compute Cloud* [9], and *low-priority VMs* of *Microsoft Azure* [4]. Although based on the same principle, each provider has a slightly different manifestation of this offering. For example, Amazon employs a sophisticated auction system where resources are claimed through a bidding process. In contrast, Google and Microsoft offer such resources for a fixed price that is significantly lower than the price of traditional resources. In this paper, we assume a prototypical fixed price model for volatile resources, derived from respective cloud offerings of Google and Microsoft. According to the conditions of many providers, we also assume that resources are not withdrawn spontaneously. Prior to resource withdrawal, a signal is emitted that notifies about the imminent retraction. In this way, cleanup operations and state storing are performed on demand, which significantly reduces the overhead. Moreover, there exists a period that guarantees the least time of resource availability, otherwise it is not charged. This also means that a minimum granularity is given for our cost model.

3   Problem Statement

Unlike executing a job on a physical on-site cluster, cloud-based virtual clusters expose direct cost visibility to the users executing jobs, i.e., the charged costs are in direct relation to resources requested. This allows flexible, fine-grained approaches for cost optimization. For example, the user can construct for every run of an application an individually configured cluster that minimizes the cost with respect to the concrete situation in which the results of the computation are needed. However, this flexibility imposes a significant burden on the user. She/he has to determine among a multitude of options the concrete configuration of the cloud-based virtual cluster.

In the first place, the employed number of processors has a significant impact on the resulting costs. An important factor that determines the optimal number of processors with respect to the monetary costs is the scalability of the parallel application at hand: At a certain scale, increasing the number of processors is not *profitable*, i.e., it is not possible to retain adequate benefits from purchasing additional processors, like an increased speedup of computation or a higher processing rate. Basically, the scalability characteristics of the application at hand must be determined by the user. This can, for example, be accomplished by measuring $T_{par}(p)$ for different numbers of processors p, using prototypical input data. Other cost-related parameters that must be considered are the ratio of reserved and volatile processors, the availability of volatile processors, and the prices for both types of processors.

In this paper, we aim to systematically simplify the process of constructing cost-optimal cloud-based clusters by formalizing their costs with a cost-model, resulting in a novel approach for cost optimization of parallel cloud computations. We discuss our cost model in detail in the next section.

4   Cost Model

Basically, a cost model for parallel cloud computing should consider pay-per-use billing and also reflect the two conflicting objectives *fast processing* versus *low monetary costs*. In our previous work, we presented a cost model that applies the concept of *opportunity costs* to model the corresponding trade-off [12]. In our case, the opportunity costs express the lost monetary profits of delayed results from computations. The cost function is given in Eq. 1.

$$C(p) = \underbrace{T_{par}(p) * p * c_\pi}_{\text{Proc. costs}} + \underbrace{T_{par}(p) * c_\omega}_{\text{Opport. costs}} \qquad (1)$$

The cloud provider's price for a processor per time unit is denoted by c_π, whereas c_ω represents the lost monetary profits of delayed results per time unit.

In this work, we extend the model to capture an execution environment consisting of reserved and volatile processors. These processor types do not only differ in terms of their price but also exhibit a different degree of availability. While a processor of type reserved is available at any time, for a processor of type volatile only a limited availability is guaranteed. Figure 1 illustrates an example of a parallel computation, employing both reserved and volatile processors. Given that a volatile processor is not available anymore, it is compensated through a (more expensive) reserved processor. Let v denote the current number of volatile processors employed for computation, and let r denote the current number of reserved processors. The total number of required processors is denoted by p, whereby $p = r + v$ holds true at any time. Referring to a single bar of this chart,

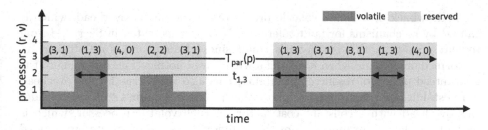

Fig. 1. Exemplary parallel computation employing volatile and reserved processors.

we will use the term *configuration*. A configuration is a tuple *(reserved, volatile)* that defines the number of utilized processors of each type.

An essential characteristic of a volatile processor is the availability α, defining the probability of being available at any given point in time. For example, volatile processors of the *Google Cloud Platform* are advertised with an availability of 85%–95%. Equation 2 defines the probability of having a configuration with v volatile processors available, out of the total number of required processors p.

$$R(v, p, \alpha) = \underbrace{(\alpha^v)}_{\substack{\text{...}v \text{ volatile procs.} \\ \text{being available}}} * \underbrace{(1 - \alpha)^{p-v}}_{\substack{\text{...}(p-v) \text{ volatile procs.} \\ \text{being unavailable}}} * \underbrace{\binom{p}{v}}_{\text{no. of comb.}} \tag{2}$$

probability of ...

Let $t_{r,v}$ denote the sum of periods spent in configuration (r, v). The total of all periods $t_{r,v}$, where execution takes place with configuration (r, v), constitute the total execution time of a parallel computation $T_{par}(p)$ (cf. Eq. 3).

$$T_{par}(p) = \sum_{i=0}^{p} t_{p-i,i} \tag{3}$$

$$t_{r,v} = T_{par}(p) * R(v, p, \alpha) \quad | \quad p = r + v \tag{4}$$

The probability $R(v, p, \alpha)$ for the configuration (r, v) further allows quantifying the fraction of $T_{par}(p)$ that is spent in this configuration, i.e, $t_{r,v}$, which is shown in Eq. 4.

With the findings from this discussion, we propose the cost function given in Eq. 5 to formalize our cost model.

$$C(p) = \sum_{i=0}^{p} \left(\underbrace{\left(T_{par}(p) * R(i, p, \alpha)\right)}_{\substack{t_{p-i,i} \\ [\text{A}]}} * \left(\underbrace{(p - i) * c_{\pi_r}}_{\substack{\text{reserved} \\ \text{processors} \\ [\text{B}]}} + \underbrace{i * c_{\pi_v}}_{\substack{\text{volatile} \\ \text{processors} \\ [\text{C}]}} \right) \right) + \underbrace{T_{par}(p) * c_\omega}_{\substack{\text{opport.} \\ \text{costs} \\ [\text{D}]}} \tag{5}$$

The total costs are comprised of the costs resulting from each configuration, determined by the period $t_{r,v}$ spent in it during execution as well as the reserved and volatile processors' prices c_{π_r} and c_{π_v}, respectively.

A drawback of utilizing volatile processors is the higher overhead, which is caused by mechanisms for fault tolerance. However, as stated in Sect. 2, during regular operation, this overhead is small since cleanup and state storing are performed on demand when receiving a withdrawal notification. Referring to the guaranteed period of resource availability, this also holds true for the overhead of re-establishing a computation on another resource. In a first step, we consider this overhead with a constant cost factor for each volatile processor, which is part of c_{π_v}. For an examination of the individual cost constituents, we divided Eq. 5 into four parts. [A], [B], and [C] are configuration specific, defining the costs of the cloud resources. Based on Eq. 4, [A] quantifies $t_{r,v}$ for each configuration and is applied in [B] (reserved) and [C] (volatile) to determine the total costs of each. Finally, [D] expresses the opportunity costs, which are independent of a computation's configurations.

5   Evaluation

For evaluating the cost models' validity, we examine different aspects of Eq. 5. Specifically, we investigate the characteristics that influence the total costs of computations for exemplary scenarios with different scalability. In each scenario, we assume a sequential execution time of $T_{seq} = 12h$ and model the parallel execution time $T_{par}(p)$ for a constant number of processors p by Amdahl's law: $T_{par}(p) = \beta * T_{seq} + \frac{(1-\beta)*T_{seq}}{p}$. The scalability of a parallel application is characterized by its sequential fraction $0 \leq \beta \leq 1$.

First, we consider five different parallel applications, which are characterized by different sequential fractions $0.01 \leq \beta \leq 0.3$. The left graph in Fig. 2 illustrates the total monetary costs $C(p)$ for parallel computations of these applications. We set the prices for reserved and volatile processors c_{π_r} and c_{π_v} as well as the availability α in accordance with the advertised ideal situation of the *Google Cloud Platform* [9]. The values of all parameters are shown in the figure. Since opportunity costs are highly application-specific, we assume the shown value for demonstration purposes. Concerning the total costs, it is apparent from this graph that all computations possess a similar behavior. Particularly, all curves of the cost function $C(p)$ have a unimodal shape, exhibiting only a single minimum. At all scales beyond this cost minimum, one would pay for inefficiently used computing resources, i.e., the return (in the form of decreasing opportunity costs) is lower than the investment for additional processors. We also see that the scalability (i.e., the sequential fraction β) has a significant influence on how strong the costs increase after the minimum is reached.

Next, we consider the influence of the opportunity costs on the total costs. As before, we examine different scenarios, which are characterized by different values of c_ω, where $0\$/h \leq c_\omega \leq 10\$/h$. The values of c_{π_r}, c_{π_v}, and α are identical to the previous scenario, whereas the sequential fraction is set to $\beta = 0.1$. The right graph in Fig. 2 illustrates the corresponding total monetary costs $C(p)$. Apparent is the strong correlation between the shape of the cost curves in both

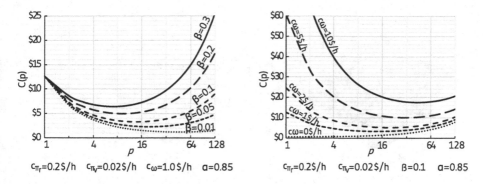

Fig. 2. Costs for parallel computations with different scalability and opportunity costs.

graphs, however, in a mirrored arrangement. This confirms that the model accurately specifies the two conflicting objectives *fast processing* and *low monetary costs*. The influence of the opportunity costs is particularly evident in the case of $c_\omega = 0\$/h$. Since there are no cost benefits at all for speeding up the computation, $p = 1$ is the cost minimal computing infrastructure. In contrast, increasing c_ω also increases the number of processors p with the cost minimal computing infrastructure, since the reduction of opportunity costs outweighs the costs for additional processors.

Next, we focus on the availability α and price c_{π_v} of a volatile processor. Particularly, we want to assess to what extent they influence the total costs. Hence, we consider two scenarios with different c_{π_v} and $0 \leq \alpha \leq 1$, while keeping the other values constant. The left graph in Fig. 3 shows the total costs for the first scenario, whereas the right graph shows the second scenario, which is characterized by an increased volatile processor price. The first one shows a clear trend of decreasing total costs as the availability of volatile processors increases. While this behavior is no surprise at all, one can furthermore observe that in the right graph it is much less pronounced. The potential benefit of employing volatile processors for parallel computations can only be capitalized if their price is significantly smaller, compared to reserved processors. If this is the case, they offer enormous economic potential for cost minimization. As illustrated in the left graph, the savings are considerable, even at lower degrees of availability.

6   Related Work

There exists a growing body of research on the utilization of cloud environments for HPC workloads. To benefit from the cloud, recent studies found that HPC applications have to be adapted to suit cloud characteristics like on-demand resource access, elasticity, and pay-per-use [7,13,15]. In [14], the authors deal with elastic scaling and investigate on a framework and runtime system for applications with dynamic task parallelism. The demand for high-performance cloud

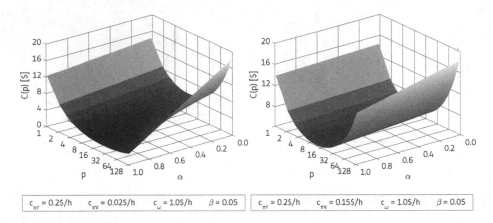

Fig. 3. Costs for parallel comp. with volatile procs. of different availability and price.

systems was also recognized by cloud providers, which launched performance-optimized VMs with InfiniBand like Microsoft *H-Series* [1]. Complementary, tools like *elasticHPC* [2] facilitate the execution of HPC workloads by automating the creation of clusters in the cloud, enabling monitoring, and providing a cost management to start and terminate jobs based on specific price constraints.

In recent years there has been considerable interest in utilizing volatile cloud resources for HPC [2,5]. Several studies investigated the benefits for various classes of parallel applications, covering traditional applications that employ MPI [17], as well as decoupled MapReduce applications [16]. Contrary to our work, the focus of most of these studies has been mainly on bidding strategies and automated bidding processes.

Cost modeling in the domain of parallel- as well as cloud-computing has been the topic of several studies during the last decade. Current cost models for cloud-based web-applications are typically based on pay-per-use and defined in terms of monetary costs [8,18]. For parallel computations costs are more abstractly defined, using performance metrics like total processing time [10]. The authors of [11] put together both concepts, extending the model for parallel computations towards pay-per-use of the cloud model. Our previous study [12], presents a cost model for parallel cloud applications to determine the monetary costs based on both execution time and utilized cloud resources.

7   Conclusion

In this paper, we presented a cost model for quantifying the monetary costs of parallel computations, performed in cloud-based environments that consist of both reserved and volatile resources. To adequately model the costs, we addressed a wide range of economic aspects. Specifically, we considered the trade-off between availability and price of volatile processors in the context of costs caused by delayed results of a computation. Our evaluation revealed that volatile processors offer enormous economic potential that can be harnessed for cost minimization. Thus, our approach helps HPC users to exploit the potential of cost-saving further when employing cloud resources for executing their parallel applications. In future work, we plan to extend our cost model towards auction-based pricing models for volatile resources like the Amazon EC2 spot instances.

References

1. Availability of H-series VMs in Microsoft Azure. https://azure.microsoft.com/en-us/blog/availability-of-h-series-vms-in-microsoft-azure/
2. ElasticHPC. http://www.elastichpc.org/
3. HPC Cloud Hits Petaflop. https://www.schrodinger.com/news/schrodinger-partners-cycle-computing-accelerate-materials-simulation-using-cloud
4. Microsoft Azure Low-Priority VMs. https://docs.microsoft.com/en-us/azure/batch/batch-low-pri-vms
5. Spotinst HPC. https://spotinst.com/solutions/hpc/
6. Amazon: Amazon EC2 Spot Instances (2014). https://aws.amazon.com/ec2/spot/
7. Da Rosa Righi, R., Rodrigues, V.F., Da Costa, C.A., Galante, G., De Bona, L.C.E., Ferreto, T.: AutoElastic: automatic resource elasticity for high performance applications in the cloud. IEEE Trans. Cloud Comput. **4**(1), 6–19 (2016)
8. Deelman, E., Singh, G., Livny, M., Berriman, B., Good, J.: The cost of doing science on the cloud: the montage example. In: Proceedings of the ACM/IEEE Conference on Supercomputing (2008)
9. Google Cloud: Preemptible VMs. https://cloud.google.com/preemptible-vms/
10. Grama, A., Kumar, V., Karypis, G., Gupta, A.: Introduction to Parallel Computing, 2nd edn. Addison-Wesley, Boston (2003)
11. Gupta, A., Milojicic, D.: Evaluation of HPC applications on cloud. In: Proceedings of the 6th Open Cirrus Summit. IEEE (2012)
12. Haussmann, J., Blochinger, W., Kuechlin, W.: Cost-efficient parallel processing of irregularly structured problems in cloud computing environments. Cluster Comput. (2018). https://doi.org/10.1007/s10586-018-2879-3
13. Kehrer, S., Blochinger, W.: A survey on cloud migration strategies for high performance computing. In: Proceedings of the 13th Advanced Summer School on Service-Oriented Computing. IBM Research Division (2019)
14. Kehrer, S., Blochinger, W.: TASKWORK: a cloud-aware runtime system for elastic task-parallel HPC applications. In: Proceedings of 9th International Conference on Cloud Computing and Services Science (2019)
15. Rajan, D., Canino, A., Izaguirre, J.A., Thain, D.: Converting a high performance application to an elastic cloud application. In: Proceedings of the 3rd IEEE International Conference on Cloud Computing Technology and Science (2011)
16. Taifi, M.: Banking on decoupling: budget-driven sustainability for HPC applications on auction-based clouds. ACM SIGOPS Oper. Syst. Rev. **47**(2), 41–50 (2013)
17. Taifi, M., Shi, J.Y., Khreishah, A.: SpotMPI: a framework for auction-based HPC computing using Amazon spot instances. In: Xiang, Y., Cuzzocrea, A., Hobbs, M., Zhou, W. (eds.) ICA3PP 2011. LNCS, vol. 7017, pp. 109–120. Springer, Heidelberg (2011). https://doi.org/10.1007/978-3-642-24669-2_11
18. Viana, V., De Oliveira, D., Mattoso, M.: Towards a cost model for scheduling scientific workflows activities in cloud environments. In: Proceedings of the IEEE World Congress on Services (2011)

Bill Estimation in Simplified Memory Progressive Second Price Auctions

Danielle Movsowitz-Davidow[1]([✉])(iD), Nir Lavi[2](iD),
and Orna Agmon Ben-Yehuda[2,3]([✉])(iD)

[1] Computer Science Department, University of Haifa, Haifa, Israel
dmovsowi@campus.haifa.ac.il
[2] Computer Science Department, Technion—Israel Institute of Technology,
Haifa, Israel
dl8.nir@gmail.com, ladypine@cs.technion.ac.il
[3] Caesarea Rothschild Institute for Interdisciplinary Applications
of Computer Science, University of Haifa, Haifa, Israel

Abstract. Vertical elasticity, the ability to add resources on-the-fly to a
virtual machine or container, improves the aggregate benefit clients get
from a given cloud hardware, namely the social welfare. To maximize
the social welfare in vertical elasticity clouds, mechanisms which elicit
resource valuation from clients are required. Full Vickrey-Clarke-Groves
(VCG) auctions, which allocate resources to optimize the social welfare,
are NP-hard and too computationally-complex for the task. However,
VCG-like auctions, which have a reduced bidding language compared
with VCG, are fast enough. Such is the Simplified Memory Progressive
Second Price Auction (SMPSP). A key problem in VCG-like auctions is
that they are not completely truthful, requiring participants, who wish
to maximize their profits, to estimate their future bills. Bill estimation
is particularly difficult since the bill is governed by other participants'
(changing) private bids.

We present methods to estimate future bills in noisy, changing, VCG-
like auction environments. The bound estimation method we present
leads to an increase of 3% in the overall social welfare.

Keywords: Bill estimation · Progressive second price auction ·
Resource allocation · Multi armed bandit problem

1 Introduction

Cloud providers give their clients the illusion of elastic resources: "just ask for
more, and the cloud shall provide". However, virtual machines (VMs) or containers in the cloud are located on physical machines. Unless they are live-migrated,

---

Nir Lavi—The work was done while the author was a student at the Computer Science
Dept., Technion.

K. Djemame et al. (Eds.): GECON 2019, LNCS 11819, pp. 54–62, 2019.
https://doi.org/10.1007/978-3-030-36027-6_5

their vertical elasticity—the ability to extend the resources on the same system—is limited first by the physical boundaries of the machine, and furthermore by the resource consumption of neighboring clients.

During 2017, the major providers introduced vertical CPU elasticity using the term "burstable" (Amazon [4], Azure [12], and Google [8]). The industry offered vertical elasticity for CPU first, because it is easy to evict and allocate on-the-fly. This is done using mature tools at the system's level, such as cgroups and CFS [5]. Vertical elasticity of storage resources, such as RAM and SSD, is the hardest, since their eviction takes a toll. Hence, the allocation of storage resources should be modified less often, to allow clients to benefit from the resources prior to its eviction.

Resources that are divided to a small number of units can be auctioned to optimize the social welfare—the aggregate benefit that all clients draw from the resource—using a VCG auction [6,9,13], as done for last level cache (LLC) ways [7]. In this auction, the clients bid with their valuation for each good—how much each good is worth to them. The host chooses the allocation which maximizes the social welfare and charges each client according to the damage it causes to its neighbors, such that it is in the client's best interest to tell the truth and enable the host to optimize the sum of true valuations.

A RAM auction is more complicated. RAM is a divisible good, which can be viewed as continuous or as composed of millions of small chunks. When viewed as millions of chunks, the complexity of a full VCG auction is prohibitive for practical purposes.

The Simplified Memory Progressive Second Price (SMPSP) [1,2] auction has a reasonable complexity on the provider's side ($O(n \log(n))$), because it is only VCG-like. In a VCG-like mechanism, clients do not bid using their full valuation functions. Instead, they use simplified bids, representing their specific resource requests: a maximal quantity q and a unit price p. The client's choice of a bid price p as a function of q is usually truthful, and simple [3]. However, the choice of quantity is harder—this is where the computational burden lies. Each client wants to choose a bid that wins the auction and optimizes its performance and profit goals. Since the unit price and quantity are coupled, the chosen quantity must correspond to a unit price that is likely to win, and that is likely to yield the maximal profit. Only by estimating the bill, can the client predict its profit and optimize it by choosing its bid quantity.

Our contribution is a method for clients to estimate their next bill in an SMPSP auction. Future bills depend on private bids made by other auction participants, which might change their preferences and consequently their bids over time. We detect such changes in a noisy environment by tracking and analyzing historical data, and focusing on the notable effect of environmental changes on the bill and minimal winning unit price. As a result, clients in an SMPSP auction now successfully respond to changing conditions in a noisy environment, improving the overall social welfare by 3% on average.

The code is free and available from https://bitbucket.org/danimovso/ginseng-open/.

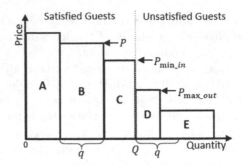

Fig. 1. Auction results. Each bid is represented by a rectangle whose height and width are the client's p and q.

2   Allocation and Payment in the SMPSP Auction

In the SMPSP auction the host (the software running on the physical machine, on behalf of the provider) sorts the participating clients' bids in a descending price order (see Fig. 1) and allocates RAM to those in the interval $[0, Q]$. This is the allocation which optimizes the social welfare. The allocation's social welfare is the sum of areas that belong to clients who were allocated RAM. To determine a client's bill the host first calculates the social welfare, and subtracts the specific client's valuation for the allocation of the resources it got. The host then repeats the process, excluding the specific client. The client's bill is the difference between these two results. Visually, if the client was allocated a quantity of q, its payment will be the area under the plot in the interval $[Q, Q + q]$.

3   Client Strategy

SMPSP clients need to translate their valuation into a bid. Unlike PSP [10] clients, SMPSP clients do not hear all the bids and therefore need to estimate what their bill would be for every bid they make.

To help clients estimate their future bills, at the end of each auction round the host provides two *borderline bid results*, as depicted in Fig. 1. p_{min_in} denotes the minimal unit price offered by a client that was allocated a positive amount of RAM. p_{max_out} denotes the maximal unit price offered by a client that did not receive its full requested quantity of RAM.

We consider a single auction round in which Q MB of RAM are offered for rent, and focus on a single client with a valuation function $V(\cdot)$ for RAM. For simplicity, V depends only on the quantity of RAM allocated to the client, and w.l.o.g., $V(0) = 0$.

The client examines options for a bid quantity q in the interval $[0, Q]$. For each option q, it performs the following stages:

1. Compute the truthful bid price, the mean unit valuation $p(q) = \frac{V(q)}{q}$, which is the best choice in a steady state, according to [3].

2. Filter out q if the resulting $p(q)$ is unlikely to win any resources.
3. Estimate $bill(q)$, the bill for the quantity q, assuming the auction is won.

Of the remaining options, the client bids with the $(q, p(q))$ pair with the smallest q that maximizes the profit:

$$q = min\left(argmax_q\left(V\left(q\right) - bill\left(q\right)\right)\right). \tag{1}$$

For the bill estimation in Step 3 we examine three approaches: (1) Use the last unit price paid by the client. (2) Use a weighted average (with a time-dependent decay) of the latest unit prices paid by the client. (3) Perform additional computations on each historical data piece; use a feedback loop to learn and adjust the results (in Sect. 4).

4   Bound Estimation

To estimate its own bill, denoted by $bill$, a client gathers data about the effect other clients' have on its bill. After each auction round, the client can adjust its estimation using the announced borderline bids. E.g., clients who where allocated some RAM in the previous round can use p_{max_out} together with their actual bill (denoted by $bill'$) and allocation (denoted by q') to deduce the average unit price in the interval $[Q, Q + q']$.

In the bound estimation approach, the client bounds its future bill from above and below by extrapolating data which was possibly recorded under different circumstances, and is not necessarily accurate. Finally, the client learns to correct the interpolation between the bounds according to the general shape of the allocation plot.

The analysis in this section relies on the following statements, which result from the concavity and monotonicity of the valuation functions: The first, $p_{max\_out} \leq p_{min\_in}$. The second, if $q_1 < q_2$, then $p(q_1) \leq p(q_2)$.

Let us denote the client's change in the requested amount of RAM by $\Delta q = q - q'$. The estimated bill can be bound on the basis of Δq, assuming that bids from the rest of the clients stay the same. We will analyze the cases where Δq is positive or negative separately.

In the following sections, "our" client, whose bill we are estimating, is described by the rectangle marked "A" in the figures.

4.1   Increased Demand

When $\Delta q > 0$ and the client's request is fully satisfied, the client's bill increases. The client's estimated bill is the lowest (Fig. 2) when all the newly unsatisfied clients (indicated by the rectangle "C") are clients who bid with unit price p_{min_in}. Hence, the estimated lower bill bound is:

$$bill \geq bill' + \Delta q \cdot p_{min\_in} \tag{2}$$

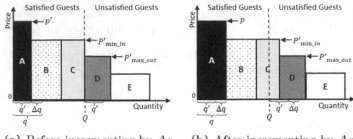

(a) Before incrementing by Δq (b) After incrementing by Δq

Fig. 2. Visualizing client A's estimation of the lowest bill bound when the rest of the clients do not change their bid. $\Delta q > 0$.

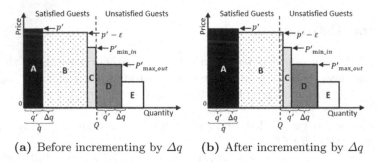

(a) Before incrementing by Δq (b) After incrementing by Δq

Fig. 3. Visualizing client A's estimation of the highest bill bound when the rest of the clients do not change their bid. $\Delta q > 0$.

The client's estimated bill is the highest (Fig. 3) if only one client bid unit price p_{min_in} and received only δMB, such that $\delta \to 0$ (the rectangle "C"), and another client (the rectangle "B") received an amount of memory when bidding for the unit price $p' - \epsilon$, such that $\epsilon \to 0$. Hence, the estimated upper bill bound is:

$$bill \leq bill' + \Delta q \cdot p(q). \tag{3}$$

4.2   Decreased Demand

In cases where $\Delta q < 0$, the client's bill decreases. The client's estimated bill is the lowest (Fig. 4) when all the unsatisfied clients affecting our client's bill bid with the unit price p_{max_out} (the rectangle "D"). If our client decreases its RAM request by $|\Delta q|$, then the rest of the clients in the interval $[Q, Q + \Delta q]$ are allocated RAM. Since the clients are sorted in a descending order, the average unit price decreases. Hence, the estimated lower bill bound is:

$$bill \geq bill' + \Delta q \cdot p_{max\_out}. \tag{4}$$

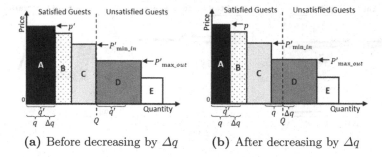

(a) Before decreasing by Δq (b) After decreasing by Δq

Fig. 4. Visualizing client A's estimation of the lowest bill bound when the rest of the clients do not change their bid. $\Delta q < 0$.

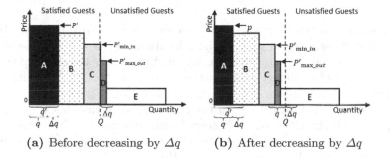

(a) Before decreasing by Δq (b) After decreasing by Δq

Fig. 5. Visualizing client A's estimation of the highest bill bound when the rest of the clients do not change their bid. $\Delta q < 0$.

The client's estimated bill is the highest (Fig. 5) when the client who bid p_{max_out} receives only δMB, such that $\delta \to 0$ (rectangle "D"), and the rest of the clients in the interval $[Q, Q + \Delta q]$ bid with the unit price $\epsilon \to 0$. Hence, the estimated upper bill bound is:

$$bill \leq bill' \cdot \frac{q}{q'}. \tag{5}$$

This is because the unit price can only drop, since the bids with the higher unit price affect the bill less.

4.3 Interpolating the Bounds

Where between the bounds would the actual bill be? The interpolation depends on the shape of the allocation plot in the vicinity of the Q boundary which affects the bill change computation. The shape of the allocation plot is the shape of the function formed by the top of the allocation rectangles. The concavity of the allocation plot affects the distance of the bill from the bounds. When $\Delta q < 0$, the shape of the allocation plot to the right of the Q boundary affects

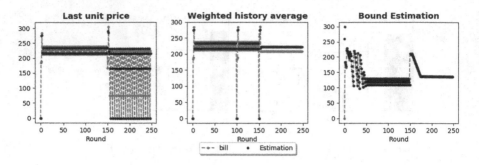

Fig. 6. The accuracy of the estimation algorithms. A typical trace of one VM's actual bill and its estimation, for each of the methods.

the interpolation: if the allocation plot is concave (downward), the lower bound will be a better estimate (Fig. 4), if the allocation plot is convex (downward), the upper bound will be better (Fig. 5). When $\Delta q > 0$, it is the shape of the plot to the left of the Q boundary that matters. The upper bound dominates when it is concave (Fig. 3), and the lower—when it is convex (Fig. 2).

The client does not need to learn the exact shape of the allocation plot—it is enough to learn its effect on the interpolation. Hence, the client validates its prior estimates of upper and lower bounds against its actual bill: it expresses the previous actual bill as a linear interpolation:

$$\frac{bill'}{q} = (1 - \alpha)\frac{L_{n-1}}{q'_{n-1}} + \alpha\frac{U_{n-1}}{q'_{n-1}}, \tag{6}$$

where L_{n-1}, U_{n-1} and q'_{n-1} denote the lower bound, upper bound and requested RAM quantity of the previous round, respectively. The interpolation coefficient, α, is extracted from the validation and used to predict the future bill,

$$bill = (1 - \alpha)L_n + \alpha U_n. \tag{7}$$

The reuse of a past value of the interpolation coefficient α relies on the assumption that the environment changes slowly, and thus the shape of the allocation plot remains more or less the same, at least for a small quantity change $|\Delta q|$.

5   Evaluation

To evaluate the bill estimation methods, we conducted a series of experiments, each with a different estimation method used by all guests. In each experiment, Ginseng [3] auctioned RAM among 10 VM clients using an SMPSP auction. Each VM ran the elastic version of memcached, a key-value storage application which is widely used on clouds. The elastic version[1] can dynamically adjust its RAM footprint on-the-fly, so its valuation function for RAM is concave, monotonically

---
[1] Available from https://github.com/ladypine/memcached.

rising. Its performance, defined by the rate of successful query responses, was measured using memaslap, which reports its progress every second. The valuation function of each guest was the performance multiplied by a factor, which was drawn from a Pareto distribution: a characteristic economic distribution. We used an index of 1.36, according to Levy and Solomon [11] and as used in earlier work [1,3].

Each experiment lasted 150 auction rounds, each taking 12 seconds. The experiments all started after a warm-up time of 100 rounds, in which auctions did not take place, allowing memcached's cache to stabilize. During each experiment, the valuation functions of 5 of the 10 participating VMs changed, once, to introduce noise.

The accuracy of the estimation methods is presented in Fig. 6. The previous unit price method and the weighted history average method do not converge, and induce fluctuations in the bill. Adjoined by needless allocation changes, this hurts the VMs' ability to utilize the RAM. The bound estimation method converges, and the bill it induces on the system is more stable.

Bill prediction inaccuracy leads to a sub-optimal allocation, which takes its toll. First, it prevents the SMPSP auction from optimizing the social welfare: the RAM is not allocated to the best possible clients. Second, an instable allocation means that RAM has to be reclaimed more often. Frequent RAM reclamation hurts the application's ability to make use of the RAM, thus hurting the overall performance and social welfare achieved by the physical machine. In this set of experiments, the "previous unit price" method increases the social welfare by 0.2%, compared with the "weighted history average" method. The "bound estimation" method increases it by 3% compared with the "weighted history average" method.

6 Conclusion and Future Work

An accurate bill prediction algorithm is essential for the stability and social welfare optimization of a VCG-like auction. The bounds estimation algorithm predicts the bill in an SMPSP auction better than others, and converges to the actual bill. Improving the bound estimation algorithm by gathering additional and relevant historical data, remains for future work.

Acknowledgments. This work was partially funded by the Amnon Pazi memorial research foundation, and supported by the Israeli Ministry of Science & Technology. We thank Orr Dunkelman for fruitful discussions. We also thank the Caesarea Rothschild Institute for Interdisciplinary Applications of Computer Science in the University of Haifa for their support. This research was also partially supported by the Center for Cyber, Law and Privacy and the Israel National Cyber Directorate.

References

1. Agmon, S., Agmon Ben-Yehuda, O., Schuster, A.: Preventing collusion in cloud computing auctions. In: Coppola, M., Carlini, E., D'Agostino, D., Altmann, J., Bañares, J.Á. (eds.) GECON 2018.: preventing collusion in cloudcomputing auctions, vol. 11113, pp. 24–38. Springer, Cham (2019). https://doi.org/10.1007/978-3-030-13342-9_3
2. Movsowitz, D., Funaro, L., Agmon, S., Agmon Ben-Yehuda, O., Dunkelman, O.: Why are repeated auctions in RaaS clouds risky? In: Coppola, M., Carlini, E., D'Agostino, D., Altmann, J., Bañares, J.Á. (eds.) GECON 2018. LNCS, vol. 11113, pp. 39–51. Springer, Cham (2019). https://doi.org/10.1007/978-3-030-13342-9_4
3. Agmon Ben-Yehuda, O., Posener, E., Ben-Yehuda, M., Schuster, A., Mu'alem, A.: Ginseng: market-driven memory allocation. In: Proceedings of the 10th ACM SIGPLAN/SIGOPS International Conference on Virtual Execution Environments, VEE 2014, pp. 41–52. ACM, New York (2014). https://doi.org/10.1145/2576195.2576197
4. Amazon: Amazon EC2 burstable performance instances. https://aws.amazon.com/ec2/instance-types/#burst. Accessed 25 July 2018
5. CFS scheduler. https://www.kernel.org/doc/Documentation/scheduler/sched-design-CFS.txt. Accessed 22 Oct 2017
6. Clarke, E.H.: Multipart pricing of public goods. Public Choice **11**(1), 17–33 (1971)
7. Funaro, L., Agmon Ben-Yehuda, O., Schuster, A.: Ginseng: market-driven LLC allocation. In: Gulati, A., Weatherspoon, H. (eds.) 2016 USENIX Annual Technical Conference, USENIX ATC 2016, Denver, CO, USA, 22–24 June 2016, pp. 295–308. USENIX Association (2016). https://www.usenix.org/node/196287
8. Google: Google cloud compute engine pricing. https://cloud.google.com/compute/pricing. accessed 07 June 2019
9. Groves, T.: Incentives in teams. Econ.: J. Econ. Soc. **41**(4), 617–631 (1973)
10. Lazar, A., Semret, N.: The progressive second price auction mechanism for network resource sharing. International Symposium on Dynamic Games and Applications 05 1999
11. Levy, M., Solomon, S.: New evidence for the power-law distribution of wealth. Phys. A: Stat. Mech. Appl. **242**(1), 90–94 (1997). https://doi.org/10.1016/S0378-4371(97)00217-3. http://www.sciencedirect.com/science/article/pii/S0378437197002173
12. Microsoft: Microsoft azure AKS b-series burstable VM. https://azure.microsoft.com/en-us/blog/introducing-b-series-our-new-burstable-vm-size/. accessed 25 July 2018
13. Vickrey, W.: Counterspeculation, auctions, and competitive sealed tenders. J. Financ. **16**(1), 8–37 (1961)

Voting for Superior Services:
How to Exploit Cloud Hierarchies

J.-Ch. Grégoire[1]([⊠]) [iD] and Angèle M. Foley[2] [iD]

[1] INRS-EMT, Montréal, QC, Canada
gregoire@emt.inrs.ca
[2] Wilfrid Laurier University, Waterloo, ON, Canada
ahamel@wlu.ca

Abstract. Cloud architecture spreads services throughout several levels from user-close edge to deep cloud, and while this allocation of resources offers versatility and power, it also presents a challenge: where should each aspect of the service be located? Related to this question is, who should decide? A user-centric approach would invite input from the user, and our model allows users to formulate preferences and submit these to the operator through a voting process wherein they express their preferences for the quality of the services they use. The outcome of the vote is a selection of services and related quality levels which receive preferential treatment.

This process is distinctive in that it operates with only partial information, which may be as much information that can be reasonably obtained. At the same time, it blends well with information that an operator can collect, statically or in realtime, for the user as well as from content and/or application providers.

Keywords: Cloud infrastructures · Voting · Task offloading · User experience · Quality of perception · Net neutrality

1 Introduction

Internet services are seemingly never good enough for the user–never fast enough, never massive enough, never private enough. To address this, the responsive Internet service provider (ISP) will attempt to improve some aspect of service, a goal that is increasingly easier through the flexibility offered by modern cloud-based infrastructures. But which aspect and by how much? At the same time today's users are savvy and skeptical. Can they trust the service provider to understand their needs and make improvements that are in their best interests, rather than in the best interest of the service provider? In an environment where it seems the only control the user has is to switch providers, we aim to give some control back to the user through a straightforward voting mechanism, and to incentivize him or her to exercise this control.

On the technical front, cloud architecture has evolved to cover several levels of performance and scale. From the original, few in number, deep-cloud infrastructures, providers (ASP) have steadily deployed new datacentres closer to their

© Springer Nature Switzerland AG 2019
K. Djemame et al. (Eds.): GECON 2019, LNCS 11819, pp. 63–70, 2019.
https://doi.org/10.1007/978-3-030-36027-6_6

customers, at the edge of the Internet, to support growth and also improve performance [4]. At the same time, ISPs, and especially wireless access providers (WAP), have deployed their own datacentres, following a similar pattern, and also in closer relation with technological evolution: the 5th generation cellular architecture includes the possibility of deploying a cloud even closer to customers (Mobile Edge Cloud, MEC) [3]. Other proposals (fog, mist, cloudlet...) have pushed this idea even further for specific applications, such as the Internet of Things (IoT) [5]. This evolution, or devolution, poses challenges in terms of *where* to locate services, a problem often referred to a *task offloading*.

There is some experience that could be brought to bear on this problem. Internet Service Providers (ISP), including WAP, have a long history of collaboration with companies specializing on content delivery (CDN), such as Akamai, to deploy servers within their networks to improve reduce latency of delivery and bandwidth consumption for their customers [8]. Such agreements, while being very effective, have however been rather restricted in scope as service support essentially consists of content caching, with very restricted interactions with customers who only "pull" content from the caches, but do not run any applications.

Thus some content can be moved, and some expertise can decide how to do this, but still some issues remain. The business case for CDN is quite straightforward as, beyond Web access, content delivery is now the foundation for "streaming" applications and has been offered as a essential element of the cloud-based virtualized infrastructure offerings by the likes of Amazon, Google or Microsoft. It is quite conceivable that such offerings will be available closer to customers. However, one must also take into consideration cost elements—as we get closer to customers the size of the infrastructure diminishes and its cost increases because of a number of factors such as the increased marginal cost of infrastructure or the added reliability constraints. Moreover, whereas with content delivery it was possible for access providers to "deal" with a unique reseller, this has become increasingly more complicated with the diversity of platforms, including large scale providers with content of their own (e.g. Amazon with Twitch, Google with YouTube), or independent providers (e.g. FaceBook, Netflix), especially with constraints of net neutrality and customer privacy.

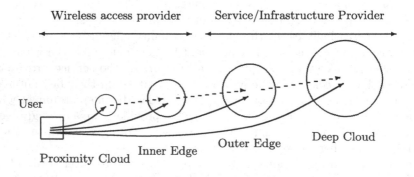

Fig. 1. Architectural view.

The challenge is therefore to decide how to manage the cloud resources to give the best service, or rather the better experience to users, considering that better performance (i.e. proximity) is associated with increased procurement costs and limited resources. Furthermore, this situation involves multiple players, with different relationships: The WAP has to satisfy its customers, while at the same time dealing with multiple service providers. Figure 1 illustrates the issue: the user can get their services from a number of different clouds, operated by either the WAP or some ASP. While the closest one may deliver better quality, getting the service from the deep cloud may still be adequate in most cases. And who gets to decide—the various internet players, or the users themselves?

The essential question, which we address here, is to find a way to determine how to allocate resources closer to the user, that is, in the access domain, in a way that best benefits user experience. In this work, we consider a user-centric perspective on resource allocation, which takes into account user preferences and needs. We allow user input through votes on their preferences, and the WAP in turn uses that information to allocate its cloud resources in a way to tries to meet its customers' needs. We show how this can be achieved with very simple mechanisms and a low computational overhead.

Our proposal is further developed in the next Section. Then, in Sect. 3, we discuss how to use the user votes to determine what level of service to aim for. In Sect. 4 we discuss the implications of these choices. Then finally in Sect. 5 we provide a short conclusion and a discussion of future work.

2   Proposal

We begin with a number of assumptions about the context in which this work applies and then describe how voting can be integrated into it.

2.1   Assumptions

Neutrality. We consider that the access operator supplies an infrastructure over which providers can deploy services and applications either in an AaaS or IaaS (application or infrastructure as a service) model. We do not concern ourselves with the nature of this infrastructure.

Further, the WAP does not attempt to give any advantage to any ASP through a specific agreement with the latter, i.e. it is trying to achieve some degree of net neutrality in that respect. The goal we want to support here is to satisfy customers' preferences, while protecting their privacy. Similarly, customers should not be paying extra for that "feature" as everyone is benefiting.

Privacy. We consider that the access operator must protect, to the best of its abilities, the privacy of its customers, in terms of location and preferences, and must limit the amount of information sent to the provider. The WAP would give the ASP the opportunity to deploy services and/or content either at proximity or at the inner edge of its network, but without revealing specific locations. This does not preclude what users themselves could choose to reveal to the ASP.

Four Stages. As shown in Fig. 1, we consider four different cloud infrastructures: two within the WSP domain, two for the ASP. While there could be more in practice we consider that, with current trends in networking and infrastructure virtualization, this number reflects a realistic diversity and is sufficient to illustrate our purpose.

Also, as we get closer to the user, resources (CPU, storage) are more limited and it is not possible to meet the needs of all ASPs, as would (arguably) be the case at the edge. The proximity cloud is a constrained resource.

Autonomy and transparency. Also for reasons of flexibility and privacy, we assume that it is entirely the WAP's decision to deploy services on the proximity edge and this decision (and its effects) are transparent to the ASP.

Service Diversity. Newer generation wireless networks (5G and beyond) offer opportunities to deploy interactive applications with strict latency requirements as well as large numbers of sensors/actuators and their related support software, with possible integration into new technologies such as cooperative-robots (cobots [6]) or existing ones like games. While streaming in its many forms (e.g. news, music, video, ...) will remain the dominant form of traffic for a while, there is a clear trend towards these more demanding applications which will generate more out-bound traffic and proximity computation: We are expecting increased diversity in service offerings, which contributes to the relevance of this work.

Flexible Quality. We assume that applications adapt to the network resources available to deliver the "best" quality possible, i.e. they have a flexible delivery to try to match the best quality of perception achievable. Such possibilities have been demonstrated in multimedia applications and are supported by the DASH protocol for streaming video [7], and the concept has been generalized [9].

2.2   Voting

We propose a model whereby users formulate their preferences to the operator, who then uses them to decide how to best allocate its resources. This can be assimilated to a voting problem, with partial information. Note that users can only vote for services they actively use, as opposed to just services of interest or occasional use.

An argument could be made for several different kinds of voting approaches. Users might vote for a single, preferred level of service. Or they might use approval voting to signify which levels are acceptable [2]. We could also envisage a system whereby users ranked services according to preferences. We chose a simple, straightforward system of voting on upper and lower bounds of acceptable service, as explained below. It is important to recognize also that by specifying the bounds at both extremes, i.e. specifying a range, we expect that users feel less pressure to inflate their requests in order to be sure of getting acceptable service.

The WAP collects offers from ASP into a set of *services*, for which it can provide preferential (i.e. through its own infrastructures) access to its customers. Each service s has a set of *profiles* $P^s = \{p_i^s\}$ as well as a total order relation, $\prec^s$ over P^s, which is meant to capture a ranking of *quality*, perceived or quantitative, i.e. $p_i^s \prec^s p_j^s$ expresses that preference p_i^s has lower quality (ranking) than p_j^s. Finally, each profile is associated with resources in CPU and storage, which apply to each instance, while the service similarly has CPU and storage overhead.

User input is required for the services to determine the *popularity of service* and to assess the *service quality* as ranked by the service provider and based on quality of perception. In order to get the feedback for this second one, we solicit user votes for two qualities: minimum acceptable level of service and ideal level of service. The ranges for these could be variable, depending on the particular service, but would likely be in the 1–5 to 1–10 range, as this would provide sufficient options for users to discriminate, but not so many as to overwhelm them with choice. Further, we assume that the lowest quality is always available through the ASP's infrastructure, without any intervention from the WAP. Lowest and highest quality profiles are represented by $\perp$ and $\top$, respectively (see Fig. 2).

In the next section, we present how this information is used by the WAP.

3   The Quality Parliament

Once the users have provided their rankings, the next issues are to identify the key services and to determine how to combine the quality criteria to obtain a Minimum and an Ideal to recommend to the service provider.

For the first step, service selection, we can rank services from most to least popular based on the votes. Since the WAP's primary purpose (in our context) is to please its customers, it is straightforward that targeting the services most required would please the larger number of users. As is often the case when dealing with ranked data, we assume that the user choices follow a Zipf distribution.

Quality selection is more complicated, as we can expect quality requests, which are based on subjective assessments, to cover a range of values. Figure 2 shows a potential shape of the distributions for Minimum and Ideal values with an underlying understanding that users will respect the intent of having two values—an assumption we will revisit below.

For each of these distributions we isolate the peaks, which would correspond to the modes of the votes, and select these as the values for which we offer service. As a side note we point out that by selecting the mode, rather than calculating the average or the median, we are differentiating ourselves from approval voting (in the case of average) and majority judgement (in the case of median) [1]. Certainly mode is applicable in this case because of the continuous nature of the "candidates." In a normal election there is no order to the candidates— if you select candidate 4 and candidate 3 wins, you are no happier than if any other candidate had won—but in our scenario, if you want service level 4 and you receive service level 3, you are only slightly disappointed. We use this continuous nature to our advantage.

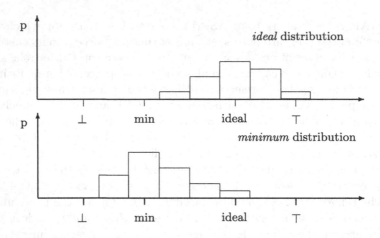

Fig. 2. Potential distributions of Minimum and Ideal values.

Having the ranking of the service, and the pair (Minimum, Ideal) for each service, we can sketch out an allocation algorithm as shown in Algorithm 1:

Algorithm 1. Resource Allocation Algorithm

---

1 <u>Allocate</u> (S, P);
  Input : List of services S ordered by decreasing preference, matching list P of
          (minimum, ideal) pairs for each service.
  Output: Set of allocated services A, with matching quality level
2 $A = \Phi$;
3 **forall the** $S_i \in S$ **do**
4 $\quad$ **if** *Resources avalable* **then**
5 $\quad\quad$ Add S_i to A at quality minimum.
6 $\quad$ **end**
7 **end**
8 **while** *Resources Available* **do**
9 $\quad$ Incrementally try to increase quality of services in A, from most popular to
    least popular.
10 **end**

This algorithm follows a straightforward structure: first try to allocate as many services as possible, giving precedence to the most popular. Then use the remaining resources to improve the quality offered, again from most to least popular. Also, we anticipate running the algorithm repeatedly; that is, allowing users to vote several times, based on the quality they currently experience. This gives users further control, allowing them to fine-tune their votes. It also gives the ASP feedback on how user satisfaction is met with current service levels.

4 Discussion

Many elements relevant to the expression of Algorithm 1 must be elaborated further. We focus only on the most critical ones here.

Fairness. The algorithm grants all services equal treatment, simply based on their vote-established order, no matter what their specific needs and popularity are. Nevertheless, it is straightforward to add positive biases for more popular services and/or negative biases for more demanding services in the model presented above, should such an approach be preferred.

Truthfulness. One concern with any system that asks for user input is whether or not the users will be *truthful*. In a case such as this, where users are being asked about their best case scenario, what is the incentive for them to be truthful? Surely all will claim they need the most extreme features and benefits? In our scenario two factors mitigate this. First, it will be clear to users that there are limited resources. It is not possible to supply every maximal demand, and choices will have to be made. If the users do not supply truthful and accurate information with which to make the choice, the service provider will do it, possibly arbitrarily. Second, the idea of an "interval of acceptability" with the minimum acceptable at one end, and the ideal at the other end, encourages the user to be flexible, generous, and honest. The user can express his or her wildest dreams, while at the same time being realistic (one might even say altruistic).

  As this is work-in-progress, we have not had an opportunity to examine truthfulness incentives from a game theory perspective, but it would be interesting to do so, possibly using ideas from work on iterated Prisoner's Dilemma, or possibly using principles of mechanism design.

Resource allocation and locality. There is a perspective that the proximity cloud should preferably be allocated to low latency, possibly critical applications in partnership with other companies/agencies (e.g. emergency services, cities) but we suppose that it is not necessarily the case. It could also be reserved in part for the WAP's own service, but we can always assume residual capacity. One practical consequence is that resources may not be uniformly available across the proximity infrastructure, which in turn could result in heterogeneous deployments, supported by the proximity-inside cloud dual model.

  We have not made any assumption on whether the algorithm should be run at the more local (proximity edge) or more global (inside edge) level but it can safely be accepted that, while service popularity trends would be globally true, there is room for more local discrimination. In such cases, the algorithm could be adapted to work across multiple levels.

  Heterogeneous deployments could present challenges for mobile users, however, and this specific issue will require further investigation.

Voting Interface Users need an interface to register their preferences. Let us first recall that a partnership must exist between access provider and service providers for a vote to be significant. Thus, the WAP knows which services are available as well as the quality levels which could, in theory, be offered. It then becomes straightforward for the WAP to present this information to its customers through a proprietary app, which could possibly—with the customer's permission—monitor the usage of services and use this information to set voting preferences. This app could also be used to illustrate the different quality levels offered.

5   Conclusion and Future Work

While ASPs have found value in expanding their cloud infrastructure towards their users, they need to partner with ISP/WAP to reach the proverbial last mile (or last km). WAPs themselves face the challenge to properly allocate tasks on their own cloud infrastructures, balancing extra performance with higher costs. Who should decide how this trade-off is balanced?

Our answer is to propose a simple voting procedure that provides information to the ISP while also giving confidence to the users. We incorporate that procedure into an algorithm that would output a recommended service level, and we discuss the benefits of this system in terms of fairness and resource allocation. As this is work-in-progress, many issues remain to be explored in future work, including handling mobility and the likelihood of truthful rankings by the users.

Acknowledgements. This work was supported by the Canadian Tri-Council Research Support Fund. Authors were each supported by their own individual NSERC Discovery Grants.

References

1. Balinski, M., Laraki, R.: Majority Judgment: Measuring, Ranking, and Electing. MIT press, Cambridge (2011)
2. Brams, S.J., Fishburn, P.C.: Voting Procedures. Handbook of Social Choice and Welfare. vol. 1, pp. 173–236 (2002)
3. Hu, Y.C., Patel, M., Sabella, D., Sprecher, N., Young, V.: Mobile edge computing–a key technology towards 5G. ETSI White Paper 11(11), 1–16 (2015)
4. Islam, S., Grégoire, J.C.: Giving users an edge: a flexible cloud model and its application for multimedia. Future Gener. Comput. Syst. 28(6), 823–832 (2012)
5. Oteafy, S.M., Hassanein, H.S.: IoT in the fog: a roadmap for data-centric IoT development. IEEE Commun. Mag. 56(3), 157–163 (2018)
6. Peshkin, M.A., Colgate, J.E., Wannasuphoprasit, W., Moore, C.A., Gillespie, R.B., Akella, P.: Cobot architecture. IEEE Trans. Robot. Autom. 17(4), 377–390 (2001)
7. Sodagar, I.: The MPEG-DASH standard for multimedia streaming over the internet. IEEE MultiMed. 18(4), 62–67 (2011)
8. Vakali, A., Pallis, G.: Content delivery networks: status and trends. IEEE Internet Comput. 7(6), 68–74 (2003)
9. Vakili, A., Grégoire, J.C.: QoE management for video conferencing applications. Comput. Netw. 57(7), 1726–1738 (2013)

Energy-Aware Dynamic Pricing Model
for Cloud Environments

Peini Liu[1], Gusseppe Bravo[1], and Jordi Guitart[1,2(✉)]

[1] Barcelona Supercomputing Center (BSC), Barcelona, Spain
{peini.liu,gusseppe.bravo,jordi.guitart}@bsc.es
[2] Universitat Politecnica de Catalunya (UPC), Barcelona, Spain

Abstract. Energy consumption is a critical operational cost for Cloud providers. However, as commercial providers typically use fixed pricing schemes that are oblivious about the energy costs of running virtual machines, clients are not charged according to their actual energy impact. Some works have proposed energy-aware cost models that are able to capture each client's real energy usage. However, those models cannot be naturally used for pricing Cloud services, as the energy cost is calculated after the termination of the service, and it depends on decisions taken by the provider, such as the actual placement of the client's virtual machines. For those reasons, a client cannot estimate in advance how much it will pay. This paper presents a pricing model for virtualized Cloud providers that dynamically derives the energy costs per allocation unit and per work unit for each time period. They account for the energy costs of the provider's static and dynamic energy consumption by sharing out them according to the virtual resource allocation and the real resource usage of running virtual machines for the corresponding time period. Newly arrived clients during that period can use these costs as a baseline to calculate their expenses in advance as a function of the number of requested allocation and work units. Our results show that providers can get comparable revenue to traditional pricing schemes, while offering to the clients more proportional prices than fixed-price models.

Keywords: Pricing model · Energy consumption · Cloud computing

1 Introduction

Cloud computing has consolidated as a paradigm for the on-demand provisioning of computing resources to end users over the Internet. These services are executed in virtual machines (VMs) hosted in large-scale data centers, which have become greedy consumers of energy to provide those services. Greenpeace [1] estimates that data centers energy use can grow up to 1012 billion kWh by 2020, which is a 3x increment regarding their energy consumption in 2007. The cost of this enormous amount of energy has turned into the primary cost driver for data centers. Belady [6] estimates that the annual amortized energy costs in

© Springer Nature Switzerland AG 2019
K. Djemame et al. (Eds.): GECON 2019, LNCS 11819, pp. 71–80, 2019.
https://doi.org/10.1007/978-3-030-36027-6_7

a data center for a single server exceeded the cost of the server itself in 2008. Consequently, any cost model for the Cloud should be energy-aware.

Cloud computing was originally devised as a utility computing paradigm, where the VMs had to be offered to the end users in a pay-as-you-use manner, i.e. the user pays only for the resources really consumed [8], such as any other utility service like water and electricity. However, commercial Cloud providers [4,12,14] typically charge their clients in a pay-as-you-go manner, i.e. the user pays a fixed value per unit of time for the VMs, whether he is using them or not [8]. Whereas those fixed prices encompass the operational costs of the provider, they are oblivious about the real energy cost to run each specific VM.

We claim that Cloud providers must offer an energy-aware and proportional dynamic pricing model to their users. Prices must be calculated dynamically because both the energy consumed in the data center (which depends on the number of clients and the amount of resources each of them uses) and the price of that energy vary over time (e.g. in Spain the energy price varies per hour [15]). Prices must be proportional so that users are charged according to their actual energy impact, i.e. clients using more energy should pay more.

Some works [2,3,8,11,13] have proposed cost models for VMs that can account for their individual energy impact. However, this energy cost is calculated after the termination of the VM, once the full energy usage profile of the VM and the provider's placement decisions about that VM are known. This impedes some of the advantages of fixed prices models discussed before, such as predictability, i.e. clients can know the cost of running their VMs before running them because it only depends on the client's behavior, and fairness, i.e. two identical VMs launched at the same time and with the same duration will pay the same.

This paper presents a pricing model for virtualized Cloud providers that is energy-aware, proportional, predictable, and fair. Our model builds upon the concepts of Allocation Units, which quantify the amount of virtual resources that are allocated to the VMs, and Work Units, which quantify the amount of work executed by using those resources. Our model dynamically derives the energy costs per Allocation Unit and per Work Unit for each time period. They account for the costs of the provider's static and dynamic energy consumption by sharing out them according to the virtual resource allocation and the real resource usage of running VMs for the corresponding time period. Newly arrived clients during that period can use these costs as a baseline to calculate their expenses in advance as a function of the number of requested allocation and work units.

2   Related Work

Pricing models in Cloud Computing have been broadly classified as subscription-based (clients reserve resources in advance for a specific period of time by paying a fixed price up-front), pay-per-use (resources are provided on-demand and clients are charged a fixed price per unit of time on usage basis), and hybrid (combination of subscription-based and pay-per-use) [10]. However, commercial Cloud providers might classify their prices differently depending on their customers' requirements. For example, Amazon [4] offers On-Demand, Reserved, and Spot Pricing Instances, being the former the most popular among the clients. Other providers such as Azure and Rackspace support similar pricing schemes [12,14]. None of these commercial providers consider the real energy cost to run the VMs when charging the clients.

Some works [2,3,8,11,13] have proposed cost models for VMs that account for their individual energy impact, but this is calculated after the termination of the VM, thus a client cannot estimate in advance how much it will pay.

Aldossary and Djemame [2] proposed a pricing model charges the customer based on the actual resource usage per unit including the energy consumption. Their model distributes the dynamic energy among the VMs according to their utilization, but the static energy is distributed evenly among VMs, independently of their size. Furthermore, they use the average power to calculate the energy consumption, which is not very accurate when resource usage fluctuates.

Hinz et al. [8] presented a cost model which accounts for the individualized energy cost for each VM according to its CPU and network usage. As a novelty, it includes also a shared cost from common hypervisor management operations, which is proportionally distributed among VMs according to their number of virtual processors (as they do also with the static energy).

Kurpicz et al. [11] presented a model for energy-proportional accounting for VMs which determines their dynamic energy costs by using the real utilization of the resources and divides the static energy costs proportionally to the number of virtual processors of the VM. To offer some cost predictability to users, the model reports a lower and an upper bound of the VM total cost, but these bounds are very coarse-grained.

3 Problem Statement

Our purpose is to define a pricing scheme that determines how much a given virtual machine j will pay if it runs for a time period of D hours. We define this cost as $C_{VM}^{j}(D)$. As listed in the top part of Table 1, the user must only provide as inputs the number of requested Allocation Units by the VM and the number of Work Units to be executed by the VM.

We define the number of Allocation Units of a VM j (AU_{VM}^{j}) as the product of its number of virtual processors ($VCPU_{VM}^{j}$) and its amount of memory (RAM_{VM}^{j}), which are normalized with respect to the capabilities of an Amazon m1.small VM (i.e. $VCPU_{VM}^{M1} = 1$ core and $RAM_{VM}^{M1} = 1.7\,\text{GB}$). According to this, AU_{VM}^{j} is calculated as shown in Eq. (1). The number of virtual processors and the amount of memory of VMs are the critical parameters that determine the number of VMs that can be allocated in a physical host.

$$AU_{VM}^{j} = \frac{VCPU_{VM}^{j}}{VCPU_{VM}^{M1}} \cdot \frac{RAM_{VM}^{j}}{RAM_{VM}^{M1}} \tag{1}$$

We define the number of Work Units of a VM j (WU_{VM}^{j}) as the number of millions of instructions to be executed by the VM.

Table 1. Parameters used by the model.

Symbol	Description
$VCPU_{VM}^j$	Number of virtual processors of VM j
RAM_{VM}^j	GB of RAM of VM j
AU_{VM}^j	Number of Allocation Units needed by VM j (calculated as in Eq. (1))
WU_{VM}^j	Number of Work Units to be executed by VM j
$E_{DC}(t)$	DC total energy consumption during time period t (in Joules)
$ES_{DC}(t)$	DC static energy consumption during time period t (in Joules)
$ED_{DC}(t)$	DC dynamic energy consumption during time period t (in Joules)
$E_H^i(t)$	Energy consumption of host i during time period t (in Joules)
$EI_H^i(t)$	Energy consumption of host i during time period t when idle (in Joules)
$AU_{DC}(t)$	Number of awarded Allocation Units in the DC during time period t
$WU_{DC}(t)$	Number of Work Units executed in the DC during time period t
$AU_H^i(t)$	Number of awarded Allocation Units in host i during time period t
$WU_H^i(t)$	Number of Work Units executed in host i during time period t
$E_{AU}(t)$	Energy consumption for each AU during period t (in Joules)
$E_{WU}(t)$	Energy consumption for each WU during period t (in Joules)
$C_{AU}(t)$	Cost of energy consumed per AU during period t (in €/kWh)
$C_{WU}(t)$	Cost of energy consumed per WU during period t (in €/kWh)
PI_H^i	Average power consumption of host i when idle (in Watts)
$MIPS_H^i$	Performance of host i (in Millions of Instructions per second)
$P_H^i(t)$	Instantaneous power consumption of host i at time t (in Watts)
U_H^i	Instantaneous CPU utilization of host i at time t ($\in [0,1]$)
$N(t)$	Number of active hosts during time period t
$VMs_H^i(t)$	Amount of VMs on host i during time period t
$Price(t)$	Energy price during time period t (in €/kWh)
T_S	Time elapsed between two samples (in seconds)
$NS(t)$	Number of samples during time period t; $NS(t) = t/T_S$

The provider offers the energy costs per Allocation and Work Unit for the time when the VM has been submitted (t_0). Next section describes how the provider accounts for these costs. The client can use them as a baseline to calculate their expenses in advance as a function of the number of requested Allocation and Work units, as follows: $C_{VM}^j(D) = (AU_{VM}^j \cdot C_{AU}(t_0) + WU_{VM}^j \cdot C_{WU}(t_0)) \cdot D$.

4 Pricing Model

To derive the energy costs per Allocation Unit and per Work Unit for each time period, our model calculates a number of parameters for each time period. They are introduced in the second part of Table 1. The model requires a number of input parameters that must be introduced by the provider. Some of these parameters are obtained by calibrating the data center in a profiling stage (see third part of Table 1), others are gathered periodically by monitoring the data center status (see fourth part of Table 1), and the rest are configuration parameters or other external inputs (see bottom of Table 1).

4.1   Energy Consumption Model

Our model must account first for the total energy consumption of the data center during each time period t $(E_{DC}(t))$, which can be calculated as the sum of the energy consumption from all the active hosts during that period, as shown in Eq. (2). The energy consumption of host i during time period t results from integrating all the power consumption of host i during that time period. Given that we do not have the continuous function describing that power consumption but a set of samples of its value, we do the calculation as presented in Eq. (3), where $P_H^i(t_k)$ is the k-th sample of the power consumption of host i.

$$E_{DC}(t) = \sum_{i=1}^{N(t)} E_H^i(t) \tag{2}$$

$$E_H^i(t) = \int_1^t P_H^i(t)dt = T_S \cdot \sum_{k=1}^{NS(t)} P_H^i(t_k) \tag{3}$$

The energy consumption of the data center $(E_{DC}(t))$ comprises both the static energy consumption $(ES_{DC}(t))$ due to keeping the hosts on and the dynamic energy consumption $(ED_{DC}(t))$ spent by all the running VMs to do their work, as shown next: $E_{DC}(t) = ES_{DC}(t) + ED_{DC}(t)$.

The static energy consumption of the data center $(ES_{DC}(t))$ is the sum of the idle energy consumption of all the active hosts. These come from their average idle power consumption during time period t as shown in Eq. (4).

$$ES_{DC}(t) = \sum_{i=1}^{N(t)} EI_H^i(t) = \sum_{i=1}^{N(t)} PI_H^i * t \tag{4}$$

The dynamic energy consumption of the data center $(ED_{DC}(t))$ is calculated from the total and the static energy consumption for the data center during time period t as follows: $ED_{DC}(t) = E_{DC}(t) - ES_{DC}(t)$.

4.2   Energy-Aware Cost Model

The provider dynamically and periodically calculates its prices for an Allocation Unit (AU) and a Work Unit (WU) to reflect the variability in the electricity price and the energy consumption (due to changing workloads).

The static and dynamic energy costs are shared out according to the virtual resource allocation and the real resource usage of running VMs for the corresponding time period. This will result in a cost per Allocation Unit $(C_{AU}(t))$ and a cost per Work Unit $(C_{WU}(t))$ for that time period.

$C_{AU}(t)$ is calculated from the energy consumption per Allocation Unit during time period t as follows: $C_{AU}(t) = Price(t) \cdot E_{AU}(t)/3600000$. As shown in Eq. (5), $E_{AU}(t)$ is derived from the static energy consumption of the data center $(ES_{DC}(t))$, which was calculated in the previous section, and the number of awarded Allocation Units to all the running VMs in the data center $(AU_{DC}(t))$, which is the sum of all the Allocation Units awarded in all the active hosts during time period t ($AU_H^i(t)$). As shown in Eq. (6), it can be calculated as the awarded Allocation Units from all the running VMs on each host i, where $VMs_H^i(t)$ represents the number of running VMs in host i during the time t and AU_{VM}^j is the number of Allocation Units of VM j.

$$E_{AU}(t) = \frac{ES_{DC}(t)}{AU_{DC}(t)} \tag{5}$$

$$AU_{DC}(t) = \sum_{i=1}^{N(t)} AU_H^i(t) = \sum_{i=1}^{N(t)} \sum_{j=1}^{VMs_H^i(t)} AU_{VM}^j \tag{6}$$

$C_{WU}(t)$ is calculated from the energy consumption per Work Unit during period t as follows: $C_{WU}(t) = Price(t) \cdot E_{WU}(t)/3600000$. As shown in Eq. (7), $E_{WU}(t)$ is derived from the dynamic energy consumption of the data center ($ED_{DC}(t)$), which was calculated in the previous section, and the number of Work Units executed in the data center ($WU_{DC}(t)$), which is the sum of the units executed in all the hosts during period t ($WU_H^i(t)$), as shown in Eq. (8).

$$E_{WU}(t) = \frac{ED_{DC}(t)}{WU_{DC}(t)} \tag{7}$$

$$WU_{DC}(t) = \sum_{i=1}^{N(t)} WU_H^i(t) \tag{8}$$

The number of Work Units that a host can execute depends on its performance capability. In this paper, we have defined a Work Unit as 1 million of instructions to be executed, and hence, we measure the performance of hosts using MIPS. According to this, the number of Work Units executed in host i during time period t ($WU_H^i(t)$) depends on the maximum performance of host i ($MIPS_H^i$) and the host utilization during time period t while running VMs (U_H^i). Without loss of generality, we measure the host utilization as its CPU utilization, since the CPU is the highest contributor to the power consumption of a host. However, our model could be easily extended to consider also the utilization of other resources. Given that we do not have the continuous function describing the CPU utilization of host i during time period t but a set of samples of its value, we calculate $WU_H^i(t)$ as shown in Eq. (9), where $U_H^i(t_k)$ is the k-th sample of the CPU utilization of host i (between 0 and 1).

$$WU_H^i(t) = MIPS_H^i \cdot \int_1^t U_H^i(t)dt = MIPS_H^i \cdot T_S \cdot \sum_{k=1}^{NS(t)} U_H^i(t_k) \tag{9}$$

5   Experiments and Evaluation

5.1   Experimental Setup and Workload

A data center comprising 200 high-performance hosts has been simulated with CloudSim-plus [7]. Each host consists of two Intel Xeon 8180M processors with

Table 2. Configuration of tasks.

Task type	Amount	Instructions
1	500	15000000
2	500	20000000
3	500	28000000
4	500	35000000

Table 3. Configuration of VMs.

VM type	vCPU	MIPS	RAM
m4.Large	2	5120	8 GB
m4.xLarge	4	10240	16 GB
m4.2xLarge	8	20480	32 GB
m4.4xLarge	16	40960	64 GB

28 cores each, two 128GB PC42400U RAM DIMM, and two disks 2.5–3840 GB-SATA, providing a computing performance of 143360 MIPS. Its idle and maximum rated power have been reported as 109.11 and 578.85 W, respectively [9]. The electricity fee paid by the data center is calculated according to the electricity price, which varies every hour [15]. The sampling period T_S is 5 min.

The workload comprises 2000 tasks of 4 types according to their number of instructions, as shown in Table 2. Tasks are allocated randomly into 2000 VMs, which can be categorized into 4 types according to Amazon EC2 [4], as shown in Table 3. The placement of each VM is decided by the simulator according to its resource requirements. We assume batch tasks with mid-high average utilization [5] as shown in Fig. 1. To reflect the daily varying utilization, tasks are assumed to arrive according to the distribution in Fig. 2. Depending of the size of the task, its CPU utilization, and its placement, each task will run from 2 to 7 h.

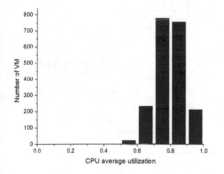

Fig. 1. CPU utilization distribution.

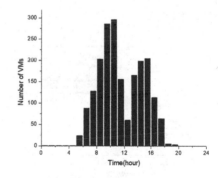

Fig. 2. Task start time distribution.

5.2 Results and Evaluation

Using the above settings, we simulate one day of the provider's execution. Figures 3 and 4 show how the cost per AU and per WU change during the experiment. The cost per AU is related to the resource allocation and the static energy consumption in the data center and the cost per WU is related to the real CPU usage from all the running VMs and their dynamic energy consumption.

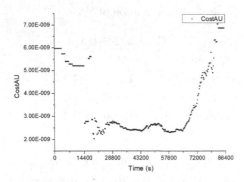

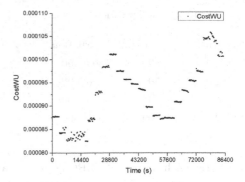

Fig. 3. CostAU changing over time.   **Fig. 4.** CostWU changing over time.

We compare our model with a fixed-price model like Amazon's [4], and a usage-based price model, such as Aldossary's [3]. We include also an optimal price that is calculated as the cost of the dynamic energy consumed by the VM. The idea of considering only the dynamic energy cost comes from the concept of energy-proportional computing (i.e. energy should be consumed in proportion to the amount of work performed) [5]. We evaluate the total revenue for the provider. We also assess the proportionality by checking how far the price of each VM is from its optimal price.

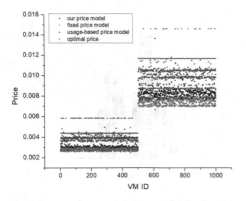

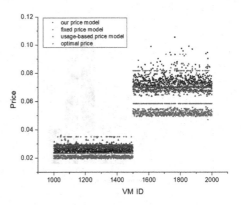

Fig. 5. Price of each VM (smaller sizes).

Fig. 6. Price of each VM (bigger sizes).

As shown in Table 4, all the models provide comparable revenue. Figures 5 and 6, which display the price of each VM (ordering them by size), show that our model is the closest to the optimal for small and midsized VMs. Only big VMs pay proportionally more because they are charged for their impact in the static energy consumption. The figures confirm that the fixed model does not consider the real energy cost when pricing each VM. The usage-based model does it, but it does not allow clients to estimate their price in advance as our model does.

Table 4. Revenue comparison for the pricing models

	Our price model	Fixed price model	Usage price model
Revenue	56.107 €	56.113 €	56.111 €

6   Conclusions

In this paper, we have presented a pricing model for virtualized Cloud providers that is energy-aware, proportional, predictable, and fair. Our model dynamically derives the energy costs per Allocation Unit and per Work Unit for each time period. Newly arrived clients during that period can use these costs as a baseline to calculate their expenses in advance as a function of the number of requested allocation and work units. Our results demonstrate that providers can get comparable revenue to traditional pricing schemes, while offering fairer and more proportional prices to the clients than fixed-price models. Our future work will consider in the model the utilization of other resources apart from the CPU, and perform a more complex evaluation using client traces from real providers.

Acknowledgments. This work was partially supported by Lenovo as part of Lenovo-BSC collaboration agreement, by the Spanish Government under contract TIN2015-65316-P, and by the Generalitat de Catalunya under contract 2017-SGR-1414.

References

1. Green, M.I.T.: Cloud Computing and its Contribution to Climate Change. Greenpeace International, Amsterdam (2010). Report
2. Aldossary, M., Djemame, K.: Energy consumption-based pricing model for cloud computing. In: 32nd UK Performance Engineering Workshop, pp. 16–27 (2016)
3. Aldossary, M., Djemame, K.: Energy-based cost model of virtual machines in a cloud environment. In: 2018 Fifth International Symposium on Innovation in Information and Communication Technology (ISIICT), pp. 1 8 (2018)
4. Amazon Web Services: Amazon EC2 Pricing. http://aws.amazon.com/ec2/pricing/
5. Barroso, L.A., et al.: The Datacenter as a Computer: An Introduction to the Design of Warehouse-Scale Machines, 2nd edn. Morgan and Claypool Publishers, San Rafael (2013)
6. Belady, C.L.: In the Data Center, Power and Cooling Costs More Than the IT Equipment It Supports. Electronics Cooling, February 2007
7. Filho, M.C.S., et al.: CloudSim Plus: a cloud computing simulation framework pursuing software engineering principles for improved modularity, extensibility and correctness. In: 2017 IFIP/IEEE Symposium on Integrated Network and Service Management (IM), pp. 400–406, May 2017
8. Hinz, M., et al.: A cost model for iaas clouds based on virtual machine energy consumption. J. Grid Comput. **16**(3), 493–512 (2018)
9. HUAWEI: Huawei server power calculator. http://support.huawei.com/onlinetools-web/ftpa/indexEn?serise=2

10. Kansal, S., et al.: Pricing models in cloud computing. In: 2014 International Conference on Information and Communication Technology for Competitive Strategies, ICTCS 2014, pp. 33:1–33:5 (2014)
11. Kurpicz, M., et al.: How much does a VM cost? energy-proportional accounting in VM-based environments. In: 24th Euromicro International Conference on Parallel, Distributed, and Network-Based Processing, pp. 651–658, February 2016
12. Microsoft Azure: Linux Virtual Machines Pricing. https://azure.microsoft.com/en-us/pricing/details/virtual-machines/linux/
13. Narayan, A., Rao, S.: Power-aware cloud metering. IEEE Trans. Serv. Comput. **7**(3), 440–451 (2014)
14. Rackspace: Cloud Servers Pricing and Cloud Server Costs. http://www.rackspace.co.uk/cloud/servers/pricing
15. Red Electrica de España: Active Energy Invoicing Price. https://www.esios.ree.es/en/pvpc?date=17-05-2017

Resource, Service and Communication Federations

Architecture and Business Logic Specification for Dynamic Cloud Federations

Ram Govinda Aryal[1](✉), Jamie Marshall[2], and Jörn Altmann[1]

[1] Seoul National University, Seoul, Republic of Korea
aryal.rg@gmail.com, jorn.altmann@acm.org
[2] Amenesik SARL, Saint-Pierre-lès-Nemours, France
ijm@amenesik.com

Abstract. Cloud federations have been seen as a possible solution for the volatility in the number of user requests and for the anti-competitive externalities of the economies of scale in the cloud service sector. In order for a federation to exist in the commercial market, an efficient mechanism for resource and revenue sharing is of paramount importance. In this paper, we design the architecture and specify the business logic for the dynamic operation of such federation platforms. The architecture and federation business logic specification include components, a federation SLA management framework, and revenue sharing mechanisms. It can also offer appropriate incentives to cloud providers for joining a federation. With such dynamism in the platform, cloud providers have the ability to automatically form and dissolve federations, to maintain resource compatibility, and to self-adapt to policies for managing contractual and economic relationships between federation members. This helps in streamlining the overall business process without being dependent on existing business relationships between service providers, between service providers of a federation, and between service providers and customers. This can encourage cloud providers to join in and be benefitted from the federation, thereby contributing to moving cloud computing to the next level.

Keywords: Dynamic cloud federation · Cloud brokerage · Revenue sharing · Cloud interoperability · Cloud federation management · Shapley value · Cloud resource sharing · Revenue sharing · Federation service level agreement

1 Introduction

Although the effectiveness of the multitenancy model of cloud computing is proven [1], limitations exist with respect to inefficient resource utilization, restricted resource scaling, and discrimination by economies of scale. Cloud federation addresses many of these limitations by aggregating cloud resources [2–5]. Cloud federation can be considered as a voluntary arrangement among cloud providers, in which they agree to interconnect their infrastructure for sharing their resources among each other [2].

Besides marketplaces [6, 7], cloud federation has been seen as a possible solution for the volatility in the number of user requests and for the anti-competitive externalities of the economies of scale in the cloud service sector [8, 9]. Dynamic cloud

© Springer Nature Switzerland AG 2019
K. Djemame et al. (Eds.): GECON 2019, LNCS 11819, pp. 83–96, 2019.
https://doi.org/10.1007/978-3-030-36027-6_8

federations allow small cloud providers to collaborate and gain economies of scale [10]. It also helps to ensure users' quality of service and to minimize costs [11]. By joining a federation, a cloud provider can also provide guaranteed availability of customer applications through reliable multi-site deployments [5].

Due to its promises, Cloud federation has been the area of research interest in recent years [1]. Despite these promises and ample research, it is important to state that there is no functional federation available in the commercial market. Extensive research has been done on optimizing the performance of federations and on dealing with challenges, such as resource sharing and interoperability [12–14]. Factors hindering providers to adopt cloud federation have also been investigated [2, 15].

To form a federation, cloud providers need to perceive additional benefits and minimal risk in joining the federation. After a thorough review of the cloud federation literature [11, 16–18], several factors were identified as important for incentivizing federations and coalitions. Revenue sharing issue has been acknowledged as one of the important factors. Revenue sharing governs how resources are shared to collectively generate revenue and how the collectively generated revenue is distributed.

Revenue sharing becomes more complicated with various innovative efforts, such as service composition for any application from a number of cloud providers and moving a virtual machine from one provider to another, in order to address the resource contention at a provider or to address dynamicity in an application footprint. As this phenomenon complicates the revenue sharing mechanism, it calls for tools that can dynamically manage contractual and economic relationships between members and provide a federation business logic for revenue allocation. Therefore, it can be stated that an effective and fair revenue sharing mechanism is required to encourage the formation of a cloud federation [39].

Previous research on architecture [3, 4, 19, 20], resource allocation, and on revenue sharing [17, 21–24] do not seem to analyze the problem from this perspective. This article deals with the architecture design and the business logic specification required for the formation and management of a dynamic cloud federation in the context of the BASMATI[1] cloud federation platform [25]. Dynamism in this context entails the ability to automatically form and dissolve federations, to maintain resource compatibility, to self-adapt to policies, and to achieve real-time situational data management. Our contribution includes (i) an architecture design of cloud federations that includes components and their interactions for SLA management and revenue sharing, and (ii) a specification of the federation business logic.

The paper is organized as follows. Related works are presented in Sect. 2. Requirements for dynamic cloud federation are presented in Sect. 3. In Sect. 4, the general architecture for dynamic cloud federation management is given. Section 5 extends Sect. 4 by detailing out the components for dynamic cloud federation management. Finally, the conclusion is presented in Sect. 6.

---

[1] BASMATI – Cloud Brokerage Across Borders for Mobile Users and Applications.

2 Related Works

Buyya et al. state three properties, which, they believe, are required at minimum to make the cloud federation effective [26]. It should (i) allow clouds in the federation to dynamically expand resources when needed; (ii) allow resource commercialization for providers with unused resources and providers in need to consume them; and (iii) deliver services with quality of service as specified in the SLA.

A number of studies deal with the architecture that supports the federation of cloud resources [3, 4, 19, 20]. Ferrer et al. present challenges for reliable and scalable service platforms and architectures that support dynamic and flexible cloud service provisioning. They also developed a toolkit for cloud infrastructure and service providers that seek to optimize the cloud service life cycle [3]. Rochwerger et al. propose a cloud architecture that supports cloud federation and management of business services [4]. The proposed model facilitates a service-based economy, in which on-demand cloud services and resources are managed across clouds transparently. An architecture for a cloud broker, named CompatibleOne is proposed by Yangui et al. The architecture, which is based on open standard, aims at assisting end users of cloud services in choosing appropriate cloud providers for their applications by considering various factors and a large number of providers in the cloud service market [19]. The federation architecture of Carlini et al. supports horizontal and vertical integration of cloud platforms, regardless of technology. It aims to minimize the user burden on using cloud services that belong to different cloud providers and increase efficiency [20].

There is various research on resource allocation and revenue sharing in the context of cloud federations as well [17, 21–24]. A participation-based method is proposed by Niyato et al. [22]. It uses a stochastic linear programming approach to a coalitional game for the formation of an optimal and stable coalition. The coalition is formed taking into account internal users demand and coalitional cost. Spot pricing, which is an auction-based method is proposed by Samaan et al. [17]. This method models cloud providers' interactions as a repeated game played among a set of selfish providers, who aim at maximizing individual benefits. These providers interact with each other, to sell their unused resources in the spot market with individual profit maximization objectives. This method is applicable in non-cooperative settings, where smaller providers are discriminated due to economies of scale. Hassan et al. [23] proposes a varied form of the auction method, in which the auction is carried out with the aim of social welfare maximization rather than maximization of individual benefit. For the maximization of social welfare, a game model is proposed that looks for a set of cloud providers with low energy cost. As with other auction models, this has a negative effect on the fairness in revenue sharing. The method proposed by Hassan [21] includes a coalitional formation game that aims to maximize social benefits. It employs a hybrid method that combines participation-based methods and auction methods for revenue sharing. Provider resources are selected in such a way that the total cost is minimized. A broker fixes the revenue rate. It then receives a number of VM offers from cloud providers on that rate. Revenue rate is adjusted (increased or decreased) according to the actual participation of cloud providers and an optimal value is reached in a number of iterations. This method compromises individual freedom, and it is unfair as large providers can operate at low cost through economies of scale. How the offset revenue (profit) is distributed is not explained. A revenue sharing scheme in a cooperative setting is proposed by Mashayekhy et al. [24]. Their resource selection uses integer programming in a way that maximizes federation profit by minimizing cost. The revenue is allocated in proportion to their contribution, which is derived from the market share. Fairness may be an issue as market share is only considered for value estimation, discriminating new entrants, who may even contribute substantial resources but lack substantial market share.

3   Requirements for Dynamic Cloud Federation Management

3.1   Cloud Application Requirements

A customer's cloud application and its requirements are introduced to the cloud management platform as TOSCA documents, describing technical characteristics, the topology of the required configuration, the service level objectives, and the constraints that are to be ensured and imposed.

3.2   Federation Business Logic Requirements

Federation business logic requirements, which are described in the federation business logic specification document, state service level agreements at the federation level and requirements for sharing revenue among federation members.

Federation Service Level Agreements Requirements. As a federation service level agreement (FSLA) is a derivation, or specialization, of the international standard known as WS-Agreement [27], it needs to describe a new service description element, which can be used to describe the technical and commercial details of a mono- or bi-directional relationship between two federation members [15]. The resulting agreement, when introduced into either, or both, of the partners, need to guide the actions of the component of the platform responsible. The actions should comprise the automated management of the technical and commercial aspects of the subsequent mutual interactions between the partners. These technical and commercial aspects include availability, price, placement, deployment, billing of resources, as well as a reference to the cost and revenue sharing mechanism.

Revenue Sharing Mechanisms Requirements. Revenue sharing is the distribution of profits and costs between stakeholders of a business or an organization. Although it is an existing concept, it has to be transformed and popularized in the context of platform-based content provisioning over the Internet [28]. Content can comprise, for example, applications, advertisements, music, and videos.

   In the case of a commercial cloud federation, in which cloud service providers and application service providers work together in a cooperative manner for the collective provision of added value application service to their collective customers, cost and revenue sharing must be clearly defined.

Cost and revenue sharing mechanisms are important for cloud federations due to two factors. Firstly, cloud providers need an effective revenue sharing mechanism, which encourages them to participate in a federation. That means cloud providers will cooperate, if they receive a benefit [17, 29, 30].

Secondly, it determines how the allocation of revenue is performed. A fair system is needed, which ensures a proper compensation of all cloud providers for the number of resources that they invested in the federation [31]. For this study, fairness is defined as self-centered inequity aversion. This term relates to the behavior, at which "people resist inequitable outcomes; i.e., they are willing to give up some material payoff to move in the direction of more equitable outcomes" [18].

4 Architecture for Dynamic Cloud Federation Management

The cloud federation management proposed involves four components: the Cloud Management Platform, the Application Controller, the Federated Cloud Management, and the components handing the edge and cloud providers. The cloud management platform is the central component, interacting with the other components. The components and their primary relationships are shown in Fig. 1.

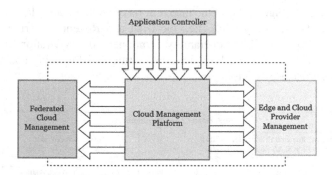

Fig. 1. Interaction of the cloud management platform with the federated cloud management component, using the federation business logic specification document, the application controller component and the edge and cloud provider management component.

Cloud Management Platform. The cloud management platform processes the cloud application requirements document (Sect. 3.1). It is also responsible for providing a deployment abstraction layer for the realization of resource deployment on existing public cloud providers and edge providers through edge and cloud provider management component, which is nowadays referred to as fog computing.

Application Controller. The application controller is responsible for the management and coordination of applications and their deployed and deployable application states. Following the requirements specified in the application description, the application controller uses a collection of application states, which allow resilient life cycle management of the application and its required resources.

Federated Cloud Management (Using the Federation Business Logic Specification Document). This abstraction layer, when employed by multiple, individual commercial cloud service providers allows for automation of resource and revenue sharing between these providers. They are referred to as federation of cloud service providers, and each provider is referred to as a federation member. The core of the federated cloud management is the federation business logic specification document (Sects. 3.2 and 5).

Cloud and Edge Provider Management. It is responsible for the localization and exploitation of cloud and edge computing resources. This component encapsulates multiple private cloud interface technologies to be able to use specialized data centers for certain application-specific needs. This component allows interconnecting to the major commercial cloud platforms, namely Amazon Web Services (AWS EC2 and ECS), Microsoft Windows Azure, Google Compute (GCE and GKE), IBM Soft Layer, Cloud Sigma and other secondary cloud providers such as RackSpace, OVH, HP, DELL, to name but a few. These commercial vendors offer infrastructure as a service. Each provider publishes either a proprietary API or an adaptation of an Open API such as OpenStack, OpenNebula or Eucalyptus.

5 Specification of the Federated Cloud Management

The following figure (Fig. 2) shows the interactions of the federated cloud management component and its sub-components (i.e., the Cost and Revenue Sharing Mechanism component, the Cross-Cloud Interoperability component, the Federation SLA Manager component, and the Application Provider Accounting and Invoicing component) and the cloud management platform.

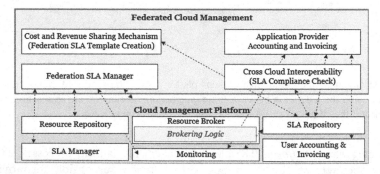

Fig. 2. Detailed specification of the federated cloud management, using the federation business logic specification document, and its interaction with the cloud management platform.

5.1 Federation SLA Manager

The federation-service level agreement (F-SLA), through which a cloud provider offers its resources within the federation, also describes the price of the corresponding offer of resources. Any service provider, which consumes resources made available through the federation, is required to make payments to the corresponding federation members providing these resources and presenting the relevant invoicing. The following figure (Fig. 3) depicts an example of how a F-SLA is used to control and manage relationships between the federation members, when they join a federation of cloud service providers.

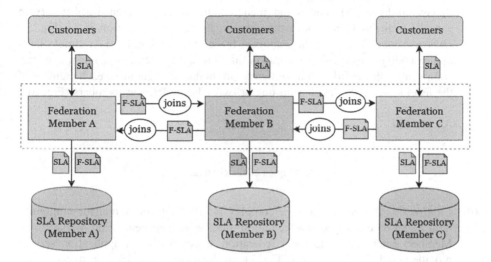

Fig. 3. Example of F-SLA based management of sharing between federation members.

Cloud providers (i.e., federation members) perform the service provisioning to customer applications based on a service level agreement (SLA) reached between the two parties. In a cloud federation scenario, theses SLAs may need to be served by federation members (e.g., Federation Member B or C of Fig. 3) other than the receiving one (e.g., Federation Member A of Fig. 3). In that case, the original SLA reached by the receiving cloud provider and the customer need still to be fulfilled. This requires for SLAs at a federation level (F-SLA) between the cooperating cloud providers, in addition to the SLA with the customers. Thus, as depicted in Fig. 3, the Federation SLA Manager of a federation member need to maintain two different types of SLAs in the SLA repository. The first group of SLAs is related to the applications of its own customers. The second group of SLAs is related to the customer applications of other federation members under the terms of the F-SLA.

The federation SLA manager has also to handle the construction and coordination of cloud service federation configurations, which are enabled through the FSLA. Seven of those configurations are:

(a) *Simple Half-Duplex Configuration* is the simplest configuration, where an application service provider is allowed access to the cloud capacity of a cloud service provider for the delivery of application services to its customers (Fig. 4).

Fig. 4. Simple half-duplex configuration.   **Fig. 5.** Simple full-duplex configuration.

(b) *Simple Full-Duplex Configuration* is the logical extension to the simple half-duplex configuration. Federation members make use of their surplus service capacity available to each other through complementary federation SLAs (Fig. 5).

(c) *Duplex Chain Configuration* combines basic building blocks (i.e., simple half-duplex configuration and the simple full-duplex configuration) in a chain together, composing a linear federation configuration. In this configuration, each member of the federation is in relation with one or two other federation members (Fig. 6).

Fig. 6. Duplex chain configuration.

(d) *Captive Configuration* is a more complex but probably more realistic configuration. It can be envisaged if a federation member (called Federation Management Member) enters into individual federation agreements with application service providers and cloud providers (Fig. 7). In this case, the federation management member would be responsible for dispatching service requests to the individual federation members, A, B, C, D, and E.

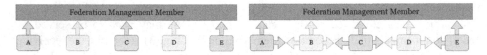

Fig. 7. Captive configuration.   **Fig. 8.** Captive duplex chain configuration.

(e) *Captive Duplex Chain Configuration* is an extension to the preceding configurations. In this configuration, federation members are exposed to and managed through a central authority (i.e., the federation management member) for their introduction to the federation. The federation management member provides them with a federation resource catalog, which would allow them to establish point-to-point operations between members as and when required (Fig. 8).

(f) *Multipoint Full-Duplex Configuration* is a further enhancement to the duplex chain configuration. In this configuration, all federation members are effectively connected to all other federation members (Fig. 9). All members of the federation would enter into bi-lateral, full-duplex service level agreements with all other members. It should be noted that the total number of relationships and their accompanying agreements increase exponentially with the size of the federation.

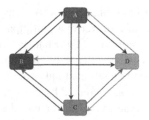

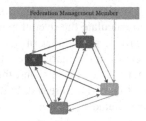

Fig. 9. Multipoint full-duplex.   **Fig. 10.** Captive multipoint.

(g) *Captive Multipoint* is an extension to the *multipoint full-duplex* configuration and can be adapted to incorporate a central federation management member (Fig. 10). It allows for an efficient collection of specific data and an efficient management of the members.

5.2 Cost and Revenue Sharing Scheme

Depending on the cost and revenue sharing mechanism implemented, it has to be considered that federation members, who bring consumable resources to the federation, such as virtual machines, disk space, network bandwidth, IP addresses, application licenses, incur costs for the resources that they provide. Therefore, in any sharing mechanisms, it is normal to expect that the federation members, who provide these resources to the federation for use by other federation members, are reimbursed at least at cost value or, to some degree, with a financial gain.

Sharing Algorithm. There are several well-known mechanisms for cost and resource sharing in game theory models. However, each one of them provides different benefit, fairness, and stability values to the collaborations [29, 30]. This may affect how the federations are created and, even, how they are dissolved. The sharing algorithm is described in the federation business logic specification document as part of the F-SLA. In the following, we introduce 3 different mechanisms of cost and revenue sharing: assigned resources mechanism, outsourcing mechanism, and Shapley value mechanism.

With the *assigned resources mechanism*, each cloud provider obtains a revenue share in proportion to the resources contributed (proportional revenue sharing mechanism) [31]. This mechanism is particularly strong in its fairness. This is a simple mechanism to implement, as it only considers the resource contributions of collaborating cloud providers for calculating the revenue share. Besides, it allows for combining resources that could not be sold separately [30].

The *oursourcing mechanism* has often been considered in connection with cloud federations, as they have been seen as a way for cloud providers to outsource some of their businesses to other cloud providers. Following this logic, collaborating cloud providers can implement a mechanism, by which the outsourcing provider will get a percentage of the revenue or a fixed fee. This revenue sharing allows a cloud provider to keep some of the revenue of the business it secured, even though it would not be able to fulfill it alone [30].

The *Shapley value mechanism* is named after Lloyd Shapley, who proposed a method to calculate the overall gain of all alternatives of a player that participates in a game with a large number of agents [18]. In cloud computing, the Shapley value is used to represent the marginal contributions of any cloud provider to the federation. In contrast with other mechanisms, this mechanism allows federations to allocate revenue according to the value created. In the simplest form, the value created by each provider can be calculated based on the resources that were made available for cloud service composition. Using this mechanism, other types of contributions (e.g., data center location, customer base) can also be considered as value additions to federations [30].

Calculation of Charges. For calculating the charges, a formula (i.e., a pricing scheme) is used that is expressed within the F-SLA, using WS-Agreement [27]. This formula is read by the invoicing and accounting component, to calculate the final charge and balance of payments. The invoicing and accounting component has to obtain the required input for the formula and calculate the corresponding charges based on the formula.

All actions performed by cloud providers and application service providers, for which an element of cost has been defined, result in a financial transaction being debited and credited to the accounts of the involved parties, for the amount described in the terms of the F-SLA or SLA. Invoice processing, often referred to as transaction collation, is performed on an account by account basis. It is performed by the accounting service of each platform operator. The resulting invoices are issued to the customers and the consumers of services, whether external or internal to a federation. All customers are liable for payment.

Due to the distributed and fully automated nature of the federation and the cloud abstraction technology provided, it can be envisaged that certain members of the federation could specialize in the management of accounting, invoicing, and cost and revenue sharing [32].

With respect to federation members, who provide application services to customers and their end users, they will invoice their customers for the services that they provide. This revenue stream is negotiated and decided between the customer and the application service provider and is clearly expressed in the terms of the SLA. For this, the charges can either be simply calculated based on the data collected for a specific customer or require the collection of accounting data from other members of a federation.

6 Validation

To validate the architecture and mechanisms proposed, we performed a simple simulation for observing the revenue distribution characteristics in federations.

For this, we considered a scenario of application deployment in one of the aforementioned federation types (i.e., the captive configuration) and performed an analysis of revenue sharing as per one of the approaches mentioned, namely the Shapley value mechanism. Figure 11 shows the application deployment scenario for that configuration.

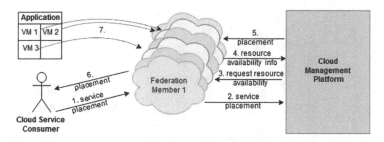

Fig. 11. Application deployment scenario for a captive configuration.

The application deployment scenario comprises 7 interactions: (1) The cloud service customer, who requires the deployment of its application, submits a service placement request to a cloud provider, who is a member of a cloud federation that (in our scenario) comprises of six providers of different capacities and characteristics. (2) The federation member forwards it to the cloud management platform. (3) The cloud management platform requests resource availability information from all federation members, (4) who respond within a certain time period, (5) and, based on these responses, calculates an optimal service placement plan by following an optimization technique, as the one described in [33]. The cloud management platform will take an account of the service provisioning, based on which the revenue shares are allocated to federation members using the Shapley Values mechanism (Sect. 5.2). (6) The cloud service customer is informed about the placement plan. (7) The federation members, who are considered in the placement plan, are triggered to deploy the plan.

With this, we observe how the capacity utilization and earning per unit resource change for each federation members in comparison to the case when they worked individually. The results are shown in Fig. 12.

The results of our simulation show that, for most of the providers (i.e., all providers except for provider Pr6), federation enables an increase of the providers' utilization ratios (Fig. 12a) and, hence, the earning per unit resource (Fig. 12b). Considering the sum of resource utilizations as well as the sum of earnings per unit resource, it is obvious that cloud federation improves the social welfare of the system of cloud providers in the market.

The results suggest that the federation operates properly as per the proposed architecture and the specified federation business logic. They also suggest that a proper federation business logic can increase the revenue stream for many federation members and can increase the social welfare of the system of cloud providers in a cloud computing market.

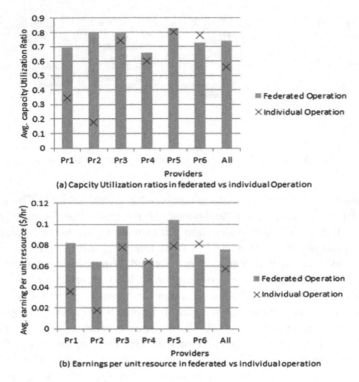

(a) Capcity Utilization ratios in federated vs individual Operation

(b) Earnings per unit resource in federated vs individual operation

Fig. 12. Comparison of federated vs. individual operation.

7 Conclusion

Federation platform operators require mechanisms for dynamic resource and revenue sharing, as they provide the motivation for cloud providers to participate in federations. Resource and revenue sharing mechanisms determine how cloud providers in a federation share their computational resources and, more importantly, the monetary benefits from the collaboration. Within this article, we presented the architecture and the federation business logic specification for such a mechanism. It allows for the formation of dynamic cloud federations.

The proposed architecture and the federation business logic specification follow the idea of an automated cloud federation management together with a cost and revenue sharing mechanism. In particular, the federation business logic describes the workings of the federation SLA management and the revenue sharing mechanism. A federation business logic enables offering incentives to cloud providers for joining federations and opens up opportunities for new sharing mechanisms.

With respect to the architecture proposed, cloud providers have the ability to automatically form and dissolve federations, to maintain resource compatibility, and to self-adapt to policies for managing contractual and economic relationships between members. Through this, a business process can dynamically be set up, independent of whether there are already business relationships between service providers, and between service providers and customers.

Overall, the proposed architecture and federation business logic specification enable cloud federations that can address specific, economic-related needs of cloud customers as well as their federation members.

Acknowledgements. The Institute of Engineering Research at Seoul National University provided research facilities for this work.

References

1. James Cuff, A.M., Llorente, I.M., Hill, C.: Future challenges in federated cloud computing (2017). https://rcc.harvard.edu/future-challenges-federated-cloud-computing. Accessed 03 Apr 2018
2. Haile, N., Altmann, J.: Risk-benefit-mediated impact of determinants on the adoption of cloud federation. In: PACIS Proceedings, p. 17 (2015)
3. Ferrer, A.J., et al.: OPTIMIS: a holistic approach to cloud service provisioning. Futur. Gener. Comput. Syst. **28**(1), 66–77 (2012)
4. Rochwerger, B., et al.: The reservoir model and architecture for open federated cloud computing. IBM J. Res. Dev. **53**(4), 1–4 (2009)
5. Petcu, D.: Consuming resources and services from multiple clouds. J. Grid Comput. **12**(2), 321–345 (2014)
6. Bany Mohammed, A., Altmann, J.: A funding and governing model for achieving sustainable growth of computing e-infrastructures. Ann. Telecommun. des télécommunications **65**(11–12), 739–756 (2010)
7. Altmann, J., Courcoubetis, C., Risch, M.: A marketplace and its market mechanism for trading commoditized computing resources. Ann. Telecommun. des télécommunications **65**(11–12), 653–667 (2010)
8. Altmann, J., Kashef, M.M.: Cost model based service placement in federated hybrid clouds. Futur. Gener. Comput. Syst. **41**, 79–90 (2014)
9. Mohammed, A.B., Altmann, J., Hwang, J.: Cloud computing value chains: understanding businesses and value creation in the cloud. In: Neumann, D., Baker, M., Altmann, J., Rana, O. (eds.) Economic Models and Algorithms for Distributed Systems. AS, pp. 187–208. Birkhäuser Basel, Basel (2009). https://doi.org/10.1007/978-3-7643-8899-7_11
10. Kim, K., Kang, S., Altmann, J.: Cloud goliath versus a federation of cloud davids. In: Altmann, J., Vanmechelen, K., Rana, O.F. (eds.) GECON 2014. LNCS, vol. 8914, pp. 55–66. Springer, Cham (2014). https://doi.org/10.1007/978-3-319-14609-6_4
11. Hassan, M.M., Hossain, M.S., Sarkar, A.M.J., Huh, E.-N.: Cooperative game-based distributed resource allocation in horizontal dynamic cloud federation platform. Inf. Syst. Front. **16**(4), 523–542 (2014)
12. Heilig, L., Buyya, R., Voß, S.: Location-aware brokering for consumers in multi-cloud computing environments. J. Netw. Comput. Appl. **95**, 79–93 (2017)
13. Haile, N., Altmann, J.: Evaluating investments in portability and interoperability between software service platforms. Futur. Gener. Comput. Syst. **78**, 224–241 (2018)
14. Risch, M., Altmann, J.: Capacity planning in economic grid markets. In: Abdennadher, N., Petcu, D. (eds.) GPC 2009. LNCS, vol. 5529, pp. 1–12. Springer, Heidelberg (2009). https://doi.org/10.1007/978-3-642-01671-4_1
15. Breskovic, I., Maurer, M., Emeakaroha, V.C., Brandic, I., Altmann, J.: Towards autonomic market management in cloud computing infrastructures. In: CLOSER, pp. 24–34 (2011)

16. Jeferry, K., et al.: Challenges emerging from future cloud application scenarios. Procedia Comput. Sci. **68**, 227–237 (2015)

17. Samaan, N.: A novel economic sharing model in a federation of selfish cloud providers. IEEE Trans. Parallel Dis. Sys. **25**(1), 12–21 (2014)

18. Roth, A.E.: The Shapley value: essays in honor of Lloyd S. Shapley. Cambridge University Press, Cambridge (1988)

19. Yangui, S., Marshall, I.-J., Laisne, J.-P., Tata, S.: CompatibleOne: the open source cloud broker. J. Grid Comput. **12**(1), 93–109 (2014)

20. Carlini, E., Coppola, M., Dazzi, P., Ricci, L., Righetti, G.: Cloud federations in contrail. In: Alexander, M., et al. (eds.) Euro-Par 2011. LNCS, vol. 7155, pp. 159–168. Springer, Heidelberg (2012). https://doi.org/10.1007/978-3-642-29737-3_19

21. Hassan, M.M., Al-Wadud, M.A., Fortino, G.: A socially optimal resource and revenue sharing mechanism in cloud federations. In: IEEE 19th International Conference on Computer Supported Cooperative Work in Design, pp. 620–625 (2015)

22. Niyato, D., Vasilakos, A.V., Kun, Z.: Resource and revenue sharing with coalition formation of cloud providers: game theoretic approach. In: 11th IEEE/ACM International Symposium on Cluster, Cloud and Grid Computing, pp. 215–224 (2011)

23. Hassan, M.M., Abdullah-Al-Wadud, M., Almogren, A., Song, B., Alamri, A.: Energy-aware resource and revenue management in federated cloud: a game-theoretic approach. IEEE Syst. J. **11**(2), 951–961 (2017)

24. Mashayekhy, L., Nejad, M.M., Grosu, D.: Cloud federations in the sky: formation game and mechanism. Trans. Cloud Comput. **3**(1), 14–27 (2015)

25. Altmann, J., et al.: BASMATI: an architecture for managing cloud and edge resources for mobile users. In: Pham, C., Altmann, J., Bañares, J.Á. (eds.) GECON 2017. LNCS, vol. 10537, pp. 56–66. Springer, Cham (2017). https://doi.org/10.1007/978-3-319-68066-8_5

26. Buyya, R., Ranjan, R., Calheiros, R.N.: InterCloud: utility-oriented federation of cloud computing environments for scaling of application services. In: Hsu, C.-H., Yang, L.T., Park, J.H., Yeo, S.-S. (eds.) ICA3PP 2010. LNCS, vol. 6081, pp. 13–31. Springer, Heidelberg (2010). https://doi.org/10.1007/978-3-642-13119-6_2

27. Risch, M., Altmann, J.: Enabling open cloud markets through WS-agreement extensions. In: Wieder, P., Yahyapour, R., Ziegler, W. (eds.) Grids and Service-Oriented Architectures for Service Level Agreements, pp. 105–117. Springer, Boston (2010). https://doi.org/10.1007/978-1-4419-7320-7_10

28. Haile, N., Altmann, J.: Structural analysis of value creation in software service platforms. Electron. Mark. **26**(2), 129–142 (2016)

29. Aryal, R.G., Altmann, J.: Fairness in revenue sharing for stable cloud federations. In: Pham, C., Altmann, J., Bañares, J.Á. (eds.) GECON 2017. LNCS, vol. 10537, pp. 219–232. Springer, Cham (2017). https://doi.org/10.1007/978-3-319-68066-8_17

30. Romero Coronado, J.P., Altmann, J.: Model for incentivizing cloud service federation. In: Pham, C., Altmann, J., Bañares, J.Á. (eds.) GECON 2017. LNCS, vol. 10537, pp. 233–246. Springer, Cham (2017). https://doi.org/10.1007/978-3-319-68066-8_18

31. El Zant, B., Amigo, I., Gagnaire, M.: Federation and revenue sharing in cloud computing environment. In: International Conference on Cloud Engineering, pp. 446–451 (2014)

32. Caracas, A., Altmann, J.: A pricing information service for grid computing. In: 5th Workshop on Middleware for Grid Computing at the 8th International Middleware Conference (2007)

33. Aryal, R.G., Altmann, J.: Dynamic application deployment in federations of clouds and edge resources using a multiobjective optimization AI algorithm. In: International Conference on Fog and Mobile Edge Computing, pp. 147–154 (2018)

Towards an Architecture Proposal for Federation of Distributed DES Simulators

Unai Arronategui, José Ángel Bañares$^{(\boxtimes)}$, and José Manuel Colom

Aragón Institute of Engineering Research (I3A),
University of Zaragoza, Zaragoza, Spain
{unai,banares,jm}@unizar.es

Abstract. The simulation of large and complex Discrete Event Systems (DESs) increasingly imposes more demanding and urgent requirements on two aspects accepted as critical: (1) Intensive use of models of the simulated system that can be exploited in all phases of its life cycle where simulation can be used, and methodologies for these purposes; (2) Adaptation of simulation techniques to HPC infrastructures, as a method to improve simulation efficiency and to have scalable simulation environments. This paper proposes a Model Driven Engineering approach (MDE) based on Petri Nets (PNs) as formal model. This approach proposes a domain specific language based on modular PNs from which efficient distributed simulation code is generated in an automatic way. The distributed simulator is constructed over generic simulation engines of PNs, each one containing a data structure representing a piece of net and its simulation state. The simulation engine is called *simbot* and versions of it are available for different platforms. The proposed architecture allows, in an efficient way, a dynamic load balancing of the simulation work because the moving of PN pieces can be realized by moving a small number of integers representing the subnet and its state.

Keywords: Simulation federation · Distributed simulation · Dynamic load balancing

1 Introduction

Complex systems require large scale simulations that can be very demanding in terms of computational resources. This requirement has produced a growing interest in the use of Cloud for distributed simulation. Moreover, the proliferation of IoT devices for sensing real world and connecting the physical and digital world have broaden the interest in that is called *pervasive*, or *ad hoc* distributed simulation [12]. It promotes the extensive use of simulation for closing the loop in control systems that reacts to changes in the environment.

Economic principles guide the conception and management of these complex systems when they are analyzed under the perspective of Resource Allocation

© Springer Nature Switzerland AG 2019
K. Djemame et al. (Eds.): GECON 2019, LNCS 11819, pp. 97–110, 2019.
https://doi.org/10.1007/978-3-030-36027-6_9

System (RAS). RAS are discrete event systems in which a finite set of concurrent processes share in a competitive way a finite set of resources. Improving the management of the own resources to support more efficient services with less cost, and to promote the interoperability between organizations for sharing resources and services is the object of study in different domains such as logistic, manufacturing, healthcare system, or cloud computing. It is essential to support decision making and providing high quality of services [17]. The synergic combination of simulation and formal models for functional, performance, and economical analysis are necessary for an efficient an reliable design and/or optimization.

In DES the model evolution happens at discrete points in time by means of simulation events. Large scale systems require distributed simulation to speedup the execution, and to federate the system simulator with other simulators specialized in different aspects interacting with the system under study such as users, external environments, or simply others well studied systems already running. A distributed DES simulation is performed through the partition of the simulation model in a set of logical processes (LPs) that interact exchanging time-stamped messages. Each LP ensures that all its internal events are processed in time stamp order.

However, important challenges has hampered the extensive use of distributed simulations, and therefore, the use of cloud computing by the simulation community [12]. Beyond an efficient management of computational resources for a distributed simulation, the modelling is the most costly task [6]. Most of the cost of developing a distributed simulation deals with the time required in specifying, trying it out, and tuning the simulation.

This paper continues our previous work on distributed simulation of discrete event systems [2] focusing on an holistic vision of the problem considering all facets that must be considered. The paper focuses on the role of languages in a MDE approach, proposes a micro-kernel providing services for distributed simulations, presents the algorithms for an efficient distributed interpretation of TPN models, and shows the architecture to federate a micro-kernel's system with other simulator engines and the environment.

2   Related Work

Cloud Federation purpose is the interconnection of cloud computing environments of two or more service providers to increase their market share and provide a more efficient management of their resources by collectively load balancing traffic and accommodating spikes in demand [14]. Current solutions provides a seamless exploitation of heterogeneous distributed resources, and brokerage solutions to find the most suitable resource to run an application [5]. Using higher levels of abstraction, such as software as a services (SaaS), supposes a different perspective of federation based on the interoperability or ability of SaaS systems on one cloud provider to communicate with SaaS systems on another cloud provider [19]. At this level of abstraction, the focus is on functional aspects, reusing developed functionality, and the efficiency of resource management is hidden to the developer. Additionally, semantic interoperability is the most important barrier to the adoption of SaaS systems in cloud computing.

Simulation Federations supposes a pragmatic approach to promote reusability and solve semantic interoperability in the domain of distributed simulations. Try to solve semantic interoperability for SaaS in general is an ambitious tasks. The High Level Architecture (HLA) is an architecture framework for distributed simulation that solves the interoperability and reusability of heterogeneous simulations [21]. A federated simulation conforms to the HLA standard and implements the interfaces specified in the standard to participate in a distributed simulation execution. To solve semantic interoperability, all federated simulations share a common specification of data communication. The federation object model (FOM) specifies object attributes and interactions, and during the simulation all joined federated shall interact with a broker using a Publish/Subscribe Pattern. However, computational resources are hidden to the programmer, and the HLA framework does not provide any mechanism to prevent imbalances. Federation migration become a fundamental mechanism for large-scale distributed simulations [3].

Distributed simulation is a consolidated discipline that faces unprecedented levels of complexity and scale in many fields [11]. Current challenges are presented in [12], which include the analysis of conservative and optimistic strategies in the cloud that has been the focus of recent works. Among the most important challenges to translate distributed simulation to the cloud is the definition of modelling languages that can be easily translated to efficient parallel and distributed simulation code. The purpose of a MDE approach is to model at the higher level of abstraction to increase productivity, and the role and semantic of languages used for modelling and supporting the MDE approach are relevant [21]. The strategy is to model the application with domain-specific languages (DSL). The use of formal models can play an important role in MDE approaches, and PN has shown to be a suitable formalism for specifying DESs. PN has been applied to different domains, providing different level of abstractions for modelling domains such as workflows, business processes, manufacturing, health systems or communication networks. The possibility to automatize the analysis using software tools has been extensively used for proposing good partitioning algorithms and estimate the lookahead in distributed simulations [9, 10, 16].

3 Language-Based View of MDE for Developing Distributed Simulation Applications

An holistic methodological approach based on formal models for the development of applications over cloud resources was presented in [20]. This MDE approach manages the complexity of developing the logic of a complex system taking into account functional and not functional requirements, and gradually incorporating restrictions imposed by the underlying hardware. In the case of DES on the cloud, sharing resources implies interferences caused by the limited isolation of

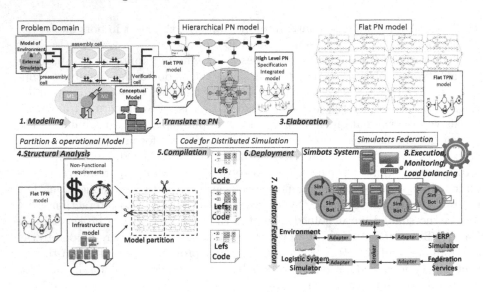

Fig. 1. MDE approach for developing a distributed simulation applications.

virtualization technologies, and with high coupled components it is clear that the execution speed is bounded by the slowest component. The impact of performance variability of resources and the incorporation of mechanism for load balancing are essential in the case of distributed simulation on the cloud. Figure 1 shows the stages of the MDE approach presented in [2]: (1) **Modelling** with a DSL language that provides the basic, usually graphical, primitives/modules that composes an application in the specific domain. Interactions with the environment or external simulators are also modelled. (2) The **modular** construction gives rise to a *hierarchical PN* model. (3) An **elaboration** process translates this high level PN specifications into a *flat model*, (4) The structural analysis of the flat model in combination with an utility function, which combines the speedup of simulations and the cost of computational resources, provides an initial **partition** of the model, (5) Model partitions are **compiled** into efficient code based on the idea of linear enabling function (LEF), (6) *Partitions* are deployed in the **system of simbots**, and finally, (7) in the case of interaction with the environment or other simulators, the simbots system is **federated** with them.

Focusing on the semantics aspects of a language for simulation, the translation of model specifications to meaningful distributed code must preserve the behaviour. Leaving out aspects of hierarchy, composition, or abstraction levels, the dimensions that should be considered in a system are the static structure and the dynamic behaviour. These aspects has been traditionally considered as separated models: static models represent concepts, attributes, relations, and conceptual hierarchies such as UML class diagrams; and dynamic models are presented specifying sequence of actions (workflows), transitions systems (state-charts), and protocols of interaction using events, states, and transition states. An important research work has been developed trying to integrate models that represent these facets of the system [1, 13].

Our main hypothesis to define our design principles for DES simulation applications are the following: **(1)** We propose only **events**, and **event dependencies** as the minimum required to represent and manage the system behaviour. The identification of a minimal set of basic primitives/concepts to represent the time flow mechanisms that control the generation of a model's behavior over time will facilitate the interoperability of simulators and the minimum information required that must be migrated to support the load balancing of simulation work. **(2)** A **model execution** based on its interpretation separates the model specification from the simulator, which is essential for scaling simulations [22]: The model is not wired with the simulator, which enables the portability of the model to other simulators and rise interoperability at a high level of abstraction. Additionally, balancing load works can be facilitated between simulators interpreting the same simulation code. **(3)** Algorithms and methods from distributed programming techniques can be integrated independently of the model interpreter, which facilitates **reusing models** and federation of simulators. **(4)** Dependencies and structural information in combination with event logs (**event sourcing** [8]) are relevant for qualitative and quantitative analysis. An analysis of these structural information is relevant for developing an initial partition, and evaluating the number of resources required to simulate a model in an estimated time, and the cost related with these decisions. However, workload varies in time during simulations. It is required combining structural information with the monitoring and recording of every state change as events in an event log.

4   Simbots: Distributed Simulation Micro-kernels

In order not to be locked-in specific simulation services to be able to use heterogeneous cloud infrastructures, and even embed these simulation services into IoT devices, it is needed a core invariant portion of DES simulation services that can be executed in heterogeneous devices. The use of micro-kernels specialized in simulation avoids to develop entirely the systems from scratch [18]. We will call *simbots* to our micro-kernels implementing LPs. A simbot is an *actor* defined as an lightweight process that communicates with other simbots through message passing. The actor model was originally constructed for distributed computations and has well-known successful implementations such as the Erlang language, and more recently frameworks like the Akka event-driven middleware [15]. The success of the actor model to afford scalability is the lacks of shared memory between actors, which only interact by means of asynchronous immutable messages. Actors are isolated from each another and are thread safe.

The **architecture of a simbot** is presented in Fig. 2. Messages are sent asynchronously to the simbot's **mailbox**, and these are retrieved from the mailbox with a receive statement or pattern-matching construction that filter events, control messages and LEFs code received from other simbots. The **Communication Interface** (*CI*) ensures that internal or external events of the simbot

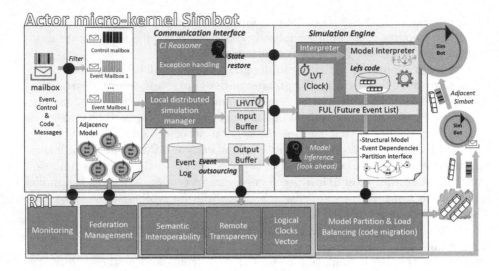

Fig. 2. Simbot: architecture of a micro-kernel for distributed simulations.

are processed in time stamp order. Section 4.1 explains the synchronization algorithm in detail. In the figure, we can observe that the *local simulation manager* defines a logical horizontal virtual time ($LVHT$) and feeds the simulation engine with the events received from neighbour simbots, executing a simulation step with the local simulation engine until the local virtual time (LVT) reaches the $LVHT$. Every internal and external event is stored in order in an *event log* using a pattern called *event sourcing*, which allows to restore the state from disk on failure recovery, such as the case of an out of order event received. The *CI reasoner monitors* the simbot and orchestrates the recovery of a failure, a change in the adjacent topology, or a load balancing of code with neighbour simbots.

The **Simulation Engine** interprets the model. Figure 5 presents the algorithm to interpret a TPN model represented with LEFs code. The interpreter can be replaced by another interpreter simulating different models using the same interface between the CI and the interpreter.

Different dynamic load balancing approaches have been proposed for distributed simulation [7]. The main objective is to minimize the delay generated by redistributing the load and migrating the code of a federate to a destination physical resource. LEFs code facilitates the migration of code between simbots with lightweight messages. Load balancing services based on the movement of code between interpreters is only possible if they use the same codification. It introduces different levels of federation with different layers of interoperability. Finally, the interpreter has a *model inference reasoner* that use the structural information to calculate the lookahead to allow neighbour simbots to advance their LVTs. It also uses the PN state equation (an algebraic computation) to compute, in an efficient way, a restored state in case of failure recovery.

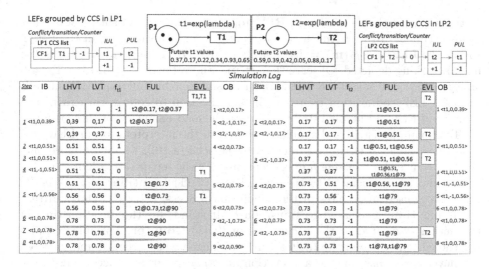

Fig. 3. Distributed simulation log.

The bottom of Fig. 2 presents a middleware, the **Runtime Interface** (*RTI*) in HLA terminology, providing the services required for supporting different levels of simulation service federation. The *federation management component* knows when federates join or leave the federation, and manages the way to keep the system running when the topology of the federation changes. Following a multi-layered federation scheme, in the case of a simbot system the *remote transparency* component, manages pair-wise communications directly between pairs of Simbots. Every Simbot and transition has a virtual address. If for example, the simbot system participates as a federate in an HLA federation, the *Semantic Interoperability* component translates the simbots events and the enabling of transitions into HLA object attributes and interactions. The *Federation Management* component deals with the HLA Federation, and the *Remote Transparency* components interchange messages by means of the event bus of an HLA middleware following the publish-subscribe pattern (see Fig. 6). Finally, the *Model-Partition* and *monitoring components* support the mechanism for load balancing between simbots, and can participate in the migration of simulation code to physical resources in a federation. The *Logical Clocks Vector* component allows to capture order and causal precedence of events to orchestrate the simulation and the management of control events in the case of failure or code migration.

4.1   Distributed Interpretation of a LEF Code

Compilation translates a transition in Timed Place/Transition nets specification into an event dependency network based on the idea of **Linear Enabling Function (LEF)** [4]. A LEF allows to characterize when a transition is enabled (an event can occur) with a simple linear function fo the marking. A LEF of a transition t is a function $f_t : \mathbf{R}(\mathcal{N}, \mathbf{m_0}) \longrightarrow \mathbb{Z}$, that maps each marking $\mathbf{m}$ belonging to the set of reachable markings, $\mathbf{R}(\mathcal{N}, \mathbf{m_0})$, to an integer, in such a way, that t can occur for $\mathbf{m}$, iff $f_t(\mathbf{m}) \leq 0$. For example, for transition $T1$ in the net of Fig. 3, the LEF is: $f_{T1}(\mathbf{m}) = 1 - (\mathbf{m}[P1]), \forall \mathbf{m} \in \mathbf{R}(\mathcal{N}, \mathbf{m_0})$, where $\mathbf{m_0}$ is the initial marking depicted. Observe that at $\mathbf{m_0}$, the value of $f_{T1}(\mathbf{m_0}) = -1 <= 0$ and $f_{T2}(\mathbf{m_0}) = 0 <= 0$, i.e. both transitions are enabled at $\mathbf{m_0}$. More details in [2]. A LEF codification translate the specification to code with a **minimal workload** that can be migrated to support the load balancing of simulation.

To explain a distributed simulation based in the interpretation of LEFs, we reproduce the TPN example presented by Ferscha in [10], where $T1$ represents the occurrence of a *machine failure* event, and $T2$ the repair rate. Figure 3 shows the codification associated to each transition, t': (1) **Identifier** of t'. A *global name* recognised in all sites of the simulation process; (2) $\tau(t')$. **Deterministic firing time** associated to transition t'. It stands for the duration time of the action associated to the occurrence of t'; (3) **Counter.** Variable containing the current value of the LEF $f_{t'}(\mathbf{m})$, initialized with $f_{t'}(\mathbf{m_0})$, and updated whenever the transition – or a transition affecting it – occurs, according to the received Updating Factor; (4) **Immediate Updating List** ($IUL(t')$). Set of transitions whose LEFs must be updated after the occurrence of t' containing the corresponding Updating Factor to be sent; and (5) **Projected Updating List** ($PUL(t')$). Set of transitions whose LEFs must be updated after the occurrence of t' containing the corresponding Updating Factor to be sent. The firing of transitions represents internal events of the simulation engine, and using the event dependency information, it is possible to update the enabling of internal transitions and external transitions. The distributed simulation is coordinated by means of the interchange between simbots of time-stamped messages, which represents how to update the enabling of external transitions when a transition fires.

To exploit parallelism, the model example is partitioned in two LPs: LP_1 and LP_2. *Future Lists* in each partition represent respectively the sequence of exponentially distributed random times ($exp(\lambda = 0.5)$) for $T1$ and $T2$. The bottom of Fig. 3 shows the logs (events recording) of a conservative distributed simulation. Gray boxes shows the variables of the simulation interpreters of distributed simbots executing LP1, and LP2, and white sides shows the input and output buffers, and the steps executed by the respective distributed simulation managers. Figure 4 shows a conservative distributed *simulation manager* algorithm sketch that invokes the interpreter algorithm, and Fig. 5 shows the algorithm that implements a step of the *simulation interpreter*. The *simulation interpreter* is executed until the LVT reaches the $LHVT$.

For simplicity, the **simulation manager** in Fig. 4 shows only the reactive behaviour when an event is received in an actor-like style. The **Start** message (`line 1-10`) initializes the *simulation manager*. It initializes the Event List (EVL) that contains the initial list of enabled internal transitions, it also initializes to zero all time stamps received from adjacent simbots (`Adj`), and it sends the lookahead value to each transition in PUL_{ext}, which contains the list

```
 1: when Start() is received                                    ▷ Initialize Simbot
 2: VT ← 0; FUL ← {};
 3: for all (t ∈ PUL_ext) do
 4:     Adj[t] ← 0;
 5:     t ! < 0, lookahead(t) >
 6: end for
 7: for all (t ∈ LEFs) do
 8:     if (f_t(M) ≤ 0) then insert(EL, t);
 9:     end if
10: end for
11:
12: when Event(t,UF,ts) is received                             ▷ Event Received
13: Adj[t] ← ts;
14: insert-FUL (t, UF, ts);
15: if allReceived(Adj) then
16:     LVTH=min(Adj);
17:     Simulate(ts);
18:     for all (t ∈ PUL_ext) do
19:         if (t ∈ FUL) then
20:             t ! < UF, ts >; remove-FUL(t);
21:         else
22:             t ! < 0, lookahead(t) >;
23:         end if
24:     end for
25: end if
```

Fig. 4. Generic algorithm sketch of the distributed simulation manager.

of transitions in adjacent simbots that can be affected by transition fires in the simbot.

When an **Event** message is received, the *simulation manager* executes a simulation step of the *simulation interpreter* algorithm in Fig. 5. The first step of the *simulation manager* is to update the received time stamp of transition in Adj (line 13), and it translates the external event of the *Input Buffer* (IB) to the *Future Updating List* (FUL) (line 14), which plays the role of the future event list in an event-driven simulation. The function *insert-FUL()* maintains events ordered by time stamp. Every event in the FUL has a pointer to the transition to be updated, the updating factor $UF(t' \to t)$ delivered by each fired transition $(t \in (t'^\bullet)^\bullet)$, and the *time* at which the updating must take effect. In the log shown in the figure, UFs are removed from the FUL to avoid redundant information. Following, the event processing checks that a message has been receive from each adjacent simbot (allreceived(Adj), line 15). In this case, the minimum time stamp (ts, line 16) is used as $LHVT$ to execute a **simulation step** of the interpreter. After this, messages are inserted in the *Output Buffer* (OB) for each transition in PUL_{ext}. Then, the *simulation manager* empties the OB and sent asynchronous messages to all adjacent Simbots to allow them advance their simulations trusting not to receive messages with smaller timestamp in the future. When transitions in adjacent simbots must be updated, the message contains the $t'^\bullet$ identifier, the UF and the ts (line 20). In other case, the message contains a zero UF value, and the lookahead time stamp (line 22). The algorithm can be improved by reducing the number of messages [11].

When the *simulation manager* executes a conservative strategy, the model requires to exploit the **lookahead** information to speedup the simulation. The

```
 1: procedure Simulate(LVHT)
 2:     while (LVT <= LVTH) do
 3:         if (head-FUL.time > clock) then VT ← head-FUL.time          ▷ Update Virtual Time
 4:         end if
 5:         while (head-FUL.time = VT) do                               ▷ Update Event List
 6:             t ← head-FUL.pt; f_t(M) := f_t(M) + head-FUL.UF;
 7:             if (f_t(M) ≤ 0) then insert(EL, t);
 8:             end if
 9:             head-FUL ← pop(FUL);
10:         end while
11:         EVL ← Sort(EVL, CCS, Strategy);              ▷ prioritizes transitions in conflict int EVL
12:         for all (t' ∈ EL) do                                      ▷ Fires enabled transitions
13:             if (f_{t'}(M) ≤ 0) then                         ▷ Checks transition is enabled yet
14:                 for all (t ∈ IUL(t')) do
15:                     f_t(M) ← f_t(M) + UF(t' → t);
16:                     if (t = t' and f_t(M) ≤ 0) then                 ▷ Avoids race conditions
17:                         insert-FUL (t, 0, τ(t) + clock);
18:                     end if
19:                 end for
20:                 for all (t ∈ PUL(t')) do
21:                     insert-FUL (t, UF(t' → t), τ(t') + clock);
22:                 end for
23:             end if
24:         end for
25:     end while
26: end procedure
```

Fig. 5. Simulation interpreter of a LEFs-coded TPN

lookahead comes directly from the net structure [10]. To calculate the lookahead for every external transition, the sample use the precomputed *future list* of random firing times. The lookahead of a transition is calculated as the minimum time-stamp of events that reference this transition in the FUL, and the times that result for the addition of the times in the future list and the LVT taking into account a number of times equal to the enabling degree of transition.

The **simulation interpreter** in Fig. 5 executes the interpreter until the $LVHT$. First, it advances the LVT until the time stamp of the first event in the FUL (line 3-4). Then, the algorithm updates all LEF values with UF in the events of the FUL that has the current LVT, and inserts enabled transitions in the EVL (lines 5-10). *head-FUL* is a pointer to FUL, *pop(FUL)* pops and returns the head of FUL, and we access the fields of events in FUL using the dot notation. Following, the algorithm deals with all enabled transitions in *coupled conflict sets (CCS)* (line 11), solving conflicts by sorting enabled transitions according to some defined strategy. A CCS is a structural transitive relation that goups transitions that share some previous input place. Then, the interpreter takes all enabled transitions in the EVL firing enabled transitions in order (lines 12-24), solving in this way conflicts.

For every enabled transition, the algorithm immediately applies IUF updating factors, which represents removing tokens from previous places, once a transition occurs (lines 14-19), but insert events in PUL, which represent that tokens will be appear in posterior places at future clock time (lines 20-22). Then, all LEFs values of transitions in the FUL with the same time-stamp of the current LVT are checked, and enabled transitions are inserted in the EVL. As

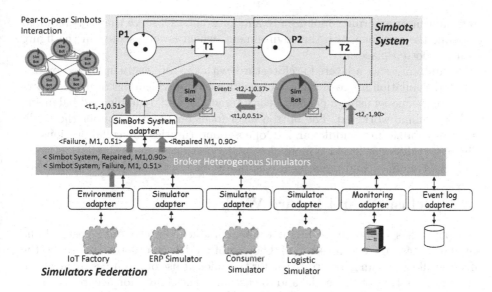

Fig. 6. Architectural approach for federation of heterogeneous simulators.

it was highlight in [2], LEFs make unnecessary the representation and updating of the marking of the PN model, and the construction of the marking of the PN after the occurrence of a sequence of transitions can be easily done collecting a log containing the occurrence of transitions each one labelled with the simulation time. The occurrence sequence and the net state equation (an algebraic computation) can be used to compute the reached marking from the initial one.

Only a mailbox is associated with a simbot, which allow to adapt the algorithm to support dynamic topologies of simbots, or use optimistic strategies incorporating an exception handling mechanism.

5   Architectural Approach for Federating Simulators

The need to build more scalable and interactive simulations considering all involved aspects (devices, humans and environment), require the expertise from several groups to be combined, and to consider more realistic scenarios. It forces to reuse legacy simulation components, and use component with varying degrees of fidelity depending of the required precision of results.

Reusability implies a different architectural approach to have heterogeneous cooperating simulators of Cloud services. Reuse is regarded by many organizations as the top driver for the adoption of SOA, which is fulfilled under the mediation of a brokering structure. This is the underlying idea of the HLA standard for distributed simulation, which provides services for information exchange and synchronization between simulations that together form a federation. Figure 6 shows the simbots system federated with heterogeneous simulators through a broker, and adapters that translate events and interactions coming from the environment or external simulators to simbot events. Observe that it is required to define the interface with the environment, which is represented in the figure with the dotted places.

Figure 6 presents a layered architecture, with the top layer supported by distributed simulation micro-kernels, which efficiently provide a distribute interpretation of the model using a pear-to-pear interaction, and dynamic load balancing with a minimal workload. The botton layer focus on the reuse under the mediation of a brokering middleware. It opens opportunities for collaborations an alliances at different levels: a more close collaboration to share simulation workload using simbots, and more open collaborations reusing different simulators.

6   Conclusions and Future Work

The paper has proposed an architecture to reduce the economic costs of the simulation task for two reason: (1) The use of models in different phases of the lifecycle allow to plan good strategies for the efficient use of resources by means of a previous analysis of the model and to customize the simulation according to the structure of the model to be simulated; (2) The implementation of a distributed simulation to take advantage of the availability of resources, and making an efficient use of the resources by the dynamic partitioning of the model to be simulated.

Moreover, the paper proposed an additional line of economic costs reduction by the connection of several existing simulators running in heterogeneous platforms. This connection try to reduce costs of model construction delegating some parts of the model to those included in existing simulators and interpreting this delegated parts as the environment of our system. To do that in the paper a mechanism for the federation of DES simulators is proposed and integrated in the simbots designed.

A compiler for ordinary Timed PN and a prototype in Akka of the distributed Simbot actor has been developed. The use of ordinary Timed PN in the modeling of large complex DES can lead to models of unmanageable size. Immediate future work includes the use of high-level models that support modularity and hierarchy, and the implementation of a compiler that explores the top-down design hierarchy and builds an interconnection table until it reaches the building blocks of the design: events, and event dependencies.

The partition of the resulting flat model, the deployment of compiled code, and the development of mechanism to support the monitoring and load balancing redistribution of code between adjacent actors are the immediate steps to to show experimentally the adequacy of the architectural proposal for an efficient distributed interpretation of the model.

Acknowledgments. This work was co-financed by the Aragonese Government and the European Regional Development Fund "Construyendo Europa desde Aragón" (COSMOS research group, ref. T35_17D); and by the Spanish program "Programa estatal del Generación de Conocimiento y Fortalecimiento Científico y Tecnológico del Sistema de I+D+i", project PGC2018-099815-B-100.

References

1. Agha, G.A., De Cindio, F.: Concurrent Object-Oriented Programming and Petri Nets: Advances in Petri Nets. Springer, Heidelberg (2001). https://doi.org/10.1007/3-540-45397-0
2. Bañares, J.Á., Colom, J.M.: Model and simulation engines for distributed simulation of discrete event systems. In: Coppola, M., Carlini, E., D'Agostino, D., Altmann, J., Bañares, J.Á. (eds.) GECON 2018. LNCS, vol. 11113, pp. 77–91. Springer, Cham (2019). https://doi.org/10.1007/978-3-030-13342-9_7
3. Boukerche, A., Grande, R.E.D.: Optimized federate migration for large-scale HLA-based simulations. In: Proceedings of 12th IEEE/ACM International Symposium Distributed Simulation and Real-Time Applications, pp. 227–235, October 2008
4. Briz, J.L., Colom, J.M.: Implementation of weighted place/transition nets based on linear enabling functions. In: Valette, R. (ed.) ICATPN 1994. LNCS, vol. 815, pp. 99–118. Springer, Heidelberg (1994). https://doi.org/10.1007/3-540-58152-9_7
5. Carlini, E., Dazzi, P., Mordacchini, M.: A holistic approach for high-level programming of next-generation data-intensive applications targeting distributed heterogeneous computing environment. Procedia Comput. Sci. **97**, 131–134 (2016). http://www.sciencedirect.com/science/article/pii/S1877050916321068. 2nd International Conference on Cloud Forward: From Distributed to Complete Computing
6. Chandy, M.K.: Event-driven applications: costs, benefits and design approaches (2006)
7. De Grande, R.E., Boukerche, A.: Dynamic balancing of communication and computation load for HLA-based simulations on large-scale distributed systems. J. Parallel Distrib. Comput. **71**(1), 40–52 (2011)
8. Debski, A., Szczepanik, B., Malawski, M., Spahr, S., Muthig, D.: A scalable, reactive architecture for cloud applications. IEEE Softw. **35**(2), 62–71 (2017)
9. Djemame, K., Gilles, D.C., Mackenzie, L.M., Bettaz, M.: Performance comparison of high-level algebraic nets distributed simulation protocols. J. Syst. Archit. **44**(6–7), 457–472 (1998)
10. Ferscha, A.: Tutorial on parallel and distributed simulation of Petri Nets. In: Performance Tools 1995, Heidelberg, Germany, September 1995
11. Fujimoto, R.M., et al.: Parallel discrete event simulation: the making of a field. In: 2017 Winter Simulation Conference (WSC), pp. 262–291, December 2017
12. Fujimoto, R.M.: Research challenges in parallel and distributed simulation. ACM Trans. Model. Comput. Simul. **26**(4), 22:1–22:29 (2016)
13. Gómez, A., Merseguer, J., Di Nitto, E., Tamburri, D.A.: Towards a UML profile for data intensive applications. In: Proceedings of the 2nd International Workshop on Quality-Aware DevOps, pp. 18–23. ACM (2016)
14. Haile, N., Altmann, J.: Evaluating investments in portability and interoperability between software service platforms. Future Gener. Comput. Syst. **78**(P1), 224–241 (2018)
15. Haller, P.: On the integration of the actor model in mainstream technologies: the scala perspective. In: Proceedings of the 2nd Edition on Programming Systems, Languages and Applications Based on Actors, Agents, and Decentralized Control Abstractions, AGERE! 2012, pp. 1–6. ACM, New York (2012)
16. Nicol, D.M., Mao, W.: Automated parallelization of timed Petri-Net simulations. J. Parallel Distrib. Comput. **29**(1), 60–74 (1995)
17. Paščinski, U., Trnkoczy, J., Stankovski, V., Cigale, M., Gec, S.: QoS-aware orchestration of network intensive software utilities within software defined data centres. J. Grid Comput. **16**(1), 85–112 (2018). https://doi.org/10.1007/s10723-017-9415-1

18. Perumalla, K.S.: μsik - a micro-kernel for parallel/distributed simulation systems. In: Workshop on Principles of Advanced and Distributed Simulation (PADS 2005), pp. 59–68, June 2005

19. Rezaei, R., Chiew, T.K., Lee, S.P., Aliee, Z.S.: A semantic interoperability framework for software as a service systems in cloud computing environments. Expert Syst. Appl. **41**(13), 5751–5770 (2014)

20. Tolosana-Calasanz, R., Bañares, J.Á., Colom, J.M.: Model-driven development of data intensive applications over cloud resources. Future Gener. Comput. Syst. **87**, 888–909 (2018)

21. Topçu, O., Durak, U., Oğuztüzün, H., Yilmaz, L.: Distributed Simulation: A Model Driven Engineering Approach. SFMA. Springer, Cham (2016). https://doi.org/10.1007/978-3-319-03050-0

22. Zeigler, B.P., Praehofer, H., Kim, T.G.: Theory of Modeling and Simulation: Integrating Discrete Event and Continuous Complex Dynamic Systems. Academic Press, Cambridge (2000)

Neutral and Non-neutral Countries in a Global Internet: What Does It Imply?

Patrick Maillé[1]([⊠]) and Bruno Tuffin[2]

[1] IMT Atlantique, IRISA, UMR CNRS 6074, 35700 Rennes, France
`patrick.maille@imt.fr`
[2] Inria, Univ Rennes, CNRS, IRISA, Rennes, France
`bruno.tuffin@inria.fr`

Abstract. Network neutrality is being discussed worldwide, with different countries applying different policies, some imposing it, others acting against regulation or even repealing it as recently in the USA. The goal of this paper is to model and analyze the interactions of users, content providers, and Internet service providers (ISPs) located in countries with different rules.

To do so, we build a simple two-regions game-theoretic model and focus on two scenarios of net neutrality relaxation in one region while it remains enforced in the other one. In a first scenario, from an initial situation where both regions offer the same basic quality, one region allows ISPs to offer fast lanes for a premium while still guaranteeing the basic service; in a second scenario the ISPs in both regions play a game on quality, with only one possible quality in the neutral region, and two in the non-neutral one but with a regulated quality ratio between those.

Our numerical experiments lead to very different outcomes, with the first scenario benefiting to all actors (especially the ones in the relaxed-neutrality region) and the second one mainly benefiting mostly to ISPs while Content Providers are worse off, suggesting that regulation should be carefully designed.

Keywords: Net neutrality · Service differentiation · Game theory · Regulation

1 Introduction

The network neutrality debate has been raging for close to two decades and is still a very sensitive issue worldwide. Basically, network neutrality is "the principle that traffic should be treated equally, without discrimination, restriction or interference, independent of the sender, receiver, type, content, device, service or application". This type of definition was introduced by the Federal Communications Commission, the regulator in the US in 2005, and by the European Union in 2014, among others. It is part of the principles for an open Internet

© Springer Nature Switzerland AG 2019
K. Djemame et al. (Eds.): GECON 2019, LNCS 11819, pp. 111–123, 2019.
https://doi.org/10.1007/978-3-030-36027-6_10

according to which resources available on the Internet should be easily accessible to all entities. The debate has been highlighted in 2005 with Ed Whitacre, CEO of the Internet service provider (ISP) AT&T, complaining that distant content providers (CPs) were using his network without financially participating to its infrastructure maintenance and upgrade, while at the same time the proportion of telecommunications economy coming from advertisement and going to CPs was increasing. The threat to differentiate traffic or even block some services raised a lot of protests. Since, numerous attempts to discriminate traffic have been observed, such as ISP Madison River Communications fined in 2005 for preventing its clients from using VoIP in competition with its own "voice" offer, Comcast blocking in 2007 BitTorrent (P2P) traffic, or the recent exclusion of some traffic from data caps in wireless subscription offers (the so-called zero rating). For more on Net neutrality and its history, the reader is advised to look at [5, 7–9, 11, 13, 14] and references therein.

An important issue barely addressed in the literature is that while neutrality principles are imposed in many countries, it is not the case everywhere. As of March 2019, we can define two, and even three sets of countries regarding net neutrality[1]:

– Countries having passed laws to protect neutrality; this includes all European Union, Canada, most of South America, Japan, India, etc. Remark though that rules are more or less strict depending on the country; for example some authorize sponsored data (that is, the possibility for content providers to pay for their traffic and exclude it from the users data cap) while other don't.
– Countries against neutrality as recently the USA, or other big countries such as Russia, China, etc. Claimed reasons are not always the same: economic efficiency in the USA, control of content/traffic by deep packet inspection in China, or congestion control in Russia.
– Countries still in the process of deciding, such as Australia or Uruguay.

As a consequence, in a global Internet, some ISPs are allowed to differentiate service for their users but also of traffic of CPs originated or going through their country. This difference of rules could end up with differentiated services for users located in a foreign and neutral country, even if neutrality is imposed and applied there. This issue is particularly exacerbated by the recent decision, in 2017, of the authorities in the USA to repeal neutrality. The USA being the origin or intermediate of an important part of worldwide traffic, it seems to us that studying the relations between countries applying different neutrality policies is becoming particularly important.

Our goal is therefore to investigate what it implies on all actors (ISPs, CPs, users) to have both neutral and non-neutral countries. To start, we will limit ourselves in this paper to two interacting countries. The actors we consider in each country are CPs, potentially deciding between classes of service for their traffic, ISPs deciding connection prices for given qualities of service (QoS) offered

---

[1] See https://en.wikipedia.org/wiki/Net_neutrality_by_country for an exhaustive list or https://www.reddit.com/r/MapPorn/comments/7k9wus/status_of_net_neutralit y_around_the_world2060x1400/ for an instructive map.

to CPs, and users with demand level depending on the QoS they experience. The interactions between countries come from users requesting traffic to CPs in their own and also in foreign countries, and from traffic having to go through ISPs in the two countries, potentially applying different neutrality policies. Non-cooperative game theory [4, 12] is used to analyse the interactions of selfish actors. The question we would like to answer is: Is there a "winner" with such a hetero-geneous situation? We wish to compare the output with the situation of a fully neutral Internet.

The literature on modeling and analysis of network neutrality through game theory has been extensive (see among others [1–3, 6, 9, 10] and references therein), trying to answer various questions, but to our knowledge no work has been deal-ing with the impact of interactions between countries applying different rules. Again, given the current tendency of countries to evolve in different political directions, this is becoming an issue of primary interest.

The results provided in this paper highlight how the specifics of net neutrality regulation relaxation can affect all actors, including those in the region where neutrality remains enforced. Our numerical results show in particular that if the non-neutral ISP still has to offer the same quality as the neutral ISP (in addition to an improved quality), then all actors are likely to benefit from the relaxation, while only the non-neutral ISP would benefit if it is given more freedom (even its hosted CPs would prefer the all-neutral situation).

The remainder of the paper is organized as follows. Section 2 introduces our two-zones, several-CP model with the available strategies and utility functions for all actors. We then investigate in Sect. 3 the case when the non-neutral ISP can only offer a high-quality service in addition to the basic one (the one in the neutral zone). In Sect. 4 we analyze numerically, on the same instance, what happens when the regulator imposes a given ratio between the low-quality and high-quality services offered by the non-neutral ISP, while the neutral ISP fixed its quality to maximize its revenue. We provide conclusions and suggest direc-tions for future work in Sect. 5.

2   Model

2.1   Topology and Actors

The topology we study in this paper is described in Fig. 1. We consider two geographic areas, with a single ISP and several CPs in each one; the set of CPs in the neutral (resp., non-neutral) area is denoted by $\mathcal{L}_N$ (resp., $\mathcal{L}_D$). We assume a peering relationship between the two ISPs. We will consider that net neutrality is enforced in one area, while neutrality constraints will be relaxed in the other one. The neutral area may correspond to the European Union and the non-neutral one to the United States, after net neutrality regulations have been repealed.

2.2   Service Qualities and Prices

Let q_N be the performance level offered by the neutral ISP, and assume that the non-neutral ISP can offer two different quality levels, namely q_L and q_H

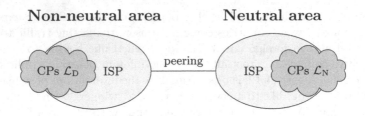

Fig. 1. Topology

(with $q_L > q_H$). We assume $q_N, q_L, q_H \in [0,1]$. Without loss of generality, the higher the value of q, the better the performance. The per-unit-of-volume prices (paid by CPs to their host ISP) are p_N (in the neutral area), and p_L and p_H for performance levels q_L and q_H, respectively, in the non-neutral area.

Prices will be assumed fixed, imposed by the regulator(s) or decided through competition: we only focus on quality levels as decision variables for ISPs.

2.3 CP Demands and Utilities

CPs also have a per-unit-of-volume gain (from advertisement) a_ℓ for CP ℓ. Each CP has a volume demand coming from its own area, plus another one coming from the other area, both depending on the offered performance q (defined just after). Let $D_i^j(q)$ be the demand of content of CP j from customers in area i. We will for example later consider the standard linear expressions $D_i^j(q) = \beta_i^j + \alpha_i^j q$. Users in area i and looking at CP j located in that same area just need to use the local ISP. Thus $q = q_i$, the performance at ISP i chosen (if a choice is available) by that CP. On the other hand, when accessing the CP j from the other area, traffic goes through both ISPs, and overall performance is assumed to be the product of the two ISP qualities $q = q_N \cdot q_D$, so that a null quality at a network leads to a null quality along the path, and a perfect quality at a node (that is $q_N = 1$ or $q_D = 1$) reduces the overall quality to the quality of the other node along the path.

The utility of CP ℓ in the non-neutral area is the difference between its advertising revenue and payments to its ISP, both of which are proportional to its total demand:

ℓ in non-neutral area $\Rightarrow$

$$U_\ell^C = (a_\ell - p_{k_\ell}) \left(D_D^\ell(q_{k_\ell}) + D_N^\ell(q_{k_\ell} q_N) \right),$$

where $k_\ell \in \{L, H\}$ is the performance level chosen by the CP.

Similarly, the utility of a CP ℓ in the neutral area is given by

ℓ in neutral area $\Rightarrow$

$$U_\ell^C = (a_\ell - p_N)D_N^\ell(q_N) + (a_\ell - (p_N + p_{k_\ell} - p_L))D_D^\ell(q_N q_{k_\ell}),$$

with decision $k_\ell \in \{L, H\}$ representing the quality that the CP has selected for its flows reaching the non-neutral zone. Note that we assume that if the CP selects the high quality, it then has to pay an extra $p_H - p_L$ per demand unit to the non-neutral ISP.

2.4   ISP Utilities

The revenues of ISPs are made of the gain from the volume of data flowing through it, minus the cost for maintaining a network with the given performance level. We therefore get, for the ISP in the neutral area,

$$U_N^I = p_N \sum_{\ell \in \mathcal{L}_N} \left(D_N^\ell(q_N) + D_D^\ell(q_N q_{k_\ell})\right) - f_N,$$

and for the ISP in the non-neutral area we obtain

$$U_U^I = \sum_{\ell \in \mathcal{L}_N} (p_{k_\ell} - p_L) D_D^\ell(q_N q_{k_\ell}) + \sum_{\ell \in \mathcal{L}_D} p_{k_\ell} \left(D_D^\ell(q_{k_\ell}) + D_N^\ell(q_{k_\ell} q_N)\right) - f_D,$$

where f_N and f_D are the cost functions. We assume that the cost borne by an ISP is made of the demand level at the quality times the (unit) cost $c_i(q_i)$ ($i \in \{N, H, L\}$) to provide this level:

$$f_N = \left(\sum_{\ell \in \mathcal{L}_N} (D_N^\ell(q_N) + D_D^\ell(q_N q_{k_\ell})) + \sum_{\ell \in \mathcal{L}_D} D_N^\ell(q_{k_\ell} q_N)\right) c_N(q_N)$$

$$f_D = \left(\sum_{\ell \in \mathcal{L}_D : k_\ell = L} [D_D^\ell(q_L) + D_N^\ell(q_L q_N)] + \sum_{\ell \in \mathcal{L}_N : k_\ell = L} D_D^\ell(q_N q_L)\right) c_D(q_L)$$

$$+ \left(\sum_{\ell \in \mathcal{L}_D : k_\ell = H} [D_D^\ell(q_H) + D_N^\ell(q_H q_N)] + \sum_{\ell \in \mathcal{L}_N : k_\ell = L} D_D^\ell(q_N q_H)\right) c_D(q_H).$$

Remark that total demand through a network is composed of the total demand of subscribers to this network, but also of the demand of users of the other network to CPs in this local network.

The cost functions c_N and c_D will be assumed increasing convex, with value 0 at 0 and $+\infty$ at 1. The typical example we will use is $c_N(q) = c_D(q) = \alpha \frac{q}{1-q}$ with some conversion rate α.

2.5   Analysis of the Interactions

Each actor takes its own decision, but not at the same time scale. We end up with a Stackelberg game, where:

1. ISPs play a game on performance levels, the one in the neutral area choosing q_N, the one in the differentiated area choosing q_L and q_H (prices being fixed, as described previously);

2. The CPs decide the class of service in the differentiated zone;
3. Demand is computed depending on those strategies.

The game is played by backward induction, i.e., each decision maker is assumed to be able to anticipate the outcome of the later stages when selecting an action.

2.6 Different Ways of Relaxing Neutrality

We take as a reference basis the situation where both areas are neutral, and investigate what happens when one region allows some non-neutral behavior from its ISP. To avoid extremely unfair behaviors, we assume that there remains some (relaxed) regulation regarding the non-neutral ISP's actions. For example, we may assume that the ISP may only offer an *improved* service in addition to that of the reference situation (our first scenario), or that the regulator imposes a *fixed quality difference* between the high- and low-quality services. Of course, other rules can be imagined, but we think those two are sufficiently simple and realistic to be worth considering.

3 A First Scenario: Opening to Non-neutrality in a Zone from an All-Neutral Situation

In this section, we investigate some possible outcomes when, from a situation where both zones are neutral and provide the same quality q_N, the possibility of creating fast-lanes is opened in one zone while the minimum quality should remain q_N. This could for example correspond to the situation in the United States, where previous neutrality recommendations have been repealed.

With our previous notations, this corresponds to q_N being fixed, and the new decision variable being q_H.

The other parameters are also assumed fixed, with values given below.

p_L	p_H	p_N	α
0.5	0.6	0.5	0.02

Those values have been chosen quite arbitrarily, but so that the players' strategies have an impact. We nevertheless think they can be realistic.

The sets of CPs are $\mathcal{L}_N = \{1_N, 2_N, 3_N\}$ and $\mathcal{L}_D = \{1_D, 2_D, 3_D\}$. We consider linear demand functions for CPs, given in Table 1. In particular, we are considering pairs of CPs, i.e., CPs that have the same demand functions in both regions and only differ by being attached to the neutral or the non-neutral ISP. This will help analyze whether a given CP prefers being hosted by a neutral or a non-neutral ISP. We also consider three kinds of CPs, with one kind (CPs 1_N and 1_D) equally of interest in both areas, and each of the two other types mainly of interest for users in one area: CPs 2_N and 2_D rather target users in the non-neutral area, while CPs 3_N and 3_D produce content that interests mostly users in the neutral area.

We display in Fig. 2 the utilities of all CPs when q_H varies, with $q_N = q_L$ fixed. We first remark that, as expected, when $q_H = q_N$ each CP is better off being hosted in the region where most of its demand lies:

Table 1. CP demand functions and advertisement revenue factors.

CP index	CP location	CP adv. rev. a	Demand in neutral region	Demand in non-neutral region
1_N	Neutral ISP	1	$0.1 + 1.0q$	$0.1 + 1q$
2_N	Neutral ISP	1	$0.05 + 0.5q$	$0.2 + 2q$
3_N	Neutral ISP	1	$0.1 + 1.0q$	$0.036 + 0.36q$
1_D	Non-neutral ISP	1	$0.1 + 1.0q$	$0.1 + 1q$
2_D	Non-neutral ISP	1	$0.05 + 0.5q$	$0.2 + 2q$
3_D	Non-neutral ISP	1	$0.1 + 1.0q$	$0.036 + 0.36q$

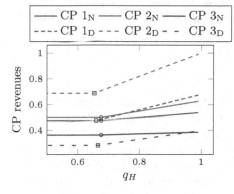

Fig. 2. CP utilities versus q_H, for $q_L = q_N = 0.5$. The situation when $q_H = 0.5$ corresponds to the all-neutral case. The marks highlight the values after which a CP selects q_H rather than q_L.

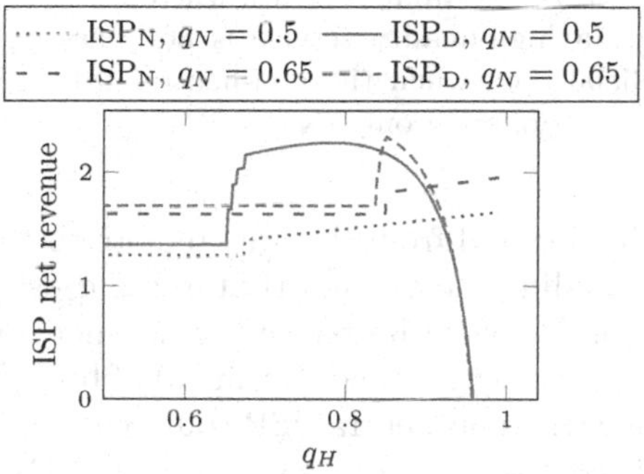

Fig. 3. ISP revenues versus q_H when $q_L = q_N$.

- being equally attractive in both regions, CPs 1_N and 1_D get the same utility, suggesting that a "virtual CP1" considering where to locate its service would be indifferent;
- similarly, a "virtual CP2" (resp., CP3) asking the same question would compare the utility of our CPs 2_N and 2_D (resp., CPs 3_N and 3_D) and prefer to be in the situation of CP 2_D (resp., 3_N). This was to be expected, since CPs will seek to minimize the multiplicative impact of qualities on the demand from the alien area.

As q_H increases, for our parameter values each CP opts for the improved quality after a certain point (indicated in the figure). Note that the values for this point conform to the intuition: a CP will switch sooner to high-quality if the impact on its demand is larger, i.e., if its target market is in the non-neutral zone and if the CP is itself hosted in the non-neutral zone. For the same reason, the improved quality q_H favors more the CPs located in the non-neutral area than their neutral-area-located counterparts, due to the multiplicative term in

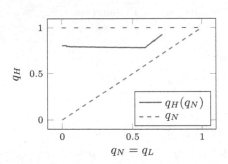

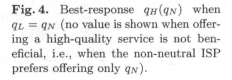

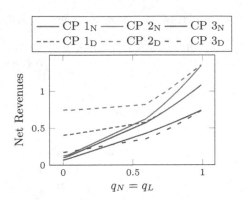

Fig. 4. Best-response $q_H(q_N)$ when $q_L = q_N$ (no value is shown when offering a high-quality service is not beneficial, i.e., when the non-neutral ISP prefers offering only q_N).

Fig. 5. CP utilities (revenues) versus $q_N = q_L$, with best-response q_H from the non-neutral ISP.

the demand from the area remote to the CP. When q_H becomes high, all CPs – including the one mostly targeting users in the neutral area, our "virtual CP3" – prefer being hosted in the non-neutral area than the neutral one.

The net revenues (utilities) of both ISPs are also plotted in Fig. 3, illustrating how the non-neutral ISP could choose its high-quality level q_H. We notice some discontinuities, corresponding to CPs switching from low-quality q_L to high-quality q_H. Those switches first have no noticeable impact on the neutral ISP, but then a positive impact since demand increases with q_H; however we do not consider here what would happen if CPs decide to switch regions (as we pointed out above, the non-neutral ISP becomes more attractive to CPs as q_H increases).

Finally, in Figs. 4, 5 and 6 we vary the common value of q_H and q_L, and consider that the non-neutral ISP selects the quality q_H maximizing its net revenue: that best-response quality q_H is plotted in Fig. 4, while Figs. 5 and 6 show the utilities of the actors. As could be expected, when the "low-quality" levels $q_N = q_L$ is high enough, a high-quality level does not make a significant enough difference, and is therefore not implemented by the non-neutral ISP. With our parameter values, this happens when q_N exceeds 0.71. Note also that before that point, the optimal q_L is not monotone in q_N: it first slowly decreases for low values of q_N, but for q_N high enough there seems to be a need to maintain q_H a certain level above q_N to keep attracting CPs, i.e., justifying the price difference, as illustrated in Fig. 3 when $q_N = 0.65$.

The impact on each individual CP is shown in Fig. 5: when the neutral (basic) quality is low, all CPs prefer being hosted by the non-neutral ISP since they can benefit from its high-quality level and the corresponding demands. However, when that basic quality increases, the gain from the high-level quality q_H is less significant, and after some threshold (around 0.35 for our example) the CP mainly targeting users in the neutral zone prefers to be hosted in that zone. The

CP targeting the non-neutral area always prefers being hosted by the non-neutral ISP, while the CP equally demanded in both regions prefers the non-neutral one until the non-neutral ISP non longer offers service differentiation.

We also display in Fig. 6 the revenues of both ISPs, and the cumulative revenues of the CPs in each zone. This allows to see what an advantage it is for an ISP to be allowed to offer an improved service; we also see the two regimes (when it is beneficial for the non-neutral ISP to offer $q_H > q_N$, and when it is not).

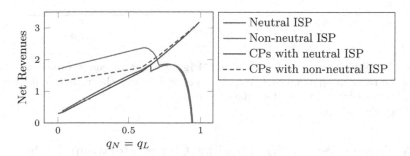

Fig. 6. ISP and cumulative CP utilities (revenues) versus q_N, with best-response q_H.

Finally, in Figs. 7 and 8 we compare the all-neutral situation (when the same quality q_N is offered in both areas) to the partially neutral one studied here, where a high-quality q_H can be offered in the non-neutral region. We observe that for our parameters, relaxing the neutrality constraint benefits to all actors, except (for a small range of values of q_N) the neutral ISP. All CPs benefit from that relaxation, in particular those hosted by the non-neutral ISP. Note however, again, that we did not consider CP mobility in our model (CPs that would switch ISPs).

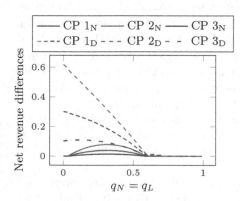

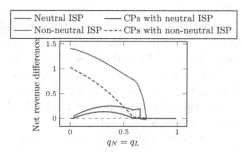

Fig. 7. CP utilities (revenues) differences when switching from an all-neutral situation to a non-neutral ISP optimizing q_H, versus $q_N = q_L$.

Fig. 8. ISP utilities (revenues) differences when switching from an all-neutral situation to a non-neutral ISP optimizing q_H, versus $q_N = q_L$.

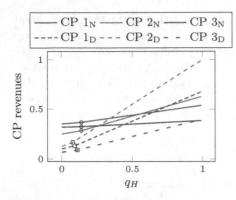

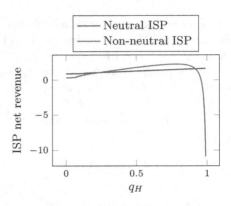

Fig. 9. CP utilities versus q_H, for $q_N =$ 0.5 and the ratio q_H/q_L fixed to 2. The marks show after which value of q_H the CPs prefer q_H over q_L.

Fig. 10. ISP revenues versus q_H, for $q_N = 0.5$ and the ratio q_H/q_L fixed to 2.

4   A Second Scenario: Quality Game Between ISPs, with a Fixed q_H/q_L Ratio in the Non-neutral Region

We now consider a different scenario, where both ISPs play a non-cooperative game on their qualities–the neutral ISP chooses q_N and the non-neutral ISP chooses q_L and q_H–but a fixed ratio between q_H and q_L is imposed to the non-neutral ISP, to avoid excessive differences between basic and improved services. For the numerical investigations, we consider the same CPs with their specificities (location and demand functions) as in the previous scenario. They are given in Table 1.

When the quality q_N is fixed and the non-neutral ISP varies q_H (and q_L to maintain the quality ratio), the utilities of the CPs are plotted in Fig. 9. We observe the same trend as with the previous scenario: the CPs hosted in the non-neutral region prefer the "higher quality" q_H over q_L sooner (i.e., for smaller values of q_H) than their counterparts hosted in the neutral region. Also, CPs whose main demand lies in the non-neutral region switch sooner to q_H. Another thing worth noting is that for all CPs, the switching point is below the quality value q_N in the neutral network: here even if q_H cannot be said to be high quality, CPs still choose it to avoid the worse quality q_L.

The net revenues (utilities) of both ISPs are also plotted in Fig. 10, illustrating how the non-neutral ISP could choose its high-quality level q_H. For our numerical values, the non-neutral ISP should choose a high quality around 0.8, and therefore a basic quality 0.4.

However, in this scenario we do not consider q_N fixed but rather determined through a non-cooperative game played between ISPs. To analyze that game, we plot the ISP best-responses (q_H *versus* q_N, since q_L is directly determined by q_H) in Fig. 11, which exhibits continuous best-response that intersect at only one point, a (stable) Nash equilibrium. Note that the best-response q_H is above

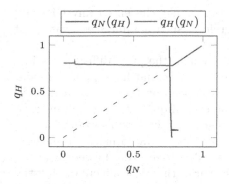

Fig. 11. ISP best-responses when the ratio q_H/q_L is fixed to 2.

Fig. 12. Equilibrium qualities when the ratio q_H/q_L varies.

q_N, and seems to equal q_N when q_N is large enough. Here at the equilibrium we have $q_H > q_N$.

We then vary in Fig. 12 the regulated ratio q_H/q_L, and plot the equilibrium values of the qualities. The resulting revenues of ISPs and CPs are displayed in Figs. 13 and 14. The figures highlight two regimes:

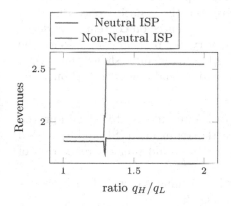

Fig. 13. ISP net revenues at equilibrium when the ratio q_H/q_L varies.

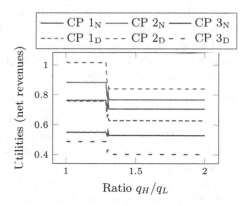

Fig. 14. CP net revenues at equilibrium when the ratio q_H/q_L varies.

- when the ratio q_H/q_L is low, the non-neutral ISP cannot set a significantly higher quality q_H to justify the price difference, and all CPs prefer the basic quality q_L. The results therefore do not depend on the specific value of the regulated ratio, provided it is low enough. Note that the equilibrium quality q_L, the one all CPs choose, is slightly below the quality of the neutral ISP, even though their price is the same. That regime is actually equivalent to the all-neutral equilibrium (when the ratio is 1, i.e., no differentiation is allowed);

we have the same qualities (except q_H, that is not chosen by any CP) and the same utilities for stakeholders. Therefore, such a limited relaxation of neutrality constraints has no impact.

– When the regulated ratio q_H/q_L is large enough, the price difference is justified by the quality difference, hence all CPs select that high-quality. Again, as a result the equilibrium qualities do not depend on the regulated ratio in that regime. Note that in this regime, the chosen quality in the non-neutral zone q_H is strictly above the one in the neutral zone. It is also worth noting that both ISPs–even the neutral one–prefer this regime over the all-neutral situation, while it is the opposite for CPs: all of them were better off in the all-neutral setting than in this relaxed scenario, the most affected being the CPs hosted in the non-neutral zone.

Between those two regimes, there is a small range of values for the regulated ratio, where some CPs would select q_L and others q_H. The impacts on the actors in that limited range are less clear.

5   Conclusions

Changing the net neutrality rules in a part of the Internet may affect actors in other parts; in this paper we have focused on a simple scenario with two domains having different regulations, and have investigated the resulting decisions from ISPs (in terms of offered qualities) and the consequences on content providers.

The specifics of the new rules can lead to very different outcomes. With the same parameter values, our numerical analysis has for example shown that, when a non-neutral ISP can offer two qualities q_H and q_L and a neutral ISP only one quality q_N:

– if we impose $q_L = q_N$, i.e., non-neutrality is only allowed to offer improved service, then all stakeholders–in particular the non-neutral ISP and its hosted CPs, but also the other ones to a lesser extent–would prefer a relaxation of neutrality rules;
– if a given ratio q_H/q_L is imposed, then either nothing is changed with respect to the neutral situation, or all CPs are worse off.

Those results suggest that regulatory decisions about relaxing net neutrality rules should be made with great care, taking into account the whole ecosystem that is affected.

The setting described in this paper opens several perspectives for future work. A first direction would be to develop the analytical study of the model proposed here rather than investigate numerical examples. Also, one can imagine other versions of regulation to constrain the non-neutral ISP in other ways, with the objective to favor user welfare, CP innovation, or fairness among users or among CPs.

References

1. Altman, E., Legout, A., Xu, Y.: Network non-neutrality debate: an economic analysis. In: Domingo-Pascual, J., Manzoni, P., Palazzo, S., Pont, A., Scoglio, C. (eds.) NETWORKING 2011. LNCS, vol. 6641, pp. 68–81. Springer, Heidelberg (2011). https://doi.org/10.1007/978-3-642-20798-3_6
2. Coucheney, P., Maillé, P., Tuffin, B.: Impact of reputation-sensitive users and competition between ISPs on the net neutrality debate. IEEE Trans. Netw. Serv. Manag. (2013)
3. Coucheney, P., Maillé, P., Tuffin, B.: Network neutrality debate and ISP interrelations: traffic exchange, revenue sharing, and disconnection threat. Netnomics 1(3), 155–182 (2014)
4. Fudenberg, D., Tirole, J.: Game Theory. MIT Press, Cambridge (1991)
5. Lenard, T.M., May, R.J. (eds.): Net Neutrality or Net Neutering: Should Broadband Internet Services be Regulated. Springer, New York (2006). https://doi.org/10.1007/0-387-33928-0
6. Ma, T.T.B., Chiu, D.M., Lui, J.C.S., Misra, V., Rubenstein, D.: On cooperative settlement between content, transit, and eyeball internet service providers. IEEE/ACM Trans. Netw. 19(3), 802–815 (2011)
7. Maillé, P., Reichl, P., Tuffin, B.: Internet governance and economics of network neutrality. In: Hadjiantonis, A.M., Stiller, B. (eds.) Telecommunication Economics. LNCS, vol. 7216, pp. 108–116. Springer, Heidelberg (2012). https://doi.org/10.1007/978-3-642-30382-1_15
8. Maillé, P., Simon, G., Tuffin, B.: Toward a net neutrality debate that conforms to the 2010s. IEEE Commun. Mag. 54(3), 94–99 (2016)
9. Maillé, P., Tuffin, B.: Telecommunication Network Economics: From Theory to Applications. Cambridge University Press, Cambridge (2014)
10. Njoroge, P., Ozdaglar, A., Stier-Moses, N., Weintraub, G.: Investment in two sided markets and the net neutrality debate. Technical report DRO-2010-05, Columbia University, Decision, Risk and Operations Working Papers Series (2010)
11. Odlyzko, A.: Network neutrality, search neutrality, and the never-ending conflict between efficiency and fairness in markets. Rev. Netw. Econ. 8(1), 40–60 (2009)
12. Osborne, M., Rubinstein, A.: A Course in Game Theory. MIT Press, Cambridge (1994)
13. Schulzrinne, H.: Network neutrality is about money, not packets. IEEE Internet Comput. 22(6), 8–17 (2018)
14. Wu, T.: Network neutrality, broadband discrimination. J. Telecommun. High Technol. (2003)

Economic Assessment, Business and Pricing Models

Sensing as a Service Revisited: A Property Rights Enforcement and Pricing Model for IIoT Data Marketplaces

Jan-Terje Sørlie and Jörn Altmann[(⌂)]

Seoul National University, Seoul 08826, South Korea
jorn.altmann@acm.org

Abstract. The Industrial Internet of Things (IIoT) has become a valuable data source for products and services based on advanced data analytics. However, evidence suggests that industries are suffering a significant loss of value creation from insufficient IIoT data sharing. We argue that the limited utilization of the Sensing as a Service business model is caused by the economic and technological characteristics of sensor data, and the corresponding absence of applicable digital rights management models. Therefore, we propose a property rights enforcement and pricing model by utilizing digital watermarking in combination with product versioning to address the IIoT data sharing incentive problem.

Keywords: Industry 4.0 · Industrial Internet of Things · Sensing as a Service · IIoT data marketplace · Digital rights management · Digital watermarking

1 Introduction

1.1 Background

In 2011, the German government launched its *Industrie 4.0* initiative to *"drive digital manufacturing forward by increasing digitization and the interconnection of products, value chains and business models"* [1]. The fourth industrial revolution has now become widely accepted as the era, in which technologies like cyber-physical systems and cognitive computing will enable a significant increase in operational efficiency and productivity [2].

Much of these digitization efforts can be attributed to our desire to interconnect the physical and digital worlds and describe the environment in a language that computers can understand to utilize their superior capabilities [3]. Such capabilities become prevalent with technologies like big data analyses, which can increase functionality and quality in products and services by revealing patterns and correlations that were previously invisible [4]. Big data is also a key source for machine learning, which is the heart of artificial intelligence [5]. Indeed, advanced data analytics has been found to be the most pursued approach to technology innovation, which is yet another indication of data itself becoming an indispensable asset [6].

Although vast amounts of digital information are already being collected and processed, fundamental Industry 4.0 prerequisites such as connectivity and interoperability

© Springer Nature Switzerland AG 2019
K. Djemame et al. (Eds.): GECON 2019, LNCS 11819, pp. 127–139, 2019.
https://doi.org/10.1007/978-3-030-36027-6_11

have been lagging behind due to cybersecurity concerns and technological incompatibility in industrial environments [7]. The EU Commission supports this hypothesis [8] and provides funding to the development of common interfaces to overcome technological barriers to a successful digital economy [9]. However, the levels of information transparency as envisioned for Industry 4.0 cannot be achieved through digitization and technological compatibility alone. Multiple studies have assessed the economic grounds and associated business models and incentives for trading digital information in the form of sensor data. For instance, Sensing as a Service (S^2aaS) was anticipated in [10] as an Internet-connected sensor network offering commercial data access services. This model has later been covered in detail and linked to the Internet of Things paradigm [11], which is one of the key frameworks supporting the fourth industrial revolution [12].

Central to the S^2aaS business model is the concept of IoT data marketplaces [13]. The key motivation behind such marketplaces is to create platforms, on which data streams from different connected devices, that otherwise may remain unexploited or stored in silos, can be traded for increased value creation [14]. We will consider such IoT devices as physical or virtual sensors capable of exchanging data over the Internet. Although some scholars also include actuators under the IoT umbrella [15], we limit our scope to only cover sensors as a part of the Sensing as a Service business model.

That said, various definitions of IoT allow for many interpretations including personal devices and applications focusing on more user-centric convenience than significant gains in operational efficiency and productivity. Therefore, we will use the term Industrial Internet of Things (IIoT), which can be considered as a subcategory of IoT. Due to the lack of a widely accepted definition of IIoT, we will assign this term to what the EU Commission defines as machine-generated, non-personal raw data [16]. We use the term industrial to emphasize the value propositions for various industries, although the actual data may be collected in non-industrial environments like in private, connected cars [17].

Prior research highlights many use-cases for data-driven applications across a wide range of industries and underlines the benefits in increased sharing of data as a non-rivalrous good [2, 18, 19]. However, a recent communication by the EU Commission addressing ownership and access rights of IIoT data, expresses concerns that current limitations in data sharing means that we are not taking full advantage of the emerging data-driven economy [20]. This EU communication has sparked a debate on the property and access rights of IIoT data as well as why privately held sensor data is not sufficiently shared [21]. This study adds to that debate.

1.2   Problem Description

Information harvested by IIoT devices is expected to enable a wide range of smart applications within domains like utility metering, logistics, supply chains, agriculture, power grids, traffic and building controls [18] as well as an overall increase in manufacturing efficiency [2]. Despite these business opportunities, the limited presence of data sharing through IIoT marketplaces is evident [20]. While some economic articles suggest that the main barrier to increased data sharing is the lack of knowledge on how data can be exploited [20], we believe the rapid increase in production and use of IIoT data suggests otherwise. In addition, the presence of online (I)IoT data marketplaces featuring common interfaces indicates that technological incompatibilities have already been overcome [9].

Prior studies on S^{2}aaS and (I)IoT data marketplaces pay little attention to fundamental prerequisites for any economic transaction, namely pricing [35, 36], well-defined property rights, and associated mechanisms to enforce them [11, 13–15]. On the other hand, the more economically oriented debate following the EU communication on data ownership does not seem to fully acknowledge the technological aspects of this issue. For instance, (I)IoT data streams are sometimes classified as an excludable good [20], which is contrary to the general understanding of digital information goods being relatively non-excludable [19]. In fact, we argue that sustainable data sharing is actually inhibited by the current *de facto* non-excludable characteristics of IIoT data streams. We believe the critical function of enforcing property rights of such data has fallen in the shadow of the academic debate on who should be granted access to data in the absence of copyright protection [22].

1.3 Research Objective and Question

Based on these shortcomings, our research objective is to combine the related and sometimes even conflicting elements of pricing strategies and property rights enforcement in one digital rights management model for IIoT data, and we ask how this combination can contribute to more economically viable IIoT data trading.

1.4 Methodology

From the findings of our literature review, we first support the need for property rights enforcement and pricing models [34–36] that are specifically adapted to IIoT data streams. Then, we propose a combined model for this purpose due to the absence of adequate alternatives in prior works. Lastly, we analytically analyze the relationship between the proposed watermarking technique and product versioning strategy with the aim to obtain economic incentives for increased IIoT data sharing.

1.5 Contributions

This study provides a model to remedy the IIoT data sharing incentive problem. The model includes a novel watermarking mechanism for sensor data that supports transparent product versioning in terms of predictable quality implications. In addition, we illustrate an important relationship between IIoT data versioning and property rights enforcement by introducing the quality gap for product versioning and how it can be optimized from the perspective of data owners. The academic motivation is to close the knowledge gap between the technologically oriented works and the more recent economic articles concerning (I)IoT data sharing.

1.6 Structure

The remainder of this study is organized as follows: a brief literature review on the economic aspects and property rights enforcement methods for IIoT data are presented in Sect. 2. In Sect. 3, we summarize the key takeaways from our literature review to support the proposed model. We then introduce a digital watermarking technique as a core element in the proceeding economic analyses. In Sect. 4, we utilize our model in an analytical analysis to answer our research question. Section 5 summarizes and concludes our findings.

2   Literature Review

The IIoT data marketplace enables raw data streams to be traded between stakeholders before value-added services like analytics, aggregation or combination of data have been provided [13]. Thus, IIoT data can be considered as a digital information good. As with information in general, determining the price of data streams is quite different from pricing physical goods due to the negligible marginal cost of production in combination with the portability and wide variety of value propositions [33, 37]. As Shapiro and Varian [23] proclaimed, *"information is costly to produce but cheap to reproduce"*. Information is also frequently referred to as being easy to create but hard to trust, and easy to spread but hard to control.

Therefore, assigning and enforcing property rights as well as embedding provenance is a crucial task in the market for relatively non-excludable and non-rivalrous data streams [19]. However, IIoT data are, in general, not protected by copyright law [22], and property rights must therefore be sought through contract law. This lack of absolute protection means that IIoT data is especially vulnerable to unwanted copying and distribution in secondary markets [24]. Unless data owners aim to transfer the entire ownership, contracts preventing buyers from copying and distributing the same data stream is critical to maintain economic incentives to collect and share data. Otherwise, a malicious buyer could exploit the arbitrage opportunity and resell data streams to multiple buyers at a lower price than the original good.

However, due to the doctrine of privity, which is commonly practiced in contract law, the rights or obligations of a contract are only binding to the parties signing the contract. This means that contract law may not be sufficient to prevent a third-party from legally redistributing data streams against the will of the original owner. This is why adding provenance to digital goods can be an effective barrier to so-called piracy by embedding traceability to the party that was initially responsible for the breach of contract [25].

Unfortunately, digital rights management of IIoT data is substantially more challenging compared to software and multimedia because replication and tampering is technically difficult to control [5]. Regardless of encryption mechanisms for secure transportation and user authentication for access control, the information contained in IIoT data streams must eventually be revealed to the consumer, which in turn enables virtually effortless reproduction. This is a clear distinction from digital media files carrying images, music and video where the perceived value is largely driven by its analogue consumption by humans. For instance, apparently invisible watermarks can be implemented in audio files at frequencies outside the human hearing range, or in middle-frequency parts of images [26]. However, unlike images and audio files, digital watermarks in IIoT data streams would necessarily impose a visible difference in the good. A single number can simply not hold more information than its intrinsic numerical value unless the value itself or its metadata have been altered. Still, digital watermarking remains as the only relevant protection measure for IIoT data streams [27].

All digital watermarking techniques face a trade-off between three conflicting goals: maximizing rate of information imbedding; minimizing distortion of the original data; and maximizing the robustness against attacks by malicious agents aiming to erase traceability [25]. Furthermore, the robustness of watermarking can be classified into four main categories [28]: removal attacks where information is sufficiently damaged; geometric attacks targeting the watermark detection mechanism; cryptographic attacks where the watermark is decoded and then removed or distorted; and protocol attacks aiming to alter the watermark information.

In a state-of-the-art review of techniques for digital watermarking, Panah et al. [27] list applicable approaches for embedding provenance in non-media or unstructured information in the form of streamed, complex data. In this relation, interpacket delay and data point sequence alteration-based methods are generally assumed to cause excessive loss of value in many IIoT data applications. The remaining approaches that appear to be more viable for IIoT data are based on alteration of less significant bits in specific datapoints. Forward reference searches from original works in this domain [29, 30] do not reveal any recent additions in this category. Table 1 summarizes watermarking methods applicable to IIoT data and their potential shortcomings with respect to the scope of this study.

Table 1. Relevant watermarking methods for IIoT data streams

Method	Potential weakness	Reference
LSB embedding in selected extremes	Limited generality and invisibility	Sion, Atallah and Prabhaka [29]
Metadata and LSB embedding	Insignificant bits can be attacked by removal with limited loss of value	Chong, Skalka and Vaughan [30]
Data point sequence alteration	The sequence of data points is considered to be critical for many applications	Xiao, Sun, Li, Wang, Xia and Liang [31]
Variable interpacket delay	Interpacket delays are considered to be critical for many applications and are often fixed	Sultana, Shehab and Bertino [32]

3 Model

3.1 Assumptions

In designing a model to embed provenance in IIoT data streams for the purpose of making contract infringement unattractive, we assume that IIoT data is privately held, and that the original owner seeks profit maximization by maintaining its monopolistic power in an open IIoT data marketplace. This means that the owner has an interest in preventing buyers from reproducing and distributing the data stream in secondary markets unless they are authorized to do so. However, we also expect the presence of malicious agents, who are willing to violate these contract terms and technologically attack any property rights enforcement mechanisms to remove traceability.

An example of an IIoT data stream covered by this study is the speed of a connected car, which is part of core functionality needed to safely operate the vehicle in addition to being of potential interest to others. For instance, developers of autonomous driving systems may utilize this information in combination with other variables. On the other hand, the same data stream can also be valuable to insurance companies when investigating an accident or for personalized pricing policies based on driving behavior. In this multi-stakeholder scenario, it is natural to assume that the insurance company prefers a lower level of precision than the software developer, if the data stream is made available at a lower price through product versioning. Therefore, we will utilize so-called quality discrimination by applying versioning of the data stream as a measure to maximize profits as supported by prior literature [5].

Regarding the perceived value of the data stream, we will assume that utility is expressed as a linear function of quality. Moreover, we generalize quality to be described as the precision of the data stream. Hence, the perceived value of a data stream can be expressed as a linear function of the number of digits precision per data point. The precision level is the only quality factor considered alterable because timestamps may in many cases express critical information that, together with the completeness of the time series, must remain reliable regardless of any watermark application [27]. We also assume that all attacks on watermarks attempt to maintain as much as possible of the original data stream and, thus, its quality. Lastly, we assume that IIoT data streams are a byproduct of operating a product or process and, thus, being created regardless of their presence on the IIoT data marketplace.

3.2 Watermarking Technique

We propose a digital watermarking technique based on alternation of less significant digits because this approach is assumed to represent the ideal trade-off between the three conflicting goals of watermarking [27]. However, as opposed to related works in [29] and [30], we put additional emphasis on the ability for the watermarking technique to provide transparent product versioning in terms of predictable quality implications. These requirements are motivated by our line of argument that there is a need for viable property rights enforcement and pricing models to facilitate increased IIoT data sharing. The applied watermarking principles are inspired by the concepts of Quantization Index Modulation [25].

Function. We propose a combined product versioning and watermarking technique based on rounding operations. In more detail, the technique is based on deterministic alternation between two different rounding tie-break conventions. Tie-breaking rules are needed when rounding a digit that is exactly half-way between preceding integers. That is, if 9.5 should be rounded to 9 or 10, or if 95 should be rounded to 100 or 90. If there were not for least significant digits equal to 5, all round-off errors would be symmetric by always rounding to the nearest preceding integer. The default rounding mode in the technical standard for floating-point arithmetic IEEE 754 is "round half to even". This means that a midway floating point will be rounded to the nearest even integer value. In other words, 9.5 is rounded to 10 and 8.5 is rounded to 8. This method has no positive/negative bias and no bias toward/away from zero and will minimize the sum of expected errors. A similar tie-breaking rounding convention featuring the same properties is "round half to odd".

The proposed watermarking technique is named Deterministic Alternation Between Integer Tie-breaks (DABIT). DABIT implements a seemingly invisible repeating watermark in IIoT data streams consisting of real numbers with or without fractions provided the sensor data points are expressed by two or more digits. The method works by altering between the two aforementioned tie-breaking rules according to a predefined sequence for every encountered tie-break. The embedded watermark represents a 64-bit binary code identifying the initial buyer of the data stream. A "round half to even" tie-break expresses a binary 1, and a "round half to odd" operation expresses a binary 0. In this way, DABIT enables close to non-biased watermarking of data streams with a negligible loss of precision. By comparing a DABIT-encoded data stream with the original time series, every case of a tie-break rounding would express a part of the watermark. Thus, the full data stream does not necessarily need to be kept as reference. The watermark embedding algorithm is conceptualized as a Python function below, in which the precision of each data point of a data stream is reduced by one digit:

```
# x[] is an unwatermarked data stream
# y[] is the resulting watermarked data stream
# t is the timestamp
# i[] is the 64 bit watermark
# n is the watermarking sequence number

if int(repr(x[t])[-1]) == 5:
  if i[n] == 0:
    y[t] = RoundHalfToOdd(x[t])
  else:
    y[t] = RoundHalfToEven(x[t])
  n += 1
else:
```

Robustness. In this section, we will discuss the robustness of DABIT against potential geometric, removal, cryptographic, and protocol attacks that are relevant to IIoT data streams. The robustness of DABIT against geometric attacks targeting the watermark detection mechanism is relatively strong. This is due to the rigorous relationship between the original data stream and the watermarked version in terms of both timestamps and the order of data points. Hence, in case timestamps were slightly altered in a geometric attack, a sophisticated watermark detection mechanism may still recognize the sequence of data points as a reference to where the watermark is embedded. In case of an alternation of the order of data points by a malicious agent and, thus, an increase in the difficulty of detecting a watermark, a higher quality loss is the consequence compared to other strategies.

Given that the unwatermarked data stream is not known and the value of the least significant digit of the original data stream is unpredictable, the DABIT watermark is arguably invisible to any malicious agent. However, the technique is potentially vulnerable to cryptographic and subsequent protocol attacks if different agents buy the same data stream with the purpose of averaging them or otherwise comparing each data point to detect and possibly alter the watermark. That said, this is also the case of most watermarking methods. A certain level of protection against such attacks can be achieved by utilizing strategic watermarks, but the actual construction of the watermark lies outside the scope of this study.

Lastly, removal attacks are arguably the most relevant threat against DABIT, because this mode of attack is in line with our assumption that minor noise in data points results in the lowest perceived quality loss for IIoT data streams. We will not consider removal attacks such as averaging adjacent data points, which would harm the frequency of the data stream, nor the complete removal of selected data points, which would not be a viable approach for attacking an invisible watermark. Instead, we identify relevant removal attacks as being rounding, truncation or adding noise to less significant digits of the data stream. Common for these three removal attacks is their aim to reduce precision of the data stream while maintaining other quality attributes such as timestamps and completeness of the time series. To simplify the assessment of these attacks, we combine these three attack modes in one worst-case scenario, where a given number of the least significant digits are removed with a rounding operation.

One of the key features of DABIT that helps withstanding the aforementioned removal attacks, is that even if the watermark is initially embedded in the least significant digits, the watermark will occasionally spread to more significant digits as well. Given a uniform distribution of least significant digits between 0–9, every 100th rounding operation is expected to affect the second least significant digit. Every 1000th rounding operation will affect the third least significant digit and so on. This effect makes the watermark fairly robust against attacks on less significant digits, but it also illustrates the exponentially increasing difficulty to recover the watermark for every digit being attacked by a malicious agent.

3.3 Economic Reasoning

The Quality Gap. The proposed model includes a quality discriminating approach, which is a common technique to accommodate different utilities of consumers of digital products [5]. For this approach to result in profit maximization, it becomes essential to identify the optimal difference in quality between product versions offered on the marketplace. We define this difference as the quality gap.

We will only consider the gap between the two product versions A and B, because any lower levels of quality than version B would not be able to compete with attacked and illegally distributed versions of A, which would obtain superior quality in this scenario. Arguably, it pays off for the data owner to pursue watermark reconstruction of illegally distributed versions of product A as long as the costs of these efforts increase consumers' perceived loss of value caused by the watermark attack. This is because any costs of pursuing malicious agents that exceeds consumers' combined willingness to pay for the quality difference between the original and the illicit good cannot be expected to be recovered. When these two cost functions are in equilibrium, the property rights holder is indifferent between pursuing malicious agents through watermark reconstruction and offering an authentic substitute of the illicit good on the marketplace (product version B). This authentic good can match the precision level of illicit goods while still providing greater value due to its authenticity.

Cost of Watermarking (CoW). We define cost of watermarking as the sum of two main cost factors: embedding cost and reconstruction costs. These costs, which are faced by the property rights holder, include the computing power, labor, and quality loss associated with these activities. Embedding cost is the cost of implementing the watermark through a rounding operation, which is a linear cost function expressed by a cost parameter ρ multiplied with the number of rounding operations x per data point (ρx). At the time of reconstruction of the watermarked, this cost is fixed ($c = \rho x$). Reconstruction costs are expressed as an exponential function with cost parameter a and the number of digits x that have been attacked by a malicious agent. In other words, the number of rounding operations applied per data point by the attacker. The exponential property is attributed to the exponentially increasing size of data that needs to be collected and processed in order to detect traces of the watermark for every digit of precision that has been attacked.

$$CoW = c + a\,10^x \tag{1}$$

Cost of Attacking (CoA). Malicious agents are facing two main factors in their cost function: the actual attack operation and the resulting loss of value of the data stream. Costs associated with performing the attack are considered to be equivalent to the costs of the initial watermark embedding process faced by the property rights holder (ρx). This is because we assume the attack to be performed as a rounding operation that reduces the precision level of the data stream by x digits. The cost of quality reduction means the overall consumer-perceived loss of quality of the data stream expressed with cost parameter b. This loss is caused by an attack of the watermark that results in a loss of x digits precision. Due to the invisibility of the watermark, the attack must remove x digits from all data points. According to our general assumption of a linear utility function, this cost function is also linear.

$$CoA = \rho x + b x \tag{2}$$

4 Analytical Analysis

4.1 Equilibrium Between CoW and CoA

To identify the optimal versioning strategy for the described scenario, we determine the equilibrium between the cost of watermarking (CoW) and the cost of attacking (CoA).

This equilibrium helps identifying the quality level, at which product version B should be introduced to support the market value of product version A. Figure 1 illustrates the location of this equilibrium.

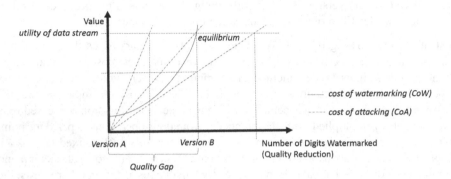

Fig. 1. Potential equilibrium between CoW and CoA

One equilibrium can occur before there is a full digit quality gap, thus when no DABIT watermark can be added. A second equilibrium between the two cost functions CoW and CoA can occur at a greater optimal quality gap between product version A and B. The following equation can be used to identify all equilibria between the two cost functions at different cost parameters:

$$CoW = CoA \tag{3}$$

4.2   Determining the Optimal Quality Gap

For simplification, without loss of generality, we assume the costs of rounding for the data owner (c) to be zero, resulting in:

$$a\,10^x = \rho x + b x \tag{4}$$

To expresses the ratio between the cost parameters a, b, and ρ at different quality gaps x between product version A and B, we construct function y. We name this function the quality gap function:

$$y = a/(\rho + b) = x/10^x \tag{5}$$

If the cost parameters are known, the optimal gap between the two product versions can be determined by tracing a horizontal line from any given cost ratio y and observe for which values of x the line intersects with the quality gap curve. Figure 2 illustrates an example on how the ideal quality gap is identified, if the cost ratio $y = 0.02$:

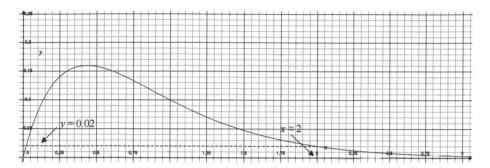

Fig. 2. The quality gap curve

We ignore the left-most optimal quality gap because it occurs at less than one digit difference in precision where no product versioning can be applied. The right-most optimal quality gap for the suggested cost ratio occurs at approximately $x = 2$, hence at two digits difference in precision between product version A and B.

Further inspections of the first derivative of the quality gap function y with respect to x reveals that the quality gap function is applicable for cost factor ratios in the interval $(0, 0.43]$. We also appreciate that the limit of the quality gap function y is 0, as x approaches infinity. In other words, as consumers' willingness to pay for precision (b) grows infinitely larger than the per data point cost of watermark reconstruction (a), the ideal quality gap approaches infinity. That said, the actual quality gap is practically limited by the number of digits per data point of the data stream.

5   Conclusion

There is little doubt that the use-cases for shared IIoT data streams are many and that great advancements in operational efficiency and productivity are likely to be in the public interest. However, we have argued that regulatory uncertainties as well as economic and technical characteristics of IIoT data streams raise the need for specialized protection mechanisms before privately held data will be shared at a significant scale.

Our economic analysis shows how a theoretical approach for implementing provenance through digital watermarking in data streams can create a basis for more commercially viable IIoT data marketplaces despite the presence of malicious agents. The key takeaway from this study is the relationship between perceived value of data streams and the efforts associated with enforcing property rights, and how this relationship can be utilized in profit maximizing pricing strategies. These results emphasize that there are more considerations to be made when assessing watermarking techniques for IIoT data streams than just the technological features alone.

Acknowledgements. The Institute of Engineering Research at Seoul National University provided research facilities for this work.

References

1. EU, Digital Transformation Monitor, Industrie 4.0, Germany, January 2017
2. Lu, Y.: Industry 4.0: a survey on technologies, applications and open research issues. J. Ind. Inf. Integr. **6**, 1–10 (2017)
3. Guth, J., Breitenbücher, U., Falkenthal, M., Leymann, F., Reinfurt, L.: Comparison of IoT platform architectures: a field study based on a reference architecture. In: Cloudification of the Internet of Things (CIoT), pp. 1–6 (2016)
4. Golchha, N.: Big data-the information revolution. Int. J. Adv. Res **1**(12), 791–794 (2015)
5. Liang, F., Yu, W., An, D., Yang, Q., Fu, X., Zhao, W.: A survey on big data market: pricing, trading and protection. IEEE Access **6**, 15132–15154 (2018)
6. Ringel, M., Zablit, H., Grassl, F., Manly, J., Möller, C.: The Most Innovative Companies 2018, The Boston Consulting Group, January 2018
7. Kim, Y., Chang, H.: The industrial security management model for SMBs in smart work. J. Intell. Manuf. **25**(2), 319–327 (2014)
8. Kerber, W., Schweitzer, H.: Interoperability in the digital economy. J. Intellect. Prop. Inf. Technol. Electron. Commer. Law **8**, 39 (2017)
9. Bröring, A., Schmid, S., Schindhelm, C.K., Khelil, A., Käbisch, S., Kramer, D., Teniente, E.: Enabling IoT ecosystems through platform interoperability. IEEE Softw. **34**(1), 54–61 (2017)
10. De Cristofaro, E., Ding, X., Tsudik, G.: Privacy-preserving querying in sensor networks. In: Proceedings of 18th International Conference on Computer Communications and Networks, pp. 1–6 (2009)
11. Zaslavsky, A., Perera, C., Georgakopoulos, D.: Sensing as a service and big data. arXiv preprint arXiv:1301.0159 (2013)
12. Khan, M., Wu, X., Xu, X., Dou, W.: Big data challenges and opportunities in the hype of industry 4.0. In: 2017 IEEE International Conference on Communications (ICC), pp. 1–6 (2017)
13. Mišura, K., Žagar, M.: Data marketplace for internet of things. In: 2016 International Conference on Smart Systems and Technologies (SST), pp. 255–260 (2016)
14. Perera, C.: Sensing as a service for internet of things: a roadmap (2017). Lulu.com
15. Perera, C.: Sensing as a service (S2aaS): buying and selling IoT data. arXiv preprint arXiv: 1702.02380 (2017)
16. Zech, H.: Building a European data economy. IIC – Int. Rev. Intellect. Prop. Compet. Law **48**(5), 501–503 (2017)
17. Kerber, W., Frank, J.: Data governance regimes in the digital economy: the example of connected cars (2017). SSRN 3064794
18. Marjani, M., Nasaruddin, F., Gani, A., Karim, A., Hashem, I.A.T., Siddiqa, A., Yaqoob, I.: Big IoT data analytics: architecture, opportunities, and open research challenges. IEEE Access **5**, 5247–5261 (2017)
19. Rafaeli, S., Raban, D.R.: Information sharing online: a research challenge (2005). SSRN 999993
20. Kerber, W.: Rights on data: the EU communication 'building a european data economy' from an economic perspective (2017)
21. Richter, H., Slowinski, P.R.: The data sharing economy: on the emergence of new intermediaries. IIC-Int. Rev. Intellect. Prop. Compet. Law **50**(1), 4–29 (2019)
22. Wiebe, A.: Protection of industrial data–a new property right for the digital economy? J. Intellect. Prop. Law Pract. **12**(1), 62–71 (2016)

23. Shapiro, C., Carl, S., Varian, H.R.: Information Rules: A Strategic Guide to the Network Economy. Harvard Business Press, Boston (1998)
24. Pantelis, K., Aija, L.: Understanding the value of (big) data. In: 2013 IEEE International Conference on Big Data, pp. 38–42 (2013)
25. Chen, B., Wornell, G.W.: Quantization index modulation: a class of provably good methods for digital watermarking and information embedding. IEEE Trans. Inf. Theory 47(4), 1423–1443 (2001)
26. Hsu, C.T., Wu, J.L.: Hidden digital watermarks in images. IEEE Trans. Image Process. 8(1), 58–68 (1999)
27. Panah, A.S., Van Schyndel, R., Sellis, T., Bertino, E.: On the properties of non-media digital watermarking: a review of state of the art techniques. IEEE Access 4, 2670–2704 (2016)
28. Voloshynovskiy, S., Pereira, S., Pun, T., Eggers, J.J., Su, J.K.: Attacks on digital watermarks: classification, estimation based attacks, and benchmarks. IEEE Commun. Mag. 39(8), 118–126 (2001)
29. Sion, R., Atallah, M., Prabhaka, S.: Rights protection for discrete numeric streams. IEEE Trans. Knowl. Data Eng. 18(5), 699–714 (2006)
30. Chong, S., Skalka, C., Vaughan, J.A.: Self-identifying sensor data. In: Proceedings of the 9th ACM/IEEE International Conference on Information Processing in Sensor Networks, pp. 82–93 (2010)
31. Xiao, X., Sun, X., Li, F., Wang, B., Xia, Z., Liang, W.: Watermarking-based intellectual property protection for sensor streaming data. Int. J. Comput. Appl. Technol. 39(4), 213–223 (2010)
32. Sultana, S., Shehab, M., Bertino, E.: Secure provenance transmission for streaming data. IEEE Trans. Knowl. Data Eng. 25(8), 1890–1903 (2012)
33. Rohitratana, J., Altmann, J.: Impact of pricing schemes on a market for software-as-a-service and perpetual software. Future Gener. Comput. Syst. 28(8), 1328–1339 (2012)
34. Altmann, J., Varaiya, P.: INDEX project: user support for buying QoS with regard to user's preferences. In: 6th International Workshop on Quality of Service (IWQoS 1998) (1998)
35. Caracas, A., Altmann, J.: A pricing information service for grid computing. In: MGC 2007, 5th International Workshop on Middleware for Grid Computing (2007)
36. Altmann, J., Rupp, B., Varaiya, P.: Effects of pricing on Internet user behavior. Netnomics 3(1), 67–84 (2000)
37. Stiller, B., Almeroth, K., Altmann, J., McKnight, L., Ott, M.: Content pricing in the internet. Comput. Commun. 27(6), 522–528 (2004)

Dominant Business Model Patterns of Regional IaaS Providers – An Exploratory Multiple-Case Study

Sebastian Floerecke[(✉)] and Franz Lehner

Chair of Information Systems (Information and IT Service Management),
University of Passau, Passau, Germany
{sebastian.floerecke, franz.lehner}@uni-passau.de

Abstract. The fast growing worldwide market for Infrastructure as a Service (IaaS) has long been increasingly dominated by the few globally acting hyperscalers. In turn, the market share and number of small and medium-sized regional IaaS providers have been declining over the past years. This battle for market shares has, however, been astonishingly widely neglected in research. The goal of this paper is therefore to identify and analyze the dominant business model patterns of regional IaaS providers in Germany and compare them regarding their long-term survival prospects. Based on an exploratory multiple-case study with 18 successful regional IaaS providers, two dominant business model patterns were identified: Whereas customizers consciously pursue a business model being considerably different from the hyperscalers by particularly addressing the discrepancy between the hyperscalers' standardized offerings and more individual customer requirements, superscalers exhibit several similarities with the hyperscalers and thus act in direct competition. Due to a missing unique selling proposition, except the guaranteed sole data storage in Germany, but at a higher price, superscalers might fall victim to the market consolidation significantly stronger. While scholars obtain a first classification schema of regional IaaS providers which opens up fruitful areas for future research, practitioners get inspirations for their business model innovation process.

Keywords: Cloud computing · Infrastructure as a Service (IaaS) · Regional IaaS providers · Business models · Business model patterns · Hyperscalers · Customizers · Superscalers · Exploratory multiple-case study

1 Introduction

Infrastructure as a Service (IaaS) is the fundamental layer of cloud computing delivering basic infrastructure services to customers via networks. IaaS services include hardware (e.g., computation, storage and network) and software (e.g., operating systems and virtualization technologies) components [1]. IaaS is currently the fastest growing cloud computing market segment globally [2], but at the same time the service model with the least research on from a business perspective [3]. The low level of research is astonishing as the IaaS market composition is unique: According to a recent study by Gartner [4], a leading American research and advisory company, the worldwide IaaS market is

© Springer Nature Switzerland AG 2019
K. Djemame et al. (Eds.): GECON 2019, LNCS 11819, pp. 140–153, 2019.
https://doi.org/10.1007/978-3-030-36027-6_12

dominated by the few globally acting hyperscalers, in particular Alibaba, Amazon Web Services (AWS), Google and Microsoft. Their IaaS offerings are primarily characterized by a high level of standardization and a comparably low price [5]. In 2017, the hyperscalers' global market share was about 75%, showing a clearly rising tendency [6]. The rest of the IaaS market is shared by several large international and national IT companies and a multitude of small and medium-sized providers [7]. The latter mostly restrict their IaaS services to one country, one region or even only one city [8]. But although the IaaS market has been growing enormously since its inception, the market share and number of the regional IaaS providers have been declining over the past years [6, 7]. A major reason for this development is that basic IaaS services – without extensions such as managed or platform services – have become a commodity [3, 8]. Commodities are products and services that are highly standardized and to a large extent equivalent with respect to functionality and quality, irrespective of the specific vendor [9]. The IaaS providers simply use similar hardware, operate at similar locations and offer similar basic IaaS services. Therefore, the price has turned into the central decision criterion for customers [3]. As the regional IaaS providers do, however, not possess the huge server farms, they are unable to achieve the necessary economies of scale in order to keep up in the price competition with the hyperscalers. As a way out, regional IaaS providers have to design and implement business models that differ from the hyperscalers to survive in the long term [8].

Whereas the cloud computing-specific literature on success-driving business model characteristics has generally grown over the recent years, e.g., [3, 10, 11], the specific competition between regional IaaS providers and the hyperscalers has been widely neglected. Only Floerecke and Lehner [8] proposed eight initial hypotheses on business model characteristics for regional IaaS providers for counteracting the increasing market consolidation. However, the study covered only parts of the business model and remained on a high level of abstraction, i.e., it did not take into account that there are fundamentally different types of regional IaaS providers pursuing various business models and that their individual prospects of success hence may vary.

Beyond this background, this paper addresses the following research question: **What dominant business model patterns of small and medium-sized regional IaaS providers exist and how are their long-term survival prospects in view of the growing dominance of the hyperscalers?** To this end, an exploratory multiple-case study [12] with 18 regional IaaS providers in Germany is conducted, which recorded profitable revenue growth over the past years, notwithstanding the precarious market situation. In expert interviews with high-level company representatives their business models are analyzed in-depth using the Business Model Canvas (BMC) [13]. The business model patterns of regional IaaS providers are derived by examining the individual business models for matches. Their respective survival prospects are evaluated based on the hyperscalers' business models, the customer demand and already foreseeable future market and technological developments.

The rest of this paper is organized as follows: Section 2 contains the background on cloud computing, business models and business model patterns. In addition, the development of the global as well as the German IaaS market is described. Third, the research design is explained in detail. Fourth, the derived dominant business model patterns of regional IaaS providers are depicted based on the BMC's components. Fifth, their central differences and their long-term survival prospects are discussed critically. Moreover, arguments for and against the survival of regional IaaS providers in general are given and weighed against each other. The paper concludes with a brief summary, limitations, contributions and an outlook on future research.

2   Background

2.1   Cloud Computing

Literature has come up with numerous definitions of cloud computing over the years, either with a stronger business or technical focus [14]. The technical orientated definition of the National Institute of Standards and Technology (NIST) has become the standard both in science and practice in the meantime. According to NIST, "*[c]loud computing is a model for enabling ubiquitous, convenient, on-demand network access to a shared pool of configurable computing resources (e.g., networks, servers, storage, applications, and services) that can be rapidly provisioned and released with minimal management effort or service provider interaction*" [1]. Cloud services are classified into three service models: Infrastructure as a Service (IaaS), Platform as a Service (PaaS) and Software as a Service (SaaS). IaaS supplies infrastructural resources (compute, storage and network). PaaS allows developing and deploying applications based on a software development environment with programming languages, libraries and tools. SaaS refers to directly usable applications. These service models form layers that are interrelated and build upon each other [15]. Cloud services on each service layer can be delivered via four main deployment models, namely as public, private, hybrid and community cloud [16]. The general key characteristics of cloud services are on-demand self-service, broad network access, resource pooling, rapid elasticity and service measurement. These characteristics distinguish cloud services from traditional on-premise IT solutions [1].

Research on cloud computing has rather focused on the technical aspects so far. Significantly less consideration has been given to the major changes within the business perspective of IT provisioning [5, 17]. The most frequently addressed business issues are adoption, cost, trust and privacy, legislation and ethics [18]. This technical focus is astonishing, because cloud computing has fundamentally changed the way IT resources are implemented, provided and used [15, 16]. Several scholars hence regard cloud computing as a co-evolution of computing technology and business models [3].

2.2   Business Models and Business Model Patterns

No commonly accepted definition of the term "business model" has been established to date [19]. Besides textual definitions there exists a component-based view, which dominates the discussion on business models. According to that, a business model is a system comprising a set of interrelated components or partial models for depicting, implementing and evaluating the business logic of a company [20]. The business model concept builds upon central theories, in particular, the transaction cost theory, the resource-based view, the cooperation theory and the strategic network theory [21]. According to Amit and Zott [22], this cross-theoretical perspective is necessary as no existing theory can fully explain value creation alone. Business models have long taken a central role in explaining the differences in company performance [20, 23]. It has been shown that the same technology can result in significantly different economic output, depending on the way it is marketed by a business model [24]. Companies therefore differentiate and compete rather through business models and less through products or processes [25].

The scientific literature provides a variety of cross-industry and industry-specific business model frameworks, which include design options for various subsets of components [23]. A comprehensive and widespread cross-industry framework among both researchers and practitioners is the Business Model Canvas (BMC) [13]. The BMC comprises nine components: value propositions, key resources, key activities, partner network, customer segments, channels, customer relationships, revenue streams and cost structure. The BMC as a whole offers a common instrument to describe, visualize, evaluate and adapt business models [13].

Business model patterns are "[...] business models with similar characteristics, similar arrangements of business model Building Blocks, or similar behaviors" [13]. The use of business model patterns provides an efficient way to undertake business model innovation by drawing upon aspects that have already been proven to be successful for other firms and industries [26]. The importance of this concept is underlined by the finding that around 90% of all business models are a recombination of existing business model patterns [25]. However, business model patterns must not be misunderstood. They do not focus on imitating, but rather support creativity and efficiency within the business model innovation process [27]. Beyond this background, several scholars (e.g., [25, 28]) have proposed various, partly overlapping collections of cross-industry and industry-specific business model patterns. Research on business model patterns in the cloud domain is nascent. Only Labes, Erek and Zarnekow [29] identified four patterns, which, however, are mainly based on leading international providers and do not distinguish between the cloud service models.

In general, research on cloud business models has widely neglected so far that the cloud ecosystem entails a multitude of companies, which offer a variety of products and services such as IaaS, PaaS and SaaS and additionally act, e.g., as integrator, aggregator or consultant and thus are characterized by a high degree of heterogeneity [30]. An undifferentiated, ecosystem role-independent analysis of cloud business models therefore has only a low level of explanatory significance [3]. The majority of ecosystem role-specific studies has focused on SaaS providers [11]. The battle for market shares between regional IaaS providers and the hyperscalers has been largely ignored. Only Floerecke and Lehner [8] proposed eight initial hypotheses on business model characteristics for regional IaaS providers. However, the authors mainly only addressed the value propositions component and remained on a high level of abstraction, i.e., they did not take into account that there are fundamentally different types of regional IaaS providers pursuing various business models and that their individual prospects of success hence may vary. A more fine-granular categorization schema of regional IaaS providers is missing and therefore derived in this study.

2.3   IaaS Market Development

According to a current study by Gartner [2], the worldwide cloud market is projected to grow 17.5% in 2019 to total 214.3 billion USD, up from 182.4 billion USD in 2018. With regard to the three cloud service models, SaaS will remain the largest segment with 94.8 billion USD, followed by IaaS with 38.9 billion USD and PaaS with 19.0 billion USD. For all three segments, substantial growth rates are predicted over the next years. IaaS is the fastest-growing segment, with an estimated growth rate of 27.5% in 2019. In particular the hyperscalers – Alibaba, Amazon Web Services (AWS), Google and Microsoft – benefit from this massive growth [2]. In 2017, their global market share was 75%, with the trend clearly rising [6]. Figure 1 shows the development of global market shares of the hyperscalers in comparison with the rest of the providers in the IaaS segment between 2015 and 2017.

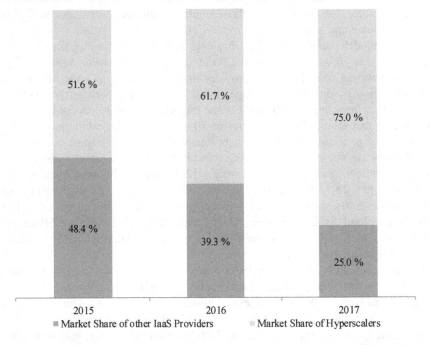

Fig. 1. Development of global market shares in the IaaS segment between 2015 and 2017 [6].

Figure 2 illustrates the development of the global IaaS market volume between 2015 and 2017 – once with and once without the hyperscalers. Whereas the market volume of the rest of IaaS providers increased slightly from 2015 to 2016, a significant reduction can be noted in 2017 – despite the enormous growth of the overall IaaS market. As can be seen, both provider categories follow an opposite trend, whereby the difference between them is growing.

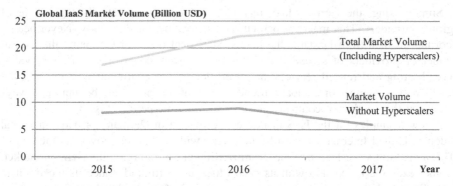

Fig. 2. Development of the global IaaS market volume (in Billion USD) with and without the hyperscalers between 2015 and 2017 [31].

Limited to Germany, the following picture emerges: According to a recent study by Information Services Group [7], a leading American technology research and advisory firm, German companies are going to invest around 1.4 billion Euro in IaaS in 2019. This represents a 30% increase compared to the previous year. The IaaS segment in Germany thus grows even faster than globally. Also here the hyperscalers are extending their market dominance: The German IaaS revenue of AWS is estimated to grow by 40% in 2019, Microsoft by 60% – i.e., significantly faster than the total market segment. Together with Google, the third largest IaaS provider, almost two thirds of the German IaaS market is dominated by these three American companies. Alibaba is, at least at present, playing only a minor role. The remaining third is shared among particularly IBM, Deutsche Telekom and Oracle, and the multitude of small and medium-sized regionally operating IaaS providers [7].

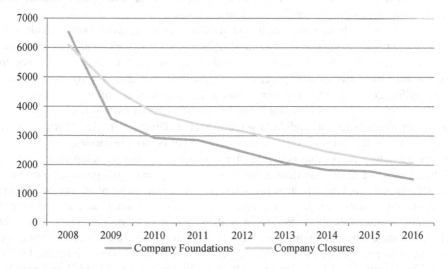

Fig. 3. Number of company foundations and closures in the information services segment in Germany between 2008 and 2016 according to destatis.

Summarizing, the German IaaS market still has a comparatively high share of regional providers. This makes it particularly interesting for this study. Nevertheless, according to data from Destatis, the federal statistical office of Germany, the overall number of providers of so-called information services, consisting of IaaS services, server hosting and related services, has been decreasing continuously between 2008 and 2016. The number of company foundations was, except at the beginning, always lower than the number of company closures in this time period (Fig. 3).

A few examples for the IaaS market consolidation in Germany provide anecdotal evidence: United Internet acquired Profit Bricks with its 120 employees at the end of 2017, a medium-sized IaaS provider from Berlin concentrating on the German market. Another example is Dogado with its head office in Dortmund. Since its inception in 2001, Dogado has taken over eleven providers of IaaS and related services, such as WebControl and Hostingparadise, and now has around 100 employees.

3 Research Design

In order to identify and analyze the dominant business model patterns of regional IaaS providers in Germany and to compare them regarding their individual survival prospects in the precarious market situation, an exploratory multiple-case study according to Yin [12] was conducted. Case studies are particularly suitable to investigate widely unexplored areas, to answer "why", "what" and "how" questions and to learn about the state of the art and generate theories from practice [32]. All these three conditions apply to this study. In expert interviews with high-level company representatives, their business models were analyzed in-depth using the BMC. The business model patterns were derived by examining the individual business models for matches. Their respective survival prospects were evaluated by comparing them with hyperscalers' business models, the customer demand and already foreseeable future market and technological developments stated by the interviewees.

The units of analysis were small and medium-sized regional IaaS providers in Germany. Potential companies had to have at least one IaaS service in their portfolio and have recorded profitable revenue growth over the past years. In order not to unnecessarily limit the sample space, the size constraint of 250 employees (EU Recommendation 2003/361/EC) has been weakened and companies up to 400 employees have been approved. As no comprehensive list of German IaaS providers exists, a Google search for potential candidates was conducted. The 64 identified providers were contacted by contact form on their website, via e-mail or private message on the Xing networking platform. On that occasion, the IaaS-specific sales development over the last five years was asked. As there is no ranking of regional IaaS providers and only few of them report business figures, the sales growth served as proof of success. This is the most commonly used proxy for company success for small and medium-sized companies in literature [33]. Providers with stagnant or shrinking sales were not included as the central intention of business model patterns research is to identify those that have been proven to be successful [25, 26]. The selection procedure resulted in 18 cases. The companies employ between 10 and 400 persons (mean: 112) and are distributed over nine of the 16 federal states in Germany. Three companies have more than

250 employees. This is, however, not regarded as conflicting with the research question as each of them is a division of a corporation that accounts for only a small proportion of the company's total workforce and focus exclusively on IaaS. With regard to the cloud service models, seven companies offer solely IaaS, eight IaaS and SaaS and three IaaS, PaaS and SaaS. The representative of each company was required to be responsible or at least co-responsible for the initial development and/or the continuous innovation of the business models and to have knowledge specific to the company's IaaS business segment. The final interview partners were eight managing directors and/or founders, three department managers, three product managers, three sales representatives and one business developer. They have been with the company for about ten years on average.

Due to the application of the BMC, the interview guide was largely predetermined. In the first part, general information about the person and the company was collected. Moreover, the current and expected future competitive situation between regional IaaS providers and the hyperscalers in Germany was analyzed. In the second part, the characteristics of the single BMC's components of the respective company and the reasons for this specific choice were asked. The third part addressed recently undertaken as well as planned business model adaptations and the intentions behind them.

The 18 interviews took place between October and December 2018. The interview language was German. All interviews were conducted by phone. The interview duration ranged from 29 to 62 min (mean: 45 min). When conducting the interviews, the laddering technique [34] was applied whenever appropriate, so that the interviews were rather guided conversations. All interviews were recorded, transcribed and anonymized. The data analysis was performed using qualitative content analysis by Mayring [35] with the tool MAXQDA. In this process, for all companies the specific BMC was created and subsequently examined for overarching patterns.

4 Two Dominant Business Model Patterns of Regional IaaS Providers in Germany

Two dominant business model patterns of regional IaaS providers in Germany were identified during the analysis. The first and significantly larger group in the sample will be referred to as customizers. These firms are characterized above all by a high degree of customization and a highly personal customer service. The second group offers particularly highly standardized basic IaaS services through automated business processes. Due to the similarity of their business model to hyperscalers but smaller company size, this group is named superscaler. Hereafter, the two business model patterns are first described textually and then summarized and compared graphically.

4.1 Customizers

The key element of customizers' value propositions are customer-specific cloud solutions. Based on the specific requirements, the company structure and the IT landscape of the customer a custom-tailored solution concept is developed and implemented. To this end, customizers additionally have integration, transition and multi-cloud services in their portfolio. Beyond that, customizers generate a significant percentage of their sales with managed services. Managed services are basic IaaS services extended by additional components, such as monitoring, update, security or backup services, based on clearly defined service level agreements. The scope can range from individual items to a complete IT outsourcing. Overall, customizers' offerings are almost entirely based on private clouds. Their customers are mainly medium-sized but also small firms, starting from around 100 employees, with limited technical IT expertise and therefore with a high dependence on provider support. Even smaller companies and private customers do not fall within their scope as their individual approach is commonly too expensive for these groups. The clients are from all industries and predominantly located in the region with a maximum distance of about 200 km. With regard to pricing models, customizers usually offer fixed prices, whereby the total price is frequently broken down to the employee level (pay-per-user). In the contract negotiations and the design of the pricing model, they take customers' wishes, general conditions and business models into account. As customizers mainly offer customized cloud solutions and managed services, they sell their services personally, not via self-service. Customizers build and maintain long-term and personal customer relations, where they continuously further develop and improve the individual cloud solutions in use. Each customer commonly has a firmly assigned contact person. Two thirds of the analyzed customizers operate an own data center, the rest rents server space at a specialized third-party provider. Due to their comparatively low level of automation and scalability, the employees are the most important and at the same time the most expensive resource. The personnel thus are the business model's bottleneck resource.

4.2 Superscalers

In the center of superscalers' value propositions are highly standardized basic IaaS services without the possibility of customer-specific adaptations. Customers can only choose out of a predefined set of variants. Superscalers offer both public and private clouds, but private clouds are significantly more demanded. They commonly do not offer any integration, transition or multi-cloud services. Instead of focusing on medium-sized companies and setting a lower bound of customer size, superscalers target a larger segment of small and medium-sized enterprises from all industries as well as private customers throughout Germany. In contrast to the customizers' clients, their customers usually possess IT skills and hence can find, book and deploy the IaaS services on the provider's website. The customer relationships are aimed towards online business without personal contact. Consequently, superscalers can serve significantly more customers compared to customizers. Nevertheless, superscalers offer service and help desks for answering questions that arise while ordering and using the IaaS service. As the IaaS services are provisioned automatically, process automation is particularly important. Superscalers commonly offer multiple pricing models: Flexible, monthly usage-based offers and fixed monthly prices and flat rates, similar to customizers. Superscalers operate own data centers and although they describe personnel as an important resource, automated business processes are decisive. The major cost drivers are hardware and electricity – staff costs are of minor significance.

Figure 4 summarizes and compares the two business model patterns based on the BMC's components. Not all of the nine components are listed: In case of key activities, it is attributable to a certain redundancy with respect to other components. Regarding the partner network, the business model patterns do not fundamentally differ from each other. Both have similar suppliers for software (e.g., operating systems and virtualization software) and hardware (e.g., servers). Further types of partnerships, e.g., with consulting firms or other IaaS providers, exist only in exceptional cases.

BMC's Component	Customizer	Superscaler
Value Propositions	• Customer-specific cloud solutions • Integration, transition and multi-cloud services • Managed services • Private clouds	• Standardized basic IaaS services without the possibility of customer-specific adaptations • Private and public clouds
Customer Segments	• Medium-sized, but also small companies (>100 employees) with limited technical IT expertise • Located in the region (maximum distance: 200 km) • All industries	• Small and medium-sized companies as well as private customers (with technical IT expertise) • Located throughout Germany • All industries
Customer Relationships	• Long-term, personal customer relationships • Firmly assigned contact person	• Both short and long-term, impersonal customer relationships • Changing contact persons (help-desk)
Channels	• Personal sale process	• Self-service sale process via website
Revenue Streams	• Fixed prices • Customer-specific pricing models	• Both usage-based and fixed prices
Cost Structure	• Personnel as major cost driver	• Hardware and electricity as major cost drivers
Key Resources	• Personnel as key resource • Own or rented data centers	• Process automation as key resource • Own data centers

Fig. 4. Comparison of dominant business model patterns of regional IaaS providers.

5 Discussion

The two dominant business model patterns of regional IaaS providers in Germany differ widely from each other. Customizers consciously pursue a business model that is considerably different from the hyperscalers. They occupy a niche in the IaaS market by particularly addressing the existing discrepancy between the hyperscalers' standardized offerings and more individual customer requirements. This approach could ensure their survival. Closer inspection, however, shows that the customizers' offerings do not correspond with the key characteristics of cloud computing, such as self-service, rapid elasticity and service measurement. It is rather a traditional server hosting model that is labeled as cloud service for marketing reasons (cloud washing).

By contrast, the superscalers' business models exhibit many similarities with the hyperscalers and thus they act in direct competition with them. Superscalers do not offer customer-specific adaptations within any BMC's component. Customers can only select one option out of predefined alternatives. In view of the fact that basic IaaS services have become a commodity, the future of superscalers can be viewed particularly critically. With the exception of the guaranteed exclusive data storage in Germany, they do not have a unique selling proposition, but demand a significant higher price. It probably is just a matter of time until the hyperscalers find ways, e.g., by defining specific cooperation forms, to bypass the Cloud Act, which obliges them to provide requested data stored on servers regardless of whether it is stored in the USA or abroad. Compared to customizers, superscalers can thus be expected to fall victim to the market consolidation to a significant larger extent. One representative of a customizer summed up the superscalers' situation this way: *"[...] to believe that we could build a data center and offer IaaS in competition with AWS is ridiculous."*

Overall, the study participants were convinced that the general willingness of customers to buy IaaS services locally will further decrease. This expectation is particularly based on four already foreseeable future developments, stated by the interviewees: First, the hyperscalers will presumably further reduce prices by exploiting their growing economies of scale which will lead to a growing price difference. Second, the hyperscalers are expected to increasingly address medium-sized companies and facilitate the ordering, configuration und usage process also for persons with low IT expertise. This will be given priority at latest once a certain saturation level of the global IaaS market has been reached. Third, the hyperscalers will likely continue to expand their modular cloud portfolio at a fast pace and thus cover more and more special cases. Superscalers will not be able to keep up with this breadth of the portfolio and customizers will be confronted with a reduction of their niche. Fourth, a far greater number of digital natives with a higher level of IT know-how will work in customer firms, who will not depend so much on the personal and individual support of particularly the customizers.

Putting all these aspects together let appear a further IaaS market consolidation and an increasing domination of the hyperscalers almost unavoidable. If the hyperscalers indeed dominate nearly the entire IaaS segment in future, it can be assumed that they will raise their prices and reduce investments in research and development, in order to achieve higher profits. It is therefore of utmost importance from a total customer perspective that the regional IaaS providers can maintain their place in the cloud ecosystem. Otherwise, it is according to Floerecke and Lehner [8] likely that the IaaS market will become subject of governmental regulations, similar to other utility markets, such as the gas and electricity market, as a consequence of the lack of competition.

In spite of this negative outlook, there are also positive developments from the viewpoint of regional IaaS providers: Particularly customizers might profit from the rising shortage of skilled IT professionals in Germany, which has recently reached a new all-time high of 82.000 job vacancies [36]. It can be expected that several small and medium-sized companies will therefore have to downsize their IT departments and to increasingly use cloud services. In this situation, the support of customizers will presumably be further needed in future. Two aspects speak in favor of both types of regional IaaS providers: First, especially in Germany, where many companies are still skeptical towards cloud computing because of privacy and security issues [37], a data center in the region guaranteeing that the data is exclusively stored in Germany, without a non-European mother company, will find its supporters. Second, regional data centers might gain importance due to the increasing usage of edge computing as key technology for industry 4.0, where a high bandwidth and a low latency are indispensable. In summary, the ultimate outcome of this competition for market shares is still open. Although the hyperscalers are clearly in the leading position, the regional IaaS providers can actively influence the outcome by their business model design.

6 Conclusion

Based on an exploratory multiple-case study with 18 successful regional IaaS providers in Germany, two dominant business model patterns were identified, analyzed and compared regarding their survival prospects in the difficult market conditions. Whereas customizers consciously pursue a business model being considerably different from the hyperscalers by particularly addressing the discrepancy between the hyperscalers' standardized offerings and more individual customer requirements, superscalers show several similarities with the hyperscalers and thus act in direct competition. Due to a missing unique selling proposition, except the guaranteed exclusive data storage in Germany, but at a higher price, superscalers might fall victim to the market consolidation to a significant larger extent. Overall, there are many indications that the general willingness of customers to buy IaaS services locally will further decrease.

This study is the first that explored business model patterns of regional IaaS providers. Scholars thus obtain a classification schema which opens up areas for future research. This is also the first study that investigated arguments for and against the survival of regional IaaS providers. As a practical contribution, superscalers are sensitized regarding the urgent necessity to reconsider and adapt their current business models. As a whole, the use of the two business model patterns provide practitioners an efficient way to undertake business model innovation by drawing upon business models or single characteristics that have already been proven to be successful.

However, this study is not free of limitations: First, whereas the majority of cases could be identified as customizers, the number of superscalers was small. Superscalers should hence increasingly be addressed in future. A second limitation is the small sample size, whereby this exploratory study cannot claim to have identified all existing dominant business model patterns. In the case selection process, providers were identified that solely offer managed services based on hyperscalers' IaaS services or act as their direct resellers. Although such aggregators were not included as none of them has reported revenue growth in the recent years, they are surely a worthwhile topic for future research. Third, the geographic scope of case sites and interviewees was restricted to Germany. It is necessary to investigate the regional IaaS market in other countries in order to address country-specific particularities. Fourth, it was neglected that several providers do not solely offer IaaS, but also PaaS and SaaS. This can also be a source for differentiation and should hence be included in future studies.

Scholars should specifically investigate how superscalers could modify their business models in order to achieve stronger differentiation from the hyperscalers. In general, it might be interesting to examine the fight for market shares from the hyperscalers' perspective. Moreover, it should not be forgotten that the IaaS market also contains large international and national IT companies, neither hyperscalers nor regional providers, whose business models should be analyzed in detail as well.

To conclude, despite the undoubtedly difficult and in future probably even more critical situation for regional IaaS providers, it is very likely that there will always be a place for them in the cloud ecosystem. This applies primarily to customizers, but also to superscalers, provided they begin to adapt their business models. Decisive for the survival of regional IaaS providers in general will be that they quickly respond to changing business models of the hyperscalers and customer demand and thus, are constantly seeking for new market niches. Acting in direct competition with the hyperscalers certainly will be a hopeless endeavor in the long-run.

References

1. Mell, P., Grance, T.: The NIST Definition of Cloud Computing. NIST (2011)
2. Costello, K.: Gartner Forecasts Worldwide Public Cloud Revenue to Grow 17.5 Percent in 2019. Gartner (2019)
3. Floerecke, S., Lehner, F.: Success-driving business model characteristics of IaaS and PaaS providers. Int. J. Cloud Comput.: Serv. Arch. (IJCCSA) **8**(6), 1–22 (2018)
4. Costello, K., Hippold, S.: Gartner Forecasts Worldwide Public Cloud Revenue to Grow 17.3 Percent in 2019. Gartner (2018)
5. Herzfeldt, A., Floerecke, S., Ertl, C., Krcmar, H.: Examining the antecedents of cloud service profitability. Int. J. Cloud Appl. Comput. (IJCAC) **9**(4), 37–65 (2019)
6. Statista: Vendor Share of the Public Cloud Infrastructure as a Service (IaaS) Market Worldwide from 2015 to 2017. Statista (2018)
7. ISG: ISG Provider Lens Germany 2019 – Cloud Transformation/Operation Services & XaaS. ISG (2018)
8. Floerecke, S., Lehner, F.: Business model characteristics for local IaaS providers for counteracting the dominance of the hyperscalers. In: 15th International Conference on Economics of Grids, Clouds, Systems, and Services, Pisa, Italy (2018)
9. Bruhn, M.: Commodities im Dienstleistungsbereich: Besonderheiten und Implikationen für das Marketing. In: Enke, M., Geigenmüller, A. (eds.) Commodity Marketing: Grundlagen – Besonderheiten – Erfahrungen, pp. 58–77. Gabler, Wiesbaden (2011). https://doi.org/10.1007/978-3-8349-6388-8_3
10. Labes, S., Hanner, N., Zarnekow, R.: Successfull business model types of cloud providers. Bus. Inf. Syst. Eng. **59**(4), 223–233 (2017)
11. Floerecke, S.: Success factors of SaaS providers' business models – an exploratory multiple-case study. In: 9th International Conference on Exploring Service Science, Karlsruhe, Germany (2018)
12. Yin, R.K.: Case Study Research: Design and Methods. Sage Publications, Thousand Oaks (2018)
13. Osterwalder, A., Pigneur, Y.: Business Model Generation: A Handbook for Visionaries, Game Changers, and Challengers. Wiley, New Jersey (2010)
14. Madhavaiah, C., Bashir, I., Shafi, S.I.: Defining cloud computing in business perspective: a review of research. Vis.: J. Bus. Perspect. **16**(3), 163–173 (2012)
15. Marston, S., Li, Z., Bandyopadhyay, S., Zhang, J., Ghalsasi, A.: Cloud computing – the business perspective. Decis. Support Syst. **51**(1), 176–189 (2011)

16. Armbrust, M., Fox, A., Griffith, R., Joseph, A.D., Katz, R., Konwinski, A., Zaharia, M.: A view of cloud computing. Commun. ACM **53**(4), 50–58 (2010)
17. Herzfeldt, A., Floerecke, S., Ertl, C., Krcmar, H.: The role of value facilitation regarding cloud service provider profitability in the cloud ecosystem. In: Khosrow-Pour, M. (ed.) Multidisciplinary Approaches to Service-Oriented Engineering, pp. 121–142. IGI Global, Hershey (2018)
18. Senyo, P.K., Addae, E., Boateng, R.: Cloud computing research: a review of research themes, frameworks, methods and future research directions. Int. J. Inf. Manag. **38**(1), 128–139 (2018)
19. Goyal, S., Kapoor, A., Esposito, M., Sergi, B.S.: Understanding business model – literature review of concept and trends. Int. J. Compet. **1**(2), 99–118 (2017)
20. Veit, D., Clemens, E., Benlian, A., Buxmann, P., Hess, T., Spann, M., Kundisch, D., Leimeister, J.M.: Business models – an information systems research agenda. Bus. Inf. Syst. Eng. **56**(1), 55–64 (2014)
21. Morris, M., Schindehutte, M., Allen, J.: The entrepreneur's business model: toward a unified perspective. J. Bus. Res. **58**(6), 726–735 (2005)
22. Amit, R., Zott, C.: Value creation in e-business. Strat. Manag. J. **22**(6–7), 493–520 (2001)
23. Wirtz, B., Pistoia, A., Ullrich, S., Göttel, V.: Business models: origin, development and future research perspectives. Long Range Plan. **49**(1), 36–54 (2016)
24. Zott, C., Amit, R.: Business model design: an activity system perspective. Long Range Plan. **43**(2–3), 216–226 (2010)
25. Gassmann, O., Frankenberger, K., Csik, M.: Geschäftsmodelle entwickeln: 55 innovative Konzepte mit dem St. Galler Business Model Navigator. Carl Hanser, Munich (2017)
26. Abdelkafi, N., Makhotin, S., Posselt, T.: Business model innovations for electric mobility – what can be learned from existing business model patterns? Int. J. Innov. Manag. **17**(1), 1–41 (2013)
27. Chesbrough, H.: Business model innovation: opportunities and barriers. Long Range Plan. **43**(2–3), 354–363 (2010)
28. Taran, Y., Nielsen, C., Montemari, M., Thomsen, P., Paolone, F.: Business model configurations: a five-V framework to map out potential innovation routes. Eur. J. Innov. Manag. **19**(4), 492–527 (2016)
29. Labes, S., Erek, K., Zarnekow, R.: Common patterns of cloud business models. In: 19th Americas Conference on Information Systems, Chicago, Illionis, USA (2013)
30. Floerecke, S., Lehner, F.: Cloud computing ecosystem model: refinement and evaluation. In: 26th European Conference on Information Systems, Istanbul, Turkey (2016)
31. Statista: Revenues from Public Cloud Infrastructure as a Service (IaaS) Market Worldwide from 2015 to 2017, by Vendor (in Million U.S. Dollars). Statista (2019)
32. Benbasat, I., Goldstein, D.K., Mead, M.: The case research strategy in studies of information systems. Manag. Inf. Syst. Q. **11**(3), 369–386 (1987)
33. Mendelson, H.: Organizational architecture and success in the information technology industry. Manag. Sci. **46**(4), 513–529 (2000)
34. Corbridge, C., Rugg, G., Major, N.P., Shadbolt, N.R., Burton, A.M.: Laddering: technique and tool use in knowledge acquisition. Knowl. Acquis. **6**(3), 315–341 (1994)
35. Mayring, P.: Qualitative Inhaltsanalyse: Grundlagen und Techniken. Beltz, Weinheim (2010)
36. Bitkom: 82.000 freie Jobs: IT-Fachkräftemangel spitzt sich zu. Bitkom (2018)
37. Karunagaran, S., Mathew, S., Lehner, F.: Differential adoption of cloud technology: a multiple case study of large firms and SMEs. In: 37th International Conference on Information Systems, Dublin, Ireland (2016)

SEConomy: A Framework
for the Economic Assessment
of Cybersecurity

Bruno Rodrigues[(✉)], Muriel Franco, Geetha Parangi, and Burkhard Stiller

Communication Systems Group CSG, Department of Informatics IfI,
University of Zurich UZH, Binzmühlestrasse 14, 8050 Zürich, Switzerland
{rodrigues,franco,parangi,stiller}@ifi.uzh.ch

Abstract. Cybersecurity concerns are one of the significant side effects of an increasingly interconnected world, which inevitably put economic factors into perspective, either directly or indirectly. In this context, it is imperative to understand the significant dependencies between complex and distributed systems (*e.g.*, supply-chain), as well as security and safety risks associated with each actor. This paper proposes SEConomy, a strictly step-based framework to measure economic impact of cybersecurity activities in a distributed ecosystem with several actors. Through the mapping of actors, responsibilities, inter-dependencies, and risks, it is possible to develop specific economic models, which can provide in a combined manner an accurate picture of cybersecurity economic impacts.

Keywords: Cybersecurity · Threats · Economics · Assessment

1 Introduction

The technological evolution and the rapid growth of the Internet have built a digital networked society, which today is an indispensable tool for communication and interaction on a planetary scale. As the number of devices (stationary or portable) increases, the complexity of systems that provide content or communication infrastructure also increases, especially to support the growing volume of traffic. As a result, these complex distributed systems are subject not only to several types of failures, but also to different types of cyber threats that can compromise CIA (Confidentiality, Integrity and Availability) aspects impairing, for example, entire societies whose Critical National Infrastructures (CNI) are connected to the Internet [8,14].

It is imperative to understand the economics behind cybersecurity activities. For example, the United States of America (U.S.A.) released in 2018 an estimate of costs related to malicious cyber activities of around 57 and 109 billion USD for incidents appearing only in 2016 [27]. These numbers involve not only losses at the initial target and economically linked firms derived from attacks, but also incurs in costs involving the maintenance and improvement of systems security.

© Springer Nature Switzerland AG 2019
K. Djemame et al. (Eds.): GECON 2019, LNCS 11819, pp. 154–166, 2019.
https://doi.org/10.1007/978-3-030-36027-6_13

Further, Gartner [16] corroborates with the U.S.A. estimate, predicting in 2018 a cost of 114 and 124 billion USD in 2019, representing an increase of 8% for one country only. While cost numbers are not precise on a global scale, there exist estimates, such as [18], that predict costs related to cybersecurity activities to exceed 1 trillion USD cumulatively for the five years from 2017–2021, taking into account the growing number of Internet of Things (IoT) devices.

Systems often fail because organizations do not take into account the full costs of failure, which includes two critical categories: security (prevention of malicious activities) and safety (prevention of accidents or faults) [17]. Further, system failures often leads to business being offline (*i.e.*, security is when a conscious attack is part of the game while safety is when something fails by itself). Security investments are typically complex, because malicious activities typically expose externalities as a result of underinvestment in cybersecurity, *i.e.*, they usually exploit vulnerabilities unforeseen in the design space. Safety, however, originates from requirements, which take systems failures due to unexpected events (*i.e.*, natural disaster and/or human failures) into account to prevent the loss of lives.

In a scenario where major actors desire to minimize costs while maximizing security and safety aspects [17,21], it is essential to understand all key cybersecurity risks, impacts, and mitigation measures (or the lack thereof) within an individually determined ecosystem economy [2]. Further, it is necessary to gain insight, into the uncertainty behind security investments. This paper contributes to the field of cybersecurity modeling with a framework allowing for an approximation of estimates and enabling the economic analysis of a given ecosystem's dimension concerning responsibilities and roles, while mapping systems and processes and their correlations as well as related costs. Thus, it is expected an understanding in detail how the economy is affected by cyber (in)security.

This paper is organized as follows. Section 2 provides the background, and related work providing an overview of how cybersecurity risks and threats are mapped into economics. Section 3 presents the Cybersecurity Economy Assessment framework and its stages, followed by a discussion and future work in Sect. 4.

2   Background and Related Work

Although reasons behind cyber attacks can be widely diverse, ranging from identity phishing and information security breaches to the exploiting of vulnerabilities on Critical National Infrastructures (CNI), it is notorious that these attacks have become increasingly driven by financial motives. Thus, related work focus on models analyzing economic aspects behind cyber attacks. For this reason, the U.S. Department of Defense (DoD) declares the cyberspace as the fifth dimension of defense areas, complementing the traditional land, water, sea, air warfare dimensions [15].

2.1 Cybersecurity Economics

A purely economic analysis was released in 2018 by the U.S. White House [27] revealing estimates of economic impacts in the year of 2016 (*cf.* Sect. 1), the year in which one of the largest Distributed Denial-of-Service (DDoS) attack was launched on the content provider Dyn-DNS, which interrupted the delivery of content for significant Internet services (such as Twitter, PayPal, and Spotify) for a few hours. These numbers corroborate with the influence of cyber attacks in the economy (whether it is a nation or large private organizations).

[10] presented one of the fundamental models aiming to determine an optimal cost/benefit relation to cybersecurity investments. The Gordon Loeb (GL) model is intended for investments related to various information security goals (in terms of Confidentiality, Integrity, and Availability - CIA). However, although the GL model is considered a baseline for cost optimization in the cybersecurity, it is not able to handle dynamic ecosystems, *i.e.,* mapping decisions and outcomes in a single period, and not considering the time factor.

[4] builds upon [10] providing a systematic analysis on how to compare existing security investment models and metrics. While [10] defined a general security probabilistic function, the high abstraction level of its model neglects the different security levels discussed by Böhme. In this sense, [4] offers a guideline toward building an economics assessment through its systematic approach decomposing costs of security into security levels and further associating with its benefits.

[24] describes one of the approaches cited by [4], the Return Over Security Investments (ROSI). This work offers a benchmark method to evaluate the cost/benefit relation of security investments, as well as how to obtain/measure security values used in their method. However, the authors state that it is very difficult to obtain data about the true cost of a security incident once companies often do not disclose data about security breaches or vulnerabilities. Nonetheless, similarly to [10], the work does not deepen in detail the complexities of calculating security investments/expenses.

Concerning the large degree of uncertainty in security investments, the fuzzy logic becomes the appropriate method to support the decision-making process [4]. Thus, the [25] fuzzy method translates non-linear local state spaces into linear models, *i.e.,* helping to define security cost classes in which threats can be classified and translated in a cost described by a function. Thus, modeling based on ROSI [24] and a fuzzy mapping [25, 26] will be able to deal with uncertainties of security investments.

[17] discusses under economic directions impacts of cyber attacks in a national context. He bases the analysis of attacks on CNIs that could harm or collapse its economy. Also, [17] puts those principles into perspective, which motivate these attacks and policy options to prevent or respond to attacks. Thus, he proposes regulatory options to overcome barriers in cybersecurity, such as safety regulation, post liability, and others. According to the knowledge of the authors, economically-driven frameworks for a suitable and detailed assessment are not yet in place.

2.2 Mapping of Risks and Threats

The AFCEA[1] presented a discussion on cybersecurity economics in a practical framework [1]. The framework guides private organizations and the U.S. government highlighting principles to guide investments mapping risks their associated economic impacts. Threats are categorized according to its complexity *i.e.,* sophisticated or not, and its mission criticality *i.e.,* define how specific vulnerability could impair a service/process.

Concerning the mapping of risks and threats (without a direct analysis of economic impacts), the National Institute for Standards and Technology (NIST) developed a model for guiding the investment in cybersecurity countermeasures. Specifically, NIST's Special Publication 800-37 [20] and 800-53 [19] define the Cybersecurity Risk Management Framework (RMF) including a method for assessing the implementation of controls to mitigate risk. Although 800-37 and 800-53 do not present an analysis directly related to economic aspects, the NIST framework to classify risks, as well as the AFCEA mapping of risks, allows for the establishment of economic models based on threats. Although 800-37 and 800-53 do not present an analysis directly related to economic aspects, the NIST framework (as well as the AFCEA) to classify risks, allows for the establishment of economic models based on threats.

Also, specific guides/frameworks exists for the different cyber systems and applications. For example, while NIST guides focus on the overall risks of an organization, STRIDE [9], LINDDUN [28], or DREAD [23], map each specific type of threat as well as their mitigation actions. For instance, STRIDE (Spoofing, Tampering, Repudiation, Information (disclosure), Denial-of-Service, and Elevation of Privilege) is an industrial-level methodology that comes bundled with a catalog of security threat tree patterns that can be readily instantiated [9]. DREAD is a mnemonic (Damage potential, Reproducibility, Exploitability, Affected users, Discoverability), which, although similar, represents a different approach for assessing threats [23]. LINDDUN builds upon STRIDE to provide a comprehensive privacy threat modeling [28].

Aiming at the evaluation of economic risks, [21] proposes a proactive model to simulate economic risks of CNI's with integrated operations, *i.e.,,* that links many vendors, suppliers into the same ecosystem. The authors seek to map inter-dependencies amongst actors to establish a causal relation, which can then be used to estimate economic risk under various scenarios. However, despite providing a view on the inter-dependencies between the actors, the proposed model does not consider problems that may later occur because of a rush to attain initial economic gains.

For an effective mapping of factors influencing the safety and security of an ecosystem, it is necessary to have an accurate idea of its threats, and risks. SEConomy relies on these mappings, which, for example, can be guided by the frameworks described. Further, it is necessary to understand the interdependence between systems/subsystems, which can trigger cascade failures.

---

[1] Non-profit organization serving military, government, industry, and academia.

3   SEConomy Framework

In ecosystems involving different actors ensuring certain security/safety levels is not a straightforward task. Due to the number of participants potentially managing sensitive information or critical tasks, the risk assessment of a supply chain, for example, becomes complicated [2,7]. The framework proposed (*cf.* Fig. 1) takes into consideration the economic analysis of complex systems by structuring to five stages of mapping and modeling, allowing the creation of economic models with fine-grained estimates.

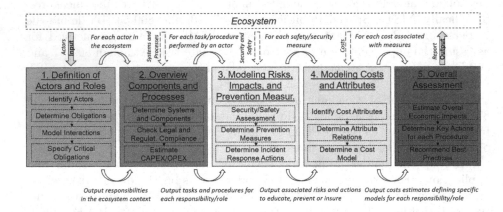

Fig. 1. SEConomy framework.

Stage 1 is concerned with the definition of actors and their functions, whose interactions should be mapped as well as which critical functions should be specified. Stage 2 to determines which systems/components and processes are performed by these actors and their legal implications for an initial attribution of investment and operating costs. Based on the mapping of actors, systems, and processes, Stage 3 is responsible for the production of risk models and possible impacts as well as preventive and training measures based, for example, on NIST risk assessment guides 800-37 and 800-53 [19,20]. Stage 4 takes into consideration this risk analysis to map costs in a fine-grained manner, *i.e.*, for each risk of each task performed by each actor previously mapped. Lastly, Stage 5 gathers outputs of Stage 4 to a produce general feedback in terms of overall economic impacts, the determination of improvement actions, and best practices.

3.1   Definition of Actors and Roles

It is possible to consider as input, for example, the production chain of an aircraft system as a complex ecosystem that requires an assurance of security and safety levels based on a detailed risk analysis of all its major control components. A comparative between Airbus and Boeing supply-chains [11] have shown, for

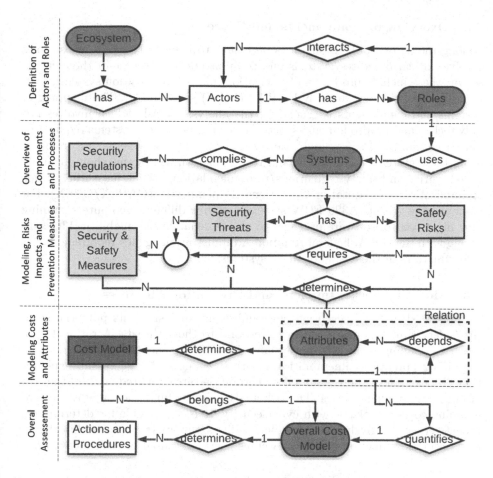

Fig. 2. SEConomy entity-relation model between stages.

example, that the manufacture of the wide-body Airbus A380 and Boeing 787 aircraft involves multiple suppliers from 30 and 67 countries, respectively. Hence, it is essential in Stage 1 to identify all actors involved in the supply chain, and their roles (and determination of which tasks/functions are critical). Figure 2 shows as a first step the identification of actors involved (*e.g.,* producers of flight control systems, software for engines) as well as their obligations and interactions with other actors. In this regard, Boeing and NIST defined a guideline on cybersecurity supply-chain risk management [22], where the organizations that provide software for their aircrafts must undergo a rigorous inspection process. It should be noted, however, that even the most rigorous processes are subject to failures as recently observed in the Boeing 737 Max accident [3].

3.2 Overview of Components and Processes

Among the actors' obligations, it is necessary to identify the ones whose roles involve critical processes/systems and components. In the case of the aviation sector, these include producers of navigation and communication systems, traffic collision avoidance, and Fly-By-Wire (FBW) systems [22]. The mapping of systems and components is crucial for the analysis of risk, which involves not only technical, but also human aspects. For example, critical systems require not only a guarantee of safety and security aspects, but also whether actors operating these systems can monitor and react. Also, these systems should comply with security and safety regulations/recommendations, which measurably leads to implications of Capital or Operational Expenditures (CAPEX/OPEX). For example, the Airbus A320 FBW system uses five different computers running four flight control software packages to ensure reliability/availability [13], complying with the U.S.A. Federal Aviation Administration agency requirements for safety matters in the design of FBW systems.

3.3 Modeling Risks, Impacts, and Prevention Measures

As presented in Fig. 2, each system requires an analysis of its potential security/safety threats, and measures to respond to these threats. A rational approach in defining what is "appropriate" involves (a) identification of risks by examining potential vulnerabilities and their chances of a successful exploitation, (b) the cost of these results if vulnerabilities are exploited, and (c) the cost of mitigating vulnerabilities. The risk analysis is the fundamental stage toward mapping costs associated with cybersecurity. It is responsible for determining, proactively or reactively, possible vulnerabilities/threats (*i.e.*, probabilities) that may occur as a function of time as well as their associated counter-measures.

Risk/Threat Assessment. SEConomy require as input the analysis of threats and risks, which can be based, for example, on frameworks such as the NIST 800-37/800-53 [19,20], and different frameworks (*cf.* Sect. 2), such as STRIDE [9], LINDDUN [28] or DREAD [23], which provide a mapping of threats into categories and their respective mitigation measures.

Mapping Dependencies (MD). The challenge is, however, to translate in a quantifiable manner risks and associated security measures in terms of costs, which includes not only estimating the probability of a threat to be successfully exploited, but also the mapping of interdependence between failures. Correlations can be mapped as the correlation between two Bernoulli random variables (A, B) as defined in [6]:

$$MD(A, B) = p_X = \frac{p_X - p_A * p_B}{\sqrt{p_A(1 - p_A) * p_B(1 - p_B)}} \qquad (1)$$

p_A and p_B denotes the probability of failure in a system A and B, respectively. These probabilities, as defined in [10], are described in values between

$p(0 \leq p \leq 1)$, representing the probability of breaches to occur under current conditions. The inter-dependence, given in Eq. (1), denotes a failure probability p_X, where p_A may lead to a failure in p_B, *i.e.*, failures or vulnerabilities in a component (p_A) under certain conditions can compromise the related components p_B.

3.4   Modeling Costs and Attributes

This stage determines measures to be taken in response to each threat and their associated costs. For example, the ROI (Return On Investment) of proactive approaches (education/training of personnel, prevention, and redundancy of critical systems) is a better economic alternative than reactive approaches (active monitoring and recovery). However, the remaining difficulty is to efficiently determine cost thresholds for CAPEX and OPEX.

Threat Exposure Cost (TEC). The SECeconomy approach is based on the ROSI (Return On Security Investment) model that determines the cost/benefit ratio related to security strategies [5, 24]: Single threat exposure costs in Eq. (2) estimate the total cost of vulnerabilities given their probable occurrences within a time frame $\Delta T \left(\frac{prob(N_{occurrences})}{time} \right)$:

$$TEC(A,B) = \Delta T * \left(\sum_{i=1}^{N_{Threats}} ThreatCost * MD(A,B) \right) \qquad (2)$$

There are two significant challenges to quantify vulnerability costs in Eq. (2): (a) economic impacts of vulnerabilities identified ($ThreatCost$) and (b) potential impacts given by $MD(A,B)$ on the K dependent systems. However, impacts on dependencies are equally not straightforward to be estimated, because the failure of one component may not always lead to the failure of another dependent system (*e.g.*, the use of a layered defense or a "sufficient" redundancy level may reduce such risks). For example, a failure in a fuel control subsystem may not always impair an aircraft's turbine, because a redundancy level of computers exists to provide input for the FBW and, typically, more than one turbine is used in a commercial wide/narrow-body aircraft.

Proactive Mitigation Cost (PMC). These costs are mapped based on proactive and reactive measures [12]. The PMC presented in Eq. (3) is relatively simpler than the reactive costs. This is because the risk vector is foreseen in assessment guides/frameworks, and their mitigation actions and associated PMCs are taken into account at system design time. Additionally, it is possible to include an $InsuranceCost$ that allows the recovery of unforeseen costs.

$$PMC(A) = \sum_{i=1}^{N_{Threat}} \Delta T * (ProactiveCost + InsuranceCost) \qquad (3)$$

Reactive Mitigation Cost (RMC). RMC are challenging to be estimated, since these failures or vulnerabilities are typically originated from unforeseen design aspects, implying on a $ReactiveCost$ to mitigate the threat and its consequences on potentially connected systems. However, the cost of reactive mitigation do not always present a linear relation with time, $i.e.$, the longer the time to perform a reactive measure not always mean that its cost will be higher. For example, in case of a vulnerability in which an attacker gains privileged access to a private network, this does not always imply that the longer time, the higher the victim's monetary loss. However, in case of a DDoS attack, there is a temporal relation taking into account that the greater the time a content provider do not provide service, the greater will be the economic damage on the victim.

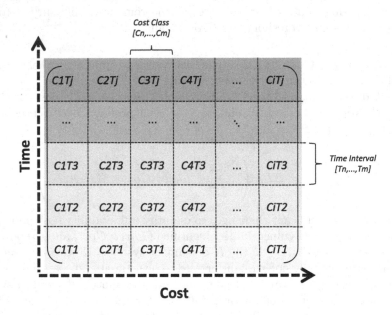

Fig. 3. MTC matrix describing time-cost classes, where $C_i T_j$ classes represent a cost function $f(x, y)$.

As described in Sect. 2, [25] proposed a type of fuzzy model, which translates local dynamics in different state space regions represented by linear models. Based on their proposal, it is defined in SEConomy different classes of RMC costs C_i in function of time T_j, whereas each class has its own cost function. Similarly to PM_{costs}, there is also the alternative to adopt an insurance model to cover potential impacts of subsystems or directly connected systems. Further, the cost of a reactive measure (and potential effects dependent systems) can be mapped in the MTC matrix ($cf.$ Fig. 3). On the one hand, data breaches are not time-sensitive, but may incur in high costs depending on how sensitive is the exposed information. Hence, a data breach could occur in a time $T1$ with a cost Ci, in which i would define the relevance of the exposed information. On the other hand, a DDoS attack is time-sensitive meaning that the longer is the time without providing services (*i.e.,* higher Tj imply in higher Ci), the higher is the economic damage expressed by the time-cost category function.

In detail, a typical fuzzy rule defined by [25] is expressed by an Event-Condition-Action (ECA) rule, where the action is expressed by a function:

$$If \ x \ is \ C \ and \ y \ is \ T \ Then \ Z = f(x, y) \tag{4}$$

C and T are defined, respectively, in terms of cost and time, in which $C_i T_j$ classes are associated with a linear cost function in the MTC matrix [26]. Cost classes are defined as $Ci = [C_n, ..., C_m]$, where n and m belongs to $\mathbb{R}_{\geq 0}$ and Time $C_z, ..., C_w$, where z and w correspond to a class time interval defined in $\mathbb{N}$. For example, a RMC that happened during a time interval "T1", can be associated, depending on the involved systems, with a cost category $C1$ defined as "low cost". Thus, a $C1T1$ is associated with a cost function of $z = F(C1, T1)$, which describes a price category. As previously mentioned, a $CiT1$ category could express, for example, a data breach. Thus, based on [25], time-cost relations can be expressed in terms classes of cost functions mapped in the MTC matrix. However, to foretell the economic impact on dependent systems, which relies on the probabilistic dependence of Eq. (1), it is necessary to consider failures/vulnerabilities which can trigger cascading failures on correlated systems/subsystems potentially impairing the functioning of the entire system, *cf.* Eq. (5).

$$RMC(A, B) = \sum_{i=1}^{N_{System}} \left(\sum_{i=1}^{N_{Threat}} \underbrace{MD(A, B)}_{\substack{\text{Probability of} \\ \text{Cascade Failures}}} * \overbrace{MTC[C_i][T_j]}^{\substack{\text{Cost Function} \\ f(x,y)}} \right) \tag{5}$$

ROSI. To benchmark the security investments is necessary to take into account initial investments in security (*i.e.,* PMC proactive measures) of a system in a given time-frame ΔT (*e.g.,* monthly), multiplied by the risks, threats which the system is exposed (T_{cost}) considering its probable occurrence (RMC). Finally, Eq. (6) calculates ROSI for a single system taking as input the threat vector (T_{cost}), mitigation costs (RMC), and initial investments in security (PMC).

$$ROSI = \Delta T * \sum_{i=1}^{N_{System}} \frac{(T_{costs} * RMC) - PMC}{PMC} \tag{6}$$

3.5   Overall Economic Assessment

In the last stage, it is necessary to calculate the overall economic impact based on ROSI from all S systems, required by R roles of A actors. Therefore, as illustrated in Fig. 2, the N economic models will define an overall estimate of costs for the entire ecosystem, as illustrated by Algorithm 1.

Algorithm 1. Overall Economic Assessment (OEA)

---

1 **begin**
2   **for** *each Actor ∈ Ecosystem*:
3   **for** *each Role ∈ Actor*:
4   **for** *each System ∈ Role*:
            /* Correlation between linked systems in Equation 1   */
5             $p(x) \leftarrow dependence(System, \forall\ linkedSystems)$
            /* Estimate exposure costs in Equation 2   */
6             $threat_{costs} \leftarrow T_{costs}(A, p(x))$
            /* Estimate mitigation (Proactive and Reactive) costs
            in Equation 3   */
7             $mitigation_{costs} \leftarrow PMCcosts(A)$
8             $mitigation_{costs} \leftarrow RMCcosts(A, p(x))$
            /* Get Overal Economic Assessment (OEA) in Equation 4
            */
9             $OEA \leftarrow ROSI(threat_{costs}, mitigation_{costs}, InitSecCost)$

---

4   Discussion and Future Work

The SEConomy proposes a framework to detail economic estimates for security measures in complex distributed systems. Despite providing estimates based on historical events and probabilities, failures and vulnerabilities in critical systems typically result in failures of sub-components or related systems, impacting the overall costs. Hence, it is also imperative to react on threats through reactive mitigation actions, and although its associated costs are not straightforward to be calculated, it is possible to map them into categories as proposed in the SEConomy.

For example, despite all recent technological advances, the introduction of a new warning component in the Boeing 737 Max caused two accidents with hundreds of fatalities [3]. Specialists stated that a software failure (*i.e.*, not properly implemented/tested) in the "Angle-Of-Attack (AOA)" sensors were triggering the flight control system to push the nose of the aircraft down repeatedly. In this regard, the calculation of risks through mutual vulnerability exposure along with other horizontal (*i.e.*, subsystems of a system) and vertical (*i.e.*, systems of another actor relations) is a complex task of potential security and safety consequences.

Thus, the presented SEConomy is a novel framework for estimating costs in complex distributed systems, which provide models for cost estimations and the mapping of relations between interdependent systems and their components. Thus, the need to refine these models especially for cybersecurity defense mechanisms becomes visible. Future work will run this refinement as well as the proposal of cyber-insurance models capable of covering the mitigation of threats not foreseen during design. Also, SEConomy will be applied for in-depth evaluations in different use cases such as Finance and e-Health sectors, while applying specific models from each sector for their respective economic estimates.

Acknowledgements. This paper was supported partially by (a) the University of Zürich UZH, Switzerland and (b) the European Union's Horizon 2020 Research and Innovation Program under grant agreement No. 830927, the Concordia project.

References

1. AFCE: The Economics of Cybersecurity: A Practical Framework for Cybersecurity Investment. The AFCE Cyber Committee (2013). https://www.afcea.org/committees/cyber/documents/cybereconfinal.pdf
2. Bauer, J., Van Eeten, M.: Introduction to the economics of cybersecurity. Commun. Strat. **81**, 13–22 (2011)
3. BBC: Boeing Admits It 'Fell Short' on Safety Alert for 737, pp. 1–3. BBC News (2019). https://www.bbc.com/news/business-48461110
4. Böhme, R.: Security metrics and security investment models. In: Echizen, I., Kunihiro, N., Sasaki, R. (eds.) IWSEC 2010. LNCS, vol. 6434, pp. 10–24. Springer, Heidelberg (2010). https://doi.org/10.1007/978-3-642-16825-3_2
5. Brecht, M., Nowey, T.: A closer look at information security costs. In: Böhme, R. (ed.) The Economics of Information Security and Privacy, pp. 3–24. Springer, Heidelberg (2013). https://doi.org/10.1007/978-3-642-39498-0_1
6. Chen, P.Y., Kataria, G., Krishnan, R.: Correlated failures, diversification, and information security risk management. MIS Q. **35**, 397–422 (2011)
7. Dynes, S., Goetz, E., Freeman, M.: Cyber security: are economic incentives adequate? In: Goetz, E., Shenoi, S. (eds.) ICCIP 2007. IIFIP, vol. 253, pp. 15–27. Springer, Boston (2008). https://doi.org/10.1007/978-0-387-75462-8_2
8. Felici, M., Wainwright, N., Cavallini, S., Bisogni, F.: What's new in the economics of cybersecurity? IEEE Secur. Priv. **14**, 11–13 (2016). https://doi.org/10.1109/MSP.2016.64
9. Garg, P., Kohnfelder, L.: The threat to our products, pp. 1–8. Microsoft (1999). https://adam.shostack.org/microsoft/The-Threats-To-Our-Products.docx
10. Gordon, L.A., Loeb, M.P.: The economics of information security investment. ACM Trans. Inf. Syst. Secur. **5**, 438–457 (2002). https://doi.org/10.1145/581271.581274
11. Horng, T.C.: A comparative analysis of supply chain management practices by Boeing and Airbus: long-term strategic implications. Master thesis, Massachusetts Institute of Technology (MIT) (2006)
12. Jentzsch, N.: State-of-the-Art of the Economics of Cyber-Security and Privacy, vol. 4. IPACSO Deliverable D4.1 (2016)
13. Kornecki, A.J., Hall, K.: Approaches to assure safety in fly-by-wire systems: Airbus vs. Boeing. In: IASTED Conference on Software Engineering and Applications (2004)
14. Maglaras, L.A., et al.: Cyber security of critical infrastructures. ICT Express **4**, 42–45 (2018). https://doi.org/10.1016/j.icte.2018.02.001. http://www.sciencedirect.com/science/article/pii/S2405959517303880. SI: CI and Smart Grid Cyber Security
15. McGuffin, C., Mitchell, P.: On domains: cyber and the practice of warfare. Int. J.: Can. J. Glob. Policy Anal. **69**, 394–412 (2014)
16. Moore, S.: Gartner Forecasts Worldwide Information Security Spending to Exceed 124 Billion in 2019. Gartner (2018). https://www.gartner.com/en/newsroom/press-releases/2018-08-15-gartner-forecasts-worldwide-information-security-spending-to-exceed-124-billion-in-2019

17. Moore, T.: The economics of cybersecurity: principles and policy options. Int. J. Crit. Infrastruct. Prot. (IJCNIP) **3**, 103–117 (2010). https://doi.org/10.1016/j.ijcip.2010.10.002.   http://www.sciencedirect.com/science/article/pii/S1874548210000429
18. Morgan, S.: 2019 Official Annual Cybercrime Report. Herjavec Group (2019). https://bit.ly/2TouUT2
19. NIST: Security and Privacy Controls for Federal Information Systems and Organizations, vol. 800, pp. 8–13. National Institute of Standards and Technology (NIST) Special Publication (2013)
20. NIST: Guide for Applying the Risk Management Framework to Federal Information Systems: A Security Life Cycle Approach. Technical report, National Institute of Standards and Technology (NIST) (2014)
21. Rich, E., Gonzalez, J.J., Qian, Y., Sveen, F.O., Radianti, J., Hillen, S.: Emergent vulnerabilities in integrated operations: a proactive simulation study of economic risk. Int. J. Crit. Infrastruct. Prot. **2**, 110–123 (2009). https://doi.org/10.1016/j.ijcip.2009.07.002. http://www.sciencedirect.com/science/article/pii/S1874548209000183
22. Robert, S., Vijay, T., Tim, Z.: Best Practices in Cyber Supply Chain Risk Management, pp. 1–14. US Resilience Project (2016)
23. Shostack, A.: Experiences Threat Modeling at Microsoft, pp. 1–11. Microsoft (2008).   https://adam.shostack.org/modsec08/Shostack-ModSec08-Experiences-Threat-Modeling-At-Microsoft.pdf
24. Sonnenreich, W., Albanese, J., Stout, B., et al.: Return on security investment (ROSI)-a practical quantitative model. J. Res. Pract. Inf. Technol. **38**, 45–52 (2006)
25. Takagi, T., Sugeno, M.: Fuzzy identification of systems and its applications to modeling and control. In: Readings in Fuzzy Sets for Intelligent Systems, pp. 387–403. Elsevier (1993)
26. Wang, H.O., Tanaka, K., Griffin, M.F.: An approach to fuzzy control of nonlinear systems: stability and design issues. IEEE Trans. Fuzzy Syst. **4**, 14–23 (1996)
27. WhiteHouse: The Cost of Malicious Cyber Activity to the U.S. Economy. White House (2018). https://www.whitehouse.gov/wp-content/uploads/2018/03/The-Cost-of-Malicious-Cyber-Activity-to-the-U.S.-Economy.pdf
28. Wuyts, K., Scandariato, R., Joosen, W., Deng, M., Preneel, B.: LINDDUN: a privacy threat analysis framework, pp. 1–23. DistriNet (2019). https://people.cs.kuleuven.be/~kim.wuyts/LINDDUN/LINDDUN.pdf

Blockchain and Network Function Virtualization Technologies

Introducing Licensing Throughout SLAs in NFV Environment

Evgenia Kapassa[1(✉)], Marios Touloupou[1], Dimosthenis Kyriazis[1],
José Bonnet[2], Carlos Parada[2], Thomas Soenen[3], and Ana Pol[4]

[1] University of Piraeus, Piraeus, Greece
ekapassa@unipi.gr
[2] Altice Labs, Aveiro, Portugal
[3] Ghent University – imec, Ghent, Belgium
[4] Quobis, O Porrino, Spain

Abstract. Software licensing is changing how organizations and individuals use software. Globally, technical and economic needs affect licensing in many ways and thus creating licensing models and techniques that reflect and serve organizations' needs, becomes an increasingly challenge in the Network Function Virtualization concept. While NFV continues emerge, it also becomes increasingly important to monitor and manage software licenses. Therefore, in this paper, a license-based architecture is introduced which aims at linking the Network Services with license models throughout SLAs. Specifically, we have introduced an interconnection between license models and SLAs, in which we aim at an efficient and flexible service orchestration in a beyond MANO SP.

Keywords: License models · SLAs · NFV · Network Services · Software licensing

1 Introduction

Telecommunication networks are an essential part of any society's infrastructure as millions of people rely on the services offered by today's telecommunication providers, expecting the arrival of commercial 5G networks to bring new capabilities. Network Function Virtualization (NFV) is expected to be the key enabler for agile network management in the upcoming 5G networks, as it will allow optimized service management through softwarization and virtualization of network components [1]. One of the leaders of the group of network operators, who introduced the NFV concept, mentions that software licenses will play a significant role in the economics of NFV [2]. As network operators push forward with virtualization in the hybrid network environment that currently exists, software license management arises as a primary challenge [3]. Licensing models and monetization of different Virtual Network Functions (VNFs) and Network Services (NSs) enable better service elasticity and better utilization of network resources, while it also starts getting attention from many companies like Google, Yahoo, Cisco and others [4]. For enterprises that rely on software to maintain a market share, the software licensing model can strongly influence the return

© Springer Nature Switzerland AG 2019
K. Djemame et al. (Eds.): GECON 2019, LNCS 11819, pp. 169–177, 2019.
https://doi.org/10.1007/978-3-030-36027-6_14

on software investment. Software licensing aims to protect both the vendor's investment by minimizing the risk of hard piracy and the enterprise's investment by minimizing the risk of auditing fines from soft piracy [5]. It is important to note that a declarative license approach is commonly used on the B2B market, particularly with telecommunications operators. This involves entrusting the software licenses with the task of controlling the use of the software in subject to the terms of the license, classifying the rights of use and the identified limits. Telecommunication operators are used to managing their software licenses and have a dedicated business process called Software Asset Management (SAM), that needs to be adapted to fit with automation processes orchestrated by NFV Management and Orchestration (NFV-MANO).

To address the aforementioned challenges, in this paper a license-based architectural approach is described, that allows efficient NS license management, in a virtualized SP. We propose an interconnection of licenses, with Service Level Agreements (SLAs) in order to introduce NFV-enabled licenses in a more efficient and flexible way. It is worth mentioned that the presented architecture is part of the SONATA (powered by 5GTANGO) Service Platform which bridges the gap between business needs and network operational management systems [6].

The rest of this paper is organized as follows. Section 2 presents the related work on the field of software licensing. Section 3 introduces the proposed license-based architecture, while Sect. 4 presents the license model followed in our approach. In Sect. 5, an end-to-end workflow is presented in order to describe in detail the overall process. The paper closes in Sect. 6 with some conclusions and future thoughts of the presented work.

2   Related Work

A substantial amount of research has been undertaken to investigate the challenges the developers face with the different approaches for using, or re-using, software, especially in the context of VNFs and NSs. Further complicating the situation, not all of the ways in which a developers may wish to make use of open source code may be allowed by the license applied to that code and the way in which the code is used may affect the resultant license of the NS being built. Therefore, licensing of VNFs and NSs is a complex task that need to be addressed at all the different layers of NFV concept. The primary opportunity is either for open source to remain popular or simply for commercial software companies to change their licensing structure to better fit virtualized computing [7]. With new license technologies like Cisco Smart Licensing [8], licensed products can be activated, and entitlements redeployed without handling special software keys or upgrade license files Service providers, network vendors and their customers would need the capabilities enabled by new licensing technologies to deliver on the promise of the intelligent, cloud-based and software-defined network and fully realize their benefits. As stated in [9], software licensing is changing how organizations and individuals purchase and use software. Thus, the authors make a general introduction on the different licensing models while they also describe how organizations and individuals can benefit from them. Such common licensing models are for example (a) Packaged: Single license purchased for a single user or machine, (b) Perpetual:

Permanent licenses purchased upfront, (c) Trial: Users are able to try the software before purchasing, (d) Server: Number of processors running determines number of licenses purchased. It is worth mentioning also the fact that ETSI NFV has published the "Report on License Management for NFV" [10]. It documents the features required to be implemented within the ETSI NFV architectural framework to support NFV license management. These features will enable any combination of commercial license management without the need for proprietary license management mechanisms. Henceforth, the authors illustrated the composability of service licenses by creating a composite service license, that is compatible with the licenses being composed. Furthermore, in [11], the authors compared SLAs and service licenses while they also proposed the phases of a service license during its life span. To make the discussion more concrete, they illustrated the proposal of a service license life cycle with a meteorological case study. At the same time, in [12], the authors have realized the interest for the integration of license management mechanisms into the software defined systems and architectures. They proposed a solution that exploits all Service-Oriented Architectures (SOA) key characteristics, trying in the same time to resolve the restrictions and to confront the weaknesses of the current License Management systems. They also defined the roles emerging from the suggested architecture and presented new business models and market opportunities.

3   License Based Architecture

This section describes the proposed license-based architecture, taking advantage of the components implemented into the SONATA (powered by 5GTANGO) SP. The SONATA (powered by 5GTANGO) SP brings, among others, the SLA Manager and increases its abilities with a Licensing Manager, a component that allows the user to obtain NS licenses and verify them during the NS instantiation. Figure 1 depicts the overall architecture) that is going to be described in this paper. The license-oriented architecture consists of (a) the Portal, (b) the Gatekeeper, (c) the SLA Manager, (d) the Licensing Manager (e) a Correlations Database and (f) the MANO Framework.

3.1   Portal

The proposed architecture is consisted of several components. In order to be accessible to the end-users, a unified Portal was implemented as a Web User Interface (WUI). The Portal is divided into sections that include Network Services, SLAs, Licensing Management, as well as an Operation section, for NS instantiation management. The main role of the Portal is to help the SP owners and operators to create business-oriented SLAs for QoS provisioning. Moreover, the Portal promotes the interconnection of the aforementioned SLAs with the desired licenses, known by the developers entered the Portal and the creators of the SLAs.

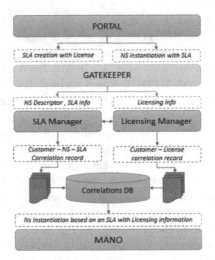

Fig. 1. Proposed license-based architecture.

3.2 Gatekeeper

While the Portal is the main web interface interacting with the SP end-users the Gatekeeper is the entry point, controlling who attempts to access the inner components (i.e. SLA Manager, Licensing Manager, MANO) and the privileges to do so. The Gatekeeper exposes API endpoints for QoS management through efficient SLAs, as well as of licenses for each NS that is going to be deployed in the SP. The Gatekeeper validates and forwards requests, for managing SLAs, to the SLA Manager (Subsect. 3.3) and for creating licenses, to the Licensing Manager (Subsect. 3.4). The Gatekeeper also serves an important and active role in implementing the MANO Framework communication interfaces (Subsect. 3.6).

3.3 SLA Manager

A key objective of NFV technologies is the provision of QoS guarantees. These guarantees are reflected to the requirements emerging from the agreements between the customers and service providers. At this point a question arises, regarding what exactly is an SLA. An SLA is a contract between the service provider and the customer, which underlines each party's responsibilities while at the same time defines the performance standards that are to be met by the provider [13, 14]. SLAs establish customer expectations regarding the service provider's performance and overall quality [15]. The proposed SLA Manager can support (a) Definition and advertising of the capabilities of network operators in SLA Template forms and (b) Agreements creation upon a NS instantiation [16]. The workflow of the SLA Management Framework is partitioned into two phases, namely (a) SLA Template Management and (b) the Information Management [17]. The SLA Template Management phase takes place prior to the NS operation, while it includes the template formulation with the appropriate Service Level

Objectives (SLO). Apart from the traditional SLOs (e.g. availability, packet loss), the SLA Manager supports licensing as a different kind of a SLO, leading to two different kinds: (a) service guarantee SLOs and (b) licensing SLOs. On the other hand, the Information Management phase starts during the NS instantiation, incorporating the SLA instance creation and the enforcement of the licenses. The SLA instance is an enforced SLA template with the instantiation information, and the relevant licensing information, that refers to the linked NS instance and the customer's information.

3.4 Licensing Manager

In the various functional domains of NFV-based network architectures, software licenses apply. In the current work, we are focusing on the software licenses for VNFs and NSs. Thus, taking into consideration the emerging NFV technologies, there is a need to include in the SLA contracts licensing information for the corresponding NSs. It is important to point out that the SLAs are business-oriented documents. Therefore, the licenses included in them, do not tend to be aligned with specific amount of resources. The licenses, as specified into the SLA Templates, focus mainly on how many scales can be used, based on the "signed" license type. It is worth mentioning that licensing is provided "as a service". The provided licenses are created per customer, and due to the fact, that are included into an SLA Template, as an additional SLO, each license corresponds to a specific NS. In this context, the Licensing Manager adopts a service-based licensing model, which links a license to a specific customer and an instantiated NS, by specifying also the number of allowed NS instances. Finally, the instantiation operation takes place with verified licenses, and orchestrated through the MANO.

3.5 Correlations Database

At this point, it should be pointed that all the presented components follow a micro-service-based architecture, therefore, a database was used in order to keep runtime information of network services, SLAs and licenses. Specifically, it keeps track of all the correlations between the generated templates and the linked NSs. At the same time, agreements information is also located in the Correlations Database, among with the end-user's authentication detail coming from the inter-communication with the Gate-keeper. Finally, the database stores the correlations between the end-user (i.e. customer), the corresponding licenses, and the number of successful instantiations, resulting from the successful placement of the service through the MANO Framework.

3.6 MANO Framework

On the bottom of the proposed architecture lies the MANO which is responsible for the orchestration and full lifecycle management of hardware resources and VNFs. In our case though, we are taking into account a customized MANO Framework, implemented into the SONATA (powered by 5GTANGO) SP, which allow the operator and the service developer to join forces in managing their lifecycles to fulfill SLAs and manage properly the corresponding licenses [18]. It exposes an API where other components, like the SLA Manager, can request lifecycle events, providing at the same time licensing information, that could be mapped to a particular amount of resources, which will be validated eventually by the Licensing Manager. As a result, MANO will use the license information for the NS instantiation and operation.

4 Proposed License Model

The model provides three types of licenses: (a) trial, which supports limited time of trying the desired NS before license is purchased, (b) public, which comes with no instantiation restrictions, and (c) private, which specifies as mandatory the purchase of a license before instantiating a NS.

- Public License: The Public License refers to an open source NS, which the descriptor (i.e. source code) is available to the end-users for instantiation free of charge. As previously mentioned, the Public License comes with no instantiation restrictions.
- Trial License: The Trial License refers to the NSs which end-users can try before they buy. Once the end-user in registered and selects to instantiate a NS with a Trial license included in the selected SLA, he or she activates the license "silently", and can use it for the time period specified in the SLA. Apart from the constrained period, the Trial License has a limited amount of free NS instances that the end-user can have it activated at the same time.
- Private License: In the proposed architecture, the Private License means that the customer needs to buy a license before instantiating a service. Additionally, this type of license specifies the number of allowed simultaneous instances per customer.

5 End to End License Workflow

In this section, it is described the end-to end workflow for establishing licenses through SLAs and enforce them after the NS instantiation. On the Customer side, there is the Portal, along with the Gatekeeper. The Gatekeeper awaits a request for an SLA creation in order to trigger the process. The sequence of interactions are depicted in the sequence diagram of Fig. 2. In detail, the steps include the following:

- Step 1: The workflow is triggered by the SP owner who enters the Portal and starts the creation of an SLA. The SP owner gives the mandatory parameters for the SLA creation (e.g. QoS parameters, expiration date etc.), selects the corresponding NS and the desired license type (i.e. public, trial, private). In case the SP owner select a trial or private license, it is mandatory to select the allowed instances as well as the valid period of the license.
- Step 2: The Gatekeeper promotes the request to the SLA Manager and the Licensing Manager.

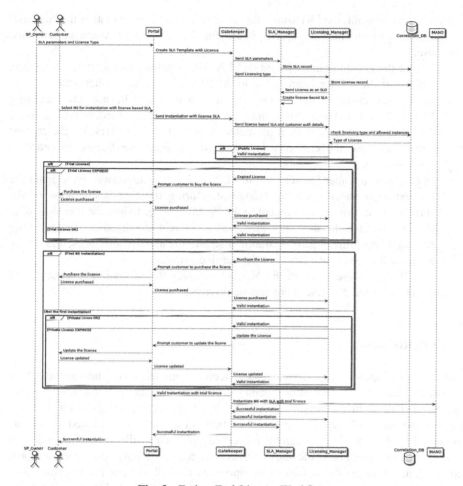

Fig. 2. End-to-End License Workflow.

- **Step 3:** The Licensing Manager receives the necessary parameters (i.e. license type, allowed instances, license expiration date) among with the customer's authentication details, and stores a license record into the Correlation Database. Additionally, it sends the license information as an additional SLO to the SLA Manager in order to include it into the SLA Template.
- **Step 4:** The SLA Manager receives the license SLO, and the SLA parameters (SLA name, QoS SLOs, SLA expiration date etc.) while it formulates the SLA Template. Additionally, it stores a record into the Correlation Database regarding the corresponding NS and the created template.
- **Step 5:** During this step, the Customer requests through the Portal a NS instantiation, specifying the desired NS and a specific SLA, with a license attached to it.
- **Step 6:** The Gatekeeper promotes the request to the Licensing Manager.

- Step 7: At this point, the Licensing Manger is responsible to validate if the customer is allowed to instantiate the service based on the selected SLA and the attached license.
  - In case the customer has selected an SLA with a public license, the instantiation request of the service is promoted to the MANO with no further action.
  - In case the customer has selected an SLA with a trial license, the Licensing Manager needs to validate it. If the license has not been expired, or not exceeded the allowed instances is then promoted to the MANO. Otherwise, the request terminates, and the customer is asked to purchase the license in order to continue.
  - In case the customer has selected an SLA with a private license, once again the Licensing Manager needs to validate it. During the first instantiation of the service, the customer is prompted to the Portal in order to buy the corresponding license. In case the customer has already bought the license, the Licensing Manager check the license expiration date and the allowed instances, and if they all are valid, the instantiation of the service proceeds.
- Step 8: If the license is valid, the MANO receives the instantiation request, and continues with the NS placement and deployment.

6   Conclusions

In the presented architecture, we consider a licensing model, taking into account both the cost constraints of the NS software and the allowed instances per customer, towards a more efficient scaling concept. In order to do so, the presented approach links the provided NSs to a selected license model, which is included into a signed SLA in an easy and flexible way. Even though the presented approach is still work in progress, the entire workflow described in the above paragraphs can be executed on a regular laptop and the code of all involved software components as well as their install instructions and documentation are available on the project's official web site [16], as well as on GitHub [17].

The next step will be to motivate service providers to engage in this critical next phase and begin developing product roadmaps to support the management of NFV licenses with the features and scalability required for telecommunications operations. In this way, the proposed architecture will be also evaluated by be tested in the NFV space.

Acknowledgements. This work has been partially supported by the 5GTANGO project, funded by the European Commission under Grant number H2020ICT-2016-2 761493 through the Horizon 2020 and 5G-PPP programmes (http://5gtango.eu). Moreover, this work has also been supported by the MATILDA project, also funded by the European Commission, under the Grant number H2020ICT-2016-2 761898 through the Horizon 2020 and 5G-PPP programs (http://www.matilda-5g.eu/).

References

1. Karl, H., et al.: DevOps for network function virtualization: an architectural approach. Trans. Emerg. Telecommun. Technol. **27**(9), 1206–1215 (2016)
2. NFV License Management: The Missing Piece of the Puzzle. https://www.cablelabs.com/nfv-license-management-the-missing-piece-of-the-puzzle
3. Latest NFV Headache: Software Licensing. https://www.tmforum.org/press-and-news/latest-nfv-headache-software-licensing/
4. Software Defined Networking Enables New Software Licensing and Business Models. https://blogs.flexera.com/ecm/2012/06/software-defined-networking-enables-new-software-licensing-and-business-models/
5. Anthony, D., et al.: A view of cloud computing. Commun. ACM **53**(4) (2010)
6. Parada, C., et al.: 5GTANGO: a beyond-MANO service platform. In: European Conference on Networks and Communications (EuCNC) (2018)
7. Cisco NX-OS Licensing Guide. https://www.cisco.com/c/en/us/td/docs/switches/datacenter/sw/nx-os/licensing/guide/b_Cisco_NX-OS_Licensing_Guide/b_Cisco_NX-OS_Licensing_Guide_chapter_010.html
8. Gangadharan, G.R., Weiss, M., D'Andrea, V., Iannella, R.: Service license composition and compatibility analysis. In: Krämer, B.J., Lin, K.-J., Narasimhan, P. (eds.) ICSOC 2007. LNCS, vol. 4749, pp. 257–269. Springer, Heidelberg (2007). https://doi.org/10.1007/978-3-540-74974-5_21
9. Gangadharan, G.R., Frankova, G., DAndrea, V.: Service license life cycle. In: International Symposium on Collaborative Technologies and Systems, pp. 150–158 (2007)
10. ETSI NFV: Network Functions Virtualisation (NFV) Release 3; Licensing Management; Report on License Management for NFV. https://www.etsi.org/deliver/etsi_gr/NFV-EVE/001_099/010/03.01.01_60/gr_NFV-EVE010v030101p.pdf
11. Carroll, S.L., Gaston, R.J.: Occupational licensing and the quality of service: an overview. Law Hum. Behav. **7**, 139 (1983)
12. Francesco, T., et al.: Multi-domain orchestration for the deployment and management of services on a slice enabled NFVI. In: IEEE Conference on Network Function Virtualization and Software Defined Networks (2018)
13. Kapassa, E., Touloupou, M., Stavrianos, P., Xylouris, G., Kyriazis, D.: Managing and optimizing quality of service in 5G environments across the complete SLA lifecycle. Adv. Sci. Technol. Eng. Syst. J. **4**(1), 329–342 (2019)
14. Touloupou, M., Kapassa, E., Symvoulidis, C., Stavrianos, P., Kyriazis, D.: An integrated SLA management framework in a 5G environment. In: 22nd Conference on Innovation in Clouds, Internet and Networks and Workshops (ICIN), pp. 233–235. 2019
15. Dräxler, S., et al.: SONATA: service programming and orchestration for virtualized software networks. In: IEEE International Conference on Communications Workshops (ICC Workshops). IEEE (2017)
16. 5GTANGO Consortium, Documentation. https://5gtango.eu/software/documentation.html
17. Kapassa, E., Touloupou, M.: The 5GTANGO SP SLA Management Repository (2019) https://github.com/sonata-nfv/tng-slamgmt/tree/v4.0

Blockchain-Enabled Participatory Incentives for Crowdsourced Mesh Networks

Elena San Miguel[1]([✉]), Roxane Timmerman[2]([✉]), Sergio Mosquera[1]([✉]),
Emmanouil Dimogerontakis[1]([✉]), Felix Freitag[1]([✉]), and Leandro Navarro[1]([✉])

[1] Universitat Politecnica de Catalunya, Barcelona, Spain
{elena.san.miguel,sergio.mosquera}@est.fib.upc.edu,
{edimoger,felix,leandro}@ac.upc.edu
[2] Ecole Centrale de Marseille, Marseille, France
roxane.timmerman@ec-m.fr

Abstract. Crowdsourced mesh networks are built, maintained and used by several participants that cooperate to provide and consume connectivity. Providers of infrastructure want to get compensation for their investments and earn tokens; users or consumers want the network to expand for improving the coverage of connectivity and stability. How do we collect funds from consumers and distribute them to providers, guaranteeing satisfaction of every participant? For that, we need of a system that coordinates the flow of economic value in mesh networks in a way that is not only transparent, automated, decentralized and secure, but also beneficial to all. We designed a new economic protocol called *Fair* to compensate providers for their investments. The key point of our model is that each provider will be paid with different prices for the forwarded traffic: the more devices a provider has, the higher its price/MB forwarded is, up to a certain limit. We implemented the model using MeshDApp, a local blockchain platform for mesh networks. Simulations show how our proposal ensures a win-win situation where the network grows and the providers are compensated for their investment. Also, continuous growth is incentivized while centralization due to few large providers controlling the network is avoided.

Keywords: Pricing · Mesh networks · Blockchain · Crowdsourcing

1 Introduction

A mesh network has a topology in which each node (router) is capable of relaying data for others. All nodes cooperate in the distribution of data throughout the network for the mutual benefit of its participants. With each participating node, the reach, throughput and resilience of the network expands. With sufficient benefits to participation, a mesh network can quickly grow to provide shared connectivity and at a much cheaper rate than a centralised topology [1].

© Springer Nature Switzerland AG 2019
K. Djemame et al. (Eds.): GECON 2019, LNCS 11819, pp. 178–187, 2019.
https://doi.org/10.1007/978-3-030-36027-6_15

Figure 1 illustrates the main components of a crowdsourced mesh network. The network infrastructure is composed by several devices (routers) that are owned by different providers, and the consumers connect to the network through any of the providers and use the infrastructure to access any of the services available in the network (e.g. Internet access service in this example).

Mesh networks have the challenge to scale in absence of economic sustainability. The toughest aspects to deal with is the trust in the agreements between peers and how to ensure the economic sustainability of this collective effort and the balance between contribution and consumption. For instance, as an example scenario and mechanism for economic sustainability, we consider the *economic compensation system* used in Guifi.net [2]. The aim is to find a balance between total resource contribution and its consumption. Currently, the above described economic compensation system is done manually: each participant declares its costs and consumption (traffic) and then the Guifi.net foundation validates this claim by cross checking it with their own network traffic measurement data and network inventory, according to the agreed list of standard costs. There is, however, room for error or manipulation. The correct application of the compensation system is critical for the economic sustainability of the network, as well as for the return of previous or future investments and maintenance.

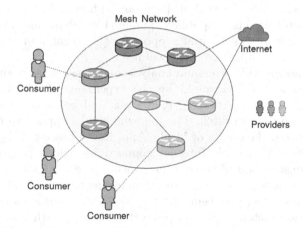

Fig. 1. A mesh network scenario where the infrastructure is owned by different providers.

Therefore, we agree that there is a need for an automated mechanism where diverse participants, providers and consumers, can pool resources with the confidence that the consumption is *(i)* accounted fairly, without discrimination and proportionally to effort and value, and that *(ii)* these calculations and money transfers are safe, automated, irreversible and shared across different participants, to avoid the cost, delays, errors and potential mistrust from manual accounting and external payments. MeshDApp[1] is a value transfer platform for mesh networks that uses a local blockchain.

---

[1] http://dsg.ac.upc.edu/meshdapp.

Our work addresses the economic sustainability problem of mesh networks. We designed and implemented a new economic model called *Fair* using Mesh-DApp. The goal of our model is to build a win-win situation for the network and the users. First, Sect. 2 presents the related work. In the Sect. 3, we present our proposed economic model called *Fair* and we evaluate the model in Sect. 4. Then we underline some discussion and future work about our work in Sect. 5 and conclude in Sect. 6.

2   Related Work

Other projects explore aspects of how mesh networks can be combined with blockchain to provide connectivity under a decentralized economic model involving independent providers and consumers of a crowdsourced network.

Our design relies on a local blockchain infrastructure that operates over an Ethereum-based lightweight consensus protocol (permissioned and low overhead, PoA). A possible alternative to this approach could be Hyperledger Fabric [3]. There are other projects in development that combine the payment in mesh networks with blockchain. Althea Mesh [4] provides last-mile connectivity for the Internet access, where routers pay each other for bandwidth using cryptocurrency payment channels. RightMesh [5] is an ad-hoc mobile mesh networking platform and protocol using the public Ethereum blockchain and RMESH tokens. AmmbrTech [6] has provided initial support for the research of MeshDApp and therefore the results will inspire their evolution.

Several studies provide economic analysis and designs for resource trading. The MeshDApp system is inspired by the experience of our research group in participating in the governance, operations and economic analysis of the Guifi.net community network [2]. The following works applied to related problems have influenced the design of MeshDApp. Route Bazaar [7] is a backward-compatible system for flexible Internet connectivity, which is inspired by the decentralised construction of trust in cryptocurrencies. It looks at agreements among Autonomous Systems with automatic means to form, establish, and verify end-to-end connectivity agreements. Tycoon [8] is a market based distributed resource allocation system based on proportional share with resource auctions for computing or storage. Request Network [9] is a decentralised network that allows anyone to request a payment (a Request Invoice) for which the recipient can pay in a secure way. Request can be seen as a layer on top of Ethereum which allows requests for payments that satisfy a legal framework.

3   *Fair* Economic Model

A key goal of our economic model is to promote the expansion of the network coverage awarding providers with a different price per MB forwarded, according to the number of devices they operate. Formalizing the model into a sentence:

The more devices a provider i has, the higher its Price/MB P_i is; up to a limit. Figure 2 shows this relation. In fact, we want to build a win-win situation where the growth of the network contributes to more stability and provides more content for users. There are several assumptions in our model:

As it is not good for the network that one provider owns too many devices, we defined a price limit. As soon as the number of devices of a provider is greater than or equal to a given parameter $Incentive$ (I), its $Price/MB$ (P) is equal to P_{max}. The two goals of this limit are to avoid monopolies (i.e. the network is not dependant on a single provider) and prevent unfair discrimination.

The incentive parameter I is proportional to the ratio of network devices versus providers, so we reward networks with providers with multiple devices, with a constant factor of 3/2 we determined experimentally, defined by Eq. 2.

To make sure prices cover minimum costs, we also fixed a P_{min} which is the price per MB forwarded that a provider with a single device would have. We decided to use a linear step function for a number of devices lower than the I parameter, but other shapes, such as an exponential form could be considered in alternative models. Finally, the price per MB forwarded of a provider i is defined by Eq. 1 when the number of devices $D_i \leq I$ or higher.

$$P_i = \begin{cases} \left\lfloor P_{min} + \frac{P_{max}-P_{min}}{I-1} \times (D_i - 1) \right\rfloor \\ P_{max} \end{cases} \tag{1}$$

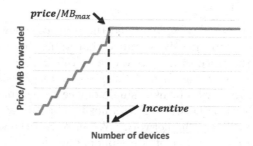

Fig. 2. $Price/MB$ of a provider under its number of devices.

We do not model the payments from consumers. We simply assume "infinite funds" in a common consumer account, assuming a subscription is paid by clients at each iteration in exchange of clients having unlimited network access. That price varies depending on the total traffic in the network during the last iteration.

4   Evaluation

In order to evaluate our economic model we performed simulation. This section presents the design of these experiments and their results.

4.1   Design of Experiments

The simulation is a test constructed as the sequential execution of the activities that take place during a day, repeated during one month. The first activity consists on getting the monitored traffic values for all devices. Then, the prices per MB per provider are computed and the charges (owed tokens) are calculated for all providers. After that, the payment to the providers is carried out taking advantage of the amount deposited in a common funds account. Finally, the providers pay the costs of maintenance of their devices and buy new devices.

We have decided to perform one iteration per day (the data is pre-processed so that we have a given amount of MB forwarded per provider, for each day). The two following subsections present the inputs of these simulation and the measurements we performed.

4.2   Inputs

Economic Models: We performed our simulation for the *Fair* economic model, and two variants, one with unlimited P_{max} (*unbounded*), and another with the same price for all providers (*fixed-price*).

Data: We used real data from the QMPSU mesh network in Barcelona. We had received (rx) and transmitted (tx) bytes for 62 devices, every hour during one month. We assumed that forwarded data (fx) is calculated as $min(rx, tx)$. Although this solution is not entirely realistic, we assume is fair enough to have values related to real traffic.

Variables: Price of a new device: We fixed the price of a new device to a proportionally value of 10^9 tokens. We assumed that a monthly cost for a provider is around 4€, and the price of a new device is 150€. Then, we calculate the cost of any provider i with the formula $Cost_i = 0.9 * (fx * P_{min})$. Indeed, it is essential for a provider who owns a single device to be able to get a benefit ($TotalReceived - Cost$). Otherwise, he will not be able to invest in the network due to lack of money. Size of the network: We performed the simulation with 2, 5 or 10 providers for each variant of the economic model.

Initial State: In the first iteration, half of the providers start with 1 device, and half start with 3 devices. This choice enables the system to have different providers at the beginning, in terms of importance in the network, to observe their developments and to discover whether it has an impact or not.

Model of Providers' Behaviors: One of *Fair*'s goals is to incentivize providers, so that they can invest in the network buying new devices. In order to evaluate the efficiency of the way this economic model incentivizes them, we have to model providers' behaviors: do they buy new devices? When? We decided to model it as follows. A provider i buys a new device when he has enough tokens ($\sharp Tokens_i \geq 10^9$), with a probability $p1 = 0.7$ or $p2 = 0.2$ depending on the number of $Devices_i$.

In fact, if the number of devices $D_i \leq I$, P_i will increase if the provider i decides to buy a new device and so, he is incentivized to do it. We modelled it with the probability $p1$. Otherwise, his P_i will be constant and would have less reasons to buy a new device. Therefore, this happens with probability $p2 \leq p1$.

In one hand, the *Unbounded* model, a provider is always incentivized to buy a new device. Therefore, the probability is $p = p1 = 0.7$. On the other hand, in the *Fixed-Price* model the incentive disappears. Therefore, the probability is $p = p2 = 0.2$.

4.3 Metrics

We evaluated the *Fair* economic model looking at 3 metrics that change over time: the size of the network, the number of tokens per provider, and the number of devices per provider.

The size of the network over time is a metric that allows us to evaluate if an economic model incentivizes efficiently providers to buy new devices and help the network grow. This is a part of the evaluation of the win-win situation desired. In fact, the bigger the network is, the bigger the stability it offers to its consumers.

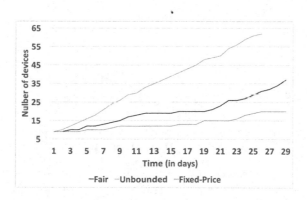

Fig. 3. Total number of devices in a network of 10 providers over time.

The number of tokens per provider over time is a measurement that lets us to evaluate the second part of the win-win situation. In fact, a provider investing in the network should be rewarded earning tokens.

Finally, the number of devices per provider over time is a measurement that makes it possible to evaluate whether the limit P_{max} is efficient or not. In fact, it should avoid monopoly and therefore, dependence of the network on a single provider.

4.4 Results

Figure 3 shows how *Fair* incentivizes the providers to invest in the network. In fact, the growth is faster than with a *Fixed-Price* model (we can observe how the deviation between the two curves increases). The growth is even faster with the *Unbounded* model, as expected. The drawbacks of this last model will be discussed later.

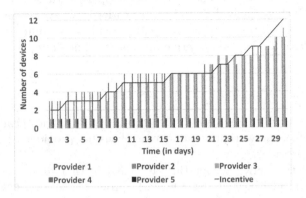

Fig. 4. Number of devices per provider over time with the *Fair* model

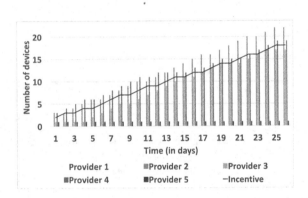

Fig. 5. Number of devices per provider over time with the *Unbounded* model

First of all, Fig. 4 shows how the limit *Incentive* is efficient. In fact, it seems that the maximum number of devices D_{max} tends to get deeply below the incentive I line throughout the time. It shows also why our economic model is fair. For instance, Provider 3 has a single device at the first iteration and has $D_{max} = 11$ devices at the end of the simulation. It proves that *Fair* places no one at a disadvantage. Then, Fig. 5 shows the biggest drawback of the *Unbounded* model: the creation of a monopoly and the difficulty of little providers to grow (Providers 1 and 5 have 2 and 1 devices at the end of the simulation, respectively). It remarks the importance of the I threshold in *Fair*, which avoids the creation of monopolies and the acceleration of differences of importance between providers. Figure 6 shows how providers slowly invest in the network in absence of an incentive.

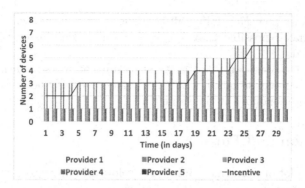

Fig. 6. Number of devices per provider over time with the *Fixed-price* model

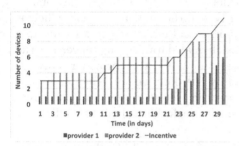

Fig. 7. Number of devices per provider over time with the *Fair* model in a network of 2 providers.

Fig. 8. Number of devices per provider over time with the *Fair* model in a network of 10 providers.

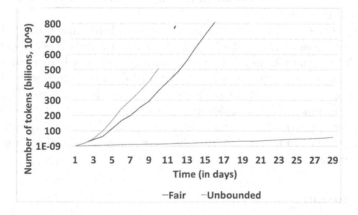

Fig. 9. Mean number of tokens per provider in a network of 10 providers over time.

Finally, Figs. 7 and 8 shows that observations made in Fig. 6 are confirmed by our experiment with other network sizes.

Figure 9 shows how *Fair* fulfils all conditions to ensure a win-win situation since it also makes possible that provider earns tokens faster than with the *Fixed-Price* model.

As a conclusion, we can state that the results of the simulation show how *Fair* ensures a win-win situation where providers invest in the network and earn tokens, avoiding monopoly at the same time.

5   Discussion and Future Work

There are still a lot of work that could be developed in order to test and validate the solution we proposed.

First of all, with the same simulation, it is crucial to design and adopt a more realistic probability distribution in order to model providers' behaviors. In fact, it would help us to evaluate the incentives in the model in a more efficient way. It would also be interesting to test it in a real environment for the same reason, and also for being able to work with real data. For instance, for the results presented in the current paper, it may be noted that provider 3 always buys a lot of devices. This could be caused by the data we are using, as it may give a significantly high number of MB forwarded for this provider. Using real data would allow us to derive more confident conclusions about the efficiency and the "fairness" of *Fair*.

Then, there are several parameters in Sect. 3 that could be analyzed, tested and optimized. For example, it would be interesting to test the use of a quadratic function or to change the definition of the I incentive. Moreover, the definition we give for fairness (incentivize providers to promote the network growth and to prevent monopoly and disadvantages for anyone within the network) could be improved and extended.

Finally, other economic models can be envisaged, because during the development of the experiments we had some ideas about alternatives or extensions. For example, we though about a crowd-funding system where each provider, if he wants to, gives a part of what it should be paid to the network. Then, this amount of money would be given to a new provider when it joins the network, as a "welcome gift". Donation from providers could also be designed as a tax, that every provider has to pay. All these possibilities are potential future work because they can be merged into the *Fair* economic model to build a more complete economic model.

6   Conclusion

In order to address the need of a system which coordinates the economic value flow of mesh networks in a transparent, automated, decentralized and secure way, we designed and implemented a new economic model called *Fair* using MeshDApp.

The goal of the model, presented in Sect. 3, is to create a win-win situation for the network and the users. This aim is enforced by *Fair* because the main idea is "The more devices a provider has, the higher its price per MB forwarded is; up to a certain limit". This incentivizes providers to invest in the network buying new devices and avoids monopoly and inequalities across providers.

The simulation results show that *Fair* makes this win-win situation possible. However, in order to validate completely our proposed solution, protocol design improvements, alternatives and experiments have to be completed as future work.

References

1. Micholia, P., et al.: Community networks and sustainability: a survey of perceptions, practices, and proposed solutions. IEEE Commun. Surv. Tutor. **20**, 3581–3606 (2017)
2. Baig, R., Dalmau, L., Roca, R., Navarro, L., Freitag, F., Sathiaseelan, A.: Making community networks economically sustainable, the guifi.net experience. In: Proceedings of the 2016 Workshop on Global Access to the Internet for All, GAIA 2016, pp. 31–36. ACM, New York (2016)
3. Selimi, M., Rao, A., Ali, A., Navarro, L., Sathiaseelan, A.: Towards blockchain-enabled wireless mesh networks, April 2018
4. Mesh, A.: Althea: an incentivized mesh network protocol. https://altheamesh.com/documents/whitepaper.pdf
5. Right Mesh. Rightmesh. https://www.rightmesh.io/docs/RightMesh_TWP5.pdf
6. AmmbrTech SRL. Ammbr network. https://ammbrtech.com/
7. Castro, I., Panda, A., Raghavan, B., Shenker, S., Gorinsky, S.: Route bazaar: automatic interdomain contract negotiation. In: 15th Workshop on Hot Topics in Operating Systems (HotOS XV), Kartause Ittingen, Switzerland. USENIX Association (2015)
8. Lai, K., Rasmusson, L., Adar, E., Sorkin, S., Zhang, L., Huberman, B.: Tycoon: an implementation of a distributed, market-based resource allocation system. Multiagent Grid Syst. **1**, 12 (2004)
9. Request Network. A decentralized network for payment requests. https://request.network/assets/pdf/request_whitepaper.pdf

BUNKER: A Blockchain-based trUsted VNF pacKagE Repository

Eder J. Scheid[(✉)], Manuel Keller, Muriel F. Franco, and Burkhard Stiller

Communication Systems Group CSG, Department of Informatics IfI,
University of Zurich UZH, Binzmühlestrasse 14, 8050 Zürich, Switzerland
{scheid,franco,stiller}@ifi.uzh.ch, manuel.keller@bf.uzh.ch

Abstract. Current projects applying blockchain technology to enhance the trust of NFV environments do not consider the VNF repository. However, the blockchain's properties can enhance trust by allowing to verify a VNF package's integrity without relying (a) on a Trusted Third Party (TTP) for remote attestation or (b) a secure database. This paper presents BUNKER, a Blockchain-based trUsted VNF packagE Repository, intended to be integrated with traditional database-based package verification environments, acting as a trusted repository containing VNF package information. Moreover, BUNKER allows users to acquire VNFs without the need of a TTP using an Ethereum Smart Contract (SC). The SC automatically transfers license fees to the vendor once a VNF is acquired, and sends the VNF package's link to the buyer before verifying its integrity.

Keywords: Network Functions Virtualization · Blockchain · Repository

1 Introduction

The deployment of Network Functions Virtualization (NFV) [11] solutions faces a major challenge regarding the incorporation of trust to end-users. For example, with the myriad of novel Virtual Network Functions (VNF) being developed, it remains an open problem on how to ensure that the VNF package being acquired by end-users is not malicious and it was not tampered with. Research has been conducted in the NFV computing environment with the introduction of Trusted Platform Modules (TPM) and remote attestation services [12]. Although these systems are able to verify the state of the NFV environment, they rely on a central database to verify the VNF's package integrity. Thus, this centralization enforces end-users to trust in the repository holding VNF packages and presenting a single point of failure and a bottleneck.

Recent Blockchain (BC) developments focused on the provisioning of trust, including Smart Contracts (SC). The BC concept was first described in 2009 in the context of the cryptocurrency Bitcoin [10]. In general, a BC is a distributed ledger where each new appended block contains transactions and information

© Springer Nature Switzerland AG 2019
K. Djemame et al. (Eds.): GECON 2019, LNCS 11819, pp. 188–196, 2019.
https://doi.org/10.1007/978-3-030-36027-6_16

(*i.e.*, the block hash) about the previous block. The most important properties of BCs are their data immutability and data decentralization [16]. The former ensures that once data is included in the blockchain, it cannot be altered or removed; while the latter provides high data availability. These properties form the perfect environment for the execution of SCs. In Ethereum [4], SCs are written in a Turing-complete programming language, called Solidity [6]. This Turing-completeness allows for the creation of complex functions and helps to enforce a variety of contracts through cryptographic principles [1]. Solidity-based SCs can be used to facilitate trusted exchanges between untrusted entities and the correct execution of programmed SC code. These properties can be used in the context of NFV to address trust deficits regarding the VNF package integrity verification.

This paper presents the design of a blockchain-based trusted VNF package repository, called BUNKER, which provides trusted and immutable information concerning VNF packages acquired by end-users. Thus, end-users are not bound to trust on a central trusted authority, but rather on a distributed and highly available data source, *i.e.*, the BC. Moreover, BUNKER allows end-users to acquire VNF packages without the need of a Trusted Third Party (TTP) and automatically BUNKER transfers the license fee to the developer or vendor. To guarantee the integrity of the VNF package, BUNKER stores the hash of the VNF package so that end-users, after receiving the VNF package, can verify whether it had been tampered with. An implementation prototype of BUNKER is available at [9].

The remainder of this paper is organized as follows. Section 2 provides an overview of related work on existing VNF marketplaces and uses of the blockchain technology for management and orchestration in the NFV context. Section 3, presents the design of BUNKER, while Sect. 4 discusses open challenges. Section 5 summarizes the paper and outlooks on future work.

2   Related Work

Currently, marketplaces providing VNF-as-a-Service (VNFaaS) have been receiving attention. FENDE [2] is a Marketplace and a Federated Ecosystem for the Distribution and Execution of VNFs. It presents to the user the compatible VNFs currently listed in a traditional central database-based repository. In addition, FENDE includes NFV management and orchestration tools, which allow users to deploy and manage licensed services in the same ecosystem. T-Nova [16] enables network operators to virtualize their network functions as well as offer them to their clients in an on-demand, per-customer model. This model allows them to provide network services to their customers without having to deploy specialized hardware on the customer's premises. A traditional database-based marketplace is available for customers to acquire and instantiate their required network services on-demand.

BC is independent of any authorization entity and establishes trust between untrusted peers. Moreover, the immutability of public BCs determines a highly suitable feature in areas where audibility is crucial. Thus, these combined properties lead to research regarding the employment of BC in the NFV context.

Virtual Machine Orchestration Authenticator (VMOA) [3] is an authentication model that establishes a trustful Virtual Machine (VM) environment. Instead of having an internal or external trusted authenticator, [3] propose to establish a VMOA BC to offload the authentication responsibility to a distributed ledger. In this system, each orchestration request is sent to a BC, authenticated and only then sent to the virtualization server. If successful, the VM manager reports the success to the BC. Each step is stored in the BC and is auditable. The implementation applies a private BC based on the Hyperledger framework. [13] proposes a BC-based NFV Management and Orchestration (MANO) solution. SINFONIA (Secure vIrtual Network Function Orchestrator for Non-repudiation, Integrity, and Auditability) is designed for data centers in which multiple network services from different clients are deployed. The BC-based NFV architecture addresses all requirements. The prototype implementation shows that the proposed architecture ensures high availability and eliminates the single point of failure. However, it is not clear where the BC nodes are located and which are the incentives for peers to maintain these BC nodes.

There have been efforts in developing marketplaces for VNF packages [2,16]. These lead to the creation of systems where users can access a VNF repository containing various packages that can be deployed easily. However, they are centralized and require that the user trusts in the database solution of the provider. [3,13] address the trust challenge by incorporating BCs into the NFV MANO, while securing the computing environment and the configurations. However, they do not extend to the VNF repository or exploit benefits of relying on a public BC. This leads to a security flaw, where malicious actors can gain access to the central VNF repository to inject malicious code. Even though VNFs are executed in a secure environment, this compromises the security of the entire system. So far, research has shown that a trusted NFV environment should extend to the VNF package repository and that the properties of public BCs are promising to address such a gap. Further, none of the approaches as listed in Table 1 (where ✓ means addressed and ✗ means not addressed) address the combination of *(a)* BC and NFV, *(b)* full decentralization, *(c)* public access, and *(d)* the incorporation of the payment of fees automatically.

Table 1. Comparison of related work

Work	Data storage	Decentralized	Public	Automatic payments
FENDE [2]	Traditional database	✗	✗	✗
T-NOVA [16]	Traditional database	✗	✗	✗
VMOA [3]	Blockchain	✓	✗	✗
SINFONIA [13]	Blockchain	✓	✗	✗
BUNKER	Blockchain	✓	✓	✓

3   BC-based Trusted VNF Package Repository

The proposed architecture of BUNKER is depicted in Fig. 1. It is composed of
two main components: *(i)* the **Graphical User Interface (GUI)**, which is
responsible for user interaction, and *(ii)* the **Smart Contract (SC)**, which
implements the main systems of BUNKER. It is worth mentioning that the NFV
MANO and NFV Infrastructure were not implemented as a third-party solutions
are able to provide them. The description of the associated components and
their internal systems is presented in details in the following sections. It should
be mentioned that BUNKER can be integrated into existing NFV solutions, such
as reverse auction mechanisms to find an infrastructure to host VNFs [7] or
orchestrators able to manage deployed VNFs [2,15].

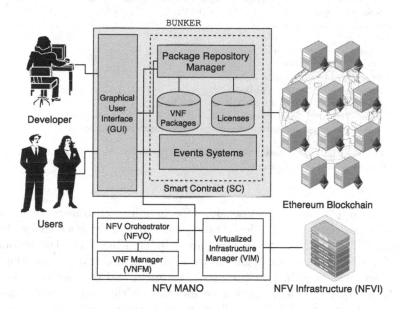

Fig. 1. Proposed BUNKER architecture.

The first component, the **GUI**, is responsible for user interaction and presenting information, such as available and acquired VNF packages, package rating, and prices. Two interaction roles with the **GUI** were identified, *users* and
developers. Users are able to acquire VNF packages to execute in their NFV
environment and submit rates for these packages. Developers are able to offer
their VNF packages by registering them in the repository. Moreover, they can
delete a VNF from the repository or update its information. To provide these
functionalities, the **GUI** implements four systems: *(i) Registration and Upgrade
System, (ii) Licensing System, (iii) Verification System*, and *(iv) Rating System*.

The *Registration and Update System* is used by developers to submit new
VNF packages to the repository. Further, developers can maintain their registered VNF packages, *e.g.*, update the package to a new version or to update

information that is stored in the repository. Table 2 presents relevant metadata and attributes of VNF packages that can be stored in the repository. In addition, the table contains examples of such attributes. This system allows vendors (*i.e.*, developers) to change attributes and to remove a VNF offering from the repository, and users to retrieve attributes from available VNF packages.

Table 2. VNF package information.

Metadata	Attributes	Example
Catalog	Package name	NexGenFirewall
	Description	IPTables-based Firewall with high performance
	Price	1.5 Ether
	Package link	https://github.com/murielfranco/firewall_repository
	Vendor/Developer	University of Zurich (UZH)
	Category	Protection
	Type	Firewall
	Licensing type	Monthly
	Version	1.0
VNF	VNF descriptor	TOSCA standard
	VNF image	Ubuntu-based
	Requirements	1 vCPU, 4 GB RAM, 6 GB Disk
	Suggested platform	CloudStack
Other	Vendor Ethereum address	0x756F45E3FA69347A9A973A725E3C98bC4db0b6a0
	Repository hash	da6e681320812a87fa7da1416119992da0a1e48e485d2f095ad19872fd6d8e1b
	Business model	Fixed price

The *Licensing System* is responsible for handling customers requests to acquire VNF packages. Figure 2 depicts the process of acquiring a package (Function buy_VNF() [9]). First, the user requests, by creating a BC transaction, a license of a VNF package through the front end. In the transaction, the customer includes the licensing fee (*i.e.*, package price) and transaction fees. The SC checks whether sufficient funds were included in the request and transfers the licensing fee to the developer. Then, it reads the package's data from the repository, emitting a licensing event containing the necessary information (*e.g.*, package link) to retrieve the VNF and to execute it in the NFV environment. Finally, the front end captures this event and retrieves the package data from the external data storage to be deployed and used in the NFV environment.

Verifying the integrity of the VNF package before deployment and execution is crucial to ensure that its code was not tampered with or its files were not corrupted. Thus, BUNKER implements a *Verification System*. This system allows verifying the VNF image's integrity by comparing the hash of the downloaded package with the hash previously generated when the package was added to the repository. Such verification can occur when a new VNF package is acquired, where the system retrieves the package and verifies it against the information stored in the trusted repository, or during *runtime*, because BUNKER offers capabilities to re-retrieve the hash and to re-verify the package integrity. This is useful before performing life-cycle operations, such as *upscaling* or *downscaling*,

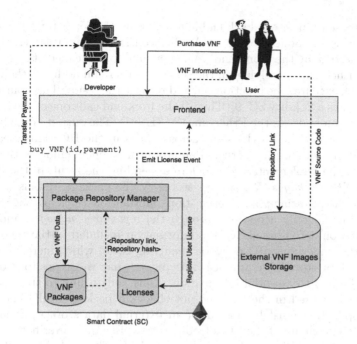

Fig. 2. Data flow of acquiring a VNF package.

to more instances. Also, it allows retrieving the VNF Descriptor (VNFD) to verify the correctness of configuration and life-cycle operations.

BUNKER allows any interested party to register new VNF packages to foster competition. However, there is no curation of the repository's offerings. This leads to a trust issue, as malicious parties may register packages that do not adhere to their specifications. Thus, customers need another way to assess the quality of an offering. For this reason, a *Rating System* was included. It allows licensees to rate a VNF package, providing feedback to future customers. The rating attributes include rating score (*e.g.*, 8.5 out of 10), summary (*e.g.*, VNF executed the promised function), advantages (*e.g.*, quick deployment), and disadvantages (*e.g.*, costly). Unfortunately, language limitations of BC-based SCs pose a challenge to verify the quality of offerings inside SCs. Nevertheless, security verification mechanisms [5] and reputation schemes [8] are planned to be studied to address such a limitation.

The second component, the **SC**, is deployed in the *Ethereum BC*, and implements the functions and data structures necessary to provide a decentralized trusted VNF package repository. This component is composed of the *(i) Package Repository Manager, (ii) Events System, (iii) VNF Packages* database, and *(iv) Licenses* database [9].

The *Package Repository Manager* is responsible for creating, managing, and maintaining VNF packages entries in the repository. It acts as an intermediate party between the user and repository, receiving all requests (*i.e.*, transactions) to the BC-based repository back end and accessing the repository as necessary. Therefore, this component offers an Application Binary Interface (ABI) for all functions needed in the front end. When a function is called, the repository manager authenticates (relying on the sender's Ethereum address) the user and if authorized, executes the function call and returns the result. This component is implemented as a Solidity SC [9]. Thus, if the front end calls one of the functions, it is executed on nodes in the Ethereum VM (EVM). The output of the functions performed by the nodes is the same across nodes in the BC. This means that the SC code is running in a trusted environment, and it enforces the correct execution of the implemented code before appending the result in the BC.

The *VNF Packages Repository* stores VNF package details (Table 2), acquired licenses, ratings, and verification information (*e.g.*, package hashes). This repository is only accessible through the *repository manager*, and as it is implemented on a BC-based SC, the information included in the repository is stored in the underlying BC network, incurring costs, which increase with the amount of data stored. In practice, this means that the repository data size should be limited to essential information. Thus, only a link to the VNF package location is stored in the BC, and not the VNF package itself. The package code or application must be hosted on an external data storage. Even though storing data externally of the BC introduces trust issues, the verification system included in BUNKER allows verifying the integrity of the packages, tackling this issue by storing an immutable hash of the VNF package.

Ethereum-based SCs allow the developers to emit events inside implemented functions. In BUNKER, the *Events System* is responsible to manage and emit events. These events are stored in the transaction's log, which is a special data structure in the Ethereum BC [6]. External applications can listen to specific SC events and perform actions upon receiving such events. BUNKER takes advantage of events by implementing an event named License. This event is emitted once a VNF is acquired and contains information, such as buyer address, VNF image link, and VNF image hash. Thus, the **GUI** constantly listens for this event to present the user with the information about the VNF that he/she acquired. Moreover, other components of the NFV MANO, such as the VNF Manager (VNFM), are able to listen to this License event [9] and automatically clone the VNF image to the user's VNF infrastructure and deploy it. In [14], it is presented the interaction of an NFV infrastructure with an SC.

4   Discussion

As described in [12], determining the VNF package integrity is a critical challenge in the setup of a trusted NFV environment. BUNKER addresses this challenge successfully without having to rely on an external Trusted Security Orchestrator (TSecO). This mitigates the single point of failure. BUNKER is based on an SC without any access control and management. As such, any interested party can use all the functions provided, given that they pay the fee needed to update the SC's state. This means that the SC is fully distributed and without the need for any dedicated management. On one hand, there is no maintenance cost because no fees have to be collected to keep the SC running. On the other hand, there is a potential for spam and fake entries that do not deliver functions promised or infringe on trademarks and intellectual property.

To provide access control and verification of vendors, BUNKER would need to be managed either by a central authority or a consortium. This increases trust in the repository's content, since the manager can verify the authenticity of vendors before any package is registered. Further, such an approach curates the repository's offerings by checking VNF packages for malicious code and verifying that the functionality complies to the specifications. However, the centralized management of the SC and the authorization of participants may be biased and against the intent of BUNKER's distributed nature. The alternative, offloading the management to a consortium, might not mitigate the problem of malicious participants and could still create conflicts of interest. Thus, the current design without an access control and an uncurated repository may face these challenges, but it reflects in full BUNKER's primary goal of removing the need for a central TTP to ensure VNF package's integrity.

5   Summary and Future Work

This paper presented the design of a novel approach for a trusted BC-based VNF package repository, called BUNKER. This repository is designed on top of the public Ethereum BC and is implemented as an SC that stores the VNFs information (e.g., VNF package hash) in the BC and allows developers to register, update, or delete VNFs, and to receive the payment of acquired packages automatically. Moreover, users are able to retrieve the content of the repository, acquire, and rate VNF packages. BUNKER provides a tamper-proof storage and since it is distributed and executed across many BC nodes, there exists no single point of failure. All these aspects contribute toward BUNKER's primary goal of providing a trusted and available VNF package repository to users and developers without the need for a centralized TTP.

Based on the details presented herein, it can be concluded that the integration of employing BCs and SCs provides for a feasible and trusted VNF package repository. However, there are challenges remaining as discussed in Sect. 4 to be addressed. Thus, future work includes *(i)* cost evaluations of BUNKER interactions, *(ii)* a security analysis (*e.g.*, VNF verification methods and cryptography to secure the repository data), *(iii)* extending the data storage to support a distributed file system, and *(iv)* an integration with an NFV solution. Overall, BUNKERas it stands today in its prototype contributes to a better understanding of a BC employment within NFV to secure NFV MANO operations.

References

1. Bocek, T., Stiller, B.: Smart contracts - blockchains in the wings. In: Linnhoff-Popien, C., Schneider, R., Zaddach, M. (eds.) Digital Marketplaces Unleashed, pp. 169–184. Springer, Heidelberg (2018). https://doi.org/10.1007/978-3-662-49275-8_19
2. Bondan, L., et al.: FENDE: marketplace-based distribution, execution, and life cycle management of VNFs. IEEE Commun. Mag. **57**, 13–19 (2019)
3. Bozic, N., Pujolle, G., Secci, S.: Securing virtual machine orchestration with blockchains. In: 1st Cyber Security in Networking Conference, CSNet 2017, Rio de Janeiro, Brazil, pp. 1–8, October 2017
4. Buterin, V.: Ethereum White Paper. https://github.com/ethereum/wiki/wiki/White-Paper. Accessed 23 Apr 2019
5. Demir, O., Xiong, W., Zaghloul, F., Szefer, J.: Survey of approaches for security verification of hardware/software systems. Cryptology ePrint Archive, Report 2016/846 (2016). https://eprint.iacr.org/2016/846. Accessed 4 July 2019
6. Ethereum Foundation: Solidity - Solidity 0.58.0 Documentation. https://solidity.readthedocs.io/. Accessed 28 Apr 2019
7. Franco, M.F., Scheid, E.J., Granville, L.Z., Stiller, B.: BRAIN: blockchain-based reverse auction for infrastructure supply in virtual network functions-as-a-service. In: IFIP Networking 2019, Warsaw, Poland, pp. 1–9, May 2019
8. Gruhler, A., Rodrigues, B., Stiller, B.: A reputation scheme for a blockchain-based network cooperative defense. In: IFIP/IEEE Symposium on Integrated Network and Service Management, IM 2019, Washington, USA, pp. 71–79, April 2019
9. Keller, M.: Blockchain-based Trusted VNF Package Repository (2019). https://github.com/mkllr888/trusted-VNF-repository. Accessed 4 July 2019
10. Nakamoto, S.: Bitcoin: A Peer-to-Peer Electronic Cash System (2009). https://bitcoin.org/bitcoin.pdf. Accessed 22 Mar 2019
11. Network Functions Virtualisation (NFV) ETSI Industry Specification Group (ISG): ETSI GS NFV-MAN 001–V1.1.1 - Network Functions Virtualisation (NFV); Management and Orchestration (2014). http://tiny.cc/NFVMANO. Accessed 1 Apr 2019
12. Ravidas, S., Lal, S., Oliver, I., Hippelainen, L.: Incorporating trust in NFV: addressing the challenges. In: 20th Conference on Innovations in Clouds, Internet and Networks, ICIN 2017, pp. 87–91, March 2017
13. Rebello, G.A.F., Alvarenga, I.D., de Teleinformatica e Automacão, G.: SINFONIA: Gerenciamento Seguro de Funcoes Virtualizadas de Rede atraves de Corrente de Blocos. In: Anais do I Workshop em Blockchain: Teoria, Tecnologias e Aplicacoes (WBlockchain - SBRC 2018), vol. 1. SBC, Brasil, pp. 0–14, May 2018
14. Scheid, E.J., Stiller, B.: Leveraging smart contracts for automatic SLA compensation - the case of NFV environment. In: IFIP 12th International Conference on Autonomous Infrastructure, Management and Security, AIMS 2018, pp. 70–74. IEEE, Munich, June 2018
15. The Linux Foundation: OPNFV: An Open Platform to Accelerate NFV. http://tiny.cc/OPNFV. Accessed 17 May 2019
16. Xilouris, G., et al.: T-NOVA: a marketplace for virtualized network functions. In: 2014 European Conference on Networks and Communications, EuCNC 2014, Bologna, Italy, pp. 1–5, June 2014

Economic Models for Cyber-Physical Systems, Industry 4.0 and Sustainable Systems

Agent-Based Appliance Scheduling for Energy Management in Industry 4.0

Ioan Petri[1](✉), Aida Yama[2], and Yacine Rezgui[1]

[1] School of Engineering, Cardiff University, Cardiff, UK
petrii@cardiff.ac.uk
[2] IMT Mines Albi-Carnaux, Ecole Mines-Telekom, Albi, France

Abstract. With the growing concerns regarding energy consumption, companies and industries worldwide are looking for ways to reduce their costs and carbon footprint linked to energy usage. The rising cost of energy makes energy saving and optimisation a real stake for businesses which have started to implement more intelligent energy management techniques to achieve a reduction of costs. As industries migrate towards more renewable energy sources and more sustainable consumption models, decentralised energy infrastructure is required where actors can manage and monetise energy capabilities.

In fish processing industries, energy is utilised to operate a range of cold rooms and freer units to store and process fish. Modelling thermal loads, appliance scheduling and integration of renewable energy represent key aspects in such industries. To enable the transition towards Industry 4.0 and to efficiently optimise energy in fish industries, multi-agent systems can provide the mechanisms for managing energy consumption and production with standalone entities that can interact and exchange energy with a view of achieving more flexible and informed energy use.

In this paper, we propose a multi-agent coordination framework for managing energy in the fish processing industry. We demonstrate how agents can be devised to model appliances and buildings and to support the formation of smart energy clusters. We validate our research based on a real use-case scenario in Milford Haven port in South Wales by showing how multi-agent systems can be implemented and tested for a real fish industrial site.

Keywords: Multi-agent systems · Appliance scheduling · Energy management · Cost · Smart industries

1 Introduction

With the emergence of distributed energy technologies for smart industries, it has become possible to manage energy more effectively based on the variation of energy profiles and mixes of energy network generation. The democratisation of the energy markets and the adoption of new consumption and production models stimulate urban and rural clusters to engage more actively in new smart grid

© Springer Nature Switzerland AG 2019
K. Djemame et al. (Eds.): GECON 2019, LNCS 11819, pp. 199–207, 2019.
https://doi.org/10.1007/978-3-030-36027-6_17

economies. Developing more informed energy practices using intelligent energy management techniques represents a method to enable users to monitor energy and to participate in a market of energy services actively. Fish industries are high consumers of energy with multiple energy-intensive appliances need to process different quantities of fish where the energy load is allocated to cold rooms and freezer units. To respond to the growing concerns related to energy use in the fish industry, a smart industry model can be implemented as a mean to help fish ports to support self-adaptability, autonomy and more informed use of energy resources. Fish processing sites usually have a cluster of buildings where each building has a set of high energy consuming appliances which need to be scheduled in relation to a fish processing operation demand [1,2].

Multi-agent systems have been proven as efficient solutions for managing energy, processes and operations across industries. Multi-agent systems pose the required autonomics and self-learning capabilities, enabling a wide range of techniques, algorithms and learning strategies needed in decentralised energy systems [3]. As energy actors are dynamic and present a range of key attributes in relation to energy profiles, demand and supply, agents can be efficiently used to coordinate such an ensemble of energy actors in accordance to an Industry 4.0 vision greatly leading to more informed use of energy and reduction of the carbon emissions [4–6]. Multi-agent systems can provide the required level of intelligence for devising smart factories, in the Industry 4.0 mission to integrate products, components and production machines and to change their behaviour accordingly by storing knowledge gained from experience [7].

In this paper, we propose a multi-agent framework for appliance scheduling in fish processing industries to achieve more decentralised and effective energy management in such industries. We present the multi-agent framework with agent properties and objectives for buildings, appliances and site entities alongside the required interaction for energy exchange and coordination. The solution is validated in the context of the Milford Port in South Wales based on which different energy management scenarios have been devised. The remainder of the paper is as follows: The related work on multi-agents for energy management is presented in Sect. 2. In Sect. 3 we present our multi-agent architecture. In Sect. 4 we describe the experimental setup for the evaluation followed by the results reported in Sect. 4. We conclude our work in Sect. 5.

2   Background and Motivation Case Study

Fish processing industries are adopting new distributed energy management solutions to achieve cost reduction while satisfying the energy demand of the fish processing units. Energy use for fish processing industries can be scheduled for direct use, such as lighting systems, heating and box washing machines or indirectly by converting the power to another form of energy, such as cooling cycles, freezing and industry equipment. To efficiently manage energy in fish industries, multi-agent applications can be used to achieve a higher order of "smartness" in energy management as reported in previous works [8–10].

To model such phenomenons in energy networks, agents can use negotiations to coordinate energy sharing and exchange to meet the demanded load of the consumption units while maintaining a level of autonomy in the site. Research studies focus more on large-scale systems where energy is consumed traditionally from the national grid without an in-depth exploration of renewable energy solutions [11,12]. Energy networks with multi-agent systems are also viewed as efficacious alternatives solutions for coordinating large industrial sites with an increasing energy load [13–15].

Milford Haven is the largest energy port in the United Kingdom and is the largest supplier of oil and gas with a capacity to supply about 30% of the UK gas demand. The port operates a fish processing industrial business that conserves and delivers vast quantities of fish to other factories and supermarkets in the UK and abroad. The principal objective of the port is to reduce energy consumption and CO_2 emissions through the implementation of a smart industry solution that can efficiently optimise energy generation and consumption. Packaway building is the main building in the port and includes several energy consuming appliances: an ice machine, a cold storage room, a box washer, lighting systems and meters. A quantity of fish is stored every day in the cold room refrigerating unit that is kept at $-5\,^{\circ}C$ throughout the night and day to preserve the fish. The ice flake produces the required quantity of ice for fish refrigeration, whereas the box washing machine is activated to clean the boxes where the fish is stored. Packaway has installed a PV system on the building's roof with 50 kW panels which serve the building with a daily energy supply.

Scheduling can allow the appliances to be used at the most advantageous time of the day, and to be scheduled based on optimised intervals in alignment with objectives related to energy optimisation and carbon emission. Using multi-agents, we implement a scheduling framework for the Packaway building that can be used to manage energy consumption in the building throughout the day.

3   Multi-layer Agent-Based Simulation Framework

We consider a set of agents $A = \{a_1, a_2, a_3, .., , a_n\}$, where each a_i represents a production or consumption unit within the Packaway building, such as ice-flake, cold-room, box washer and lighting. Each agent a_i also has a set of properties such as schedule, capacity or frequency and a set of constraints such as minimum running time and required start time. Each appliance within the Packaway building has an associated appliance agent a_i whereas the solar panel set-up is implemented by a single solar panel agent. An energy provider agent acts as the grid energy provider in the physical building (see Fig. 1). Each appliance agent has a daily demand for energy with a predefined constraint to consume the amount of energy at the lowest possible price and emitting as little carbon dioxide as possible. To achieve this, the agent can schedule its consumption in one of the four time slots of the day, consuming either solar energy produced by the solar panels of the building or energy provided from the national grid. The solar panel agent simulates the energy production of the solar panels installed on the building and informs the main building agent regularly with the amounts of energy available for appliance consumption. The interaction between the different agents is presented in Fig. 1.

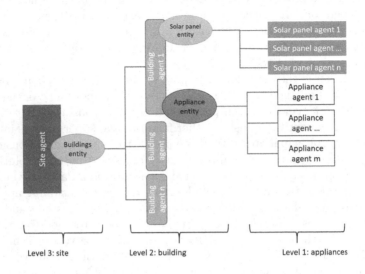

Fig. 1. The multi-agent framework with corresponding layers.

The appliance agents and solar panel agents compose the first level of the multi-agent framework. A building agent is programmed to consume the sum of all its appliance agents' consumption and produces the sum of all its solar panel agents' production. From one level of agents to the next, some of the properties are the same, such as production or consumption, but have slightly different roles and different methods to perform a required set of tasks. The multi-layer architecture also means that an agent decision can have an impact on agents from a different layer. A more detailed presentation of the multi-agent layer is presented in the following subsection.

3.1 Layers of Agents

In this section, the specifications of each layer of agents will be explained and detailed. This will provide a greater understanding of the modelling framework and the policies of interaction between different layers and agents.

The appliances layer is formed of five types of agents. There is one agent designed for each type of physical appliance in the Packaway building and one for the solar panel system. We implement agents specific for these types: 'coldroom' type, an 'iceflake' type, a 'boxwash' type and a 'light' type as well as a 'PVpanel' type where each type matches to a class in the overall implementation. Each agent matches to a physical appliance or a solar panel with a key differentiation between appliance agents and solar panel agents based on energy usage and consumption patterns.

- Static: ID, Capacity, Daily Usage
- Theoretical (dynamic): Schedules, Status
- Practical (dynamic): Consumption, Cost, CO2 emission, Log

Each appliance agent has a set of properties and a set of methods that simulate the behavior of its physical entity (appliance) and enable the interaction of the appliance with other entities in the building with decisions made on daily basis.

The buildings layer – is formed of one type of agent which acts as a manager for the appliance agents and solar panel agents. Each building agent manages a set of appliances and solar panel agents and has identifiers such as ID, weekly usage, appliances, solar panel and grid energy provider whereas the decision-making properties are related to status, production and consumption schedules, prices and CO_2 emission of solar and grid energy. There are three types of properties for a building agent; static, theoretical and practical, as presented below:

- Static: ID, Appliances, Week-usage, Solar panel, Grid provider
- Theoretical: Week-schedule, Status, Solar-schedule, Prices, CO_2
- Practical: Consumption, Production, Cost, CO2 emission, Week-stats, Logs

The building agent has properties that contain a list of appliance level agents and can be both consumers and producers of energy where the consumption consists of the sum of consumption for all the appliances in the building.

A building agent has methods to perform various actions from calculation of bills with appliances and solar panel to information retrieval and decision making and has a set of key methods for collecting information from all the appliances, solar panels and energy provider agents. This permits the building agent to update the prices and CO_2 properties and to make decisions in relation to the optimum operation schedule of an appliance (time to start, operating interval, etc).

The site layer – contains higher level agents that coordinate building agents based on consumption and production objectives. Each site agent is programmed to orchestrate information exchange between the building with a wider objective of sharing energy efficiently within the local cluster.

The decisions of the site agent are similar to an appliance or building agents but with a greater impact on the building agents and associated appliance and solar panel agents. The site agent also saves up site data in its log over which a set of methods operate to take decisions for coordinating lower level agents and to model behaviours throughout the simulation.

4   Evaluation and Results

The multi-agent framework is implemented in Matlab, where each agent is a class with functions and attributes. The multi-agent framework has been calibrated with data from the real site, where each agent has a production or consumption capacity, a set of behaviors and associated constraints. The overall simulation process is organised in three rounds starting with the initialisation of agents, then the execution of the process and lastly the optimisation of appliance schedules.

Step 1: Initialization – is the phase that sets the parameters and configures the environment for the experiments with two operations (i) agent creation and calibration with real site data including appliance agents and solar panel agents and (ii) a message board mechanism enabled to circulate information about the simulation such as prices and the CO_2 emission characteristics.

Step 2: Execution – is the main part of the program and contains the instructions to run the simulation such as the number of weeks, agents and constraints. The appliance agents work on a day time interval divided into four periods, while the building agents work on a week interval divided into several days.

Step 3: Finalization – is the phase that saves the relevant information for all the building agents, all the appliance agents and solar panel agents in a log aimed at capturing the amount of energy that agents have produced or consumed throughout the simulation.

In the experiments, we seek to optimise energy consumption and production using building level agents and appliance level agents designed and implemented based on the observations from data of the Packaway building. We have devised three scenarios where different input parameters are varied in order to observe how different factors simulated with multi-agent behaviours can impact and optimise energy production and consumption and also impacting CO_2 emissions and energy costs in fish ports. The configuration is using a default energy type, a production capacity, a price and a CO_2 emission level such as: (i) solar energy with a 2.5 kWh/day capacity, a 0.10 £/kWh price, a 32 g/kWh emission level and (ii) grid energy type with infinite capacity, 0.15 £/kWh and 66 g/kWh.

Scenario 1: Four Appliances Scheduling Strategy

This scenario investigates a default energy management plan for the Packaway building where all four appliances are optimally scheduled to support the main fish operation with an objective to consume minimum energy consumption. The scheduling mechanism for the appliance agents is based on daily usage and reflects the physical building consumption and production as retrieved from the site investigations. The overall objective of the agents is to collaborate based on a shared scheduling plan, where all the appliance agents schedules are optimised based on the time of the day, demand of fish, demand of ice and energy consumption. The experiment is configured with adequate appliance capacities and usage, as presented below, in order to assess impact on production, consumption, cost and CO_2 emissions. The configuration of the experiment is (i) Cold room with 10 kW production capacity and 70 kWh/day consumption (ii) Box wash with 50 kW capacity and 1 kWh/day, (iii) Ice flake with 32 kW capacity and 50 kWh/day and (iv) light with 0.5 kW capacity and 1 kWh/day.

As presented in Fig. 2, the experiment aims to explore the performance of the building when appliances operate at different capacities and calibration comparing to real site observations. Theoretically, the building should consume 122 kWh

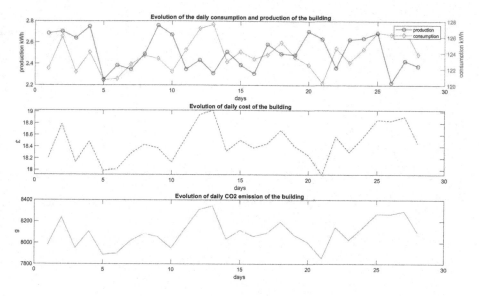

Fig. 2. Energy consumption, production, cost and CO_2 emissions with four appliances.

of energy every day based on the site observations. As we can see from Fig. 2, the daily consumption of the building varies between 120 and 128 kWh. This is a variation of less than 5% of the expected value which demonstrates that the multi-agent framework has the ability to simulate and model any building scenario with high precision and the multi-agent scheduling strategy is beneficial in terms of energy use and cost. In the scenario where four appliances operate at full capacity, the cost of the consumed energy, as well as the amount of CO_2 emitted, are proportional to the energy consumed. This is because the agent function that models energy consumption at the building level is linear as derived from historical building consumption data.

Scenario 2: Scheduling Appliances When Demand Increases
This scenario is meant to test the influence of the demand of energy on the appliances in a day interval where all four of the appliances are in operation. To test the impact of the scenario we have increased the daily energy allowed consumption of the appliances by 25%. The configuration of the experiment is (i) Cold room with 10 kW capacity and 88 kWh/day consumption (ii) Box wash with 50 kW capacity and 1.25 kWh/day, (iii) Ice flake with 32 kW capacity and 63 kWh/day and (iv) light with 0.5 kW capacity and 1.25 kWh/day.

Theoretically, the appliances should consume 153,5 kWh every day and according to the results reported in Fig. 3, energy consumption fluctuates between 150 and 165 kWh. This is a variation of nearly 8% around the desired value showing that when more energy is required for the appliance agents, the scheduling is constrained and less optimization strategies can be implemented to impact the cost and CO_2 emissions. Another general observation on the multi-agent framework is that the simulation loses in accuracy when the amounts of

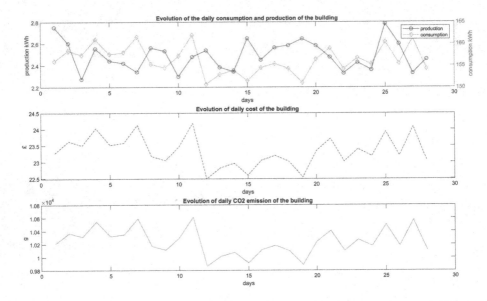

Fig. 3. Energy consumption, production, cost and CO_2 with increased demand.

energy increases which can bring additional constraints when energy needs to be optimally managed at a large scale.

5   Conclusion

In this paper, we present how agent-based appliance scheduling can be used to support more efficient energy management in fish industries. We consider that multi-agents can greatly support energy coordination in energy-intensive industries with great potential to optimise cost and reduce carbon emissions. Through experiments, we explore different appliance scheduling techniques in the attempt to devise a multi-agent based decision support system for energy site managers that is fully aligned with the latest carbon reduction governmental strategies. Fish ports need to exploit the vast potential of data-driven techniques for increasing the informational level in the ports and for enabling a more intelligent decision process as part of the Industry 4.0 transition.

The modeling of different levels of complexity in fish industries can lead to a more holistic understanding of the intrinsic energy processes and help in identifying areas of improvements. We have primarily focused on decarbonising ports and proposed a more economical strategy for managing energy and operations in fish processing industries using multi-agent systems as a mean to pave the way towards implementation of a smart industry model.

We demonstrate how a multi-agent framework can also optimise cost with energy in direct relation with the number of appliances in operation, production units, and building properties. We have also emphasised the essential techniques that can reduce consumption and make more informed use of energy produced in a fish site which can be utilized when developing the smart grid and corresponding business models.

Acknowledgments. This work is part of the EU INTERREG piSCES project: "Smart Cluster Energy System for the Fish Processing Industry", grant number 504460.

References

1. Morstyn, T., et al.: Using peer-to-peer energy-trading platforms to incentivize prosumers to form federated power plants. Nat. Energy **3**(2), 94 (2018)
2. Schleicher-Tappeser, R.: How renewables will change electricity markets in the next five years. Energy Policy **48**, 64–75 (2012)
3. El Nabouch, D., Matta, N., Rahim-Amoud, R., Merghem-Boulahia, L.: An agent-based approach for efficient energy management in the context of smart houses. In: Corchado, J.M., et al. (eds.) PAAMS 2013. CCIS, vol. 365, pp. 375–386. Springer, Heidelberg (2013). https://doi.org/10.1007/978-3-642-38061-7_35
4. Kuznetsova, E., et al.: An integrated framework of agent-based modelling and robust optimization for microgrid energy management. Appl. Energy **129**, 70–88 (2014)
5. Lee, J., Kao, H.-A., Yang, S.: Service innovation and smart analytics for industry 4.0 and big data environment. Proc. CIRP **16**, 3–8 (2014)
6. Nieße, A., et al.: Market-based self-organized provision of active power and ancillary services: an agent-based approach for smart distribution grids. In: Proceedings of 2012 Complexity in Engineering (COMPENG). IEEE (2012)
7. Shrouf, F., Ordieres, J., Miragliotta, G.: Smart factories in Industry 4.0: a review of the concept and of energy management approached in production based on the Internet of Things paradigm. In: 2014 IEEE International Conference on Industrial Engineering and Engineering Management. IEEE (2014)
8. Abras, S., Ploix, S., Pesty, S., Jacomino, M.: A multi-agent home automation system for power management. In: Cetto, J.A., Ferrier, J.L., Costa dias Pereira, J., Filipe, J. (eds.) Informatics in Control Automation and Robotics. LNEE, vol. 15, pp. 59–68. Springer, Heidelberg (2008). https://doi.org/10.1007/978-3-540-79142-3_6
9. Brazier, F., Cornelissen, F., Gustavsson, R., Jonker, C.M., Lindeberg, O., Polak, B.: Agents negotiating for load balancing of electricity use, Amsterdam, Netherlands, pp. 622–629 (1998)
10. Ygge, F., Akkermans, J.M.: Power load management as a computational market. Högskolan i Karlskrona/Ronneby...Kyoto, Japan, pp. 393–400 (1996)
11. Al-Alawi, A., Islam, S.M.: Demand side management for remote area power supply systems incorporating solar irradiance model. Renew. Energy **29**(13), 2027–2036 (2004)
12. Tolbert, L.M., Qi, H., Peng, F.Z.: Scalable multi-agent system for real-time electric power management, vol. 3, Vancouver, BC, Canada, pp. 1676–1679 (2001)
13. Lum, R., Kotak, D.B., Gruver, W.A.: Multi-agent coordination of distributed energy systems, vol. 3, Waikoloa, HI, United States, pp. 2584–2589 (2005)
14. Zhenhua, J.: Agent-based control framework for distributed energy resources microgrids, Hong Kong, China, pp. 646–52 (2007)
15. Dimeas, A.L., Hatziargyriou, N.D.: A MAS architecture for microgrids control, Arlington, VA, United States, vol. 2005, pp. 402–406 (2005)

Leveraging Quality of Service and Cost in Cyber-Physical Systems Design

Christos Kotronis[1(✉)], Anargyros Tsadimas[1], Mara Nikolaidou[1],
Dimosthenis Anagnostopoulos[1], George Dimitrakopoulos[1], Abbes Amira[2],
and Faycal Bensaali[2]

[1] Department of Informatics and Telematics, Harokopio University, Athens, Greece
{kotronis,tsadimas,mara,dimosthe,gdimitra}@hua.gr
[2] College of Engineering, Qatar University, Doha, Qatar
{abbes.amira,f.bensaali}@qu.edu.qa

Abstract. Cyber-Physical Systems (CPSs) comprise multiple cyber-parts, physical processes, and human participants (end-users) that affect them, and vice versa. During the design of such systems, it is critical for the designer to take into account the end-user-perceived quality of provided services, as well as their cost, and integrate them into the CPSs; striking a satisfactory balance between quality and affordability is critical to system acceptance. In this work, we propose a model-based approach, using the Systems Modeling Language (SysML), to explore system design, encapsulating Quality of Service (QoS) and cost aspects, as system requirements, into a core model. Via this approach, the designer can define the system structure, configure it, measure and evaluate the quality, while analyzing cost, and find the best solution(s) for a correct design. As a use case, this approach is applied to a healthcare CPS, namely the Remote Elderly Monitoring System (REMS). In that context, managing REMS QoS and cost requirements, can contribute to an effective system design and implementation, enhancing the end-user satisfaction.

Keywords: Cyber-Physical Systems · Model-based design · SysML · Quality of Service · Cost analysis · Remote Elderly Monitoring

1 Introduction

Cyber-Physical Systems (CPSs) are the integration of cyber parts, e.g., electronic system components like sensors, mechanical components, physical processes, as well as humans, i.e. the end-users that actively interact with them. During the design of such systems, the user-perceived quality of the provided services, as well as associated costs, should be taken into consideration, otherwise the system may perform poorly, inducing high expenses for its operation [2].

While several efforts have been made to design CPSs [8], the majority of them do not integrate and manage quality/cost from the early stages, i.e. from concept, to the final stages, i.e. system evaluation [10]. Among the available approaches,

© Springer Nature Switzerland AG 2019
K. Djemame et al. (Eds.): GECON 2019, LNCS 11819, pp. 208–217, 2019.
https://doi.org/10.1007/978-3-030-36027-6_18

model-based design can facilitate the designer to define and evaluate high-quality systems, providing her the means to incorporate Quality of Service (QoS) [9] and cost in a core system model, configure it, and evaluate the system (based on QoS and cost). Doing this, she can consider trade-offs between quality, usability and affordability, and create an improved and satisfactory system.

In this work, we introduce a model-based approach to effectively design CPSs, evaluating them from a QoS and cost perspective. Specifically, using the Systems Modeling Language (SysML) [17], we integrate quality and cost aspects into a core CPS model, as system requirements. The designer can choose different system design configurations, verify these requirements, and consequently, evaluate the system; if the required objectives are not achieved, the approach enables the designer to explore alternative designs, reaching a better solution. The designer follows a novel iterative step-wise process, starting from the system definition, going to its configuration, and ending to its evaluation. During this process, quality and costs are defined, measured, and evaluated, enabling the designer to check whether the system can satisfy the end-user's needs.

The Remote Elderly Monitoring System (REMS) is employed as a case study for our CPS design approach; it is a healthcare system, used by elderly individuals to measure their vital signs, while their medical condition(s) is being monitored by professional health caregivers [1]. An effective design and implementation of such CPSs [7,15] is crucial, since the elderly patients depend on high-quality healthcare monitoring services, while the system must remain affordable to them; focusing on the balance of quality and costs, results in greater satisfaction, and acceptance from the end-users. We stress that, in contrast to other works (see Sect. 2), our approach enables tuning this balance *by design*.

The paper is structured as follows. In Sect. 2, a short overview of related work is presented. Section 3 contains a description of our model-based approach, while in Sect. 4, this approach is applied to the REMS CPS use case. Finally, we conclude the paper and propose directions for future work.

2   Related Work

The need to design and implement CPSs in various domains has been expressed in [18]. In fact, CPSs should be designed –and implemented– with the goals of (i) providing adequate services to their end-users, while (ii) remaining affordable to them. Related efforts typically focus on these two goals separately [20]; however, their combination during all system stages is (a) crucial [3], and (b) remains an open challenge. For example, QoS is the quantitative index for the overall performance of provided services [9], thus it is important to be taken into consideration during the design, where it should be measured, evaluated, and preserved at a high level [16]. However, if the designer focuses solely on excellent QoS, ignoring the needed costs, the resulting system could be cost-prohibitive.

In [13], the estimation of the system's quality, requires suitable evaluation characteristics for design and analysis. An efficient way to manage quality, is via model-based approaches and a system model perspective [14], that can lead to efficient CPS design and development. While various model-based design techniques for CPSs [10] have been proposed, only few properly model and integrate critical requirements, like QoS, etc. [20] into the system. For example, the authors of [4] investigate specific QoS requirements in CPSs, while depicting some state-of-art CPS QoS models. In addition, in [6], adaptive CPSs are designed via quality requirements and parametric models, verified during system execution.

In summary, incorporating and evaluating *both* quality and cost still remains an unexplored area. To that end, our proposed model-based approach comes into play; we design CPSs, enriched with quality and cost aspects, verifying whether they are satisfied. Different solutions can be explored to reach a satisfactory system design that can balance the user-perceived QoS and cost affordability.

3   Integrating QoS and Cost Requirements into CPS Design

In this work, we focus on the effective design, configuration and evaluation of CPSs from a QoS and cost perspective, which are critical [20] in designing a system with maximal performance and user satisfaction. Specifically, our model-based approach facilitates the designer to construct a core system model, form its structure, and define QoS and cost requirements, that affect the system functionality. With those elements in place, she can explore alternative system design configurations, and evaluate the system, measuring and assessing QoS, while performing a cost analysis. External models can be integrated into the core model, providing additional information to tune or extend the defined model elements; this allows the designer to create a more practical and effective system model.

Having the CPS core model in the center, the designer performs specific actions, summarized in four stages; these form an iterative "design, configure, evaluate" process during system design. In each stage, the designer exploits constructs from the CPS model, while providing input elements –or additional models– to it. The stages are described, in detail, in the following.

Stage 1: Define the System's Structure. The designer constructs the initial CPS model; she specifies the basic components that comprise the CPS, in an abstract fashion. Specifically, an abstract system components model, containing this structure, is created as a SysML Block Definition Diagram (BDD) [5].

Stage 2: Define (a) QoS Requirements, (b) Cost Elements and Related Requirements. This is a crucial stage, since the designer integrates QoS and cost aspects into the system model. Regarding QoS, it is modeled as SysML requirements [5], within a SysML Requirement Diagram (RD) [5]. These requirements may obtain graded values, representing levels of the quality satisfaction; the desired level of each requirement is defined by the designer herself. In parallel, this stage provides an abstract costs model, comprising cost entities; system components estimate the respective cost entities, that are used to measure and hold the components expenses, e.g., their acquisition cost, etc. Following the creation of the costs model, the designer defines related graded cost requirements within a cost RD.

QoS and cost requirements are verified in following stages, based on their levels, allowing the designer to check whether the system provides high-quality services that can fully and efficiently serve its end-users, while remaining afford-able to them. For this purpose, a verification model is applied to the CPS core model, providing verification elements that measure and evaluate QoS and cost.

During this stage, the designer can also create relationships between the requirements and any other model element. The system components satisfy the defined QoS requirements, via "satisfy" connections, while the cost entities sat-isfy respective cost requirements. In addition, the verification elements evalu-ate both system components and cost entities, and verify their corresponding requirements, via respective "evaluate" and "verify" connections.

Stage 3: Configure the System. In this stage, the designer exploits the com-ponents and cost models, and chooses a pre-defined configuration for the sys-tem, that is applied to them. The selected configuration is used to populate the components' properties with specific values that lead to the verification of the requirements, assisting the system evaluation. If the designer desires to, she can select the "best" configuration/solution, that satisfies all or the majority of the defined QoS and cost requirements; this configuration, populates the compo-nents' properties with values that correspond to the "best" system design.

Stage 4: Evaluate the System. At this –final– stage, the requirements are verified and the system is evaluated. To do this, the designer exploits the verification model, using the SysML Parametric Diagram (PD) [5], i.e. a construct within the verification model, in order to check the correctness and performance of the system design, as well as evaluate the system, assessing its QoS and cost. In case the latter are not satisfactory, the designer can explore alternative system designs, in order to reach a suitable solution. The PD's purpose is to exploit the configuration-generated properties, and calculate the real requirement level, that will be compared with the desired one. Requirements which are not verified during this process, failing to deliver the required level, are properly indicated in the modeling environment so that the designer can focus on improving them.

Approach Summary. Figure 1 depicts the iterative design process, the CPS core model and the models/elements "exchange" between them. In each stage, the designer exploits constructs from the CPS model, e.g., abstract components model, and provides input, e.g., components model, enhanced with newly created properties and values, to it. Stages 1 and 2 may be considered as the "entities definition" stages, i.e. the designer defines the structure, QoS and cost entities and requirements, as well as verification elements. Stages 3 and 4 allow the designer to populate these entities with values, configuring and evaluating the CPS. The aforementioned input/output models/elements, along with their rela-tionships, e.g., the components satisfying QoS requirements, create an integrated CPS design model, enriched with structural, QoS, and cost aspects. In summary,

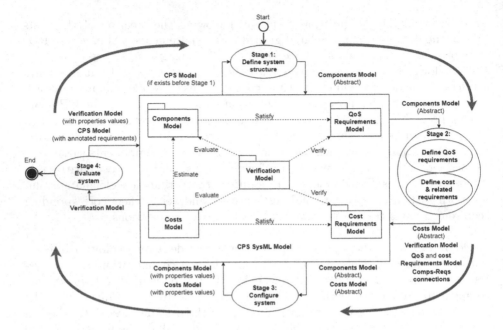

Fig. 1. Model-based approach for designing CPSs.

our approach enables the designer to: (i) define the system model, depicting the system's structure, (ii) focus on the system's QoS and cost requirements specification, as well as their verification, (iii) configure and evaluate the system model via formal methods such as parametric execution –via the PD–, and (iv) explore and decide on alternative design solutions/configurations.

4   Healthcare CPS: The REMS Case Study

In this section, we illustrate the feasibility of the proposed approach to the healthcare REMS CPS, following the associated designer steps. REMS is a representative implementation of a CPS that requires high-quality healthcare services and reduced costs, enhancing its performance and its end-users' satisfaction. As our case study, we focus only on the *Home* subsystem, where the elderly patient resides and operates the medical equipment in the context of the REMS CPS.

Define REMS Home Subsystem Structure. According to previous work [11,12], basic CPS structural elements are the *Device*, representing mechanical or electronic components, the *Aggregator*, typically representing a central unit that collects the Device(s)-generated data, and the *Layer*, i.e. the middle level for the Device(s) and Aggregator connection.

Based on these, the designer creates the REMS Home model, specifying the following structural components: (i) an *Electrocardiogram (ECG)* Device, used to measure and monitor the elderly's heart rate, and detect heart attacks, arrhythmias, etc.; (ii) a *FallDetection* Device, useful for recording the patient's acceleration and orientation, monitoring her body position (e.g., falling or standing); (iii) the Aggregator-type *IoTGateway*, that gathers and processes data, generated from the peripheral Device(s); (iv) the *ElderlyPatientHome* Layer, where the Device(s) and the Aggregator communicate. The latter is a composite component. Here, the ECG, the FallDetection and the IoTGateway are its respective parts, connected with *composition* relationships, forming the REMS Home's structure hierarchy. In Fig. 2, an excerpt of the REMS Home subsystem model is depicted; the white-colored elements represent its components.

Define QoS Requirements for REMS Home Subsystem. Based on [12], specific QoS requirement types allow the designer to define graded QoS requirements in the REMS Home model. In particular, *Time, Security*, and *SWaP* [19] types can be exploited, along with properties that describe them, i.e. a unique *id*, a *text*, and the satisfaction *level* (described in Sect. 3).

In our case, Time requirements, regarding REMS's real-time behavior, e.g., real-time transmission of patient data from medical Device(s) to an Aggregator, are specified. Moreover, Security requirements, ensuring secured data, and SWaP, regarding the components' energy consumption, e.g., battery lifetime, and size properties, e.g, Device portability, are defined. Figure 2 illustrates the blue-colored *RealTimeTransmission* Time requirement, with id = "4", a text describing the need for this requirement, and the desired "real-time" level.

Define Cost Entities and Requirements for REMS Home Subsystem. To design REMS from a cost perspective, and integrate cost aspects into its model, cost entities and related requirements are specified by the designer. Considering a CPS's capital expenditures (CapEx) and operation expenses (OpEx), she can define *CapEx* and *OpEx* cost entities, along with a *value* property, to assess the system components' worth, and a *measurement unit*, i.e. the currency. Similarly to the QoS requirements, *Costing*-type requirements can be specified; cost entities must satisfy these requirements. For example, in Fig. 2, the white-colored *LayerCapEx* holds the Layer's value and currency; thus, the ElderlyPatientHome estimates this CapEx cost entity, which in turn satisfies the *LayerAcquisition* Costing requirement, regarding the components' overall purchase.

Define Verification Elements for REMS Home Subsystem Requirements. Along with the requirements' definition, the designer must designate elements, suitable to verify each requirement, and thus, assess desired QoS and cost levels. To do that, the real QoS (or cost) level value must be calculated, stored, and compared to the desired level. For this purpose, two verification elements are defined; one used for calculation, and the other for storing the real value. A *VerificationReqFormula* is created for each requirement, holding the expression –typically, an inequality– to calculate the real level. These expressions are primarily used in the requirements' verification process, thus, formulas refine the textual QoS/cost requirements. For example, Fig. 2 shows the formula for the patient data

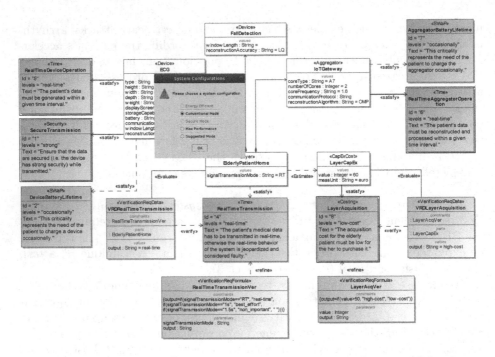

Fig. 2. REMS Home subsystem model configuration and evaluation. (Color figure online)

RealTimeTransmission level. If the corresponding property has "RT" value, then the output level is "real-time"; in case of delay, the value is "best effort" or worse.

Configure REMS Home Subsystem. At this step, the designer configures the system, populating the components' and cost entities' properties with appropriate values; this leads to the system's evaluation. Specifically, the modeling environment provides a list of pre-defined configurations to the designer, allowing her to choose one for each component or the overall system. After her decision is applied, specific components' properties are automatically populated with pre-constructed values, regarding the chosen configuration. For example, in Fig. 2, the designer selects the "Conventional Mode" configuration; in this mode, among other features, patient data is generated, transmitted, and processed in real-time. Upon selection, values related to real-time behavior are automatically incorporated into its properties, i.e. Layer's *signalTransmissionMode* is "RT" (Real-Time), etc. These values are used as input to the VerificationFormulas expression, in order to calculate them and extract the real requirement level.

To assist the designer further, an external tool provides the "best" configuration option; this enables the automated calculation and pre-population of the model elements properties' values, so that all QoS and cost requirements are satisfied, and the designer-specified levels are achieved. When the designer selects this configuration, the calculated results return back to the modeling environment as values that effectively correspond to the "best" system design.

Evaluate REMS Home Subsystem via Its Requirements Verification. At this step, the designer exploits the VerificationFormulas, to calculate expressions, and the *VerificationReqData* elements, as placeholders for the extracted real QoS/cost levels. The PD, mentioned in Sect. 3, is used to receive input parameters, insert them to a formula expression, execute it, extract the resulting value, and store it for further analysis (here, the system evaluation). Each PD is created within a VerificationReqData; this element's only property is the output of the expression's calculation. In addition, these elements verify corresponding requirements and evaluate the system components via respective relationships.

Finally, the –calculated– real requirement level is compared to the desired one, leading to the requirements' verification, and, thus, the evaluation of the system. In Fig. 2, the calculation of the formula that refines the RealTimeTransmission requirement, returned "real-time" as the output value, stored in the related VerificationData; this value is compared to the desired QoS level (also "real-time"). Since the real value is at least as good as the desired value, this requirement is verified. In parallel, regarding the cost requirement, the calculated "high cost" value is worse than the "low cost" desired level. Note that when a requirement is not verified, it is annotated in the model with a red-colored frame. In this case, the modeling environment alerts the designer, recommending appropriate actions she can take, like choosing another configuration.

5 Conclusions

In this work, we proposed a model-based approach to attack the challenge of integrating quality and costs into CPSs, during their design, as well as balance these concepts, in order to provide high-quality system services, while costs remain tolerable for the user. The approach comprises different steps that a designer can follow, enabling her to: (i) create a core system model, enriching it with structural elements, and QoS and cost aspects, in the form of requirements, (ii) configure the system, (iii) evaluate the system, via the verification of the requirements, assessing both quality and costs, (iv) exploit alternative design configurations, improving the user-perceived QoS, and consequently, improving the CPS. This approach was applied to the REMS, a healthcare CPS; the designer followed the workflow from the system concept and definition, to specific REMS QoS and cost requirements specification, to its configuration and evaluation. As future work, we plan to apply the approach to other CPS domains, where designing them from a quality perspective, is crucial for their users.

Acknowledgments. The authors wish to acknowledge Qatar National Research Fund project EMBIoT (Proj. No. NPRP 9-114-2-055) project, under the auspices of which the work presented in this paper has been carried out.

References

1. Baig, M.M., Gholamhosseini, H.: Smart health monitoring systems: an overview of design and modeling. J. Med. Syst. **37**(2), 98 (2013)
2. Brauner, P., Valdez, A.C., et al.: On studying human factors in complex cyber-physical systems. In: Mensch und Computer 2016-Workshopband (2016)
3. Broy, M., Schmidt, A.: Challenges in engineering cyber-physical systems. Computer **47**(2), 70–72 (2014)
4. Dillon, T., Potdar, V., Singh, J., Talevski, A.: Cyber-physical systems: providing Quality of Service (QoS) in a heterogeneous systems-of-systems environment. In: 5th Digital Ecosystems and Technologies Conference, pp. 330–335. IEEE (2011)
5. Friedenthal, S., Moore, A., Steiner, R.: A Practical Guide to SysML: The Systems Modeling Language. Morgan Kaufmann, Burlington (2014)
6. García-Valls, M., et al.: Pragmatic cyber physical systems design based on parametric models. J. Syst. Softw. **144**, 559–572 (2018)
7. Haque, S.A., Aziz, S.M., Rahman, M.: Review of cyber-physical system in healthcare. Int. J. Distrib. Sens. Netw. **10**(4), 217–415 (2014)
8. Hehenberger, P., Vogel-Heuser, B., et al.: Design, modelling, simulation and integration of cyber physical systems: methods and applications. Comput. Ind. **82**, 273–289 (2016)
9. ISO: IEC 25000 software and system engineering-software product quality requirements and evaluation (square)-guide to square (2005)
10. Jensen, J.C., Chang, D.H., Lee, E.A.: A model-based design methodology for cyber-physical systems. In: 2011 7th International Wireless Communications and Mobile Computing Conference, pp. 1666–1671. IEEE (2011)
11. Kotronis, C., Nikolaidou, M., et al.: A model-based approach for managing criticality requirements in e-health IoT systems. In: IEEE 13th Conference on System of Systems Engineering (SoSE). IEEE (2018)
12. Kotronis, C., Routis, I., et al.: A model-based approach for the design of cyber-physical human systems emphasizing human concerns. In: IEEE International Congress on Internet of Things (2019, to be presented)
13. Merino Laso, P., Brosset, D., Puentes, J.: Monitoring approach of cyber-physical systems by quality measures. In: Magno, M., Ferrero, F., Bilas, V. (eds.) S-CUBE 2016. LNICST, vol. 205, pp. 105–117. Springer, Cham (2017). https://doi.org/10.1007/978-3-319-61563-9_9
14. Liu, Y., Peng, Y., et al.: Review on cyber-physical systems. IEEE/CAA J. Autom. Sin. **4**(1), 27–40 (2017)
15. Monisha, K., Rajasekhara Babu, M.: A novel framework for healthcare monitoring system through cyber-physical system. In: Internet of Things and Personalized Healthcare Systems. SAST, pp. 21–36. Springer, Singapore (2019). https://doi.org/10.1007/978-981-13-0866-6_3
16. Mourtzis, D., Vlachou, E.: Cloud-based cyber-physical systems and quality of services. TQM J. **28**(5), 704–733 (2016)
17. Object Management Group - SysML: System Modeling Language (2018). https://www.omg.org/spec/SysML/
18. Sanislav, T., Miclea, L.: Cyber-physical systems-concept, challenges and research areas. J. Control Eng. Appl. Inform. **14**(2), 28–33 (2012)

19. Thales Defense & Security, Inc.: Design considerations for size, weight, and power constrained radios. In: 2006 Software Defined Radio Technical Conference and Product Exposition (2006)
20. Zheng, C., Le Duigou, J., et al.: Multidisciplinary integration during conceptual design process: a survey on design methods of cyber-physical systems. In: DS 84: 14th International Design Conference, pp. 1625–1634 (2016)

Conceptual Modeling for Corporate Social Responsibility: A Systematic Literature Review

Otília de Sousa Santos[1], Patrício de Alencar Silva[1(✉)],
Faiza Allah Bukhsh[2], and Paulo Gabriel Gadelha Queiroz[1]

[1] Programa de Pós-Graduação em Ciência da Computação, Universidade Federal Rural do Semi-Árido (UFERSA), Mossoró, Rio Grande do Norte, Brazil
otilia.santos@alunos.ufersa.edu.br,
{patricio.alencar,pgabriel}@ufersa.edu.br
[2] Department of Computer Science, University of Twente, 7500AE Enschede, The Netherlands
f.a.bukhsh@utwente.nl

Abstract. Enterprises have been challenged to adopt practices of sustainability to benefit shareholders and society with goods standing much beyond monetary profit or required by law. In combination with environmental and economic concerns, Corporate Social Responsibility (CSR) has become an option to leverage businesses with good reputation and to attract sustainability-aware market segments. In line with such a demand, this paper presents a systematic literature review of conceptual modeling studies referring explicitly to certifications, laws or norms of CSR. The more specific research goal of this work is to discover ontologies for representing CSR best practices, design patterns or policies. In total, 921 peer-reviewed papers were analyzed, from which only 17 were considered relevant for data extraction. The main result of this work is the identification of a research gap in explicit knowledge representation of CSR practices for Information Systems design, which ought to be filled to complement the (dominant) economic perspective on sustainability.

Keywords: Conceptual modeling · Corporate Social Responsibility · Sustainability · Ontology

1 Introduction

Normally, corporate strategies include sustainable practices to minimize risks related to the reputation of businesses, market instability or compliance to regulations [1]. According to Carrol (1979), *"for a definition of social responsibility to fully address the entire range of obligations business has to society, it must embody the economic, legal, ethical, and discretionary categories of business performance"* [2]. Corporate Social Responsibility (CSR) creates perspectives on doing businesses that are both profitable and socially rewarding. This definition is extended by Cai et al. (2011), who elaborate on a variation of CSR named Logistics Social Responsibility (LSRS), which is particularly important in Value Chain Management for returning value to society

© Springer Nature Switzerland AG 2019
K. Djemame et al. (Eds.): GECON 2019, LNCS 11819, pp. 218–227, 2019.
https://doi.org/10.1007/978-3-030-36027-6_19

from the extraction of primary resources to the delivery of final products and services to the final consumers [3].

CSR practices can be used by enterprises to leverage reputation in sustainability-aware markets, ultimately leading to profit increase. This paper reports on a systematic literature review on conceptual modeling explicitly referring to certifications, frameworks, guidelines, laws, norms and ontologies for describing CSR practices or business policies. Among all the conceptual modeling approaches, ontologies are of special interest in this research for enabling group communication and establishing the basis for linguistic contracts. Hence, this report is aimed to synthesize the quest for conceptual modeling approaches in general to somehow describe CSR business practices. In Sect. 2, we describe the protocol grounding this systematic review. We describe the review process in detail in Sect. 3. In Sect. 4, present and discuss the review findings and results. Some limitations and conclusions are summarized in Sect. 5.

2 Systematic Review Protocol

The systematic review protocol used in this research combines major guidelines proposed by Biolchini et al. [4] and some minor recommendations defined by Kitchenham et al. [5]. The protocol prescribes *research goal, scope, research questions, search strategy, study selection criteria* and *search terms*, as described as follows.

2.1 Research Goal and Scope

The motivation of this work is an ongoing research project about enriching Value Network Modeling with CSR concepts. Our research goal is to discover and classify contributions on conceptual modeling approaches for CSR. Such contributions might include case studies, certifications, frameworks, laws, modeling patterns, or, in the best case, ontologies for representing CSR business policies or practices. The classification of these approaches will provide an overview of how CSR has been treated by the conceptual modelling community, its development trends, and research gaps. This research goal is twofold: (1) *to identify norms, laws, regulations or standards for categorization of CSR practices or policies*; and (2) *to discovery conceptual modeling approaches, i.e. frameworks, modeling patterns or ontologies for representation of CSR practices or policies*. The themes included in the scope are: (1) *interventions*, e.g., models, norms or laws for CSR; (2) *population*, e.g. studies approaching CSR and social sustainability; (3) *expected results*, e.g. modeling constructs or patterns of CSR; and (4) *application*, e.g., to researchers, managers, entrepreneurs and enterprises interested in structured approaches for modeling CSR practices or policies.

2.2 Research Questions

We are particularly interested in answering the following research questions: *What are the current norms, laws, regulations or standards most commonly adopted as references to elaborate CSR practices in companies? What are the requirements for implementing CSR guidelines in practice? What conceptual modeling constructs (i.e. modeling patterns, frameworks, ontologies, etc.) available for explicit representation of CSR practices and how are these approaches classified?*

2.3   Search Strategy

The search strategy consists of the definition of selection criteria for the literature sources, identification of digital libraries to be explored and definition of search terms. These steps are elaborated as follows.

- **Selection criteria for the literature sources:** we selected these sources based on index scores in Computer Science publications, combined with opinion of scholars and practitioners in the field.
- **Digital libraries:** IEEE Xplore, ScienceDirect, Scopus and Scielo.
- **Search terms:** we followed a process of defining, testing and adapting search terms, as each digital library has its search particularities. Some of the libraries use the search term to match index papers by a few metadata (i.e. title, abstract or keywords). However, some other libraries use the search term to index papers based on a full text search or based on all the metadata describing the publication.

2.4   Digital Libraries

Four electronic database sources were used to extract data for this research: *IEEE Xplore*, *ScienceDirect*, *Scopus* and *Scielo*. Despite the peculiarities of the Web forms provided by the original search string was: ("Social Sustainability" OR "Social Responsibility" OR "Corporate Social Responsibility" OR "CSR") AND ("Ontology" OR "Conceptual Model" OR "Framework").

2.5   Quality Assessment Criteria

Studies were selected based on answers provided to our research questions. Based on those questions, we derived some quality assessment criteria for selecting the papers, categorized as *inclusion criterion* (IC), *exclusion criterion* (EC) and *quality criterion* (QC). *The inclusion criteria* comprised studies about: (1) social sustainability and CSR; (2) experiments of CSR practices in large organizations; or (3) conceptual models, frameworks or ontologies for explicit representation of CSR practices or policies. The *exclusion criteria* subsumed studies that: (1) do not answer any of our research questions; (2) do not treat social sustainability or CSR; or (3) present duplicated, incomplete or inconsistent results. The *quality criteria* regard the impact and provenance of the publication venue and were used to select: (1) peer-reviewed studies published in journals, magazines or conferences, where the average impact factor of the journal publications was 0.8; (2) studies published in papers with more than four pages; and (3) studies published in the time period ranging from 2010 to 2018.

2.6 Study Search, Selection and Classification

The study selection was part of a four-step process illustrated in Fig. 1, comprising the following stages: (1) *search*, where the search strings were submitted to the search engines of the selected digital libraries, recalling 921 papers[1]; (2) *selection*, when 60 duplicated papers were excluded, and titles, abstracts and keywords of the remaining 861 papers were reviewed, from which 711 were excluded; (3) *extraction and classification*, when a full text review was done on the 150 papers and the quality assessment criteria were applied, leaving 17 papers for the final extraction and classification stage. The data extraction aimed to identify information in the publications that could somehow answer our research questions. For each publication, we collected information about the goal of the study, motivation to include the study in the final review, and the form of the conceptual modeling contribution to CSR (e.g. laws, norms, modeling patterns, ontologies or best practices).

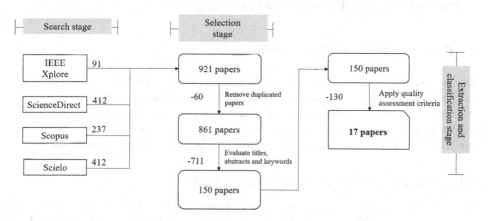

Fig. 1. Paper search and selection process.

3 General Report

The most general finding is that all the 17 studies considered for the final extraction and classification of modelling approaches are aligned with the overall goal of CSR, that is to promote sustainable social development through organizational action, under requirements defined by Ethics, society, shareholders' interests, and compliance to international law and CSR standards. However, a more specific finding is that CSR practices are normally related to many disciplines, such as *Economics*, *Ethics*, *Law* and *Stakeholder's Theories*, to name a few. These disciplines provide different perspectives on how CSR practices can be used to return value to the Enterprise. For instance, *Economic* and *Law* principles for CSR are often referred to as necessary for the

---

[1] A full list of the papers used in this research is available online at: http://bit.ly/2KWIpZN.

short-term sustainability of the organization. Regarding principles of *Ethics* and *Philanthropy*, however, these may leverage corporate reputation in a short-term, but only in a long-term may cause a positive impact on Enterprise sustainability. Moreover, from a *Stakeholder's Theory* perspective, CSR practices normally involve different types of organizational actors, such as business partners, competitors, consumers, government bodies, investors, regulators and shareholders. Nevertheless, the adoption of CSR practices by enterprises may trigger different types of conflicts amongst those organizational actors.

Additionally, it is important to observe the frequency of publications about this topic within the last decade. During the time period considered for study selection, a higher number of contributions to this research topic were published between 2012 and 2014. For reasons falling beyond the scope of this paper, the publication rate of the last year of analysis is equivalent to the one of the first year. Considering that sustainability and its three dimensions (i.e. Economic, Environmental and Social) are concerns of increasing interest for many disciplines, it is questionable why contributions of conceptual modeling for CSR have not evolved progressively.

4   Review Results and Discussion

In this section, we attempt to answer the main research questions of this study by categorizing the final 17 papers selected for data extraction and classification. The studies are organized in two subsections: one for conceptual modelling approaches (i.e. modelling patterns, conceptual frameworks, methods, ontologies, etc.) and another one for laws, norms and standards for CSR proposed by international organizations.

4.1   Conceptual Modelling Approaches for CSR

In Table 1, we summarize the contributions of conceptual modeling found for explicit representation of CSR practices. We indicate the type of Information System artifact and its context of intervention, e.g. experimental validation, implementation or knowledge and technology transfer in real-world assets.

4.2   Norms, Laws and Standards for CSR

Below, we provide an overview of international organizations and CSR documents considered as the most prominent for research in Business Information Systems:

- **Social Accountability International (SAI):** *is a global non-governmental organization advancing human rights at work. SAI's vision is of decent work everywhere, sustained by an understanding that socially responsible workplaces benefit business while securing fundamental human rights*[2].

---

[2] http://www.sa-intl.org/.

Table 1. Summary of conceptual modelling approaches for CSR.

Authors	Conceptual modeling approach	Contribution
Cazeri *et al.* [6]	A *conceptual model* to evaluate the integration between CSR practices and enterprise resource planning in Brazil, validated by experts' opinion	The conceptual model could potentially enhance CSR practices of a company in general
Venturelli *et al.* [7]	A *method* to classify the maturity level of CSR practices implemented by an organization. The method is supported by an expert system implemented with Fuzzy Logics	A CSR implementation score based on aggregation of performance indicators of three areas of the organization: human capital, business strategy and business performance measures
Mitsuzuka *et al.* [8]	A *method* to find CSR activities related to corporate value using a machine learning technique. It used 36 CSR activities from the TOYO KEIZAI database as resources	The method explains how RSC activities related to corporate value might influence one another
Malandrino and Sessa [9]	An *ontology* to describe competences necessary to implement CSR practices in enterprises. The ontology describes patterns of competency that can be used to derive key performance indicators	The ontology was used to formalize organizational practices of CSR that might lead to improvement of business performance
Guimaraes, Severo and Vasconcelos [10]	A *framework* to identify CSR resources on the business strategy level and to formulate Global Reporting Initiative (GRI) indicators	Demonstrated that CSR practices contribute to business success and increases market competitiveness
Yin and Jamali [11]	A *conceptual model* to analyze the business impact of CSR practices implemented by multinational companies operating in China	Evaluated Chinese companies regarding adherence to CSR practices
Hurtado *et al.* [12]	A *tool* that facilitates the construction of a communications framework to adjust the alignment of corporate social responsibility (CSR) in the company-stakeholder relationship	Demonstrated that a fit strategy of CSR practices might have a positive impact on corporate reputation
Krisnawati *et al.* [13]	A *conceptual model* based on GRI, Balanced Scorecard and Performance Prism indicators to asses CSR goals of a company's shareholders	The proposed model helps to assess how CSR practices could benefit each company's shareholder individually

(*continued*)

Table 1. (*continued*)

Authors	Conceptual modeling approach	Contribution
Maas and Rentiers [14]	A *conceptual framework* based mainly on the recently published ISO 26000 standard	A practical tool for organizations to perform self-evaluation and detection of gaps in their CSR policies
Raufflet, Cruz and Bres [15]	A *method* to define CSR practices in compliance to international standards	Evaluated the method regarding its effectiveness for CSR compliance checking
Yaldo et al. [16]	An *ontology* for automatic generation of GRI reports	The ontology is used for checking completeness, correctness and consistency of the concepts and relationships among the data
Na and Jian [17]	A *conceptual model* to assess the influence of CSR on brand value based on structural equation modeling for testing relations among the dimensions of CSR	Reported that consumers' perception on a company CSR practices can improve company brand value
Zhao et al. [18]	A *system* of CSR performance indicators	Provided explicit relations between CSR practices and corresponding performance indicators
Soiraya [19]	An *ontology* to classify Green Information Technology and Communication resources based on CSR reports	The ontology was used to identify patterns of configuration of Green ICT
Friendlieb and Touteberg [20]	A *framework* that involves different groups of stakeholders, both internal and external to a company, in the process of defining and evaluating CSR quality	The framework helps to produce sustainability reports to overcome the shortcomings of existing standards and guidelines
Li *et al.* [21]	A *framework* of indicator for evaluation of CSR practices, based on a blend of concepts proposed by Carol (1991) and found on the ISO 26000 standard	The model helps to assess the capability or maturity level of CSR practices of a company
Xie and Sims [22]	Identified a practical *strategy* for CSR activity management	Predicts that strategy will make multinational companies more proactive to implement CSR practices

- **International Organization of Standardization (ISO):** the ISO 26000 standard[3] characterizes the social responsibility of a company by its decisions and actions taken in benefit of society and environment, followed by ethic and transparent behavior.
- **Global Reporting Initiative (GRI)**[4]: GRI's core products are the Sustainability Reporting Standards, which are made available as a free public good. They have been continuously developed over 20 years and represent global best practice for reporting on economic, environmental and social issues.
- **World Business Council for Sustainable Development (WBCSD)**[5]: WBCSD is a global, CEO-led organization of over 200 leading businesses working together to accelerate the transition to a sustainable world. Their goal is to make member companies more successful and sustainable by focusing on the maximum positive impact for shareholders, the environment and societies.

5 Conclusions and Future Research

This study aimed to survey conceptual modelling approaches for explicit representation of CSR business practices. By applying a systematic literature review protocol, 17 studies addressing this topic more directly were identified in conjunction with some major international standards in the field. Some of these studies have been demonstrated and evaluated as effective on leveraging business with positive social reputation.

The main threats to validity of this study regards constraints on the classification of IT artifacts of interest (i.e. conceptual modelling artifacts) and the type of target publications (i.e., only peer-reviewed publications). To cope with the first issue, this study can be extended with a quest for alternative types of IT artifacts (e.g., business process models, key performance indicators, business values, use cases, business rules, etc.). For the second issue, it is possible to extend this research with non-peer-reviewed publications, e.g., software documentation, surveys, interviews, expert opinion reports or white papers. Yet, the publication rate on the research topic did not increase. This is opposite to global concerns of sustainability on the design of Information Systems.

Finally, only three ontologies were found. Ontologies enable communication and consensus not only in Information Systems, but also among people. The lack of expressive contributions in this field indicates that the conceptual modeling foundations for CSR are still premature and probably scattered through probably conflicting applications in Business Information Systems. Nevertheless, ontology validation is a research area in its own, encompassing tasks such as *verification* (of completeness, correctness and consistency), *conformance checking* (practical, theoretical or technological) and *evaluation* (of acceptance, usability and utility). The three CSR ontologies found in the literature were not reported as a result of formal ontology validation

---

[3] https://www.iso.org/standard/42546.html.

[4] https://www.globalreporting.org/.

[5] https://www.wbcsd.org/.

processes. Therefore, there is a research gap on ontologies for explicit representation of CSR vocabularies to ground the design of sustainability-aware applications in Information Systems.

References

1. Carroll, A.B.: A three-dimensional conceptual model of corporate performance. Acad. Manag. Rev. **4**(4), 497–505 (1979)
2. Carroll, A.B.: The pyramid of corporate social responsibility: toward the moral management of organizational stakeholders. Bus. Horiz. **34**(4), 39–49 (1991)
3. Cai, S., Miao, Z., Xu, D.: Sustainable development: a quest for logistics social responsibility among Chinese manufacturing firms. In: 2011 8th International Conference on Service Systems and Service Management (ICSSSM), pp. 1–6. IEEE (2011)
4. Biolchini, J.C., Mian, P.G., Natali, A.C.C., Conte, T.U., Travassos, G.H.: Scientific research ontology to support systematic review in software engineering. Adv. Eng. Inform. **21**(2), 133–151 (2007)
5. Kitchenham, B.: Procedures for performing systematic reviews, vol. 33, pp. 1–26. Keeled University, Keeled, UK (2004)
6. Cazeri, G.T., et al.: An assessment of the integration between corporate social responsibility practices and management systems in Brazil aiming at sustainability in enterprises. J. Clean. Prod. **182**, 746–754 (2018)
7. Venturelli, A., Caputo, F., Leopizzi, R., Mastroleo, G., Mio, C.: How can CSR identity be evaluated? A pilot study using a Fuzzy Expert System. J. Clean. Prod. **141**, 1000–1010 (2017)
8. Mitsuzuka, K., Ling, F., Ohwada, H.: Analysis of CSR activities affecting corporate value using machine learning. In: Proceedings of the 9th International Conference on Machine Learning and Computing, pp. 11–14. ACM (2017)
9. Malandrino, O., Sessa, M.R.: Ontology-based model sustaining competence management within corporates: competence certification in CSR. In: ICALT, pp. 525–527. IEEE (2017)
10. Guimaraes, J.C.F.D., Sivero, E.A., Vasconcelos, C.R.M.D.: Sustainable competitive advantage: a survey of companies in Southern Brazil. BBR. Braz. Bus. Rev. **14**(3), 352–367 (2017)
11. Yin, J., Jamali, D.: Strategic corporate social responsibility of multinational companies' subsidiaries in emerging markets: evidence from China. Long Range Plan. **49**(5), 541–558 (2016)
12. Hurtado, J.C.H., Ferris, X., Airman, N., Medjidie, D.: Communications and corporate social responsibility: a canvas to build its strategy. In: 2015 10th Iberian Conference on Information Systems and Technologies (CISTI), pp. 1–8. IEEE (2017)
13. Krisnawati, A., Yudoko, G., Bangun, Y.R.: Building a novel model of performance measurement system for corporate social responsibility towards sustainable development. In: 2014 IEEE International Conference on Management of Innovation and Technology, pp. 514–519. IEEE (2014)
14. Maas, S., Rentiers, G.: Development of a CSR model for practice: connecting five inherent areas of sustainable business. J. Clean. Prod. **64**, 104–114 (2014)
15. Raufflet, E., Cruz, L.B., Bres, L.: An assessment of corporate social responsibility practices in the mining and oil and gas industries. J. Clean. Prod. **84**, 256–270 (2014)

16. Yaldo, I., Dong, H., Woodbine, G., Fan, Y.: An ontological model for corporate social responsibility (CSR) reporting based on global reporting initiative GRI G4. In: Proceedings of the 25th Australasian Conference on Information Systems. ACIS (2014)
17. Na, H., Jian, L.: Research on the relationship between corporate social responsibility and brand equity—From the perspective of consumer cognition. In: 2013 International Conference on Management Science and Engineering 20th Annual Conference Proceedings, pp. 870–876. IEEE (2013)
18. Zhao, Z.Y., Zhao, X.J., Davidson, K., Zuo, J.: A corporate social responsibility indicator system for construction enterprises. J. Clean. Prod. **29**, 277–289 (2012)
19. Soiraya, B.: Semi-automatic Green ICT Ontology construction from CSR report. In: 2012 7th International Conference on Computing and Convergence Technology (ICCCT), pp. 711–714. IEEE (2012)
20. Freundlieb, M., Touteberg, F.: Evaluating the quality of web-based sustainability reports: a multi-method framework. In: 2012 45th Hawaii International Conference on System Sciences, pp. 1177–1186. IEEE (2012)
21. Li, C., Zu, B., Li, Z., Zhang, L.: Corporate social responsibility and social responsibility needs of stakeholders. In: 2011 International Conference on Remote Sensing, Environment and Transportation Engineering, pp. 192–196. IEEE (2011)
22. Xie, M., Sims, R.: An analysis of multinational corporations' corporate social responsibility strategies in China from an institutional, stakeholder and social contract perspective. In: 2011 International Conference on Business Computing and Global Informatization, pp. 278–281, July 2011

Resource Management

Efficient Multi-resource, Multi-unit VCG Auction

Liran Funaro[1]([✉]), Orna Agmon Ben-Yehuda[1,2]([✉]), and Assaf Schuster[1]([✉])

[1] Computer Science Department, Technion—Israel Institute of Technology,
Haifa, Israel
{funaro,ladypine,assaf}@cs.technion.ac.il
[2] Caesarea Rothschild Institute for Interdisciplinary Applications of Computer
Science, University of Haifa, Haifa, Israel

Abstract. We consider the optimization problem of a multi-resource, multi-unit VCG auction that produces an exact, i.e., non-approximated, social welfare. We present an algorithm that solves this optimization problem with pseudo-polynomial complexity and demonstrate its efficiency via our implementation. Our implementation is efficient enough to be deployed in real systems to allocate computing resources in fine time-granularity. Our algorithm has a pseudo-near-linear time complexity on average (over all possible realistic inputs) with respect to the number of clients and the number of possible unit allocations. In the worst case, it is quadratic with respect to the number of possible allocations. Our experiments validate our analysis and show near-linear complexity. This is in contrast to the unbounded, nonpolynomial complexity of known solutions, which do not scale well for a large number of agents.

For a single resource and concave valuations, our algorithm reproduces the results of a well-known algorithm. It does so, however, without subjecting the valuations to any restrictions and supports a multiple resource auction, which improves the social welfare over a combination of single-resource auctions by a factor of 2.5-50. This makes our algorithm applicable to real clients in a real system.

Keywords: VCG · MCMK · d-MCK · MCK · Resource allocation · Cloud

1 Introduction

Infrastructure-as-a-Service (IaaS) providers have been using auctions to control congestion via preemptible virtual-machine (VM) instances for nearly a decade [4]. A natural extension of this idea is to auction additional individual resources in an existing VM. VCG[1] [10,18,29] are appealing for this purpose, as they are *truthful*: they incentivize clients to reveal their true valuation of the

---

[1] The auction is named after William Vickrey, Edward H. Clarke, and Theodore Groves.

© Springer Nature Switzerland AG 2019
K. Djemame et al. (Eds.): GECON 2019, LNCS 11819, pp. 231–246, 2019.
https://doi.org/10.1007/978-3-030-36027-6_20

resources, which helps cloud providers accurately price their services. Moreover, VCG maximizes the *social welfare*—the aggregate valuation the clients assign to the chosen resource allocation. For private (corporate) cloud providers, maximizing the social welfare maximizes the aggregate value the in-house clients generate for the corporation [5]. Cloud clients compete for multiple resources (e.g., RAM, CPU, bandwidth), and these need to be combined in a single auction. A single resource VCG auction is computationally hard to solve [25], and a multi-resource auction is more difficult.

Other solutions, besides auctions, were proposed for mitigating congestion. Posted prices (CloudSigma) and burstable performance (Amazon, Azure, GoogleCloud, Rackspace, and CloudSigma) incentivize clients to reduce their requirements and hence reduce the congestion. Spot instances are based on the uniform price auction [2]. VCG (or generally affine-maximizer) mechanisms, however, are the only known truthful mechanisms that maximize social welfare [21,27].

The optimization problem for a single-resource VCG auction can be reduced to a multiple-choice knapsack problem (MCK), which is NP-hard but can be solved in pseudo-polynomial time via dynamic programing [20]. Many approximated, sub-optimal solutions have been proposed for the MCK problem [9,22]. However, for VCG to be truthful, an exact, optimal social welfare must be found [26]. To obtain a more efficient, exact solution for a single resource VCG auction, researchers relax the problem by requiring all the functions that describe client valuations of a resource allocation (henceforth *valuation functions*) to be monotonically increasing and concave [23,24] or usually concave [4]. Others solve the problem for a single resource when only one function is not concave but is monotonically increasing [7]. Concave valuation functions are an unrealistic requirement for cloud clients as their valuation functions have multiple inflection points [8,15,31].

In a real computational system, we may need to allocate multiple resources [12]. To auction multiple resources, we must consider the relationship between them. Usually, computing resources are complementary goods: a client who is willing to pay one dollar for an additional single unit of CPU time and RAM is unwilling to pay anything for each resource individually. Alternatively, the resources might be substitute goods: a client who is willing to pay one dollar for an additional single unit of each resource is unwilling to pay two dollars for both resources together. Thus, in both cases, the client cannot bid in an individual auction for each resource. If this client partitions its budget between two resources, it may win only one or both. A client pays for a worthless bundle if it wins only one of two complementary resources, or if it wins both substitute resources. Such a scenario will also decrease the utilization. Only a multiple resource auction that considers the clients' value for each combination of resources can both optimize the social welfare and be truthful.

Unfortunately, single resource solutions do not apply for multiple resources. The multiple resource VCG auction can be reduced to a multiple-choice, *multidimensional* knapsack problem (MCMK or d-MCK), which to the best of our knowledge has no pseudo-polynomial solutions. Similarly to MCK, MCMK also has many approximated solutions [6,16]. Such solutions provide near-optimal results: the best of them yields results within 6% of the optimal value, which does not guarantee the auction will be truthful and maximize the social welfare. Exact solutions for MCMK have been proposed via branch-and-bound algorithms (B&B) [17,19]; however, their results indicate an implicit nonpolynomial increase in runtime with respect to the number of possible allocations. These solutions were only tested empirically with small datasets and did not scale well for many clients and large, complete valuation functions.

Moreover, MCMK solutions were not designed for a VCG auction and thus do not allow efficient calculation of payments according to the VCG payment rule. To compute a winning client's payment in a VCG auction, the auctioneer must find the social welfare that could be achieved when that winning client is excluded from the auction. Solutions not tailored to VCG must compute the payments by repeatedly finding the optimal allocation for each winning client if that client had not participated in the auction. This implies a worst-case quadratic complexity with respect to the number of clients.

In this work, we implement an efficient, exact, multi-unit, multidimensional resource VCG auction. Two approaches can be considered for this problem. The resources may be treated as infinitely divisible (continuous), as Lazar and Semret [23], Maillé and Tuffin [24], and Agmon Ben-Yehuda et al. [4] do for a single resource. The other approach, which we adopt, divides each resource into identical units of a predefined size (e.g., a single CPU second can be time-shared as 1000 millisecond units). The smaller the units are, the closer the auction's result is to the continuous solution, and the higher the complexity of finding the allocation that maximizes the social welfare.

In the multi-unit, multi-resource auction, agents, representing the clients, can bid using a multidimensional valuation function, which attaches a monetary value to each number of units of each resource. To find the exact solution, the auctioneer must consider all the allocations for the number of agents and the number of resource units available. Since the number of possible divisions of resources between agents is exponential in the number of agents and resource units, iterating over them is impractical.

We present a method for solving a multi-unit, multi-resource auction without any restrictions on the valuation functions, in pseudo-near-linear time on average, over all possible realistic valuation functions, with respect to the number of clients (n) and the number of possible unit allocations for each client (N). Our algorithm's worst-case time complexity is $O(n \cdot N^2)$, as opposed to the worst-case nonpolynomial complexity of the known MCMK algorithms. Furthermore, our algorithm computes the VCG auction payments without repeating the full auction for each winning client. The payment calculation complexity is a function of N and the number of winning clients. It does not depend on the number of clients in the auction (n). Our solution is also applicable to a single resource auction and has a better average complexity than the dynamic programming solution, which is $O(n \cdot N^2)$ [20]. All of the above makes it feasible to choose a VCG auction as a resource allocation mechanism in a real system.

Our contributions are an *optimization algorithm* for the multi-unit, multi-resource allocation problem and an implementation of this algorithm. We numerically analyze its complexity in Sect. 4. We evaluate the performance of our implementation in Sect. 6 and verify the correctness of the results. We validate our results for a single resource with concave valuation functions, by comparing to Maillé and Tuffin's results, and show that separate single-resource auctions produce sub-optimal results, in contrast to multi-resource auctions, which produce optimal results.

2   The Non-linear Optimization Problem

In this paper, vectorized arithmetic operators are defined element-wise. For example, $a + b = (a_0 + b_0, ..., a_n + b_n)$, and $a \leq b \iff \forall i \in 1..R : a_i \leq b_i$. The symbols used in this paper are listed in Table 1.

In an ideal VCG auction, the auctioneer computes the exact allocation that maximizes the social welfare. Each winning client pays the auctioneer according to the damage it caused the rest of the clients—i.e., the *exclusion compensation principle*. This payment rule makes the auction *truthful*: the best client strategy is to bid with its true valuation of the resources. Thus, VCG optimizes the social welfare according to true data about client valuations.

The VCG optimization problem can be described as a non-linear optimization problem (NLP) that is *separable*, *non-convex*, and *linearly and discretely constrained*, as follows:

Separable: The sum of n separable valuation functions is maximized.

$$\text{Maximize:} \sum_{i}^{n} V_i(a_i). \tag{1}$$

Such valuation functions can be represented as a multidimensional vector.

Non-Convex: None of the separable functions (V_i) are required to be convex, concave, or even monotonic.

Linearly Constrained:

$$\sum_{i=1}^{n} a_i \leq m . \tag{2}$$

Discretely Constrained: The resource is not continuous and is divided into units. Each $a_{i,r}$ is a natural number (or zero) that represents the number of allocated units. Only a whole unit can be allocated. Hence, the V_i functions should be defined only on an even-spaced grid of the natural numbers.

3   Joint Valuation Algorithm

Funaro et al. [13] developed the *joint valuation algorithm* for finding the optimal allocation of resources in a single dimension, for monotonically increasing

Table 1. Table of symbols

n	Number of agents
R	Number of resources
m	Number of units for each resource: $(m_1, ..., m_R)$
a_i	Allocation of agent i for each resource: $(a_{i,1}, ..., a_{i,R})$
A	Set of allocations $\{a_i\}_{i=1}^n$
V_i	Valuation function of agent $i \in 1..n$
N	The number of possible allocations on which a valuation function is defined $N = \prod_{r=1}^{R} (m_r + 1)$

functions with $O(n \cdot N^2)$ time complexity. In this work, we extend this algorithm to multidimensional non-monotonic valuation functions, such that it fulfills all the constraints delineated in Sect. 2. While the complexity of a naïve extension is proportional to the square of the number of possible unit-allocation combinations (Sect. 3.3), our extension has a pseudo-near-linear time complexity on average over all possible realistic valuation functions (numerically analyzed in Sect. 4). Funaro et al. [14] prove that the algorithm produces the correct optimal allocation and the correct payments.

3.1 Finding the Optimal Allocation

To find the optimal allocation, two agents are first combined into one effective agent with a joint valuation function (Sect. 3.3). For any number and combination of goods that the two agents will obtain together, the joint function stores the optimal division of goods between them, and the sum of the valuations of these agents for this optimal division. Then another agent is joined to the effective agent, and then another, etc. This process produces a new joint valuation function at each stage, until the final effective agent's valuation function is the maximal aggregated valuation of all the agents. Its maximal value is the maximal social welfare. The optimal allocation is then reconstructed from the stored division data of the joint valuation functions.

3.2 Payment Computation

Our algorithm is efficient in the number of times that the optimal allocation must be computed. To compute a winning agent's payment according to the exclusion compensation principle, the auctioneer must determine the social welfare that could be achieved when that winning agent is excluded from the auction. This can be naïvely computed by repeatedly finding the optimal allocation for each winning agent, without its participation in the auction. Our algorithm, however, reduces the number of repetitions by using a preliminary step. It re-computes the joint valuation function by joining the agents in reverse order to that taken when first finding the optimal allocation. For each winning agent j, the joint valuation function of the rest of the agents is computed by joining the intermediate effective valuation function right before adding agent j, which includes agents $1, ..., j-1$, and the one right before adding j in the reverse order, which includes agents $j+1, ..., n$. The maximal value of this function is the maximal social welfare achievable without this agent, as required for the calculation of that agent's payment according to the exclusion compensation principle.

3.3 Joining Two Valuation Functions

To naïvely join two valuation functions, we need to find, for each possible allocation, how to best divide the resources between the two clients. For each possible allocation of the joint agents $\boldsymbol{a}_j$, there are $\prod_{r=1}^{R}(a_{j,r}+1)$ possible divisions of the resource. To compute the full joint valuation function of two clients, each with N possible allocations, the number of possible resource divisions to compare is

$$\sum_{\substack{\boldsymbol{a}_j \ s.t. \\ \boldsymbol{a}_j \leq \boldsymbol{m}}} \left(\prod_{r=1}^{R}(a_{j,r}+1) \right) = \prod_{r=1}^{R} \frac{m_r(m_r+1)}{2} = O(N^2), \tag{3}$$

for four resources, each with 15 units, $N^2 = 2^{16}$. This number of comparisons will take a few seconds to compute on a standard CPU for each joining of two valuation functions. For many clients, however, this can add up to a full hour.

The complexity of finding the optimal allocation and the payments depends on the complexity of joining two valuation functions. Let $J(N)$ denote the complexity of joining two valuation functions with N possible allocations. Then the algorithm's time complexity is $O(n \cdot J(N))$.

We can reduce the complexity of $J(N)$ by reducing the number of compared allocations. To do so, we filter out allocations that cannot maximize the social welfare. If an allocation globally maximizes the social welfare, then (1) it is *Pareto efficient*: one agent's allocation cannot be improved without hindering another's, and (2) it is also a *local optimum*: the aggregated valuation cannot be increased by taking a resource from one agent and giving it to another.

Formally, the Pareto efficiency property means that if the allocation is optimal, any left partial derivative of any single agent's valuation function is positive: $\partial_{r-}V_i(\boldsymbol{a}_i) > 0$. The local optimum property means that for an optimal allocation, any right partial derivative of any single agent's valuation function is no greater than any of the other agents' left partial derivatives: $\partial_{r+}V_i(\boldsymbol{a}_i) \leq \partial_{r-}V_j(\boldsymbol{a}_j)$. Both are true element-wise for each resource (r) dimension. Since our domain is discrete, partial derivatives are not defined. We will define the left/right partial derivatives as the difference in the values between adjacent points in the allocation space $(dr = 1$ for all the resources).

Using these properties, we restrict the search during the joining of two valuation functions. We first eliminate client allocations in which the left partial derivative of their valuation function in one of the resource dimensions is nonpositive. Second, for each possible allocation of the first valuation function, we only consider allocations of the second function in which the condition on the partial derivative is maintained. To accommodate *boundary allocations* (allocations that reside on the valuation function's domain boundary), where the left or right partial derivative is not well defined, we assign the minimal allocation (zero) a left partial derivative of infinity, and assign the maximal allocation (m_r for each resource r) a right partial derivative of zero. We do this because we cannot assign an agent with less than zero or more than the maximal quantity.

These two restrictions will eliminate most of the resource divisions to $O(N)$ comparisons instead of $O(N^2)$, as shown numerically in Sect. 4 and empirically in Sect. 6. Algorithm 1 describes the joining of two valuation functions.

Algorithm 1. Joining two valuation functions.

Data: V_i, V_j: valuation functions
Result: V_r: joint valuation function, Λ_r: the allocation that produces V_r
1 Initialize V_r and A_r to zeros;
2 Calculate V_i's and V_j's gradients and store them into an array of vectors;
3 Remove allocations such that $\partial_{r-}V_i(a_i) \leq 0$ (for each r);
4 Remove allocations such that $\partial_{r-}V_j(a_j) \leq 0$ (for each r);
5 **foreach** a_i **do**
6   **foreach** a_j *such that for each* r: $\partial_{r+}V_i(a_i) \leq \partial_{r-}V_j(a_j)$ *and* $\partial_{r+}V_j(a_j) \leq \partial_{r-}V_i(a_i)$ *and* $a_i + a_j \leq m$ **do**
7         $v_r \longleftarrow V_i(a_i) + V_j(a_j)$;
8         $a_r \longleftarrow a_i + a_j$;
9   **if** $V_r(a_r) < v_r$ **then**
10             $V_r(a_r) \longleftarrow v_r$;
11             $\Lambda_r(a_r) \longleftarrow a_i, a_j$;
12   **end**
13   **end**
14 **end**

Eliminating allocations that cannot be Pareto efficient (Lines 3 and 4 in Algorithm 1) requires verifying a simple lower limit condition on the left partial derivative in the initialization of the algorithm. The local optimum property (Line 6 in Algorithm 1), however, requires repeated elimination for each loop iteration (Line 5 in Algorithm 1) with different multi-dimensional conditions each time. This can be done efficiently using k-dimensional upper-bound data structure. An analysis of the data-structures for this purpose are described by Funaro et al. [14].

4 Complexity Analysis of Joining Two Valuations

We first show the worst-case time complexity of $O(N^2)$, which may be relevant only in unrealistic scenarios. Then, we analyze the average-case complexity over realistic valuation functions, and find it equal $O(N)$. The actual complexity is dependent on the k-dimensional data-structure construction and query time.

Funaro et al. [14] show that it is bounded by $O(N \log N + \varepsilon N)$, where ε is insignificant.

The worst case complexity of joining two valuation functions is $O(N^2)$, when for every query, the number of matching allocations is proportionate to N. This can happen, for example, when both valuation functions are linear, with an identical slope. Any of the N queries on one of the functions will return every allocation ($O(N)$), as the upper-bound limit is inclusive. This adversarial example, however, is unlikely on a real cloud, with a mixture of clients and valuation functions, and where precise linear scaling is rare. We will thus consider in the following only strictly convex/concave functions, i.e., without any precise linear parts.

To analyze the average case complexity we will assume $N \to \infty$, which approximates a smooth continuous function were the left partial derivative is equal to the right. This reduces the local optimum property to a single rule: for an optimal allocation, all the agents' valuation functions have identical identical gradients.

For concave/convex valuation functions, each gradient vector is obtained at most once. Hence, each query will match at most one allocation. For a function with one or more inflection points, each query will match a number of allocations up to the number of inflection points in the function. The number of inflection points is related to the number of hierarchies in the resource. For example, a CPU might have two inflection points: when switching from a single-core to multiple-cores, and then to multiple-chips. Memory might also have two inflection points when switching between cache, RAM and storage. Five inflection points, however, might be considered unrealistically high for computing resource valuation functions. Thus, we consider the number of possible inflection points for each resource to be a constant as it is independent on the parameters (n, N and R) and is generally small.

Also, we can consider each resource to have inflection points independently of the other resources, e.g., it is possible to switch from a single processor to a multi-processor algorithm regardless of the RAM usage. Thus, if each resource has t inflection points, we can divide the valuation function domain into $(t+1)^R$ sections, each being convex or concave. That is, each gradient vector might be obtained at most once in each of these sections. The actual number of matches is much lower than $(t+1)^R$, and is constant as shown in Sect. 6.2.

We reconcile these differences by showing that the average case, over all possible realistic valuation functions yields a constant number of matching allocations. To do this, we will assume without loss of generality that the partial derivatives on each of the inflection points and in the function boundaries distribute uniformly from zero to the maximal derivative. The partial derivatives of the required gradient will also distribute uniformly with the same boundaries. Then, for exactly two inflection points per resource, we will have three sections, each with different uniformly distributed boundaries. The probability of a single derivative that is uniformly distributed to be in these boundaries is $\frac{1}{3}$, and thus, for each resource, exactly one section is expected to have this gradient. Thus, regardless of the number of resources R, exactly one section is expected to have the required gradient (out of the total $(t + 1)^R$). Since only a single matching allocation exists in that section, the expected number of matching allocations is exactly one.

Furthermore, if we assume that the required gradient has different derivative boundaries, as we would expect in the real world, then a higher number of inflection points will yield a single matching section as well. If the first client's valuation function has a maximal derivative d times higher than the second, then $\lfloor 3 \cdot d - 1 \rfloor$ number of inflection points per resource will yield at most one matching allocation per query. Since the joint valuation function is expected to have higher derivatives with each joining, we would expect d to grow in each step, and thus reduce the number of matching allocations. This yields an average complexity of $O(N)$ over realistic valuation functions.

5 Evaluation

Here we empirically evaluate the algorithm's complexity, and verify that our implementation is efficient enough to be applicable in a real system.

5.1 Implementation Details

We implemented the joint function algorithm and Maillé and Tuffin's [24] algorithm in C++ and Python. The code is available as open source[2].

The joining of two valuation functions was implemented in C++. We implemented the naïve joining in C++ as well. Both implementations accept two R-dimensional tensors, which represent the clients' valuation functions (or effective joint valuation functions), and return an R-dimensional tensor, which is the joint valuation function. The C++ library is called (via a Python wrapper) to join the functions one by one, and the allocation and payment calculations are implemented in Python.

Our C++ implementation of Maillé and Tuffin's [24] algorithm accepts all the clients' bids and returns the optimal allocation. This C++ implementation is called once (via a Python wrapper) to compute the optimal allocations, and then again for each winning client to compute the payments.

5.2 Benchmark Dataset

We considered three different types of datasets: *concave, increasing,* and *mostly-increasing*. We produced 10 datasets of each type, each with 256 clients that participate in the VCG auction. The *concave* datasets contain concave, strictly increasing valuation functions. These datasets are used to compare our results to Maillé and Tuffin's method, where the types of valuation functions are very

---

[2] Available from: https://bitbucket.org/funaro/vecfunc-vcg.

restricted [24]. The *increasing* datasets include weakly increasing valuation functions that might not be concave. This is our main test case as real-life valuation functions may have multiple inflection points [8,15,31]. Valuation functions, however, are not expected to decrease when more resources are offered, if these resources can be freely discarded. The *mostly-increasing* datasets include valuation functions with multiple maximum points (non-monotonic). Such functions will increase for a large part of their input, but may occasionally decrease. They are realistic when the hindering resources are not disposed of, as is the case, for example, when allocating more RAM lengthens garbage collection time and performance drops [4,30]. We use these datasets to show that our algorithm performs well even with non-monotonic functions. We did not test strictly convex valuation functions as they are not realistic.

For each client, we produced an R-dimensional valuation function ($V_i : [0,1]^R \in \mathbb{R}^R \mapsto [0,\infty) \in \mathbb{R}$), which it uses as its bid. We generated R intermediate single-dimensional functions ($v_i^r : [0,1] \in \mathbb{R} \mapsto [0,1] \in \mathbb{R}$) without loss of generality, where an input value of 1 represents the entire available resource r, and an output of 1 represents the client's maximal valuation of the resource.

To compute a client's valuation function—i.e., its bid for each bundle of units—for each single-dimensional function, we sampled a vector sized according to the number of available units for each resource and computed the vectors' tensor product: $V_i = v_i^1 \otimes ... \otimes v_i^R$. This yielded an R-dimensional tensor with values in the range of $[0,1] \in \mathbb{R}$. To produce a valuation function of fewer than R dimensions ($0 < r < R$), we used the same dataset but only with the first r intermediate single-dimensional functions.

We modeled the clients' maximal valuations using data from Azure's public dataset [11], which includes information on Azure's cloud clients, such as the bundle rented by each client. Assuming the client is rational, the cost of the bundle is a lower bound on the client's valuation of this bundle. We modeled the clients' expected revenue using a Pareto distribution (standard in economics) with an index of 1.1. A Pareto distribution with this parameter translates to the 80-20 rule: 20% of the population has 80% of the valuation, which is reasonable for income distributions [28].

For each client, we drew a value from this Pareto distribution, with the condition that the value is higher than the client's bundle cost (i.e., a conditional probability distribution). We then multiplied each client's R-dimensional tensor with the maximal value drawn from the Pareto distribution, to produce the client's valuation function.

5.3   Experimental Setup

We evaluated our algorithm on a machine with 16GB of RAM and two Intel(R) Xeon(R) E5-2420 CPUs @ 1.90 GHz with 15 MB LLC. Each CPU had six cores with hyper-threading enabled, for a total of 24 hardware threads. The host ran Linux with kernel 4.8.0-58-generic #63~16.04.1-Ubuntu. To reduce measurement noise, we tested using a single core, leaving the rest idle.

6   Results

Our algorithm scales linearly to the number of possible allocations (N), for any number of resources, as depicted in Fig. 1. Although the performance differences between the concave, increasing and mostly-increasing datasets were insignificant, we can see that our algorithm performs better on the mostly-increasing dataset. This is because more allocations were eliminated in the preprocessing phase due to their negative left partial derivative. This preprocessing was included in the algorithm's runtime.

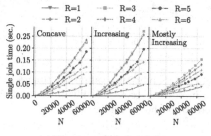

(a) Runtime of each joining.

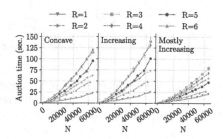

(b) Runtime of a full auction and payment calculation for 256 clients.

Fig. 1. The performance of our algorithm in each of our datasets (concave, increasing and mostly-increasing).

Adding resources results in larger vectors and thus higher complexity; at the same time, more vectors are eliminated in the preprocessing phase. This is why we see an increase in runtime for up to four resources, after which the performance begins to improve.

Figure 1b shows that the multi-resource auction is feasible even in the worst case: for concave/increasing valuation functions, and for three and four resources with 256 clients, a full auction takes less than two minutes for over 60,000 possible allocations.

6.1   Naïve Joining of Valuation Functions

The results show (Fig. 2) that the performance of the naïve approach for joining two valuation functions fits the expected curve, as shown in Sect. 3.3, for any number of resources. Figure 2 depicts the performance for the increasing dataset. The naïve joining is not affected by valuation function properties such as monotonicity. The complexity function, described in Sect. 3.3, passes through all the markers, i.e., fits the actual performance perfectly. Each line, however, had to be scaled by a different factor to fit the markers. This might be an effect of the cache prefetching combined with the C-style multidimensional array representation. The naïve joining compares each allocation a_i to all allocations

a_j s.t. $a_j \leq m - a_i$. For multidimensional valuation functions that are represented as C arrays, we will read the array non-continuously when $a_i > 0$. This will reduce the effectiveness of the cache prefetching as it relies on the continuity of the reading.

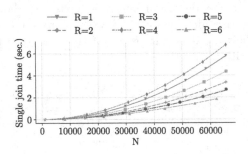

Fig. 2. The performance of the naïve approach for joining two valuation functions. Markers depict the performance with different numbers of resources. The lines are the complexity function described in Sect. 3.3, scaled to fit the markers.

6.2 Ideal Case Analysis

We ran another set of experiments on each dataset, where we counted, in each joining of two valuation functions, the number of allocations that matched the queries of the one valuation function, for each allocation of the other. Figure 3 shows the results. The number of matching allocations converges to a constant number. Thus, were we to have an ideal data structure with reasonable query and construction time, the complexity of joining two valuation functions would be $O(N)$.

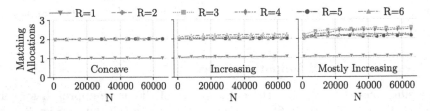

Fig. 3. The average number of matching allocations for each query for each dataset and number of resources.

6.3   Separate Single-Resource Auction

We compared our multi-resource VCG auction implementation to the alternative of performing an auction for each resource separately. We used Maillé and Tuffin's method for a single-resource auction with the concave valuation functions dataset. For each resource r, each client bid its intermediate single-dimensional valuation functions v_i^r (see Sect. 5.2). Each client's maximal valuation was treated as a budget, which was partitioned equally among its valuation functions for each resource. For example, for two resources, a client with a maximal valuation of 10 would have a maximal valuation of 5 for each of its resources.

Such an approach reduces the social welfare by over 60% on average compared to the optimum for two resources (Fig. 4). When more resources are auctioned, the social welfare decreases even further.

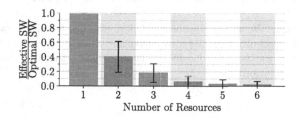

Fig. 4. The social welfare when using a separate single-resource auction normalized to the optimal social welfare. The whiskers represent the standard deviation.

6.4   Verification

To verify our implementation, we compared our algorithm's results with those of Maillé and Tuffin [24] using the concave dataset and a single resource. For all the tested numbers of units (N), our algorithm produced the same allocation and payments as Maillé and Tuffin's method.

We also compared our algorithm's results for two and more resources to those of the naïve implementation. For all the tested numbers of units (N) and resources (R), our algorithm produced identical results to the naïve implementation.

7   Conclusions and Future Work

We introduced a new efficient algorithm to allocate multiple divisible resources via a VCG auction, without any restrictions on the valuation functions. We verified the algorithm experimentally, and showed its efficiency on a large number of resources and its scalability when increasing the number of units per resource.

We analyzed how the different properties of the valuation functions affect the algorithm's performance. We showed that using only concave valuation functions negligibly decreases the complexity compared to increasing valuation functions, and that mostly-increasing ones perform the best.

The Resource-as-a-Service (RaaS) cloud [1,3] is a vertically elastic cloud model that allows providers to rent adjustable quantities of individual resources for short time intervals—even at a sub-second granularity. Our algorithm allows cloud providers to implement the RaaS model. They can deploy a multi-resource auction for allocation of additional resources in an existing VM every two minutes for up to 256 clients in a single physical machine. Our implementation can be adapted simply to use succinct valuation functions that are only defined on a small subset of the allocations. This may greatly improve the performance and might allow a sub-second auction granularity for a large number of clients. A succinct implementation might also support continuous valuation functions with good performance but unbounded complexity. Adapting the implementation for continuous succinct valuation functions is left for future work.

Acknowledgments. We thank Deborah Miller, Sharon Kessler, Hadas Shachnai, Tamar Camus, Ido Nachum, Danielle Movsowitz and Shunit Agmon for fruitful discussions. This work was partially funded by the Hasso Platner Institute, and by the Pazy Joint Research Foundation.

References

1. Agmon Ben-Yehuda, O., Ben-Yehuda, M., Schuster, A., Tsafrir, D.: The resource-as-a-service (RaaS) cloud. In: Proceedings of the 4th USENIX Conference on Hot Topics in Cloud Computing (HotCloud). USENIX Association (2012)
2. Agmon Ben-Yehuda, O., Ben Yehuda, M., Schuster, A., Tsafrir, D.: Deconstructing Amazon EC2 spot instance pricing. ACM Trans. Econ. Comput. (TEAC) **1**(3), 16 (2013)
3. Agmon Ben-Yehuda, O., Ben-Yehuda, M., Schuster, A., Tsafrir, D.: The rise of RaaS: the resource-as-a-service cloud. Commun. ACM **57**(7), 76–84 (2014)
4. Agmon Ben-Yehuda, O., Posener, E., Ben-Yehuda, M., Schuster, A., Mu'alem, A.: Ginseng: market-driven memory allocation. In: Proceedings of the 10th ACM SIGPLAN/SIGOPS International Conference on Virtual Execution Environments (VEE), vol. 49. ACM (2014)
5. Agmon Ben-Yehuda, O., Schuster, A., Sharov, A., Silberstein, M., Iosup, A.: ExPERT: Pareto-efficient task replication on grids and a cloud. In: IEEE 26th International Parallel & Distributed Processing Symposium (IPDPS), pp. 167–178. IEEE (2012)
6. Akbar, M.M., Rahman, M.S., Kaykobad, M., Manning, E.G., Shoja, G.C.: Solving the multidimensional multiple-choice knapsack problem by constructing convex hulls. Comput. Oper. Res. **33**(5), 1259–1273 (2006)
7. Bae, J., Beigman, E., Berry, R., Honig, M.L., Vohra, R.: An efficient auction for non concave valuations. In: 9th International Meeting of the Society for Social Choice and Welfare (2008)
8. Cameron, C., Singer, J.: We are all economists now: economic utility for multiple heap sizing. In: Proceedings of the 9th International Workshop on Implementation, Compilation, Optimization of Object-Oriented Languages, Programs and Systems PLE, p. 3. ACM (2014)

9. Chekuri, C., Khanna, S.: A polynomial time approximation scheme for the multiple knapsack problem. SIAM J. Comput. **35**(3), 713–728 (2005)
10. Clarke, E.H.: Multipart pricing of public goods. Public Choice **11**(1), 17–33 (1971)
11. Cortez, E., Bonde, A., Muzio, A., Russinovich, M., Fontoura, M., Bianchini, R.: Resource central: understanding and predicting workloads for improved resource management in large cloud platforms. In: Proceedings of the 26th Symposium on Operating Systems Principles, pp. 153–167. ACM (2017)
12. Dolev, D., Feitelson, D.G., Halpern, J.Y., Kupferman, R., Linial, N.: No justified complaints: on fair sharing of multiple resources. In: Proceedings of the 3rd Innovations in Theoretical Computer Science Conference, pp. 68–75. ACM (2012)
13. Funaro, L., Agmon Ben-Yehuda, O., Schuster, A.: Ginseng: market-driven LLC allocation. In: Proceedings of the 2016 USENIX Conference on Usenix Annual Technical Conference, pp. 295–308. USENIX Association (2016)
14. Funaro, L., Agmon Ben-Yehuda, O., Schuster, A.: Efficient Multi-Resource, Multi-Unit VCG Auction. arXiv e-prints arXiv:1905.09014, May 2019
15. Funaro, L., Agmon Ben-Yehuda, O., Schuster, A.: Stochastic resource allocation. In: Proceedings of the 15th ACM SIGPLAN/SIGOPS International Conference on Virtual Execution Environments, VEE 2019. USENIX Association, ACM (2019)
16. Gao, C., Lu, G., Yao, X., Li, J.: An iterative pseudo-gap enumeration approach for the multidimensional multiple-choice knapsack problem. Eur. J. Oper. Res. **260**(1), 1–11 (2017)
17. Ghassemi-Tari, F., Hendizadeh, H., Hogg, G.L.: Exact solution algorithms for multi-dimensional multiple-choice knapsack problems. Curr. J. Appl. Sci. Technol. **26**, 1–21 (2018)
18. Groves, T.: Incentives in teams. Econ.: J. Econ. Soc. **41**, 617–631 (1973)
19. Hifi, M., Sadfi, S., Sbihi, A.: An exact algorithm for the multiple-choice multi-dimensional knapsack problem. Cahiers de la Maison des Sciences Economiques b04024, Université Panthéon-Sorbonne (Paris 1), March 2004
20. Kellerer, H., Pferschy, U., Pisinger, D.: Introduction to NP-completeness of knapsack problems. In: Kellerer, H., Pferschy, U., Pisinger, D. (eds.) Knapsack Problems, pp. 483–493. Springer, Heidelberg (2004). https://doi.org/10.1007/978-3-540-24777-7_16
21. Lavi, R., Mu'Alem, A., Nisan, N.: Towards a characterization of truthful combinatorial auctions. In: Proceedings of 44th Annual IEEE Symposium on Foundations of Computer Science, pp. 574–583. IEEE (2003)
22. Lawler, E.L.: Fast approximation algorithms for knapsack problems. Math. Oper. Res. **4**(4), 339–356 (1979)
23. Lazar, A.A., Semret, N.: Design and analysis of the progressive second price auction for network bandwidth sharing. Telecommun. Syst.—Spec. Issue Netw. Econ. (1999)
24. Maillé, P., Tuffin, B.: Multi-bid auctions for bandwidth allocation in communication networks. In: IEEE INFOCOM (2004)
25. Maille, P., Tuffin, B.: Why VCG auctions can hardly be applied to the pricing of inter-domain and ad hoc networks. In: 3rd EuroNGI Conference on Next Generation Internet Networks, pp. 36–39. IEEE (2007)
26. Nisan, N., Ronen, A.: Computationally feasible VCG mechanisms. J. Artif. Intell. Res. **29**, 19–47 (2007)
27. Roberts, K.: The characterization of implementable choice rules. In: Aggregation and Revelation of Preferences, vol. 12, no. 2, pp. 321–348 (1979)
28. Souma, W.: Universal structure of the personal income distribution. Fractals **9**(4), 463–470 (2001)

29. Vickrey, W.: Counterspeculation, auctions, and competitive sealed tenders. J. Finance **16**(1), 8–37 (1961)
30. Yang, T., Berger, E.D., Kaplan, S.F., Moss, J.E.B.: CRAMM: virtual memory support for garbagecollected applications. In: Proceedings of the 7th Symposium on Operating Systems Design and Implementation, OSDI 2006, pp. 103–116. USENIX Association (2006)
31. Ye, C., Brock, J., Ding, C., Jin, H.: Rochester elastic cache utility (RECU): unequal cache sharing is good economics. Int. J. Parallel Program. **45**, 1–15 (2015)

Cloud-Based Integrated Process Planning and Scheduling Optimisation via Asynchronous Islands

Shuai Zhao[1]([✉]), Haitao Mei[2], Piotr Dziurzanski[1], Michal Przewozniczek[1], and Leandro Soares Indrusiak[1]

[1] Department of Computer Science, University of York, Deramore Lane, Heslington, York YO10 5GH, UK
shuai.zhao@york.ac.uk
[2] IBM York, The Catalyst, Baird Ln, York YO10 5GA, UK

Abstract. In this paper, we present Optimisation as a Service (OaaS) for an integrated process planning and scheduling in smart factories based on a distributed multi-criteria genetic algorithm (GA). In contrast to the traditional distributed GA following the island model, the proposed islands are executed asynchronously and exchange solutions at time points depending solely on the optimisation progress at each island. Several solutions' exchange strategies are proposed, implemented in Amazon Elastic Container Service for Kubernetes (Amazon EKS) and evaluated using a real-world manufacturing problem.

Keywords: Optimisation as a Service · Multi-objective Genetic Algorithm · Island model · Amazon EKS · Integrated process planning and scheduling

1 Introduction

In numerous real-world manufacturing scenarios, optimisation of the manufacturing plan and its scheduling seem to be ideally suited to be conducted in a cloud. Firstly, they are notorious to require substantial computation and secondly, as the optimisation process is triggered when a smart factory state changes, the needs for huge computational resources are interleaved with idle intervals. Yet the problem of cloud-based optimisation of realistic industrial problems is relatively unpopular in academia [1]. One of the reasons is the innate heterogeneity of the manufacturing process, as discussed, e.g., in [2], and hence the difficulties in proposing an optimisation framework generic enough to be applicable to a wide range of manufacturing optimisation problems.

The main ambition of the project summarised in this paper is to propose a cloud-based service capable of optimising real-world manufacturing problems ranging from discrete manufacturing (i.e., production of distinct items) to process manufacturing (i.e., production using formulations or recipes). The knowledge description regarding the smart factory and the manufacturing order to be

© Springer Nature Switzerland AG 2019
K. Djemame et al. (Eds.): GECON 2019, LNCS 11819, pp. 247–259, 2019.
https://doi.org/10.1007/978-3-030-36027-6_21

processed can be specified using a dedicated ontology, for example, based on a common ancestor ontology for generic manufacturing domain proposed in [3]. Such ontology can be then used to build an analytic description of a smart factory (aka digital twin), as proposed in [4], which then can evaluate alternative manufacturing configurations as a part of a search-based optimisation process. As this process is executed in the cloud on-demand only, the applied computing resources can be relatively powerful and large in quantity as long as the computation time is not long-lasting. It is then suitable to perform distributed computation in a cluster with several computing nodes. Among search-based optimisation meta-heuristics, the island model of genetic algorithms (GAs) is applicable to distributed execution. In this model, each node evolves a separate subpopulation to preserve the genetic diversity of the entire population. The islands exchange some individuals periodically. Typically, the number of islands is fixed [5]. Although a cloud-based realisation of a traditional island-model is quite effective [6], the underlying synchronous execution of each generation may be treated as a source of potential performance loss due to the risk of island failures, different processing time or communication latency. Removing these drawbacks was our main motivation behind proposing a new, asynchronous version of the island model, where the islands exchange their migrants only through a fast NoSQL database at time points decided by the islands based on the progress of their local optimisation process. A general algorithm is proposed and several migration strategies are implemented, deployed to a Kubernetes cluster (using Amazon EKS) and evaluated based on a real-world scenario, formulated by EU H2020 SAFIRE project partner who was in charge of the evaluation based on a real discrete-manufacturing use case.

The main contribution of this paper can be summarised as follows: (i) proposing a generic algorithm for asynchronous island model with multiple objectives, (ii) suggesting several migration strategies for the proposed asynchronous island model, (iii) proposing a cluster-based architecture following the proposed asynchronous island model in Amazon EKS, (iv) presenting experimental evaluations of the suggested migration strategies based on a real-world manufacturing scenario.

2   Related Work

Genetic Algorithms (GAs) have been arguably one of the most widely-used optimisation meta-heuristics since the seminal work of John Holland in 1960s. In GAs, a population of solutions to a particular problem is improved generation after generation, mimicking the breeding of living organisms. The solutions represented by chromosomes are selected with a probability proportional to their 'fitness', crossed over and mutated. Despite the initial population is randomly generated, the subsequent generations are increasingly closer to the optimal solution. The original GAs were executed sequentially and hence they were notorious for low speed [7]. Several techniques have been proposed to alleviate this problem, including parallel execution of GAs [5,8,9].

The typical parallelisation of GAs can be performed either at the fitness-evaluation or the population level (the island model), performed synchronously following the master-slave architecture [5]. In clouds, these approaches are beneficial only under certain conditions, since the nodes are heterogeneous and connected with links characterised with different latencies. The fitness-evaluation level parallelism is beneficial only for expensive fitness functions [8], whereas the barrier applied in the island model is detrimental when the slave nodes are unreliable or have assorted response times [9]. In order to find approaches more suitable for contemporary cloud clusters, it is beneficial to undust the research related to evolutionary Peer-to-Peer (P2P) computing, as they assume varied response time and nodes' unreliability. For example, in [10], a number of evolutionary strategies for multi-objective P2P optimisation has been evaluated, such as distributed migration decision criterion, exchange topology, number of emigrants, emigrants selection policy and replacement/integration policy. In this paper, we investigate similar criteria but for a different distributed algorithm, cloud architecture and when applied to a real-world manufacturing problem.

In the proposed solution, a custom multi-objective GA has been containerised using Docker [11], similarly as recommended in positional paper [12]. In contrast to that paper, we deployed the containers in a Kubernetes cluster [13]. The islands communicate each other using a NoSQL database rather than an open-source message broker named RabbitMQ. However, the performance of both the solutions is difficult to compare as the authors of that paper provided no implementation details nor the experimental results. In contrast, this paper describes a series of experiments based on real-world industrial scenarios.

Ma et al. employed the population-level parallelisation in [9]. Their solution followed the master-server architecture. The number of slaves was decided statically. Each slave obtained a subpopulation of the size inversely proportional to its CPU utilisation. Then the corresponding fitness values were computed and returned to the master. In the proposed solution, the number of Kubernetes worker nodes is decided dynamically using the auto-scaling facility provided by Amazon EKS, triggered with an alarm monitoring the memory usage of the nodes.

A simple yet interesting proof-of-concept GA implementation described in [14] applied the island model of GA. The islands have been executed in the serverless manner which leverages the scaling capabilities of that solution. However, no implementation details nor experimental results were provided to back the claims regarding the performance of that proposal. The serverless Function-as-a-Service facilities offered nowadays by popular cloud vendors impose strict limitations on a function execution both in timeout and consumed memory. For example, Amazon Lambda in May 2019 was limiting the maximal invocation payload, consumed memory and deployment package size to 256 KB, 3008 MB, zipped 50 MB, respectively. Hence, it is unclear whether the architecture from [14] can be applied in practice with real-world scenarios as analysed in this paper. One of the possibilities of omitting these limits in serverless execution is to use Fission, a popular framework for serverless functions on Kubernetes, as proposed in [6]. However, that paper still followed a traditional master-slave architecture with an innate barrier at the end of each optimisation stage. In contrast, the solution proposed in this paper is fully distributed and the nodes are executed asynchronously. The number of nodes is decided by the Kubernetes horizontal auto-scaler based on the node utilisation rather than the master node as proposed in that paper.

3   Asynchronous Island-Based GA with Migrations

In the island model of GA, the evolution is performed independently on a number of subpopulations by GA instances named "islands". Aperiodically, the islands exchange the migrants. The traditional island model follows a fully synchronous master-slave architecture: the iterations on all islands begin at the same time, triggered by the master node, and the iteration completion is synchronised with a barrier. However, this approach can be modified to be fully distributed. In this section, the asynchronous island-mode GA is depicted in Algorithm 1 with several migration strategies suggested.

Each island in the island mode of GA maintains its own subpopulation. It searches towards the optimal solution within a given number of execution stages, where each execution stage contains a fixed number of iterations. The optimisation engines run in each island are executed asynchronously and do not communicate directly with each other. Instead, they communicate using a light-weight database (see GA Data Service in Sect. 4), pushing their selected solutions at certain time points. At other time points, the solutions pushed by other islands are popped and applied by an island to modify its current Pareto Front approximation. Similarly to [15], a complete migration is performed by a selection and a replacement operator. The former selects the migrants to be pushed to a database and possibly later imported (popped) by other islands, whereas the latter operator selects the individuals in the Pareto Front approximation in an island that will be replaced by the migrants popped from a database so that the same population size is maintained during the entire execution. In each island, the optimisation process stops after evolving a predefined number of generations.

In this paper, four strategies for implementing the selection operator are considered, as enumerated below:

– *Generic selection* does not perform the actual selection from the current Pareto Front approximation but, instead, it randomly generates a new solution. This strategy serves as the performance baseline for the remaining selection operators.

- *Random selection* randomly selects a solution from the current Pareto Front approximation.
- *Best selection* selects the best solution from the current Pareto Front approximation. The solution quality is evaluated with the Generational Distance (GD) performance indicator from [16], which quantifies the proximity of a given solution to the ideal point.
- *Diversity selection* selects the solution with the highest diversity based on the Crowding Distance (CD) value [17], which measures the average distance between the solution and its two closest neighbours in the current Pareto Front approximation.

To maintain a fixed size of each island's population, a certain replacement operator is required to be applied during the migration. This paper considers two replacement strategies:

- *Random replacement* removes a randomly selected solution in the population of the target island.
- *Worst replacement* removes the worst solution in terms of the solution quality based on a certain quality indicator.

With the above selection and replacement operators combined, we provide, in total, eight migration strategies that can be pre-configured before the optimisation process.

Algorithm 1 starts with P randomly generated solutions and then executes for S stages, where each stage contains I iterations. After the GA island is executed in each stage, an approximation of Pareto Front, PF is updated with new non-dominated solutions (if there exist any). Then, a quality indicator[1] is applied to check the quality of the current Pareto Front approximation and is compared to that of the approximation in the previous execution stage. If the quality is not improved continuously over the prior R iterations (i.e., stuck in a local optimum), the Pareto Front approximation is *pushed* to the database by overriding the previous approximation set of this island (if it exists). In addition, after each execution stage that does not improve the Pareto Front approximation, a *pull* operation is performed to get solutions from a Pareto Front approximation from other islands, randomly selected, in the database (if there exits any). Then migrations are performed to migrate M solutions from the selected front to the current population based on a certain selection and replacement operators described previously. Lastly, the PF approximation is pushed to the database as the final optimisation result obtained by this GA island.

---

[1] We do not enforce the choice of quality indicator applied in the algorithm, but assume that a higher quality value indicates a higher quality of the optimisation result.

Algorithm 1. Asynchronous island-based GA

---

inputs   : I: number of iterations; P: number of individuals per island;
           S: number of stages; R: number of maximum stuck iterations in a row;
           M: number of solutions to migrate; CI: quality indicator;
outputs : PF: a *Pareto Front (PF)* approximation;

1 $PF = \emptyset$, s = 0, c = 0;
2 create a GA island with P randomly generated solutions;
3 **for** *s=1,...,S* **do**
4   execute the GA island for I iterations;
5   add non-dominated solutions returned into PF;
6   **if** CI *value of PF obtained after stage (s) is not higher than that of stage (s-1)* **then**
7   increment c;
           if $c == R$ **then**
8   c=0;
9   *push* the PF approximation to database;
           end
10   **for** *m=1,...,M* **do**
11   *pull* a PF approximation from a database;
12   migrate one solution from the remote set to the current population;
           end
       end
   end
13 *push* the final PF approximation to database;

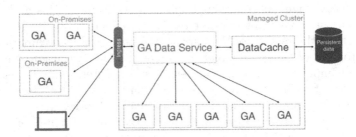

Fig. 1. The architecture of the distributed island-based GA optimisation algorithm.

4   Cloud Deployment

Section 3 described the GA with asynchronous islands. To deploy this algorithm in a cloud environment, the architecture depicted in Fig. 1 is applied. It contains the following components:

- **GA Data Service (data tier)** is responsible for the data communication between islands and storing the data in a persistent data storage.
- **Data Cache** is used to reduce the response time when the data service reads/writes data from/to the persistent storage.

- **GA Island** executes the proposed GA; it can run either on a managed cluster or on-premise.

GA Data Service is highly available and automatically scale out/in according to the load of the requests from GA islands. Additionally, the data cache is designed to use a distributed key/value storage, such as a Redis cluster or Cassandra, to support both high availability and fast data exchange.

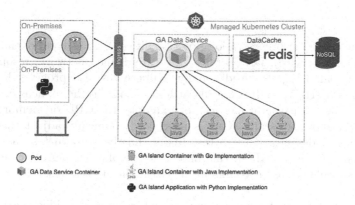

Fig. 2. The architecture of the cloud-base manufacturing Planning and scheduling optimisation system.

The micro-service architecture employed by the proposed solution decouples the components so that the whole solution can be easily deployed to any distributed system. This enables this solution to be provided as a cloud service by cloud providers and requires the minimum possible maintains.

The deployment of the proposed architecture is based on the following assumptions:

- The number of islands that are running at the same time is up to hundreds.
- These islands issue requests to data-tier servers in a sporadic fashion, i.e., the requests (both sending data to or requesting data from the data-tier) arrive with a minimum interval, longer that the data-tier servers' response time.
- The amount of data exchange between the islands and the data-tier is relateively low, up to a few MBs in a single push/pop operation.

In the past several years, Docker [11] and Kubernetes [13] are two popular techniques for containerisation and container orchestration, respectively. Docker allows applications to be shipped to any popular operating systems by creating a Docker image that is similar to a virtual file system so that the application and its dependencies are encapsulated together. A Docker image is instantiated as a running container by the underlying execution-engine, such as Docker Engine or containerd. Kubernetes is a platform running on a computer cluster,

Table 1. Cost of *push* operation with a scaled number of islands (in ms).

No. islands		2	4	8	16	32	64	128
Push	Avg.	2013.78	2012.92	2013.52	2013.79	2016.33	2014.24	2017.78
	Std.	7.61	1.62	1.66	2.20	70.89	31.80	77.69
Pull	Avg.	1000.56	1000.52	1000.54	1000.64	1002.53	1001.49	1002.56
	Std.	0.52	0.51	0.56	0.59	44.79	31.67	44.77

and provide container orchestration functionalities, such as component abstraction (e.g., Pod, Service), DNS service, software-defined network, resource allocation, load balancing etc. Additionally, Kubernetes also provides Horizontal Pod Autoscaler (HPA) to dynamically auto-scale out/in the replicas of a service component based on several metrics, for example, the CPU or memory utilisation. The Cluster Autoscaler (CA) is used to dynamically adjust the number of computing nodes in a Kubernetes cluster. Lastly, Kubernetes allows different plugins to be installed. In this paper, we employ an ingress controller to allow users/applications to communicate with the data-tier service outside of the cluster.

Docker and Kubernetes have been adopted by many providers such as Amazon AWS, Microsoft Azure, Google Cloud, and IBM Cloud. This enables us to leverage the managed Kubernetes services from these cloud providers, rather than installed locally on premises. The Kubernetes HPA and CA enable auto-scaling the components (such as the data-tier service) in our system based on the load. By creating multiple instances of service components, Kubernetes automatically handles the load balancing and re-starts a faulty container once detected. This approach enables the proposed system to be highly available during the operation.

Figure 2 depicts the deployment of the system presented in this paper. The core component is `GA Data Service`, which is responsible for data exchange between islands and also generating reports to users. It has a minimum number of instances by default to provide service high availability and scaling out/in according to the load of the requests. The islands can be implemented using any programming language, and communicate with the GA Data Service via REST API from within the cluster or outside of the cluster through the ingress. The GA Data Service stores all the data into an external NoSQL cluster and uses a Redis cluster as a cache layer.

5   Experimental Results

This section investigates the efficacy of the proposed cloud-based deployment of the GA algorithm based on the asynchronous island management model when applied to the real-world use case described in [4], in which a set of 14 metal

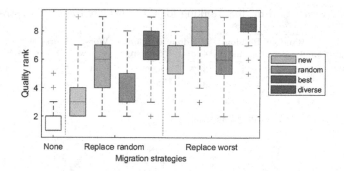

Fig. 3. Optimisation result quality ranking with different migration strategies.

parts is ordered to be manufactured in a plant equipped with 12 Wire Electrical Discharge Machining (WEDM) machines of 3 different sizes, operating in 3 various modes each. The considered optimisation problem is an example of a typical manufacturing planning and scheduling problem that can be found in any discrete manufacturing company. However, the used optimisation engine can be also applied to process manufacturing as described in [1].

We first evaluate the communication overhead of the proposed cloud architecture by measuring the response time of *push* and *pull* operations. The evaluation is conducted on Amazon Elastic Container Service for Kubernetes (Amazon EKS) run on dual-cores t2.medium instances in the AWS US-West-2 Zone spans over its all availability zones. Table 1 reports the average response time (in milliseconds) and the standard deviation for 10,000 push and pull operations. The size of data for each push and pull operations equals 590 KB (i.e., a Pareto Front approximation with 50 elements). According to the results, the overhead incurred due to communication is relatively even despite increasing the number of asynchronous islands, which repeatably issue asynchronous push and pull requests to the data service. As observed, a push operation takes about 2 s and a pull operation needs about 1 s to complete regardless the number of islands.

The following experiment investigates the efficiency of the proposed optimisation algorithm (recall Algorithm 1) with eight migration strategies described in Sect. 3. The optimisation algorithm is configured with $S = 40$, $P = 50$, $I = 20$, $R = 3$, $M = 1$. The Diversity Comparator Indicator (DCI) [18] has been used as the quality indicator CI for measuring the quality of Pareto Front approximations obtained in the subsequent execution stages. DCI quantifies the diversity of the given approximation similarly as in [1]. Five asynchronous islands have been created in the Kubernetes cluster. In total, 100 test cases have been performed for each migration strategy. A ranking has been constructed for Pareto Front approximations obtained by the evaluated migration strategies in a way that each strategy has received the number of points equal to the number of strategies with lower or equal DCI value.

As shown in Fig. 3, the strategy without any migrations (i.e., box *None*) has yielded the result with the worst quality among all the tested strategies.

Table 2. Average and median ranking for the considered migration strategies.

Migration strategy	No migration	Random + new	Random + random	Random + best	Random + diversity	Worst + new	Worst + random	Worst + best	Worst + diversity
Avg	1.596	3.38	5.73	3.75	6.69	5.44	7.82	5.74	8.22
Med	1	3	6	3	7	5	8	6	9

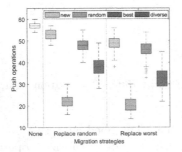 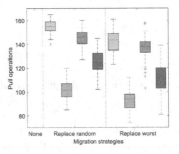

Fig. 4. Push (9 leftmost boxes) and pull (8 rightmost boxes) requests made by each migration method.

This result was expected as in this strategy there is no communication with other islands and hence it cannot obtain the performance boost via importing non-dominated solutions from other subpopulations (islands). The strategies with the random replacement operator have outperformed the ones applying the worst replacement operator (i.e., *replace worst*) regardless of the selection operator. The *diversity selection* and *best selection* operators have outperformed the remaining selection operators. In accordance with the results presented in [15], migration of the best solution has not been profitable mainly due to the risk of the premature convergence of the entire subpopulation. Instead, migration of the solutions likely to improve the Pareto Front approximation diversity (i.e., *diversity selection* and *random selection* operators) is more beneficial in the studied problem.

Table 2 summarises the average and median ranking values of all the competing strategies. As given in the table, both *random selection* and *diversity selection* operators provide higher quality ranks in average and median values. As expected, the strategy without migration has ranked the lowest. In addition, the *worst replacement* operator has yielded a better average and median quality ranking values than the *random replacement* strategy for each selection strategy. These results are in line with the results presented in Fig. 3. In addition, all the above observations have yielded a statistically significant difference according to the Sign Test with p-value threshold for statistical significance equal to 0.02.

Figure 4 reports the numbers of push and pull operations issued by each strategy. The importance of these metrics stems from the cloud communication overhead as shown earlier in Table 1. As shown on the left hand side of the figure, the *no migration, new selection* and *best selection* operators have led to a larger number of push operations than the *random selection* and *diversity selection*

Table 3. DCI comparison of the considered migration strategies.

M	None	Random + new	Random + random	Random + best	Random + diversity	Worst + new	Worst + random	Worst + best	Worst + diversity
1	0.294	0.294	0.294	0.294	0.412	0.294	0.529	0.353	0.706
2	0	0	0.048	0	0.19	0.238	0.381	0.143	0.333
3	0	0	0.143	0	0.238	0.095	0.095	0.048	0.619
4	0	0.042	0.125	0.125	0.25	0.125	0.042	0.042	0.292
5	0	0.08	0.12	0	0.28	0.12	0.12	0.04	0.24

operators. This observation indicates that the algorithm applying the former three operators is less likely to escape from local optima since both the push and pull operations are issued when an island has not improved its Pareto Front approximation for a given number of execution stages. In addition, although the *diversity selection* operator has yielded more communication requests than the *random selection* operator, it has usually led to better optimisation results (recall Fig. 3). This observation indicates that its relatively heavy communication is beneficial.

Table 3 gives the DCI quality indicator for the strategies with different numbers of solutions transferred during one migration (as specified by parameter M in Algorithm 1). Again, the *diversity selection* operator has led to the best results for all the considered M values and both the replacement operators.

In Table 4, DCI values comparing the Pareto Front approximations for different numbers of migrants, M, are presented. From this table, it can be concluded that an increased number of solutions migrated improves the final solution quality. However, having more migrants impose higher communication overheads in the cloud, as discussed earlier in this section.

Standard Amazon EC2 instances have been used as Amazon EKS worker nodes. Their ECUs[2] ranged from 13 to 68. On average, execution of a single stage has taken about 900s and hence the total EC2 cost (including the data transfer cost) has not exceeded 10 USD in any case. Additionally, AWS charged 0.20 USD per hour for using an Amazon EKS cluster in May 2019[3]. These costs

Table 4. DCI quality changes with an increased number of migrations in one *pull*.

M	Replace random					Replace worst				
	1	2	3	4	5	1	2	3	4	5
Random	0	0.292	0.208	0.292	0.333	0.13	0.174	0.304	0.304	0.348
Best	0.043	0.217	0.13	0.478	0.304	0.316	0.158	0.316	0.316	0.526
Diversity	0.115	0.154	0.308	0.308	0.192	0.083	0.208	0.292	0.25	0.375

---

[2] 1 ECU is defined as the compute power of a 1.0–1.2 GHz server CPU from 2007.
[3] The current costs can be found at https://aws.amazon.com/eks/pricing/.

are just 0.02 per cent of the total production cost of the considered parts and hence it is negligible for our business partner.

6   Conclusion

In this paper, a GA for multi-objective optimisation using asynchronous islands have been proposed. The software implementation of these algorithms has been deployed to a Kubernetes cluster (in Amazon EKS) and applied to an integrated process planning and scheduling for a real-world smart factory representing the discrete manufacturing branch. Several migration strategies have been evaluated and the most favourable selection and replacement operators have been identified. Similarly, various numbers of migrants have been analysed.

In our future work, we plan to investigate migration topologies different from the fully connected graph used in this paper, e.g. a ring. A custom scaling of the number of island based on the optimisation state is also planned. Finally, a larger set of real-world manufacturing problems is planned to be evaluated.

Acknowledgements. The authors acknowledge the support of the EU H2020 SAFIRE project (Ref. 723634).

References

1. Dziurzanski, P., Zhao, S., Swan, J., Indrusiak, L.S., Scholze, S., Krone, K.: Solving the multi-objective flexible job-shop scheduling problem with alternative recipes for a chemical production process. In: Kaufmann, P., Castillo, P.A. (eds.) EvoApplications 2019. LNCS, vol. 11454, pp. 33–48. Springer, Cham (2019). https://doi.org/10.1007/978-3-030-16692-2_3
2. Méndez, C.A., et al.: State-of-the-art review of optimization methods for short-term scheduling of batch processes. Comput. Chem. Eng. **30**(6–7), 913–946 (2006)
3. Lemaignan, S., Siadat, A., Dantan, J., Semenenko, A.: MASON: a proposal for an ontology of manufacturing domain. In: IEEE Workshop on Distributed Intelligent Systems: Collective Intelligence and Its Applications (DIS 2006), pp. 195–200, June 2006
4. Dziurzanski, P., Swan, J., Indrusiak, L.S., Ramos, J.: Implementing digital twins of smart factories with interval algebra. In: 2019 IEEE International Conference on Industrial Technology, ICIT 2019 (2019)
5. Di Martino, S., Ferrucci, F., Maggio, V., Sarro, F.: Towards migrating genetic algorithms for test data generation to the cloud (2012)
6. Zhao, S., Dziurzanski, P., Przewozniczek, M., Komarnicki, M., Indrusiak, L.S.: Cloud-based dynamic distributed optimisation of integrated process planning and scheduling in smart factories. In: Proceedings of the Genetic and Evolutionary Computation Conference. GECCO 2019. ACM, New York (2019)
7. Thierens, D.: Scalability problems of simple genetic algorithms. Evol. Comput. **7**(4), 331–352 (1999). https://doi.org/10.1162/evco.1999.7.4.331
8. Leclerc, G., Auerbach, J.E., Iacca, G., Floreano, D.: The seamless peer and cloud evolution framework. In: Proceedings of the 2016 on Genetic and Evolutionary Computation Conference, pp. 821–828. ACM (2016)

9. Ma, N., Liu, X.F., Zhan, Z.H., Zhong, J.H., Zhang, J.: Load balance aware distributed differential evolution for computationally expensive optimization problems. In: 2017 GECCO Proceedings Companion, pp. 209–210. ACM (2017)

10. Melab, N., Mezmaz, M., Talbi, E.: Parallel hybrid multi-objective island model in peer-to-peer environment. In: 19th IEEE International Parallel and Distributed Processing Symposium. pp. 9–pp, April 2005

11. Enterprise Application Container Platform. https://www.docker.com/. Accessed 19 Apr 2019

12. Salza, P., Ferrucci, F., Sarro, F.: Develop, deploy and execute parallel genetic algorithms in the cloud. In: 2016 GECCO Proceedings Companion, pp. 121–122. ACM (2016)

13. Kubernetes: Production-Grade Container Orchestration. https://kubernetes.io/. Accessed 19 Apr 2019

14. García-Valdez, J.M., Merelo-Guervós, J.J.: A modern, event-based architecture for distributed evolutionary algorithms. In: Proceedings of the Genetic and Evolutionary Computation Conference Companion, GECCO 2018, pp. 233–234. ACM, New York (2018)

15. Nogueras, R., Cotta, C.: An analysis of migration strategies in island-based multimemetic algorithms. In: Bartz-Beielstein, T., Branke, J., Filipič, B., Smith, J. (eds.) PPSN 2014. LNCS, vol. 8672, pp. 731–740. Springer, Cham (2014). https://doi.org/10.1007/978-3-319-10762-2_72

16. Ishibuchi, H., Masuda, H., Tanigaki, Y., Nojima, Y.: Modified distance calculation in generational distance and inverted generational distance. In: Gaspar-Cunha, A., Henggeler Antunes, C., Coello, C.C. (eds.) EMO 2015. LNCS, vol. 9019, pp. 110–125. Springer, Cham (2015). https://doi.org/10.1007/978-3-319-15892-1_8

17. Deb, K., Agrawal, S., Pratap, A., Meyarivan, T.: A fast elitist non-dominated sorting genetic algorithm for multi-objective optimization: NSGA-II. In: Schoenauer, M., et al. (eds.) PPSN 2000. LNCS, vol. 1917, pp. 849–858. Springer, Heidelberg (2000). https://doi.org/10.1007/3-540-45356-3_83

18. Li, M., Yang, S., Liu, X.: Diversity comparison of pareto front approximations in many-objective optimization. IEEE Trans. Cybern. 44(12), 2568–2584 (2014)

Stability Analysis of a Statistical Model for Cloud Resource Management

Mitalee Sarker$^{(\boxtimes)}$ (ID) and Stefan Wesner (ID)

Institute of Information Resource Management, Ulm University, Ulm, Germany
{mitalee.sarker,stefan.wesner}@uni-ulm.de

Abstract. In this paper, we presented a comprehensive stability analysis of statistical models derived from the network usage data to design an efficient and optimal resource management in a Cloud data centre. In recent years, it has been noticed that network has a significant impact on the HPC and business critical applications when they are run in a cloud environment. The existing VM placement algorithms lack capabilities to deploy such applications in an effective way and cause performance degradation. As a result, there is an urge for a network-aware VM placement algorithm which will consider the application behaviour and system capability. Our approach uses static models based on simple probability distribution concept and partition (number theory) to characterise and predict the resource usage behaviour of the VMs. However, the stability of those models is a key requirement to ensure a persistent placement of the VMs which can prevent their frequent migration and keep the infrastructure rigid. The paper investigates the stability of the models with respect to time. Sticky HDP-HMM method was proven highly capable to model the monitoring data with a certain accuracy. The refined data was further used to estimate the resource consumption of each VM and physical host running in the infrastructure. A stability parameter has been defined to determine the level of steadiness of the models that gives us a clear indication on whether the models can be used further to derive an optimal placement decision for new VMs. The paper ends with a discussion on instance based stability analysis and future work.

Keywords: Cloud data centre · Network · VM placement

1 Introduction

In present day, many companies and enterprises are moving towards cloud services to deploy and run their applications. This migration defines a new era which has brought revolutionary changes to the business industry and IT sectors. Cloud computing offers a set of benefits to the users such as reducing the pain of running and maintaining applications on-premise infrastructure, providing clear payment methods such as pay-as-you-go model, ensures data security and flexible resource usage and many more. Traditional approaches for provisioning resources for a certain application in cloud, look for the resource requirements of the application

© Springer Nature Switzerland AG 2019
K. Djemame et al. (Eds.): GECON 2019, LNCS 11819, pp. 260–272, 2019.
https://doi.org/10.1007/978-3-030-36027-6_22

during its deployment phase such as number of CPUs, cores, memory, storage etc. These algorithms often do not check for the network resource demands such as bandwidth requirements of an application as well as latency concern and the impact of the underlying networking infrastructure on the performance of an application [15]. Such resource allocation methods are often sub-optimal as they do not consider the time varying resource demands of the applications [14]. An inappropriate placement of a VM contributes to the performance degradation of the application running inside it, which in turn hampers the Quality of Service (QoS) promised to the customers by the cloud providers. Another concerning aspect is that, the data centres are being enhanced to a great extent by implementing commodity based hardware in order to cope with the rising migration of the applications into cloud [8]. This commodity hardware based data centres can not ensure the best performance for all applications due to diverse hardware requirements from the applications. Some cloud providers offer dedicated service for a specific set of applications such as Oracle HPC [5], Amazon HPC [17], Azure HPC [2] provide such services to HPC applications. However this approach can lead to over or underutilisation of resources due to lack of a balanced resource distribution in the whole infrastructure. Additionally, expanding a data centre with a large amount of servers, switches, routers and other equipments surely contribute to the rising energy usage that has an unavoidable impact on the climate, while the data centre provider faces high operational and maintaining cost. Hence it is extremely important to use an enhanced optimal plan for allocating resources in a data centre.

1.1 Problem Statement

According to [11], the performance of HPC applications deteriorates to a great extent during inter-node communication in cloud because of high latency induced by virtualisation overhead and low bandwidth provided by the shared network infrastructure. Besides, as stated in [3], flat or scalable network causes significant loss in performance of the system and communication intensive applications due to its principal of shared network and use of less network components in a large scale system. Considering the above mentioned issues, we formulated the major problems we aim to solve in general.

1. How to ensure better performance for resource demanding and communication intensive applications in a cloud data centre?
2. How to avoid congestion and guarantee higher bandwidth inside a cloud network infrastructure?
3. How to manage resources in a cloud infrastructure optimally?

To solve the aforementioned problems, analyse application behaviour to predict resource demands and identify system capability can play a vital role. For this reason, there is a great need of a tool which should take the time varying need for resources of the applications into account and based on that should provide optimal and fast VM allocation decisions.

1.2   Motivation

The work we have presented in this paper is highly motivated by the hypothesis mentioned in [16].

- The time varying parameters such as network bandwidth demand of a virtual machine can be described as a set of discrete data rate states including their probability of occurrence for a specific amount of time. Such discrete probability distribution models are based on the concept used to model traffic sources in statistical multiplexing in the Asynchronous Transfer Mode network [9,10].
- The probability that a new VM overbooks the network bandwidth if it is placed in a physical server can now be obtained from the overlayed probability distribution functions and placement decisions can be produced by checking the upper limit of overbooking.

We assume that the discrete data rate states to describe the communication behaviour of the applications follow a stable probability of occurrence. As a result, this hypothesis will not work for the application that requires user generated action which does not show periodicity. Our target applications currently are the HPC and DIC (Data Intensive Computing) applications whose operation modes follow a steady manner with time. To test our hypothesis, we have analysed the network resource usage behaviour of CFD (Computational Fluid Dynamics) application. We believe that the stability property exists due to the characteristic of the application.

The main goal of this research work is to calculate optimal decisions for resource distribution in a cloud data centre. However to find an optimal server list, it is not realistic to calculate all possible combination between the servers and the VMs as it will require a significant amount of time which contradicts with the core challenge of an optimisation algorithm to provide a fast and satisfactory decision. In addition to that, the obtained configuration must maintain a stable condition long enough to decrease frequent resource reallocation. Therefore the stability of a probability distribution function is essential since it leads to classify applications based on their resource demands and influences the optimal placement decisions. As the optimal decision only holds if the probability distribution functions are stable enough, they need to be observed on a regular basis to detect any sign of instability which will eventually cause an update of the models as well as a new optimal configuration. The work is also motivated by the fact that using an intelligent and optimal resource management brings economical benefit to the cloud providers, for example the number of servers can be reduced that will decrease energy consumption along with operational and maintaining cost. As a consequence of that, cloud users will receive increased offerings and provider's ranking will accelerate. Furthermore, efficient redistribution of network traffic in the infrastructure while maintaining QoS will also be ensured by the framework.

The paper is structured as follows: Sect. 2 briefly outlines the existing research work on network-aware VM placement topic. The next section describes our solution approach along with conceptual explanation of the methodologies and a short summary of the testbed. Section 4 represents and interprets the results obtained from the new approaches. Section 5 discusses about possible stability analysis based on VM instances and the last section provides us the conclusion of this paper and future work plan.

2   Related Work

In most of the research, VM placement problem in general has been defined as a NP-hard problem. Considering the importance of network in cloud resource management, a research trend on network-aware VM placement algorithm has emerged recently.

Researchers and scientists have followed multiple fundamental approaches to tackle the VM placement problem. Examples include, but are not limited to, improve the performance of a specific application in the cloud, bandwidth constraint, network-congestion control or network traffic minimisation, reduction of network latency, minimisation of network energy consumption in a data centre network architecture and prediction of workload in the cloud.

The work described in [22], focuses on the dynamic bandwidth demands of the cloud applications. Their solution estimates the bandwidth demands of a virtual cluster during application profiling. Both types of clusters with static and stochastic bandwidth demands are provided enough bandwidth of the physical link with a high probabilistic guarantee and a small risk factor. However, the efficiency of the profiling methods raises questions as it is not clear whether the application was profiled long enough to understand its resource usage behaviour. An online solution called "Kraken" has been presented in [7] which provides minimum guarantee for network bandwidth and computing resources to a virtual cluster during runtime. They consider Hadoop application and Fat-tree network topology for the evaluation of the online resource reservation scheme. However, the scalability issues of the network topology with respect to the network growth is not clearly stated. A priority-aware VM allocation (PAVA) algorithm has been presented in [18] which takes care of computing and network resource demands of the critical cloud applications in a SDN (Software Defined Networking)-enabled cloud. The critical applications are given high priority and deployed in the nearby hosts. SDN controller sets up a priority queue for the critical applications and guarantees the minimum bandwidth for them. The drawback of this method is it is controller dependent which may cause single point of failure and it does not provide fair share of the network resource.

Nowadays, time series based modelling techniques and machine learning algorithms are also gaining attention in resource allocation context [1,4,20]. The algorithms get trained by the historical resource utilisation data of the already deployed applications in cloud to identify the dynamic resource demands and usage pattern and based on their knowledge, the algorithms then allocate resources for the future applications. However, time series based approaches are time dependent and require frequent update. Training machine learning algorithms can take a significant amount of time which is often incompatible with the core cloud characteristic of faster application deployment. Also the resource usage forecasting is valid for a shorter period of time, for example, forecasting for the next 48 h [4]. These approaches often trigger resource reallocation and VM migration and eventually make the infrastructure unstable.

3   Solution Approach

The solution approach is a framework called "Allocation Optimiser" that is designed to assess the network resource requirements of the applications and based on the assessment, it will create the server environment, while considering the SLA to be served. The potential outcome would be an optimised number of physical servers for deploying VMs. A brief overview of the framework has been illustrated in [16]. We have described the main functionalities of the framework below.

- Get the current mapping between the VMs and the physical servers.
- Calculate throughput from monitored Tx and Rx data rate for each running VM for a certain period of time.
- Model the network resource (bandwidth) usage behaviour of the VMs.
- Estimate their network resource consumption for a certain amount of time.
- Calculate the stability level of the models.
- Store the stable probability models of all VMs in a database.
- Calculate per server overlay model from the VMs which are running inside it.
- Estimate the combined resource consumption for each physical server.
- Calculate the stability level of the overlay models.
- Store the stable overlay models of all physical servers in a database.
- Calculate the probability rate for overbooking the bandwidth resource per physical server.
- If a new VM deployment request arrives, check its memory requirement and based on that filter the servers.
- Match a probability model to the new VM based on its metadata, requested VM size, flavour etc.
- Determine the overlay probability above threshold for the servers with the new VM's probability model
- Use an optimisation algorithm to produce the optimal candidate server list.
- Observe the performance and update VM placement or perform migration.
- Periodically update the models.

The abovementioned workflow of "Allocation Optimiser" clearly outlines the relation between the stability analysis of probability distribution models and the computation of allocation decisions. Without a stable probability distribution function, the allocation decision will not be valid. The main optimisation goal of the framework is to reduce energy usage and cost which in turn guarantees better server and resource utilisation and longer hardware life. Allocation Optimiser also ensures improved performance of resource demanding and communication intensive applications.

The framework has two main components, Data Provider and Calculator. The principal tasks of the Calculator component have been classified into three main units, analyse time series data, derive probability distribution models and overlay models of the data rate for running VMs and physical hosts respectively as well as examine the stability level of the models and compute the optimal list of hosts for a new VM placement.

3.1   Time Series Data Analysis

Time series consists of a set of data along with their corresponding time of occurrence. To examine the network resource utilisation data, more precisely data rate, monitoring data of 7 days of two VMs has been used. The default sampling frequency of the monitoring tool, 10 s and 1 min have been applied to sample the data. As calculations on both frequency showed similar results, 1 min frequency can be used as a sample frequency since it reduces both, data values and computation time. Due to our goal to estimate the overbooking parameter of bandwidth usage per physical server, only the data rate that are in or, above Megabit per second was taken into consideration and the rest was converted into null. To use the refined data for further analysis, several methods and concepts were studied such as decomposition method, Hidden Markov Model, Peak and valley detection to model the data. The main challenge was to determine an adequate number of data rate states in order to reduce computational complexity. Among the methods, the first two were realised. The decomposition method was not able to describe the bandwidth usage behaviour accurately as some data points have zero values. However the Hidden Markov Model was identified as an effective approach for modelling the data rate. The idea of using this approach was inspired from the work mentioned in [12], where HDP-HMM (Hierarchical Dirichlet Process – Hidden Markov Model) has been applied to categorise (RTT) Round Trip Time series. We have applied Sticky HDP-HMM method for modelling the data rate since this method stabilises the irrelevant state transitions among the states of the Markov chain as stated in [6]. The concepts are briefly explained in the following chapters.

A Markov model is a stochastic model where the present value of the model is only dependent on the previous value. In a Hidden Markov Model, only the observations are visible and the states are hidden. The time series value of the data rate can be described by a HMM where $x(t)$ is the base value or the data rate state and $y(t)$ is the observation or the data rate value as depicted in Fig. 1. We assumed the number of data rate states and the parameters of the data rate specific probability distribution models as random variables on every state of the Markov chain.

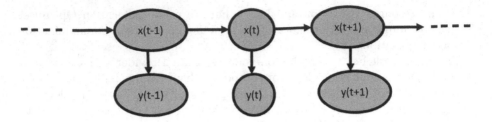

Fig. 1. Graphical representation of a HMM, where at time t, x(t) is the hidden state and y(t) is the corresponding observation.

A HMM has a diverse sets of computational problems, considering our use case, we have only focused on the determination of the single most likely sequence of states for a given sequence of observation.

A Dirichlet Process is a distribution over distributions according to [19]. Let G be a Dirichlet Process distributed as

$$G \sim DP(\alpha, G_0) \tag{1}$$

Here G_0 is a base distribution, α is a positive scaling parameter and G is a random probability measure that has the same support as G_0.

When the base distribution itself is a draw from a Dirichlet Process, it is called a Hierarchical Dirichlet Process.

$$DP(\gamma, H)$$
$$G_0 \mid \gamma, H \sim DP(\gamma, H)$$

$$G_j \mid \alpha_0, G_0 \sim DP(\alpha_0, G_0), \; for \; each \; j. \tag{2}$$

In order to define the characteristic of the states as finite and unknown, Dirichlet Processes (DP) can be used as priors. Hierarchical DP can be used through defining another layer of random variables and a "vague" prior to this layer, on which the parameters of HMM are dependent.

MCMC (Markov Chain Monte Carlo) consists of a set of sampling algorithms which are used to sample from a probability distribution.

Gibbs Sampler algorithm produces samples from the posterior distribution by checking every variable and sample from the conditional distribution of that variable while the rest of the variables are set to their present values. The algorithm for a Gibbs sampler has been presented in [21].

The aforementioned techniques have been applied to analyse the data rate states by using the steps presented in Fig. 2. We have used Scalar Gaussian for observation model since our data is 1 Dimension. In order to decrease computational complexity, we set the maximum number of states to be 10.

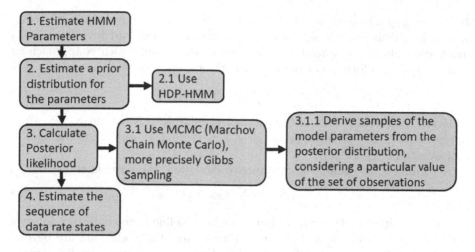

Fig. 2. Data rate states estimation by using Sticky HDP-HMM.

3.2 Stability Analysis of the Probability Distribution Models with Regard to Time

According to the probability theory, stability of a distribution is defined by the equality between a linear combination of two separate random variables and their distribution with respect to location and scale parameters.

As stated in [13], a non-degenerate distribution is called stable when the following property is fulfilled.

Let's assume X is a random variable and its independent copies are X_1 and X_2. If for any constants, a>0 and b>0, the random variable aX_1+bX_2 has the same distribution as cX+d for some constants c>0 and d, then X is declared as stable. The distribution is called strictly stable if the property is satisfied with d = 0.

For the stability analysis, we wanted to measure the fluctuations of the probability values of a distribution in time. Let's consider data rate as a random variable, X and the probability distribution function of X is P(X). Then the change in the distribution between timestamp t and t+1 can be described as

$$Y_t = P(X_{t+1}) - P(X_t) \tag{3}$$

When the probability distribution model is stable around X^*, Y will fluctuate around zero with some standard error. We have used statistical dispersion to address this issue. Statistical dispersion is the measurement of spread or, variation of a distribution from a central value. It can be described in a set of forms such as standard deviation, variance, interquartile range, mean absolute difference etc. Since we want to determine the stability level of the probability distribution models, we selected standard deviation as the stability parameter because it is capable to represent time variant volatility and takes every item of the data group into consideration. Standard deviation of a probability distribution model is defined as the square root of its variance. Standard deviation reveals information about the spread of data close to the mean, which is approaching to normality. The formula of the variance σ^2 of a discrete random variable X is

$$\sigma^2 = \sum (x - \mu)^2 P(x) \tag{4}$$

Here x represents values of the random variable X, μ is the mean of X, $P(x)$ represents the corresponding probability, and symbol $\sum$ represents the sum of all products $(x - \mu)^2 P(x)$.

According to the definition of standard deviation, the formula is

$$\sigma = \sqrt{\sigma^2} = \sqrt{\sum (x - \mu)^2 P(x)} \tag{5}$$

To determine the degree of stability, we have defined the confidence interval or stability limit as follows. The probability values of a model that are beyond these limits will be considered as unstable. However, a probability distribution model is declared as stable if its highest data rate state is in the stability limit.

$$Upperlimit : (3 \times SD) + Mean$$
$$Lowerlimit : Mean - (3 \times SD) \tag{6}$$

3.3 Test Setup and Methodology

For the testing purpose, we have set up two VMs in a cloud testbed by using a well known cloud middleware, OpenStack and run a CFD application. In the setup, one VM played the role of a master and the other VM was configured as slave VM. The VMs have 2 CPU, 4 Gb RAM and 40 Gb Disk. The operating system was Ubuntu 16.04.5 LTS with the kernel version 4.4.0-142-generic.

For collecting resource usage values, Collectd has been installed and configured in all VMs. A separate VM has been created to collect the monitoring values. Influxdb has been installed and configured in that VM. The monitoring values were captured for CPU, memory, load and network throughput utilisation. For our present analysis, we have only used the network throughput data. The capturing frequency was 10 s.

A simulation has been run for a specific amount of time in the VMs and theoretically when it ended, it restarted after a random pause from 1 s to 12 h. During the simulation, the two machines communicated with each other in the moment of the calculation phase. There are some periods of "silence" because a sleep time has been added after the end of the calculation and the start of a new one. At the end of the test, the monitoring data has been retrieved and modelled by using Sticky HDP-HMM method mentioned in Subsect. 3.1 and further used to create probability distribution models. The analysis ended with the time based stability check of the models. For both VMs, we investigated the stability level for each hour of a whole day and then for each day of a whole week. The analysis showed that both VMs were stable for consecutive 3 days and on the 4th day, a small diversion was observed at the highest data rate state. For the rest of the week, the probability models showed stable sign again.

4   Results

In this section, we showed the results for a VM called "cfd2". The state sequence of monitoring data for 1 day achieved by using the Sticky HDP-HMM method has been demonstrated in Fig. 3. The X-axis represents the time stamp index and the Y-axis shows the data rate in bit per second which has been stated as throughput in the figure. The method has created a set of data rate states which are represented by patterns of different colour in the background. The data was sampled by 1 min frequency.

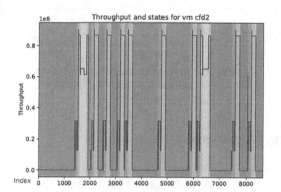 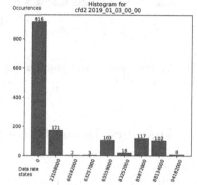

Fig. 3. State representation for 1 day monitoring data of cfd2 VM. (Color figure online)

Fig. 4. Histogram for 1 day monitoring data of cfd2 VM.

The sampled states obtained from the Sticky HDP-HMM and the corresponding data rate values have been depicted in the form of a histogram in Fig. 4, where the states have been presented in X-axis and the occurrences were depicted in Y-axis. State 0 demonstrates the events when no bandwidth was used and also the throughput values which were not considered to be significant. The unit for the data rate values are bit per second.

We have calculated the probability distribution for the same data and showed it in Fig. 5. Figure 6 summarised the stability level of the probability values of the same distribution. The X-axis illustrates the data rate states in bit per second and the Y-axis shows the corresponding mean and standard deviation values. The standard deviation with red font indicates unstable data rate state. From the figure, it is clear that the highest data rate and its nearby states are stable enough to acknowledge the distribution as stable for that day. The abovementioned results also prove that the hypothesis that has been described in Subsect. 1.2 is working for this particular CFD application, which means the network behaviour of the CFD application is predictable and can be described statistically.

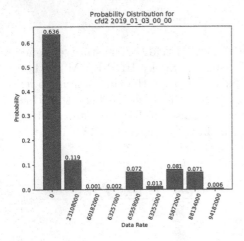

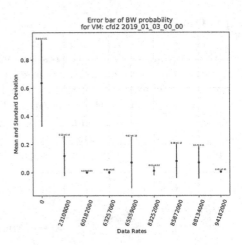

Fig. 5. Probability distribution for 1 day of cfd2 VM.

Fig. 6. Standard Deviation of probability values for 1 day of cfd2 VM. (Color figure online)

5   Instance Based Stability Analysis

This analysis aims to determine whether the VMs show same behaviour for a certain period of time. For example, VM1 and VM2 have 3 probability distribution models for a day which can be defined as $P_{VM1morning}$, $P_{VM1afternoon}$, $P_{VM1night}$ and $P_{VM2morning}$, $P_{VM2afternoon}$ and $P_{VM2night}$ respectively. VM1 and VM2 will be called stable instance if the probability distribution models are same which means the VM instances behave in the same way.

$$P_{VM1morning} = P_{VM2morning}$$
$$P_{VM1afternoon} = P_{VM2afternoon}$$
$$P_{VM1night} = P_{VM2night}$$

This analysis will lead to a more fine grained classification of the VMs with respect to their network resource consumption. In addition, with the help of the VM classification, it will be easier to detect the network behaviour of a new VM.

There exist different ways to determine whether two discrete probability distributions are same. Examples include, but are not limited to, Kullback-Leibler divergence, Kolmogorov-Smirnov test, Chi-squared test etc. Possible candidate VMs for the analysis should be the set of VMs which belong to the same user and the VMs who communicate a lot to a single VM (all-to-one). To evaluate the approach, daily network bandwidth consumption of the VMs needs to be modeled into three separate probability distributions with a time period of 8 h. The probability models should be compared to detect the level of equality.

6   Conclusion and Outlook

In this paper, we have defined stability for the network traffic models of a HPC application and with experimental results we have showed that the network behaviour is statistically predictable and quite stable for a certain period of time. The consequent steps would be to implement the techniques mentioned in Sect. 5 to analyse instance based stability for the same application. The accomplishment of this task will eventually lead to develop the main functionality of "Allocation Optimiser" framework which is to compute the optimal list of physical hosts for a new VM placement. To achieve this milestone, a theoretical analysis of a set of optimisation algorithms will be performed and a suitable algorithm will be chosen for the framework. A use case is necessary to verify the functionality of the framework and its performance should be compared with respect to other existing placement algorithms. The limitation of the framework will be evaluated in a simulation environment. Moreover, traffic models with throughput probabilities are not sufficient to be used in deriving an optimal placement decision for the VMs. We need to consider additional critical elements such as latency, jitter, buffer overflow losses and burstiness. In addition, new target applications should be determined apart from HPC and DIC applications to check the applicability of the framework.

Acknowledgements. The research leading to these results has received funding from the EC's Framework Programme HORIZON 2020 under grant agreement number 732258 (CloudPerfect).

References

1. Adegboyega, A.: Time-series models for cloud workload prediction: a comparison. In: 2017 IFIP/IEEE Symposium on Integrated Network and Service Management (IM), pp. 298–307. IEEE (2017)
2. Azure, M.: High-performance computing. https://azure.microsoft.com/en-us/solutions/high-performance-computing/. Accessed 24 May 2019
3. Balaji, P., Naik, H., Desai, N.: Understanding network saturation behavior on large-scale blue gene/p systems. In: 2009 15th International Conference on Parallel and Distributed Systems, pp. 586–593. IEEE (2009)
4. Barr, J.: New - predictive scaling for EC2, powered by machine learning. https://aws.amazon.com/blogs/aws/new-predictive-scaling-for-ec2-powered-by-machine-learning/. Accessed 25 May 2019
5. Oracle Cloud: HPC on oracle cloud infrastructure. https://cloud.oracle.com/iaas/hpc. Accessed 25 May 2019
6. Fox, E.B., Sudderth, E.B., Jordan, M.I., Willsky, A.S.: The sticky HDP-HMM: Bayesian nonparametric hidden Markov models with persistent states. Arxiv preprint (2007)
7. Fuerst, C., Schmid, S., Suresh, L., Costa, P.: Kraken: online and elastic resource reservations for cloud datacenters. IEEE/ACM Trans. Network. (TON) **26**(1), 422–435 (2018)
8. Ghiasi, A., Baca, R.: Overview of largest data centers, May 2014. http://www.ieee802.org/3/bs/public/14_05/ghiasi_3bs_01b_0514.pdf. Accessed 19 Apr 2018
9. Heyman, D.P., Tabatabai, A., Lakshman, T.: Statistical analysis and simulation study of video teleconference traffic in ATM networks. IEEE Trans. Circuits Syst. Video Technol. **2**(1), 49–59 (1992)

10. Hubner, F., Tran-Gia, P.: Quasi-stationary analysis of a finite capacity asynchronous multiplexer with modulated deterministic input. ITC-13, Copenhagen (1991)

11. Mehrotra, P., et al.: Performance evaluation of Amazon EC2 for NASA HPC applications. In: Proceedings of the 3rd Workshop on Scientific Cloud Computing, pp. 41–50. ACM (2012)

12. Mouchet, M.: Statistical characterisation of RTT series. https://labs.ripe.net/Members/maxime_mouchet/statistical-characterisation-of-rtt-series. Accessed 27 May 2019

13. Nolan, J.: Stable Distributions: Models for Heavy-Tailed Data. Birkhauser, New York (2003)

14. OpenStackCommunity: Openstack compute schedulers. https://docs.openstack.org/newton/config-reference/compute/schedulers.html. Accessed 06 June 2018

15. Popescu, D.A., Zilberman, N., Moore, A.W.: Characterizing the impact of network latency on cloud-based applications' performance (2017)

16. Sarker, M., Wesner, S.: Statistical model based cloud resource management. In: Coppola, M., Carlini, E., D'Agostino, D., Altmann, J., Bañares, J.Á. (eds.) GECON 2018. LNCS, vol. 11113, pp. 107–115. Springer, Cham (2019). https://doi.org/10.1007/978-3-030-13342-9_9

17. Amazon Web Services: High performance computing (HPC). https://aws.amazon.com/hpc/. Accessed 24 May 2019

18. Son, J., Buyya, R.: Priority-aware VM allocation and network bandwidth provisioning in software-defined networking (SDN)-enabled clouds. IEEE Trans. Sustain. Comput. 4, 17–28 (2018)

19. Teh, Y.W., Jordan, M.I., Beal, M.J., Blei, D.M.: Hierarchical Dirichlet processes. J. Am. Stat. Assoc. 101 (2004)

20. Witt, C., Bux, M., Gusew, W., Leser, U.: Predictive performance modeling for distributed computing using black-box monitoring and machine learning. arXiv preprint arXiv:1805.11877 (2018)

21. Yildirim, I.: Bayesian inference: Gibbs sampling. Technical Note, University of Rochester (2012)

22. Yu, L., Shen, H., Cai, Z., Liu, L., Pu, C.: Towards bandwidth guarantee for virtual clusters under demand uncertainty in multi-tenant clouds. IEEE Trans. Parallel Distrib. Syst. 29(2), 450–465 (2017)

Poster Session: Emerging Ideas

Genetic Algorithms for Capacity Estimation in Pluralistic Spectrum Licensing Simulations

Stephan Wirsing[✉] and Albert Rafetseder

Faculty of Computer Science, University of Vienna,
Währinger Straße 29, 1090 Vienna, Austria
{stephan.wirsing,albert.rafetseder}@univie.ac.at
https://cosy.cs.univie.ac.at/

Abstract. The regional licensing of 5G spectrum represents an exemplary use case for the huge potential of a geographically fine-grained spectrum assignment. It raises the question, whether new types of spectrum licenses could augment the current arsenal of static allocation schemes with central control. In our contribution, we introduce the use of genetic algorithms (GA) as integral part of ex-ante evaluations of new licensing schemes. We apply the method to calculate the near-optimal exploitation of available spectrum resources in the course of an academic simulation. It assesses the effects of interference-based sub-licensing contracts, also known as Pluralistic Licensing Contracts (PLCs), on mobile networks. Our findings suggest that PLCs might provide a low-effort exploitation of underutilized spectrum reserves, e.g. in sparse user populations, and constitute a highly scalable means for the pricing of externalities.

Keywords: Genetic algorithms · Pluralistic spectrum licensing

1 Background and Related Work

The recent award of 5G spectrum throughout Europe has emphasized the attractiveness of regional spectrum licenses, which can be acquired not only by Mobile Network Operators, but also by private companies to build highly customized networks on their own premises. As the award of regional spectrum adds new players to the market, it is also worth questioning the terms on which these licenses are granted. Typically, licensees have exclusive access to their spectrum, which protects them from interference, but in turn limits spectrum re-use within the license region. In contrast, general authorizations which apply for short range devices (e.g. WiFi or Bluetooth) allow a shared and more flexible band usage at the cost of reduced interference protection. Hence, *intermediate* forms of spectrum access are promising to deliver a certain degree of protection, and at the

---

The first author was supported by a netidee scholarship by the Internet Foundation Austria.

K. Djemame et al. (Eds.): GECON 2019, LNCS 11819, pp. 275–280, 2019.
https://doi.org/10.1007/978-3-030-36027-6_23

same time use the available spectrum more efficiently than exclusive licenses. In recent years, a number of approaches for *secondary* spectrum access have been developed [1], i.e. where a primary licensee has privileged access, but accepts additional spectrum users in the same band under predefined conditions. One approach for a more flexible use of radio spectrum is the Pluralistic Licensing concept presented in [2]. It provides a licensing framework based on contracts, where the tolerated interference due to secondary band usage determines the license costs. Here, we interpret Pluralistic Licensing contracts (PLCs) as the mutual agreement between primary and secondary licensees, comprising at least a specification of the permitted maximum transmit power level of the secondary, over the entire band (interference mask). We differ from the original work, as we do not preclude a contemporaneous operation of primary and secondary systems in our simulation.

2 Methodology

In real wireless systems, the joint use of spectrum causes noise, congestion, and even blocking between users, and thus precautions are taken to contain the negative effects: using robust modulation, limiting transmit powers and directionality, listen-before-talk and "cognitive" schemes etc. Given the many possible mitigation strategies, it is difficult to assess in general the impact of simultaneous spectrum use. Therefore, the approach taken in this contribution builds on

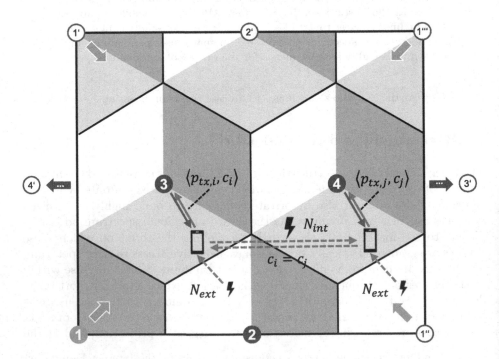

Fig. 1. Scenario model. Signal propagation is wrapped around corners.

a strongly simplified academic model, which is based on the channel capacity model, developed by Shannon [3] and interprets the primary licensee as sourcing the signal power S in the spectrum, the sub-licensee instead contributes to the noise power N. The attainable channel capacity expressed as achievable data rate R of an additive white noise Gaussian channel of the channel bandwidth B, where signal and noise interfere is given as $R = B \log_2(1 + \frac{S}{N})$. This approach allows us to extend Holland et al.'s conceptual description of Pluralistic Licensing [2] and evaluate concrete interference scenarios.

In our simulations, we address the optimal resource utilization of the *primary* mobile network. We assume constant levels of secondary interference, i.e. where secondary spectrum users fully exploit their transmit power permissions. The resulting channel and transmit power assignment problem of the incumbent is solved by means of Matlab's Global Optimization Toolbox built on [4]. We use a genetic algorithm (GA) to heuristically solve the mixed integer problem with a nonlinear objective function and nonlinear constraints (MINLP). The algorithm assigns a transmit channel index c_m (integer) and a transmit power level ρ_m (real positive number) to each link identified by the index m between a base station and a mobile station. The number of all possible and allowed links is given by the integer M. The solution vectors ρ and c contain the channel and transmit power assignments of all links within the primary's network, and hence $\rho = (\rho_1, ..., \rho_M)$ and $c = (c_1, ..., c_M)$. The assignment algorithm (see Fig. 2) uses two consecutive Genetic Algorithms (GAs) to sequentially optimize the channel assignment (GA1) and the transmit power allocation (GA2). Both GAs start from an initial set of feasible but non-optimal allocations (initial population) and iteratively valuate, select, recombine and alter individuals based on the specified objective function to create new populations.

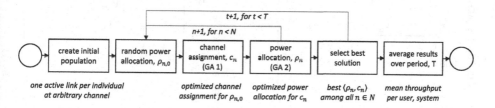

Fig. 2. Repeated application of a genetic algorithm.

3   Simulation and Results

The simulation pursues two major objectives: First, to determine the theoretical capacity c_{th} and the effective[1] capacity c_{eff} of the modeled mobile scenario

---

[1] The effective capacity considers that users are not served in excess of their demand.

for a given spectrum allocation; and second, to assess the effects on the latter, when the interference situation changes, e.g. due to secondary spectrum usage. To quantify the effects of elevated interference levels, we refer to the average throughput (data rate) per user (mobile station) that can be achieved under certain interference conditions, which are varied in terms of noise power *immissions*, that is the *received* interference power. In each scenario, we simulate four base stations, serving the same total number of $n_u = 16$ users, equally distributed over a rectangular scenario area. We consider an average demand of 500/100 kbit/s in Downlink/Uplink direction. The throughput per user device refers to the sum of both rates, i.e. 600 kbit/s.

Spectrum Increase: First, we vary the *average* number of available 200 kHz channels from 0.5 to 1.75 per user per cell in increments of 0.25 channels per user. Interference from secondary spectrum usage is constant at -123 dBm/Hz. Whereas the deviations between theoretical and effective system capacity roughly coincide for a low number of channels (see Fig. 3, left), they differ increasingly with the amount of available spectrum. The linear increase in c_{th} is in accordance with Shannon's channel capacity formula, and has been consistently computed by the algorithm, whereas c_{eff} reaches the demand limit at 1.25 channels (250 kHz) per user per cell. The individual users' service ratios (Fig. 3, right) are calculated from their *achieved* rates divided through their *demand* rates. The boxplot indicates the respective statistics (minimum/maximum values, 25-, 50-, and 75-percentiles) of the service ratio. Whilst at 0.5 channels/user the majority does not receive 50% of their demand, a number of 1.25 channels per user permit a minimum service ratio of about 90%.

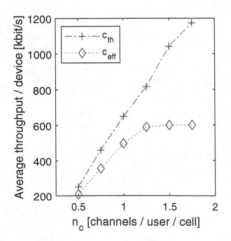 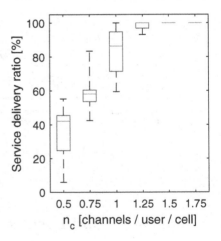

Fig. 3. Increasing spectrum cannot be fully exploited (left), but improves service delivery ratio (right).

Interference Increase: The variation of interference is conducted for several external power densities from -123 to $-33\,\mathrm{dBm/Hz}$ (see Fig. 4). We compare the effective capacities (c_{eff}) of two alternative spectrum configurations with one channel per user per cell (blue) and two channels per user (red). The results indicate a significantly higher interference tolerance of the two-channel configuration, where the average throughput starts degrading at -100 dBm/Hz and falls below 90% (540 kbit/s) at -83 dBm, marked by (b). The same threshold is reached in the one-channel configuration already at $-133\,\mathrm{dBm/Hz}$, marked by (a). Hence, the provision of additional spectrum allows to offset an increase in interference by 50 dB (a b). At point (b), the average rate of the one-channel configuration is about one half the rate of the two-channel configuration, which in both cases indicates a similar spectrum efficiency of 300 kbit/s per user per channel, or 1.5 bit/s/Hz, respectively. Beyond (b), both configurations degrade towards a throughput of zero, whereby the decrease of the two-channel configuration is two times as sharp.

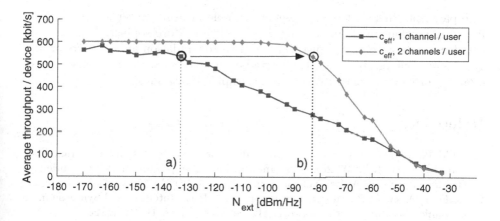

Fig. 4. Compensation of interference increase $(a - b)$.

4   Discussion and Conclusion

The presented model has been developed for academic purposes. Even though many simplifications have been made to keep it manageable, it allows a bottom-up estimate of the effective capacity of particular spectrum allocations under the assumption of an efficient utilization by network operators. At its core, the consecutive application of GA has proven a promising approach to determine the effective capacity of spectrum allocations. We were able to reproduce capacity changes due to changing spectrum and interference conditions. Our analysis of external interference was simplified by assuming to constant wideband immissions, which is reasonable for studying the effect of interference masks that could be part of Pluralistic Licensing agreements. Indeed, PLCs could be useful to exploit unused spectrum of primary licensees, who have acquired nation-wide licenses scaled to serve densely populated areas. We showed that primary licensees would effectively have the opportunity to (1) open their spectrum in sparsely populated areas and most likely offset considerably increased noise levels, or to (2) accept a lower network capacity in more dense regions, where spectrum is scarce. In both cases a more efficient use of the spectrum is achieved, as either unused capacities are made available (1) or the primary service quality is reduced to a minimum acceptable level (2). Detailed knowledge about degrading effects (as indicated by our second simulation) when interference rises thus paves the way for designing secondary usage contracts based on network externalities: If network degradation is acceptable for the primary operator, it may be willing to agree to a secondary usage, e.g. in return for a fee proportional to the effective capacity reduction (and related monetary losses) from its initial capacity c_0:

$$p(N_{ext}) = \beta(c_0 - c_{eff}(N_{ext}))$$

The payment scheme above represents a simple measure to set a price for sub-licensing portions of acquired exclusive spectrum. More sophisticated schemes could take into account the distribution of the degradation among users or user groups (e.g. charge based on the degradation of users with the lowest service quality), or contain temporal and/or geographic limitations.

References

1. Buddhikot, M.M.: Understanding dynamic spectrum access: models, taxonomy and challenges. In: 2007 2nd IEEE International Symposium on New Frontiers in Dynamic Spectrum Access Networks, pp. 649–663. IEEE (2007)
2. Holland, O., et al.: Pluralistic licensing. In: 2012 IEEE International Symposium on Dynamic Spectrum Access Networks (DYSPAN), pp. 33–41. IEEE (2012)
3. Shannon, C.E.: Communication in the presence of noise. Proc. IEEE **72**(9), 1192–1201 (1984). https://doi.org/10.1109/PROC.1984.12998
4. Goldberg, D.E., Holland, J.H.: Genetic algorithms and machine learning. Mach. Learn. **3**(2), 95–99 (1988)

Towards a Roadmap for Cloud TV Services in the Internet of Things Era

G. Dede[(✉)], D. Grigoropoulos, G. Loupatatzis, T. Kamalakis,
and Ch. Michalakelis

Department of Informatics and Telematics, Harokopio University of Athens,
9, Omirou Street, Tavros, Greece
gdede@hua.gr

Abstract. Cloud TV will play an important role in future pay-TV services and is quickly becoming the next arena for TV content providers. This emphasizes the need for a technology roadmap to address several key issues that may affect the deployment of future Cloud TV services. Taking into account an important blend of social, economic and technological factors, three alternative technologies, Internet Protocol TV, Over the Top and Smart TV have been investigated and ranked using the Analytical Hierarchy Process. The results reveal that OTT seems to take the precedence and security, privacy, accessibility, costs saving and time-to-market are crucial aspects, need to be taken into account.

Keywords: Decision making · Cloud TV · Roadmap · OTT · IPTV · Smart TV

1 Introduction

Industry 4.0 is expected to deliver significant gains in productivity by assimilating several technological advancements including cloud computing, which will play a crucial role in the era of the Internet-of-Things. The broadcasters and the communication operators who want to offer video services are faced with a daunting task: ensuring the live and on-demand video on any device. The operators that want to capitalize this change need a complete television platform based on cloud computing (Cloud TV) that drastically reduces the time to market and increases the revenues.

Cloud TV offers an effective transition for pay-TV operators who want to invest into the TV industry without much risk. The cloud based model allows companies to test and develop the platform without much expense, ensuring high availability of content and disaster recovery issues. The main objective of this paper is to investigate the cloud based TV services for the case study of Greece, offered by cloud vendors, and examine three alternative technological solutions for Cloud TV, IPTV, OTT and smart TV in order to evaluate the most appropriate solution that a pay TV operator has to follow [1]. This evaluation will help afterwards each operator to design its strategy. Towards this end, the framework of the analytical hierarchy process (AHP) [2] is used as a fundamental part of an effective technology roadmapping, [3]. The importance of the various criteria involved is evaluated and discussed revealing an important blend of economic, social and performance related aspects that may influence the deployment of

© Springer Nature Switzerland AG 2019
K. Djemame et al. (Eds.): GECON 2019, LNCS 11819, pp. 281–285, 2019.
https://doi.org/10.1007/978-3-030-36027-6_24

Cloud TV platforms. The obtained results form a key part of future Cloud TV solutions and implementations both for Greece and for other countries that have not yet deployed Cloud TV solutions as well as a useful guide for Pay TV operators in order to invest on Cloud TV services, which is the current trend for Pay-TV services. The evaluation process is implemented as part of the validation of systems in HORSE Project: a five-year research and innovation project aimed at making recent technological advancements more accessible to small and medium manufacturing enterprises [4].

2 Methodology

The hierarchy levels of AHP are presented in Fig. 1. In order to rate the alternative technologies, one must evaluate the weights of the criteria and the factors. Each expert m $(1 \leq m \leq M)$ compares all possible combinations of C_k by filling out the pairwise comparison matrix (PWC) $\mathbf{P}^{(m)} = [P_{ij}^{(m)}]$, which signify the importance of C_i compared to C_j based on nine level scale [1]. The weights $w_k^{(m)}$ of criterion C_k is calculated with the most widely adopted approach of eigenvalue problem. Assuming that the eigenvalues are ordered so that λ_1 is the largest eigenvalue, then the weight of criterion C_i is estimated by the principal eigenvector $\mathbf{x}_1^{(m)}$ as $wk^{(m)} = x_{1k}^{(m)} \left[\sum_{m=1}^{M} x_{1k}^{(m)} x_{11} \right]^{-1}$. After all the comparisons have been completed, the average weight w_k for each criterion C_k is calculated. A similar procedure is followed for the estimation of the weights of the factors f_{jk} of each criterion. Finally, the alternatives are pairwise compared according to each factor and for each alternative A_i one obtains the relative scores S_{ijk} under factor F_{jk}. The final ranking priorities A_i of each alternative are evaluated.

$$Ai = \sum_{k=1}^{N} \sum_{j=1}^{J_k} S_{ijk} f_{ijk} w_k$$

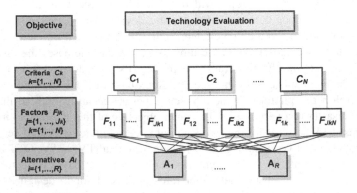

Fig. 1. AHP hierarchical model

3 Results and Discussion

In this section, the results of PWCs for the evaluation of the importance of the criteria and factors that may affect the deployment of Cloud TV are presented in Table 1. Sixteen experts, a sufficient number of participants for PWC [5], working in the field of Pay TV, with Computer Science and Electronics and/or Management background have participated in pairwise comparison surveys. |Security seems to take the precedence over the other criteria, emphasizing the need of end users for reliable products since they want to request unceasing services from anywhere and anytime without any kind of malfunction. Reliability criterion has the second highest weight, emphasizing the need to provide reliable, uninterruptible services and also high availability to customers. Reliability of cloud providers builds strong ties between the company and the customer as the uninterruptible service delivery is crucial for the customer experience.

Table 1. Criteria and factors

Criteria-factors	Description	Weight
C1 Flexibility (11,83%)		
F_{11} Interoperability	Interoperability between the different platforms	53,70%
F_{12} Portability	Portability of services to cover a wide range from different mobile devices	21,06%
F_{13} Scalability	Supports a wide range of TV channels	25,24%
C2 Usability (7,87%)		
F_{21} Accessibility	Supports highest degree of access to their clients	42,97%
F_{22} Content control	Controls the TV content to the customer	25,52%
F_{23} TV software app	The usability of the application that end-users experience	31,50%
C3 Economic Issues (10,01%)		
F_{31} Pricing model	The pricing model followed by each cloud TV provider	34,47%
F_{32} Costs saving	Stated in the contract the resources and requirements from client's side (Capex/Opex)	36,45%
F_{33} Time-to-market	The time-to-market plan that cloud vendors promise	29,08%
C4 Security (31,13%)		
F_{41} Protection	The security offered by the cloud TV vendors in relation to their infrastructure	41,11%
F_{42} IT compliance	Customer must consider the security policies of providers	17,85%
F_{43} Data security	Applicant cloud providers should explicitly state the encryption method used	41,03%
C5 Performance (15,98%)		
F_{51} Latency	Providers determine the latency to be present in broadcast of live TV programs	50,91%

(continued)

Table 1. (*continued*)

Criteria-factors		Description	Weight
F_{52}	Software	Performance of software tools for Transcoding, Encoding/Decoding, Ingestion	28,01%
F_{53}	Hardware	Technical characteristics of equipment	21,09%
C6 Reliability (23,18%)			
F_{61}	SLAs	Indicate the availability of vendors, response time in the event of problems occurs	36,21%
F_{62}	Availability	Availability of TV channels, VOD content, Smart TV applications, extra features	41,77%
F_{63}	Service management	Providers should be trustworthy, supervise and control the television services	22,02%

Regarding Flexibility, experts seem to be more concerned about the interoperability. Concerning Usability, accessibility seems to take the precedence and as far as economic are concerned, cost saving has the highest importance emphasizing its role as a motivation for potential investment. Regarding Performance, the experts seem to be more concerned about the latency rather than hardware or software factors. Software has rated as more important than hardware, as this is a little more considerable according to the performance of software tools that used to provide Transcoding, Encoding/Decoding, Ingestion of TV assets and linear TV Channels. Considering Reliability, availability is the most important factor since it is the great goal of vendors to provide any kind of variable content anywhere and anytime.

Figure 2(a), (b) presents the relative scores of alternatives for each factor and the final ranking, respectively. The scenario rating with highest importance is OTT highly rated in almost all the factors. OTT devices support flexibility, portability, functionality, rapid upgrading and adaptability to new trends and applications. OTT technology also offers low latency, content and personal data security, great usability and high performance by having 4K Ultra High Definition players installed. In addition, OTT is considered to be the most affordable solution by helping the pay-TV company to save money and increase revenue by improving cash flows. IPTV is not expected to have any more penetration to the market, assumed as a legacy technology. Although Smart TV is ranked third, it is considered as a technology of the future, because the factories of major television manufacturers have spent a lot of time to research and development (R&D) for internet connectivity and optimization of TV processors to provide as many applications as possible, including pay-TV software Apps.

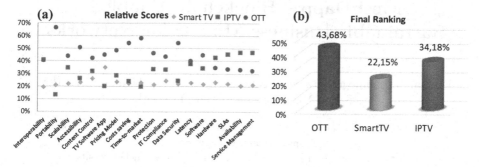

Fig. 2. (a) Relative scores, (b) Final ranking

4 Conclusion

In this paper the evaluation of the potential of three technological alternatives OTT, Smart TV and IPTV for Cloud TV implementation for pay-TV business strategy, has been carried out for the case study of Greece. The results focus on security, data protection, accessibility, costs saving and time-to-market but are also indicative for the rest of the factors. OTT takes the precedence, IPTV is ranked second, while Smart TV is considered as a longer term alternative. The growing penetration of portable devices in addition with the predictions and estimation of high video traffic through internet can motivate the OTT application in pay-TV market. Furthermore, R&D are going to improve all these functionalities and optimize new features and applications that can be supported from OTT technology providing great customer experience. This paper implements and verifies an open and transparent roadmapping model for Cloud TV investment, emphasizing on crucial interdisciplinary aspects of cloud operation The obtained results form a key part of future Cloud TV solutions and implementations both for Greece and other countries that have not yet deployed Cloud TV solutions.

Acknowledgments. The research leading to these results has received funding from the European H2020-FoF-2015 Project "Smart Integrated Robotics System for SMEs Controlled by Internet of Things Based on Dynamic Manufacturing Processes (HORSE)".

References

1. Dawi, N.M., et al.: Service quality dimensions in pay TV industry: a preliminary study. Int. Rev. Manag. Mark. **6**(4), 239–249 (2016)
2. Saaty, T.L.: Decision making with the analytic hierarchy process. Int. J. Serv. Sci. **1**(1), 83–98 (2008)
3. Dede, G., et al.: Towards a roadmap for future home networking systems: an analytical hierarchy process approach. IEEE Syst. J. **5**(3), 374–384 (2011)
4. http://www.horse-project.eu/
5. Dede, G., et al.: Convergence properties and practical estimation of the probability of rank reversal in pairwise comparisons for multi-criteria decision making problems. Eur. J. Oper. Res. **241**(2), 458–468 (2015)

MeshDapp – Blockchain-Enabled Sustainable Business Models for Networks

Emmanouil Dimogerontakis[1], Leandro Navarro[1(✉)], Mennan Selimi[1,2], Sergio Mosquera[1], and Felix Freitag[1]

[1] Universitat Politècnica de Catalunya, BarcelonaTech, Barcelona, Spain
leandro.navarro@upc.edu
[2] Max van der Stoel Institute, South East European University, Tetovo, North Macedonia

Abstract. The digital world demands a network infrastructure to supply connectivity to any participant anywhere. Sustainable networks require balanced value flows. Value is connectivity delivered at a material and service cost to compensate, involving diverse participants, ranging from consumers to providers, such as last mile access, regional transport, Internet carriers, or content providers. We focus on the case of wireless mesh networks that deliver connectivity through access points and a mesh network that routes traffic to Internet gateways, provisioned by several device owners and service operators [1–3].

The presented work is motivated by the need for balance and automation among services delivered, costs and incentives for participation in these decentralised networks. This balance is key for achieving extensible network infrastructures that can deliver widespread availability of Internet connectivity with minimal barriers of entry.

Keywords: Blockchain · Mesh networks · Network sustainability

1 Problem Statement

We explore the technological feasibility to implement business and sustainability models that combine retail pricing with wholesale cost, profit distribution and return of investment. A technical enabler is a permissioned blockchain that provides desirable properties such as trusted data feeds (oracles) about traffic and resource consumption, robust and irreversible transaction records (distributed ledger), and inexorable outcomes (smart contracts).

2 Conceptual Architecture

A mesh network provides connectivity services such as Internet access, content and local services. We need multiple network devices, such as access points (APs), routers (R), servers (S), and Internet Gateways (GW). Consumers (users) can

© Springer Nature Switzerland AG 2019
K. Djemame et al. (Eds.): GECON 2019, LNCS 11819, pp. 286–290, 2019.
https://doi.org/10.1007/978-3-030-36027-6_25

connect to network services and the Internet through AP devices in various locations, interconnected through several intermediate mesh routers. Servers deliver local services, and one or several gateway nodes are needed to deliver enough Internet connectivity.

Each device $\{AP, R, GW, S\}$ in a mesh has a cost that corresponds to an initial investment on network devices, links, servers (CAPEX) and its maintenance and operation (OPEX). This cost can fluctuate according to usage. Similarly to the electricity market, there is need for a market maker, the *mediator* agent, that finds the optimal retail service prices (e.g. the MBh equivalent to the kWh) to balance the demand and supply of connectivity across the different network infrastructure paths.

Such a system can accommodate participation, capacity, growth, variability and sustainability. While the routing protocol tries to optimize the allocation of capacity to traffic, the price optimization by the mediator agent can be used by service providers to compute retail tariffs for traffic and services offered to consumers (price plans). Examples are Internet access when including an Internet GW, or other services when combined with the matching GW/server such as voice calls, content (e.g. radio, TV, video). Each participating network device is rewarded by payments from consumers (who mediates this for later). In addition, these devices can provide connectivity and services to their owners, as both providers and consumers (prosumers).

Services satisfy consumer demand through the effort done by the supply or value chain. In the short term, there must be a balance between the charges in the consumption and the supply side. In the long term, services and the infrastructure should be socially and economically viable, satisfactory to all parts.

The main stakeholders are:

- *User:* a client of the mesh network. The user has a user interface (web browser or mobile app) and can have different roles (e.g., consumer, provider, network admin).
- *Consumer:* a user that consumes connectivity in exchange of an economic contribution according to a service contract: a customer of a retailer AP.
- *Provider:* a user that owns and provides devices $\{AP, R, GW, S\}$ to the infrastructure, or resources to supply connectivity or content services in a given local network expecting a compensation in economic or other terms.

The main components of the model are the following:

- *Mesh Network Island:* the network devices, the wireless physical connection between them, and the stack of network protocols that enable their connectivity. It is important to clarify that economic incentives are kept separate, not affecting routing and forwarding decisions driven by link quality metrics. Mixing economic with quality choices may lead to routing and forwarding convergence issues.
- *Node DB:* contains information relevant to the mesh about all the network devices.

- *Monitoring System:* responsible for monitoring the resources being used (i.e. traffic amounts) and providing the necessary data to the rest of the services.
- *Mediator:* the core agent of the model that, in every mesh island, is responsible for matching the demand and the supply of the offered service as well as maintaining the balances among the different participants. The Mediator applies the logic to compute the distribution of economic value, the *settlement* to providers in exchange of services, and determines a fair price for retail and aggregate traffic for each usage cycle.

2.1   Economic Compensation System

The aim of an economic compensation mechanism is to fairly distribute the economic value of the connectivity supplied by the network among providers: the devices and services $\{AP, R, GW, S\}$ which contributed to deliver that value. The amount received from service provision (retail) to consumers has to be distributed across the suppliers, an (approximately) zero-sum balance as in Eq. 1. Retailers (service providers) get funds (monetary units F_i) in exchange to amounts of service provision (Internet traffic or any other service or content) (as byte units B_i):

$$Collected(t) = \sum_{r=1..R} \sum_{c=1..C} (B_{r,c}, F_{r,c}) = (B, F) \text{ in period } p_t \qquad (1)$$

$$where: \quad r \text{ is a retailer among the set } R$$
$$c \text{ is a customer among the set } C$$

The tuple (B, F) has to (roughly) match the service provided by suppliers in the value chain, considering that the provision of connectivity involves multiple network hops and devices.

The accounting of traffic could be done in detailed *retail form* per client connection in each device (each client payment is split across the network devices involved in that provision), but we have selected an *aggregate form* where the sum of all user payments is split among all forwarding reports across all network devices involved in each period. That simplifies the accounting (routers only count bytes forwarded, instead of bytes per each end-client) at the price of small aggregation differences.

$$Owed(t) = \sum_{0<f<F} Settle_n(B(t, f), F(t, f)) \text{ in period } p_t \qquad (2)$$

$$where: \quad f \text{ is a forwarder among the set } F$$
$$n \text{ is a settlement event for period } p_t$$

The service fees collected in a given period can be allocated in settlements proportional to weights in terms of aggregated service (forwarding) units and fee/price units as in Eq. 2.

The goal of the *mediator* agent is to determine the settlement of owed payments in a mesh island, for each node and time, that optimize Eq. 3 for every user i as consumer (constr. 3b) or provider (device owner), where the settled retribution to each node (*Owed*) satisfies its expressed *Price* (constr. 3d), and where each device is useful, with positive utility (constr. 3c), such as by satisfying the expected rate of RoI (Return on Investment) combined with its social and economic benefits.

Payments spread across the value/service chain of network devices can be achieved according to the idea of fairness of settlements, such as proportional share [4] or Shapley value in ISPs [5]. To ensure that payments are satisfied in each cycle (constr. 3d) we use a reserve fund which allows us to keep a fund margin across payment cycles. This margin comes from the difference between the customer offered (spot) retail price and the internal aggregate network prices or costs.

$$\text{maximize} \atop c, f, t \quad U_i \quad (\forall \text{ consumer } c, \text{device } f, \text{time } t) \tag{3a}$$

$$\text{subject to} \qquad U(c,t) > 0,\, c = 1, \ldots, C, \tag{3b}$$

$$U(f,t) > 0,\, f = 1, \ldots, F, \tag{3c}$$

$$Owed(f,t) - Price(f,t) \geq 0,\, t - 0, \ldots, T \tag{3d}$$

We argue that smart contracts in a blockchain can automatically facilitate, verify and enforce the negotiation or performance of the aforementioned mechanism in a transparent and irreversible way. That can result in value transfers in the form of payments of token units. In the next section we sketch how a blockchain using smart contracts can implement the economic interaction between the components mentioned in the architecture. We materialize our design in the *MeshDapp* system.

3   Approach and Evaluation

We have implemented the models in a set of Solidity smart contracts under an Ethereum PoA permissioned and local blockchain[1], and evaluated its feasibility and operation under a simulated mesh network, as well as integrated in an experimental mesh network. We describe in the poster the overall idea and how the contract architecture has been designed.

4   Conclusions

We find the system, smart contract architecture, and the oracle to feed them with monitoring data, to be feasible and able to support the exchange of economic value in exchange of connectivity, between consumers and providers. The resulting decentralized and open model can support the sustainability of

---

[1] http://dsg.ac.upc.edu/meshdapp.

the network infrastructure and the services it provides, as well as create opportunities for local participants to generate value, both from the economic and networking perspectives.

Acknowledgements. This paper has been partially supported by the AmmbrTech Group, the Spanish government TIN2016-77836-C2-2-R and the Catalan government AGAUR SGR 990.

References

1. Braem, B., et al.: A case for research with and on community networks. ACM SIGCOMM Comput. Commun. Rev. **43**(3), 68–73 (2013)
2. Baig, R., Roca, R., Freitag, F., Navarro, L.: guifi.net, a crowdsourced network infrastructure held in common. Comput. Netw. **90**, 150–165 (2015)
3. Kabbinale, A.R., et al.: Blockchain for economically sustainable wireless mesh networks. Concurr. Comput.: Pract. Exp. e5349 (2019) cpe.5349
4. Feldman, M., Lai, K., Zhang, L.: The proportional-share allocation market for computational resources. IEEE Trans. Parallel Distrib. Syst. **20**(8), 1075–1088 (2009)
5. Stanojevic, R., Laoutaris, N., Rodriguez, P.: On economic heavy hitters: shapley value analysis of 95th-percentile pricing. In: Proceedings of the 10th ACM SIGCOMM Conference on Internet Measurement, IMC 2010, pp. 75–80. ACM, New York (2010)

Modeling, Characterising and Scheduling Applications in Kubernetes

Víctor Medel[1], Unai Arronategui[1(⊠)], José Ángel Bañares[1], Rafael Tolosana[1], and Omer Rana[2]

[1] Aragón Institute of Engineering Research (I3A),
University of Zaragoza, Zaragoza, Spain
unai@unizar.es
[2] School of Computer Science and Informatics,
Cardiff University, Cardiff, UK

Abstract. The simplification of resource management for container is one of the most important services of Kubernetes. However, the simplification of distributed provisioning and scheduling decisions can impact significantly in cost outcomes. From an economic point of view, the most important factor to consider in container management is performance interference among containers executing in the same node. We propose a model driven approach to improve resource usage in overall deployment of applications. Petri Net models, a Confirmatory Factor Analysis (CFA)-based model and a regression model allows to predict performance degradation of the execution of containers in applications. Time series indices can provide an accurate enough characterisation of the performance variations in the execution lifetime of applications. These indices can be used in new scheduling strategies to reduce the number of resources used in shared cloud environments as Kubernetes.

Keywords: Modeling · Petri nets · Confirmatory Factor Analysis · Interference · Scheduling · Containers

1 Introduction

Faster start up times and fewer required resources are the main advantages of containers compared to traditional virtual machine technologies. These have result in a higher participation of container technology in private and public clouds. Kubernetes has become the facto standard for distributed execution of applications in containers. Deployment and scheduling of applications on shared Kubernetes platforms remains activities that can be improved also in their economic angle. However, it can require a substantial effort, due to the complexity of the cloud distributed infrastructures. This paper aims to enhance a modeling path to improve these aspects of application execution to reduce resource requirements and, therefore, cost.

Our approach is the use of formal models with a twofold goal: (1) a better management of the growing complexity of current systems; (2) a high quality of

K. Djemame et al. (Eds.): GECON 2019, LNCS 11819, pp. 291–294, 2019.
https://doi.org/10.1007/978-3-030-36027-6_26

the implementation reducing the time to market. This poster presents in a cohesive way our works related with the modelling, characterisation of applications and scheduling in Kubernetes.

2   Models and Methodology

In [3,5] we presented a High Level Petri Net (reference net) based performance and management model for Kubernetes, identifying different operational states that may be associated with a "pod" and container in this system. The model is an executable specification that can be used for performance evaluation. A quantitative analysis can be conducted by a performance-oriented interpretation of the model such as throughput, utilisation rates, or queue lengths, from which is possible compute rewards functions [6].

The Reference net formalism is a special class of high level Petri net (adhered to the Nets-within-Nets paradigm). The hierarchical construction of the model allows to follow a top-down approach incorporating more details in the lower levels. However, the construction of a complete model with all the details can be an impossible task when there are a big number of factors that can affect the system's behaviour, and there is not a clear relationship between them. In this case, the usual solution for incorporating the observed behavior to the model is to annotate the model with deterministic time, probability distributions, or functions obtained from the monitoring data acquired from benchmarking. This approach can capture the whole behavior of the computational resources, and, therefore, a more precise performance analysis can be obtained. This is the case of the modelling and characterisation of applications interferences in container deployments.

Performance degradation of containers running in the same machine can be observed when resources needed for one container are used by another one. The performance loss produced by the simultaneous execution of two containers on the same host is the measure of the interference between both containers. Also, this interference is time dependent, as resource requirements vary during execution of applications.

We consider several *sources of interference* rooted on physical resources hosting the container:

- *Network usage*: all containers on a node share network access, thus they can disturb each other
- *CPU usage*: a reservation system to share the CPU proportionally is applied in most container management systems if there is contention.
- *I/O file system access*: it has similar sharing behavior as the network.
- *Cache Memory* and Memory bandwidth: Containers can provoke cache misses to others containers running in the same host, degrading memory bandwidth.

We propose a *methodology* to estimate the interferences and to obtain functions to annotate our Petri net based performance model. It consists of different steps to estimate the execution time of an application when it's co-scheduled with another one. First, the interference profile of an application can be obtained following a process where the timed interference indices are modeled using Confirmatory Factor Analysis (CFA) [1]. This model is based on the definition of human-comprehensible indices to represent resource usage. These indices are computed from data sets obtained from experiments on resource usage from different benchmark applications and are expressed as time series to show the evolution of resource usage over time.

To validate our approach we executed different applications inside a container to generate a number of different jobs, each of which represents the application executed with different input parameters. These applications represent different profiles characterized by the intensive use of a certain type of resource. The objective is to get a dataset which captures the variations of the metrics to build meaningful indices. The high correlation between the observed variables avoids using them as raw values to describe an application and to do further analysis. We follow the approach of reducing all observed variables of resource usage to four human-comprehensible indices to represent resource usage over time: *CPU usage, Memory page fault, Memory hierarchy usage* and *Intensity of memory hierarchy usage*, and characterising resource usage of applications over time with these interference indices.

Afterwards, we measure execution time of this application in time intervals while simultaneously running benchmark applications on the same machine. Then a regression model can be defined from the first two steps for each application to obtain a interference linear function that models the application. Finally, these linear functions are used to estimate interference between two application whose interference linear functions are known.

3   Interference-Aware Scheduling

When the number of tasks to schedule, at the same time, is greater than the amount of available computers in a distributed infrastruture, interference-aware scheduling is a policy that aims to minimize the performance degradation of these tasks, as explained in the previous section. The goal is to schedule, in the same machine, the tasks whose simultaneous execution produce the less performance degradation to each other.

In [4], we showed how the default Kubernetes scheduler was not suited to avoid performance degradation. Also, it was showed how a simple yet effective policy could reduce resource contention. In this work, we proposed a simple scheduling technique based on the characterisation of applications. The idea is that clients, or developers, provide informal information about the resource most intensively used by the application, and the scheduler uses that information to allocate the applications using the same resource in different machines. In our experiments, we achieved about a 20% improvement in the execution time of a simple scenario compared with the default Kubernetes non-deterministic scheduler. But it was a coarse grained approach that didn't take into account the variable requirements of resources during the execution of many applications, particularly long running applications such as services.

In Paragon [2], authors use a collaborative filtering algorithm to determine the influence of several sources of interference and propose an interference-aware scheduler. However, the main novelty of our approach compared with Paragon is that they considers interference remains constant over time.

4   Conclusions and Future Work

This paper has presented a model driven approach to reduce costs linked to resource management strategies with containers in Kubernetes, using Petri Net Models, a Confirmatory Factor Analysis (CFA)-based model and a regression model. Different methodologies applied with these models allow to predict resource usages of applications. Time series indices provide a characterisation of performance variations of applications that can contribute to enhance scheduling policies in containers platforms as Kubernetes.

As future work, in addition to the scheduler based on interference functions, we will use the petri net model with these annotations to perform different performance and cost analyzes.

Acknowledgments. This work was co-financed by the Aragonese Government and the European Regional Development Fund "Construyendo Europa desde Aragón" (COSMOS research group, ref. T35_17D); and by the Spanish program "Programa estatal del Generación de Conocimiento y Fortalecimiento Científico y Tecnológico del Sistema de I+D+i", project PGC2018-099815-B-100.

References

1. Brown, T.A.: Confirmatory Factor Analysis for Applied Research. Guilford Press, New York (2015)
2. Delimitrou, C., Kozyrakis, C.: Paragon: QoS-aware scheduling for heterogeneous datacenters. In: ACM SIGPLAN Notices, vol. 48, pp. 77–88. ACM (2013)
3. Medel, V., Rana, O., Bañares, J.a., Arronategui, U.: Modelling performance & resource management in kubernetes. In: Proceedings of the 9th International Conference on Utility and Cloud Computing, UCC 2016, pp. 257–262. ACM, New York (2016)
4. Medel, V., Tolón, C., Arronategui, U., Tolosana-Calasanz, R., Bañares, J.Á., Rana, O.F.: Client-side scheduling based on application characterization on kubernetes. In: Pham, C., Altmann, J., Bañares, J.Á. (eds.) GECON 2017. LNCS, vol. 10537, pp. 162–176. Springer, Cham (2017). https://doi.org/10.1007/978-3-319-68066-8_13
5. Medel, V., Tolosana-Calasanz, R., Bañares, J.Á., Arronategui, U., Rana, O.F.: Characterising resource management performance in kubernetes. Comput. Electr. Eng. **68**, 286–297 (2018)
6. Tolosana-Calasanz, R., Bañares, J.Á., Pham, C., Rana, O.F.: Resource management for bursty streams on multi-tenancy cloud environments. Future Gener. Comput. Syst. **55**, 444–459 (2016)

Author Index

Printed in the United States
by Bookmasters

.

Printed in the United States
By Bookmasters